Fighting like the Devil
for the sake of God

Manchester University Press

Fighting like the Devil
for the sake of God

Protestants, Catholics and the origins of
violence in Victorian Belfast

Mark Doyle

Manchester University Press

Manchester and New York

distributed in the United States exclusively
by Palgrave Macmillan

Published by Manchester University Press
Oxford Road, Manchester M13 9NR, UK
and Room 400, 175 Fifth Avenue, New York, NY 10010, USA
www.manchesteruniversitypress.co.uk

Distributed in the United States exclusively by
Palgrave Macmillan, 175 Fifth Avenue, New York,
NY 10010, USA

Distributed in Canada exclusively by
UBC Press, University of British Columbia, 2029 West Mall,
Vancouver, BC, Canada V6T 1Z2

British Library Cataloguing-in-Publication Data
A catalogue record for this book is available from the British Library

Library of Congress Cataloging-in-Publication Data applied for

ISBN   978 0 7190 7952 8 *hardback*

ISBN   978 0 7190 7953 5 *paperback*

First published 2009

18 17 16 15 14 13 12 11 10 09   10 9 8 7 6 5 4 3 2 1

The publisher has no responsibility for the persistence or accuracy of URLs for external or any third-party internet websites referred to in this book, and does not guarantee that any content on such websites is, or will remain, accurate or appropriate.

Typeset
by Action Publishing Technology Ltd, Gloucester
Printed in Great Britain
by MPG Books Group

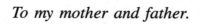

To my mother and father.

Contents

		page
List of maps and illustrations		ix
Acknowledgements		xi
List of abbreviations		xiii
	Introduction	1
1	Defending the faith: evangelicalism and anti-Catholicism	16
2	Belfast Catholics: 'a mere incohesive heap'	48
3	An unenviable notoriety: the 1857 riots	76
4	Local government and Catholic alienation	107
5	The idea of order: Dublin Castle and Belfast Protestants	129
6	The city erupts: August 1864	160
7	Glasgow: sectarian détente	192
8	Memories of violence, 1864–86	224
	Epilogue	250
	Appendix: 1864 riot ballads	255
	Bibliography	269
	Index	289

List of maps and illustrations

page

Maps

0.1 Belfast in 1861   xiv

3.1 Principal sites of the 1857 riots   77

6.1 Principal sites of the 1864 riots, 8–14 August   165

6.2 Principal sites of the 1864 riots, 15–17 August   174

6.3 Approximate route of the McConnell funeral,
   18 August 1864   179

Illustrations

8.1 The battle of the navvies   230
   Reproduced courtesy of the Deputy Keeper of the Records,
   Public Record Office of Northern Ireland

8.2 The McConnell funeral   231
   Reproduced courtesy of the Deputy Keeper of the Records,
   Public Record Office of Northern Ireland

Acknowledgements

This book is the culmination of a process that began several years ago, when I first formulated a research proposal for my thesis in the Boston College History Department. Since then I have accumulated many debts, both professional and personal, that are much too numerous to acknowledge in any satisfactory manner. The following is but a partial list of the organisations and individuals that have made this project possible.

First I would like to thank the Irish Studies Program at Boston College, which subsidised the bulk of my graduate study and funded a year of research in Ireland and the United Kingdom. Significant funding was also provided by the Harry Frank Guggenheim Foundation, the North American Conference on British Studies and the Mellon Foundation through the University of Pennsylvania Humanities Forum. The History Department at Boston College has been a constant source of inspiration, camaraderie and goodwill. Kevin O'Neill, Peter Weiler and Prasannan Parthasarathi served on my thesis committee, and much of what follows reflects their guidance and patient support. Other faculty members – including Jim Cronin, Robin Fleming, Tom Hachey, Lynn Johnson, Kevin Kenny, David Quigley and Rob Savage – offered substantial support at various stages of my graduate studies, as did the many friends I made among my fellow graduate students. Of the latter I would like especially to acknowledge Adam Chill, Anthony Daly, Meaghan Dwyer and Ely Janis, who read portions of this project and whose friendship and good humour helped push me through to the end. This book was completed during a postdoctoral year at the University of Pennsylvania, and I would like to thank the members of the Penn Humanities Forum – especially my fellow Fellows, Judith Brown, Anthony Raynsford, Camille Robcis and Llyd Wells – for their feedback and camaraderie, as well as Jennifer Conway, Gautam Ghosh, Wendy Steiner, Gary Tomlinson and Sara Varney, who extended such a warm welcome.

For their assistance with the research stage of this project, I would like to thank the staffs of the Belfast Central Library; the Borthwick Institute of Historical Research at the University of York; the Cardinal Tomás Ó Fiaich Library, Armagh; the Diocesan Archives of Down and Connor, Belfast; the Glasgow University Library; the Linen Hall Library, Belfast; the Mitchell Library, Glasgow; the National Archives of Great Britain at Kew; the National Archives of Ireland; the National Archives of Scotland; the National Library of Ireland; the Presbyterian Historical Society of Ireland; the Public Records Office of Northern Ireland; Union Theological College, Belfast; and the libraries at Boston College, Queen's University Belfast and the University of Pennsylvania. I would also like to thank David Hume and David Scott of the Grand Orange Lodge of Ireland, Schomberg House, Belfast, as well as Matthew Lamberti of the Widener Library at Harvard University.

Scholars in the UK and Ireland who have contributed directly or indirectly to the completion of this project include Paul Bew, Ambrose Macaulay, Elaine McFarland, Don MacRaild and Graham Walker. Sharon Oddie Brown, Brian Kane, Mary Lennon and many who took part in the University of Notre Dame's summer seminar in 2003 have also helped this project along, and they have my gratitude. For their patience, warmth and unfailing encouragement, my family and friends were, and continue to be, indispensable; I hope they know how much they have meant to me.

List of abbreviations

BI	Borthwick Institute of Historical Research, University of York
CSORP	Chief Secretary's Office Registered Papers (in the National Archives of Ireland)
DDC	Diocesan Archives of Down and Connor, Belfast
GOLI	Grand Orange Lodge of Ireland, Schomberg House, Belfast
LHL	Linen Hall Library, Belfast
ML	Mitchell Library, Glasgow
NAI	National Archives of Ireland, Dublin
NAS	National Archives of Scotland, Edinburgh
NLI	National Library of Ireland, Dublin
PRONI	Public Record Office of Northern Ireland, Belfast
TNA	The National Archives, Kew

Map 0.1 Belfast in 1861

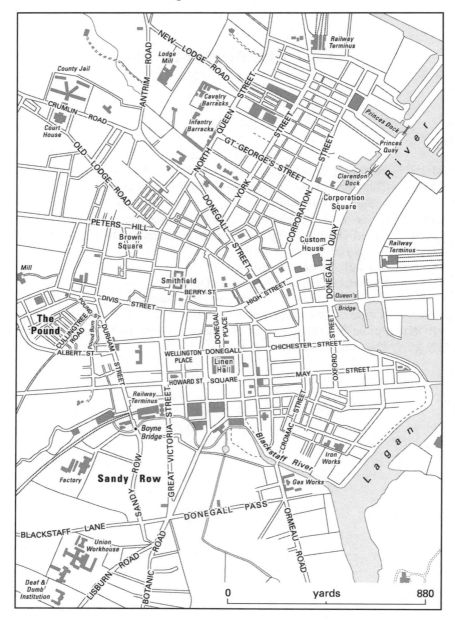

Introduction

In 1919 the Belfast journalist James Winder Good described a peculiar sort of folk memory among the working-class Protestants and Catholics of Belfast. The city's older residents, he said, passed along their knowledge about the city to young people by telling stories about violence. Gates scarred with bullet holes from long-ago riots, a corner where a sniper had once operated, a cul-de-sac in which an unfortunate company of dragoons had been successfully repulsed by stone-throwing crowds – these became landmarks of communal identity for the coming generations, reminders of collective victories or humiliations, urban monuments evoking feelings of triumph or recalling grievances to be avenged. 'Naturally youngsters,' wrote Good, 'to whom these tales and a thousand others are told, make for themselves holy places like the Mohammedans, and vow, after the fashion of Indian braves, that when their turn comes they will prove not unworthy of the traditions they have inherited.'[1]

By 1919 this tradition of violence had acquired a veneer of timelessness. Irish Protestants and Catholics had been fighting and killing one another at least since the seventeenth century, after all, and it was hardly surprising that their rivalry should carry over into the urban confines of modern, industrial Belfast. When the two sides came to blows in the city, as they often did, it seemed to many outsiders that they were simply re-enacting distant battles that the rest of the world had happily forgotten. As the twentieth century progressed, this impression – that violence in Belfast was timeless, indelible and seemingly ineradicable – grew stronger. The vicious partition riots of 1920–22, the sectarian bloodbath of 1935 and, of course, the protracted politico-sectarian warfare of the post-1968 'Troubles' often looked like little more than bloody variations on the same bleak theme. To speak, as the subtitle of this study does, of the origins of Protestant–Catholic violence in the middle of the nineteenth century seems not only inappropriate, therefore, but also slightly wrongheaded, as if one were to locate the roots of European imperialism in the Scramble for Africa. Yet the specific tradition of violence that Good observed in the Belfast of 1919 did have a discernible origin, and, like many traditions, it was the product not of ineluctable historical forces but of deliberate human action.[2] Though embedded in the centuries of conflict between Protestants and Catholics in the north of Ireland, Belfast's tradition of violence emerged at a specific historical moment, and that was very recent indeed.

This book describes that moment, focusing primarily on the period between 1850 and 1865, the time when Belfast underwent its most rapid urbanisation and experienced its first flush of industrial glory. The period was bounded at one end by the Irish famine of the 1840s and the waves of migration and evangelical anti-Catholicism that followed in its wake. At the other end, the mid-1860s opened an era of intense politicisation that led the city's rival religious traditions to attach themselves to the pro- or anti-nationalist cause. In between, working-class Protestants and Catholics adjusted to the traumas of industrialisation much as many other migrants did in many other cities, fashioning new urban identities for themselves and carving out their places in the city's evolving culture. Woven into these new identities, alongside the routines of work, faith and leisure, was a tradition of communal violence, a remnant of the sectarian battles of the countryside that was invigorated and transformed in the narrow working-class streets into something new and distinctly urban. More than half a dozen times during this fifteen-year period the industrial suburbs of west Belfast shook with violence, often for days and weeks on end. Belfast had known rioting before, but nothing of the magnitude and duration that characterised these mid-Victorian battles.

Many scholars have described the ideological and structural forces underlying this violence. Disagreements over politics and religion, underpinned by structural inequalities in power and employment, laid the foundations for these riots – indeed, according to some, these issues were what Protestants and Catholics were 'really' fighting about. Very few, however, have attempted to fill in the rest of the picture. Specifically, few have grappled with the question of why violence in particular became the mode by which people acted out their sectarian hostilities. Why violence should become a recurring, almost routine fact of urban life is a further question that is unanswerable merely by examining the 'underlying causes' of particular outbreaks of violence. To understand the peculiar embeddedness of Belfast's violence, therefore, we must adjust our focus somewhat, looking not only at the abstract forces promoting antagonism between Protestants and Catholics but also at the complex social relationships that existed among specific groups and individuals. Relationships between workers and elites, moderates and extremists, men and women, mill workers and labourers, the people and the state, and even between older and younger generations all gave form and meaning to Belfast's communal rivalries, and it was in them that its violent tradition truly resided. This is a level of analysis that brings us down from the lofty heights of theoretical antagonisms and into the narrow, grimy neighbourhoods of the city itself, where the whirring din of the factories and the commotion of the streets frequently drowned out the distant clamour of grander historical forces. Before I discuss my methods and arguments in more detail, however, it is useful first to glance at the history of Belfast up to this time and to consider more fully what made the mid-Victorian years so important. I will then briefly examine the dominant trends in the historiography of Belfast's nineteenth-century riots, concluding with a description of my own approach.

Linenopolis

Built on the site of a Norman castle near the river Lagan, Belfast was officially established in 1613 by a charter from King James I. It was one of several towns in Ireland's northern province settled by Scottish and English colonists during the so-called Plantation of Ulster, a Crown-sponsored colonisation scheme designed both to pacify Catholic Ireland and to exploit the region's economic potential. A bustling seaport from the start, Belfast quickly became the economic centre of Counties Antrim and Down, exporting beef, butter and linen to English markets in growing quantities from the late seventeenth century. The majority of the inhabitants were Presbyterians, but the Test Act of 1704 barred this group from local office, and political power accordingly fell into the hands of a tight-knit band of Anglican burgesses. Presbyterians could still practise their professions and trades, however, and together with the Anglican ruling class many became immensely prosperous merchants and professionals in the eighteenth century. Catholics, meanwhile, remained on the periphery of Belfast society, never numbering more than several hundred families in the eighteenth century and remaining largely confined to the labouring classes. Indeed, so little threat did the Catholics pose to the Protestant identity of the city that a considerable amount of tolerance was possible during these years: when Belfast's first Catholic chapel was founded in 1784, Protestants contributed £84 for its construction and paraded at its opening.[3]

The latent tensions between Presbyterians and the Anglican establishment finally erupted during the 1780s and 1790s. Although the laws barring Presbyterians from holding local office had been repealed in 1780, many Belfast Presbyterians remained resentful of the privileges enjoyed by Anglicans, and, fired by the revolutions in America and

France, they embraced a radical form of republican politics. The Society of United Irishmen, founded in Belfast in 1791, embodied their aspirations. It called for an independent, democratic Irish parliament under which all religious groups would have equal rights. Collaborating with Catholic secret societies known as the Defenders, the United Irishmen staged a revolt in 1798, but, despite some fierce fighting in Belfast's hinterland and elsewhere, the revolt disintegrated amid massive state repression and sectarian recriminations. The Act of Union, which incorporated Ireland into the United Kingdom, followed in 1801, and, while many Belfast Presbyterians continued to espouse the principles of the United Irishmen well into the nineteenth century, Belfast never again became a centre of radical politics.[4]

As the new century opened, political turmoil gave way to bounding economic prosperity. Since the 1780s Belfast's wealthy merchants had been investing their profits in cotton textile mills, exploiting the town's favourable geography and the skills of a labour force long accustomed to household linen weaving. By 1806 the cotton mills employed some 15% of the city's workforce, and other industries, such as rope works, distilling and sugar refining, had turned this commercial port into a thriving pocket of industrial prosperity in an otherwise agricultural country. Cotton remained the cloth of choice until about 1828, when the York Street mill belonging to the Mulholland brothers caught fire, and the brothers, deciding to exploit Ireland's extensive native flax production, refitted the mill for linen spinning. With linen Belfast had found its niche in an imperial economy crowded with the cotton cloths of Lancashire and Scotland, and soon linen mills were sprouting like wild flowers along the town's western edge. By 1840 there were eighteen linen mills in Belfast and its immediate hinterland, and by 1852 there were twenty-four; meanwhile, the number of cotton mills had declined to just four.[5]

Nineteenth-century Belfast was a deeply, self-consciously Protestant city, and many of its inhabitants attributed its most un-Irish prosperity and 'civilisation' to the distinctive religious traditions of its people. But with industrialisation came a flood of migrants from rural Ulster, and, as these migrants took up work in the textile mills, the religious balance of the town began to shift. Catholics, who had comprised a mere 16% of the population in 1808, grew to roughly a third by 1834, a proportion they would maintain until the last decades of the century.[6] Adding to the tension was the fact that most of the migrants, Protestant and Catholic, had come from parts of rural Ulster where sectarian violence was common, and it is therefore little surprise to find that Belfast's earliest sectarian riots followed patterns similar to those of the Ulster countryside. The first clash occurred in 1813, when the Catholic butchers of Hercules

Street attacked a group of Protestant Orangemen returning to Belfast from a procession in Lisburn. Armed with guns from a nearby public house, the besieged Orangemen fired into the crowd, killing two Protestants and wounding four Catholics.[7] At least nine other disturbances broke out over the next twenty years. Often these outbreaks accompanied Orange processions, although election-day violence was also common. For the most part these were localised skirmishes of short duration, causing minimal damage and differing little from the riots that had convulsed rural Ulster since the 1790s. All the same, they were disturbing signs that the much vaunted prosperity of Linenopolis, as civic boosters and admiring outsiders called it, was forcing together two groups who were not at all prepared to abandon their sectarian rivalries in their new urban home.

As the city became more polarised, it developed its first sectarian neighbourhoods. Catholics had long clustered near Smithfield and Hercules Street in the north-west quarter of the city centre, and, as linen mills began appearing further west, new Catholic migrants settled in the area known as the Pound, named for a cattle pound that had once stood just outside the city walls. Immediately to the south of the Pound and across a patch of waste ground was Sandy Row, a Protestant neighbourhood likewise populated by unskilled weavers and labourers. As industrial suburbs, both the Pound and Sandy Row enjoyed insalubrious reputations for their poor housing and sanitation, but they were even more notorious for their sectarian rioters: in 1852 one Protestant missionary told of his hesitation on entering Sandy Row for fear that its 'bludgeon-men' might harm him.[8] Despite their reputations, however, these were not yet homogeneous sectarian ghettoes. Protestants living in the Pound and Catholics living in Sandy Row, though rare, were not unknown even into the early 1850s.[9]

Several elements made the mid-Victorian years a pivotal time in the city's history, accelerating the trends toward polarisation and violence that had been under way for several decades. First, there was the Irish famine of 1845–49, a calamity that had been less severe in Ulster than elsewhere in Ireland, but which greatly strained Belfast's philanthropic and social institutions.[10] The collapse of the rural economy greatly spurred migration to the city and in so doing it heightened the anxieties of many Belfast Protestants who worried about the influx of ragged Catholics who, they feared, would be a drain upon the city's resources and a threat to its Protestant character. As we will see in Chapter 1, these anti-Catholic anxieties were sharpened after 1850 by the 'papal aggression' controversy in England, and, driven by the twin threats of Catholic migration at home and the machinations of Popery abroad, Belfast experienced an intense evangelical resurgence years that profoundly altered the tenor of communal relations.

A second development also had its roots in the famine. Before the 1850s most linen weaving in Ulster was done by hand, either by rural weavers or by workers living in places like Sandy Row, who wove cloth at home from yarn spun in the mills. But the famine decimated the number of rural weavers, and, as labour costs skyrocketed, Belfast's linen magnates invested in more labour-efficient power looms, greatly improving productivity and stimulating further migration to the city. By the 1860s Belfast had become the leading linen producer in the world, thanks in large part to the US Civil War of 1861–65, which starved British industry of cotton imports and created a massive new market for Belfast linen.[11] Secondary industries such as iron foundries also benefited from the expanding economy, and new factories, docks and businesses appeared almost overnight. 'The progress of Belfast has continued for the last 12 months with unabated vigor,' marvelled one foundry owner in 1853. 'It is extending on all sides. Old houses are thrown down, & new ones on an improved scale erected in their stead. New factories, & gigantic warehouses have risen up since this time last year, & no symptom of any cessation to the increase.'[12] It was also during this period that the foundations of Belfast's other great industry, iron shipbuilding, were laid. Edward Harland and Gustav Wolff, the great shipbuilders whose firm would anchor much of Belfast's later prosperity, began their partnership on the Queen's Island shipyards in 1861.[13] The rapid growth of these years prompted an unprecedented expansion in population: between 1851 and 1861 the city grew by 40%, and in the next decade it grew by another 43%. By 1871, Belfast contained some 174,000 people, nearly twice the population of twenty years before.[14]

The linen and shipbuilding industries tied Belfast's prosperity to the fortunes of the British Empire as a whole, and people of all political and religious persuasions became increasingly attuned to developments in the outside world. The US Civil War was a point of obvious interest, as were the Opium Wars with China, the nationalist struggles in Italy and the Crimean War, in which many Belfast soldiers fought.[15] Public interest in these events was facilitated by the spread of cheap newspapers (the Stamp Tax was removed in 1853, the Paper Tax in 1860) and the laying of telegraph wires to Britain, Europe and North America by 1858. Literacy rates in Belfast were higher than those in rural Ireland – although in this respect, as in many things, Protestants enjoyed an advantage over Catholics – and even the illiterate had access to information via street ballads and specially deputised newspaper readers in the factories, all of which helped to expand their horizons beyond their own neighbourhoods.[16] This was in sharp contrast to the rural world that many Belfast workers had left behind, and it created an atmosphere of widespread political awareness that framed many people's emerging identities.

It was against this background of economic and cultural vigour that a new type of urban rioting emerged. Far more serious than earlier outbreaks, these mid-Victorian riots lasted much longer and took in much more of the city's geography than had earlier clashes. They also became significantly less predictable: whereas earlier riots had usually been prompted by Orange marches or elections, the riots of the 1850s and 1860s were triggered by all sorts of events, ranging from outdoor evangelical sermons (1857) to Catholic parades in Dublin (1864) and even flower-gathering expeditions along the Blackstaff River (1865). Often they spilled over into the mills and the city centre, poisoning relationships between neighbours in the mixed streets of west Belfast and drawing in a host of participants from across the social spectrum, as well as the thousands of soldiers and policemen sent by the government to restore order. Industrial civilisation had indeed arrived in Ireland, some English observers noted wryly, but the country's ancient sectarian feuds seemed as intractable as ever.[17]

Historiographical explanations

It was the outbreak of the 'Troubles' in Northern Ireland in the late 1960s that first directed scholars' attention towards these nineteenth-century riots. The two works that most explicitly sought clues to the city's twentieth-century violence in the earlier riots were Andrew Boyd's *Holy War in Belfast* and A. T. Q. Stewart's *The Narrow Ground*, both of which argued that the patterns of conflict that took hold during this period remained the same in the 1960s and 1970s.[18] Apart from these two explicitly presentist studies, however, most scholars have tried to understand these riots on their own terms, looking for the specific ideological or structural causes that gave rise to the violence. Some, such as Sybil Baker, have proposed a long list of underlying causes, including the absence of 'normal' class warfare in Belfast, the economic and political marginality of Catholics, the partisanship of the local police force and the lack of alternative recreational outlets.[19] Others, such as Sean Farrell and Catherine Hirst, have argued instead for a single, predominating cause. For Farrell, this was 'the continuing power of Ulster's two conflicting visions of how Irish society should be structured'.[20] Hirst, the most recent historian to investigate this period, makes a similar argument, maintaining that it was political disagreements – specifically, rivalries between Catholic nationalists and Protestant unionists – that motivated Belfast's rioters from about 1834 onwards. Other factors, such as religious zealotry, were also present, says Hirst, but these were of secondary importance.[21]

Similar explanations can be found within broader studies that examine

one or the other of the city's chief religious traditions. In their study of
Ulster evangelicalism, for instance, David Hempton and Myrtle Hill have
suggested that evangelical anti-Catholicism played a major part in feeding
the riots, even if it was not a primary cause.[22] Peter Gibbon and David
Miller have likewise studied the Protestant side of the conflict, locating
the source of the riots in the growing politicisation of Protestant shipyard
workers and in the powerful Protestant ethos of self-reliance and personalistic loyalty to the monarchy, respectively.[23] The only thorough
consideration of the Catholic experience is that of A. C. Hepburn, who
argues that Catholics' status as unwelcome and vulnerable outsiders was
an important structural factor framing the violence.[24]

Each of these studies has provided valuable information on the forces
underlying these riots, and, taken together, they offer a fairly comprehensive view of the profound instability of mid-Victorian Belfast.
Competing religious, political and economic aspirations, coupled with a
set of civic structures that ensured Protestant dominance in the city while
Catholics struggled on the periphery, undoubtedly supplied the necessary
conditions for strong sectarian rivalries to develop in these years. But by
focusing primarily on underlying ideological and structural forces, these
studies have left many serious questions unanswered. Most importantly,
they have failed to explain why rioting became endemic in Belfast rather
than merely sporadic. Behind this question lie several others: what role
did violence itself play in propelling communal polarisation? What was it
about the mid-Victorian years, in particular, that caused violence to
escalate? What, finally, led these undoubtedly antagonistic groups to
express their hostilities through violence, rather than some other means?
Sectarianism alone explains very little.[25] We can easily imagine a society
in which people holding conflicting religious or political views coexist
peacefully, even when facing each other from uneven positions of political and economic power. Indeed, most societies could scarcely function
otherwise. Something more, it seems, needed to exist in order to bring
about the violent communal polarisation that took hold in Belfast during
these years.

Overall, what has been missing from these studies is an understanding
of how violence itself operates in a society – how it fits within the
contours of everyday life, how it structures social relationships, how it
provides the model and motivation for future acts of violence. One scholar
whose work offers some insights into these questions is Frank Wright,
who, in a series of studies examining nineteenth- and twentieth-century
Ulster, articulated a theory of communal violence that centred on what he
called 'communal deterrence'.[26] In essence, 'communal deterrence' is
what emerges when most members of a divided society, fearing violence

from an opposing group, gravitate toward their own side's violent extremists for protection. 'In a deterrence relationship,' Wright explains, 'all incidents of violence or humiliation between members of opposed communities are seen to have a meaning for the whole community.'[27] When representative violence of this sort emerges, ordinarily peaceful people come to acquiesce in – or actively to support – violence from their own side in order to deter violence from the other. Fear of representative violence not only divides one community from the other, therefore, but it also binds each separate community more closely together under the hegemony of its own most violent members. Applied to Ulster as a whole, Wright's model explains the province's historic violence and polarisation as the confluence of deep-rooted 'theoretical' opposition between Protestants and Catholics and immediate, 'emotive' antagonisms between individuals. Structural forces provide the foundation, in other words, but complex patterns of fear and deterrence provide the violence.

Methods and arguments

In the chapters that follow, I borrow the core of Wright's theoretical insights in order to chart the construction of a tradition of violence in Belfast's emergent working-class communities. Like Wright, I accept that important structural forces shaped the violence of this period, and I shall make frequent use of the findings of those who have already uncovered these forces to frame my own discussion. But also like Wright, I recognise that individuals' experiences of urban life and urban violence are just as important as the larger forces shaping their actions, and I shall undertake extensive analyses of a wide range of sources to determine what those experiences were. Where I differ from Wright is in the scope of the relationships I consider. For while 'communal deterrence' is undoubtedly important, it is but one of the relationships that can fuel communal violence in a divided city. To understand fully how Belfast's unique tradition of violence took shape, other sorts of relationships must be examined.

Three levels of analysis guide my study. The first concerns the networks of social relations that existed within each confessional group. Protestants and Catholics were never homogeneous blocs in the city; in addition to the obvious class divisions among them, differences of gender, ideology and occupation created multiple cleavages on both sides. These different (and often overlapping) social groupings were bound together by a web of formal and informal ties – fraternal organisations, religious bodies, political alliances, kinship and the like – that became profoundly important during moments of communal crisis. In an atmosphere of heightened sectarian tension, provocative actions by one side or the other could easily trigger these networks, and often the city found itself in the grips of a massive and prolonged struggle seemingly out of all proportion to the initial conflict. Whole neighbourhoods, often at some distance from each other, became drawn into the riots in this way, and men and women, textile workers and shipwrights, middle-class ideologues and the 'hard men' of the street corners all had roles to play. Of course, as John Bohstedt has suggested, communal networks do not always have to promote unrestrained violence; sometimes they can have a moderating influence by leading groups to adopt tacitly accepted rules of engagement.[28] In mid-Victorian Belfast, however, the opposite was the case: the strongest social networks on both sides were those that encouraged rather than discouraged violence, while those networks that might have restrained the rioters, where they were present, were simply too weak to do so.

A second level of analysis concerns the relations between the state and the inhabitants of the city. With few exceptions, most discussions of violence in nineteenth-century Belfast have ignored the role of the state during periods of rioting, even though many of the sources that scholars use to study the riots come directly from the state.[29] Often scholars have assumed that the state was what it said it was: an impartial referee whose only objective was to keep the two sides separated. But a critical reading of the sources reveals that this stance was itself guided by certain tensions and assumptions that greatly influenced the course of the violence. Tensions between local officials and the central government, compounded by profound anti-state sentiments among ordinary people on both sides, made policing these riots not merely a matter of enforcing 'law and order' but of politics as well, and in time the forces of the state became just as central to the conflict as the contending communities themselves. As I will show, the state found itself unable to contain Belfast's violence not because it lacked the might to do so, but because it failed to secure legitimacy among either community. What emerged instead was something very much like Wright's vigilante-driven 'communal deterrence' regime, although the nature of this regime varied according to the divergent experiences and aspirations of Catholics and Protestants.

The third level of analysis concerns the power of violence itself to fuel communal polarisation. To understand this process, I pay close attention to the details of the riots as they unfolded – the targets attacked, the identities of the protagonists, the role of the urban topography, the actions of the police and so forth – uncovering not only what motivated individual rioters, but also how people from different backgrounds experienced violence. In thus privileging the events of these riots, I am following in the footsteps of historians such as George Rudé and Iver Bernstein, who have argued that the secret to a riot's origins may be found in the specific nature of the violence itself.[30] I shall take this argument one step further, however, and suggest that the reason why rioting *recurred* in Belfast with such frequency had to do, in part, with the way these riots bridged the gap between combatants and non-combatants. Violent sectarianism, as we shall see, was never the occupation of more than a minority on each side, but this minority managed to establish hegemony within their communities through the specific types of violence they employed. These included the intimidation of 'moderates', the extortion of 'blackmail' from peaceable neighbours and, most importantly, the violent expulsion of outsiders in order to create communally 'pure' neighbourhoods and workplaces. The polarising power of this violence reverberated through the numerous riot stories found in newspapers, popular ballads and folk memory. To the extent that they are recoverable, I examine these narratives for evidence of how both sides made sense of, and drew lessons from, specific outbreaks of rioting. An individual's experience of violence could be either direct or vicarious, as we shall see, but that experience powerfully informed how he or she would act during future periods of rioting.

A final methodological technique should be mentioned here. Despite widespread recognition among historians that Victorian Belfast had more in common with industrial cities in Britain than with anywhere else in Ireland, few who have studied the riots of this period have considered Belfast's experience alongside that of its British peers.[31] Doing so, however, not only helps us to pinpoint those areas in which Belfast was unique, but also to identify sources of tension and identity formation that were common to other industrialising cities. Workers' traumatic experiences of migration and urbanisation, the anxieties of the middle classes about the moral state of the poor, the struggles of religious institutions to keep pace with a growing population and many other aspects of industrialisation in Britain were present in Belfast as well, and throughout this study I shall examine Belfast's emerging identities within this wider context. Towards that end, a major component of this study is an extended comparison between Belfast and Glasgow, Belfast's nearest British counterpart but one that largely escaped the sort of rioting that was so common in Belfast. Following the method employed by Ashutosh Varshney in his recent study of Hindu–Muslim violence in India, my comparison of Belfast and Glasgow examines the patterns of social interaction in a city of social violence against those in a city of social peace, the better to identify what sorts of inter- and intra-communal relations foster communal violence.[32] By considering Belfast within its British context, in other words, I am able to isolate those factors that made Belfast the uniquely violent city that it was.

One of those factors, it will become clear, was imperialism. In recent years historians have begun to re-examine the imperial nature of British rule in nineteenth-century Ireland, delineating the sinews of British economic, political and cultural domination that have long been taken for granted (often with insufficient empirical grounding) by postcolonial theorists.[33] With specific regard to Ulster, the investigation of imperial attitudes and structures has tended to focus on the twentieth century (specifically the recent 'Troubles'), and such investigations have sometimes yielded fruitful comparisons with other colonial or postcolonial societies such as those of Algeria and South Africa.[34] What has often been missing, however, is a sense of how the religious and political ideologies, mechanisms of state control and patterns of social integration that promoted conflict in Ulster differed from similar structures within Britain itself. This study does not pursue an exhaustive analysis of these differences, but by placing Belfast within its proper context – as a city that was both the most British city in Ireland and the most Irish of Britain's industrial cities – it does offer some idea of how imperial structures and mindsets helped to shape the lives of ordinary people.

The imperial dimension will become clearest when we focus on the position of the state. Historians of other parts of the British Empire have long recognised the ways in which imperial states foster communal division through state-run education, the preferential political treatment of one community over another and the categorising and solidifying of social differences.[35] Indeed, many of the world's most intractable conflicts in our own time, from Sudan to Sri Lanka, are directly traceable to such imperial experiences, but few scholars have applied such concepts to the study of nineteenth-century Ulster. Another feature of the imperial state, as several scholars have noted, is that it tends to control populations through coercion rather than consent.[36] This reflects, and in fact promotes, a crisis of legitimacy for the imperial state, making possible the emergence of competing claimants to power who usually promote their claims to legitimacy by presenting themselves as true representatives of 'the people'. Where there is more than one 'people' to be represented, however, rival loci of power often emerge that compete not only with the imperial state but also with one another. The result is profound instability and confusion as different groups strive for the allegiance of different segments of society on the basis of radically different claims to legitimacy. The multilayered violence of mid-Victorian Belfast, which drew in the state, Protestant extremists, Catholic extremists and – eventually – ordinary people on both sides, vividly illustrates these imperial side-effects.

Many other themes weave their way in and out of this discussion. The role of religious belief as a marker of difference, the adoption of clearly defined gender roles during moments of crisis and the way an urban environment structures identity and conflict are all subjects that confront us when we plunge into the social world of the Belfast working classes. I shall reflect upon these topics when they arise and, where appropriate, situate my arguments within the relevant literature from a range of academic disciplines. The principal burden of this study, however, will be to chart the emergence during these years of a unique tradition of working-class violence in Belfast that became engrained in both sides' respective communal identities. This tradition preceded the titanic political struggles between nationalists and unionists that erupted in later decades, and, indeed, it helped greatly to shape such struggles. The patterns of communal violence that appeared inevitable and timeless from the perspective of 1919 or 1969 were, in fact, part of a constructed tradition that arose from a specific historical moment. Though structured by religious, political and economic forces, this tradition resided solely within the complex relationships of the city's inhabitants.

Notes

1 James Winder Good, *Ulster and Ireland* (Dublin: Maunsel and Co., 1919), 259–60.
2 Eric Hobsbawm and Terence Ranger, eds, *The Invention of Tradition* (Cambridge: Cambridge University Press, 1983).
3 J. C. Beckett, 'Belfast to the End of the Eighteenth Century', in J. C. Beckett et al., *Belfast: The Making of the City, 1800–1914*, (Belfast: Appletree Press, 1983), 17–18; Jonathan Bardon, *Belfast: An Illustrated History* (Belfast: The Blackstaff Press, 1982), 25–8; Ian Budge and Cornelius O'Leary, *Belfast: Approach to Crisis* (London: Macmillan, 1973), 4; Philip Ollerenshaw, 'Industry, 1820–1914', in *An Economic History of Ulster, 1820–1940*, ed. Liam Kennedy and Philip Ollerenshaw (Manchester: Manchester University Press, 1985), 67; Fred Heatley, 'Community Relations and the Religious Geography, 1800–86', in Beckett et al., *Belfast* 131.
4 Bardon, *Belfast*, 47–65. On the United Irishmen in Belfast and Dublin, see Nancy J. Curtin, *The United Irishmen: Popular Politics in Ulster and Dublin, 1791–1798* (Oxford: Clarendon Press, 1994).
5 Budge and O'Leary, *Belfast*, 16–21; Ollerenshaw, 'Industry', 67–70; Bardon, *Belfast*, 66–70.
6 Budge and O'Leary, *Belfast*, 28–32.
7 *Ibid.*, 24–5.
8 W. M. O'Hanlon, *Walks Among the Poor of Belfast, and Suggestions for Their Improvement* (Belfast: H. Greer, 1853), 33–4.
9 Catherine Hirst, *Religion, Politics, and Violence in Nineteenth-Century Belfast: The Pound and Sandy Row* (Dublin: Four Courts Press, 2002), 14–18.

10 Christine Kinealy and Gerard MacAtasney, *The Hidden Famine: Poverty, Hunger, and Sectarianism in Belfast, 1845–1850* (London: Pluto Press, 2000).

11 Ollerenshaw, 'Industry', 73–7; D. L. Armstrong, 'Social and Economic Conditions in the Belfast Linen Industry, 1850–1900', *Irish Historical Studies*, 7 (1950–51), 238, 264.

12 James MacAdam, diary, 29 Dec. 1853, PRONI, D/2930/7/7.

13 Ollerenshaw, 'Industry', 89–91.

14 Budge and O'Leary, *Belfast*, 28.

15 In October 1855 the *Times* of London estimated that roughly 1,000 Belfast men had volunteered to fight in the Crimean War. David Murphy, *Ireland and the Crimean War* (Dublin: Four Courts Press, 2002), 8.

16 Frank Wright, *Two Lands on One Soil: Ulster Politics before Home Rule* (Dublin: Gill and Macmillan, 1996), 370. In 1851 the proportion of Belfast residents over the age of five who could neither read nor write was 20.4%, lower than in all nine Ulster counties apart from Antrim (in which Belfast lies). J. R. R. Adams, *The Printed Word and the Common Man: Popular Culture in Ulster, 1700–1900* (Belfast: Queen's University Institute of Irish Studies, 1987), 115–16.

17 See e.g. *Evening Post*, 8 Sept. 1857; *Daily Telegraph*, 15 Aug. 1864; and *Saturday Review*, 1 Apr. 1865.

18 Andrew Boyd, *Holy War in Belfast* (Tralee: Anvil Books, 1969); A. T. Q. Stewart, *The Narrow Ground: Aspects of Ulster, 1609–1969* (London: Faber, 1997), 143–54.

19 Sybil Baker, 'Orange and Green: Belfast, 1832–1912', in *The Victorian City*, ed. H. J. Dyos and M. Wolff (London: Routledge & Kegan Paul, 1973), vol. 2, 787–815. See also Budge and O'Leary, *Belfast*, 94–5; and Heatley, 'Community Relations'.

20 Sean Farrell, *Rituals and Riots: Sectarian Violence and Political Culture in Ulster, 1784–1886* (Lexington, Ky.: University Press of Kentucky, 2000), 129.

21 Hirst, *Religion*.

22 David Hempton and Myrtle Hill, *Evangelical Protestantism in Ulster Society, 1740–1890* (New York: Routledge, 1992), 121–8.

23 Peter Gibbon, *The Origins of Ulster Unionism: The Formation of Popular Protestant Politics and Ideology in Nineteenth-Century Ireland* (Manchester: Manchester University Press, 1975), 67–86; David Miller, *Queen's Rebels: Ulster Loyalism in Historical Perspective* (Dublin: Gill and Macmillan, 1978), 68–72.

24 A. C. Hepburn, *A Past Apart: Studies in the History of Catholic Belfast, 1850–1950* (Belfast: Ulster Historical Foundation, 1996), ch. 3.

25 Kyla Madden, *Forkhill Protestants and Forkhill Catholics, 1787–1858* (Montreal and Kingston: McGill-Queen's University Press, 2004), 3–9.

26 Frank Wright, 'Communal Deterrence and the Threat of Violence in the North of Ireland in the Nineteenth Century', in *Political Violence: Ireland in a Comparative Perspective*, ed. John Darby, Nicholas Dodge and A. C.

Hepburn (Belfast: Appletree Press, 1990), 11–28; Frank Wright, *Northern Ireland: A Comparative Analysis* (Dublin: Gill and Macmillan, 1987), 11–20; Wright, *Two Lands*, 2–11.

27 Wright, *Two Lands*, 5.

28 John Bohstedt, *Riots and Community Politics in England and Wales, 1790–1810* (Cambridge, MA: Harvard University Press, 1983), 23. See also Mark Harrison, *Crowds and History: Mass Phenomena in English Towns, 1790–1835* (Cambridge: Cambridge University Press, 1988).

29 I am referring specifically to parliamentary inquiries and the reports of policemen and magistrates. Newspapers, though not printed by the government, often relied upon policemen and other officials for their information, and there was therefore a strong pro-state bias in many of their reports as well.

30 George Rudé, *The Crowd in History: A Study of Popular Disturbances in France and England, 1730–1848* (New York: Wiley, 1964); Iver Bernstein, *The New York City Draft Riots: Their Significance for American Society and Politics in the Age of the Civil War* (New York: Oxford University Press, 1990).

31 Two notable exceptions are Baker, 'Orange and Green', and David Hempton, 'Belfast: The Unique City?', in *European Religion in the Age of Great Cities, 1830–1930*, ed. Hugh McLeod (London: Routledge, 1995), 145–64.

32 Ashutosh Varshney, *Ethnic Conflict and Civic Life: Hindus and Muslims in India* (New Haven: Yale University Press, 2002).

33 Terrence McDonough, ed., *Was Ireland a Colony? Economics, Politics, and Culture in Nineteenth-Century Ireland* (Dublin: Irish Academic Press, 2005); Stephen Howe, *Ireland and Empire: Colonial Legacies in Irish History and Culture* (Oxford: Oxford University Press, 2002); Kevin Kenny, ed., *Ireland and the British Empire* (Oxford: Oxford University Press, 2006).

34 David Miller, ed., *Rethinking Northern Ireland: Culture, Ideology, and Colonialism* (London: Longman, 1998); Pamela Clayton, *Enemies and Passing Friends: Settler Ideologies in Twentieth Century Ulster* (London: Pluto Press, 1996); Wright, *Northern Ireland*.

35 Much of the best work in this regard has been done by scholars of India. See e.g. Joya Chatterji, *Bengal Divided: Hindu Communalism and Partition, 1932–1947* (Cambridge: Cambridge University Press, 1994); Bernard Cohn, 'The Census, Social Structure, and Objectification in South Asia', in *An Anthropologist among the Historians and Other Essays*. Bernard Cohn, ed. (Delhi: Oxford University Press, 1987), 224–54; Gyanendra Pandey, *The Construction of Communalism in Colonial North India* (Delhi: Oxford University Press, 1990)

36 David M. Anderson and David Killingray, ed., *Policing the Empire: Government, Authority, and Control, 1830–1940* (Manchester: Manchester University Press, 1991); Nandini Gooptu, *The Politics of the Urban Poor in Early Twentieth-Century India* (Cambridge: Cambridge University Press, 2001), ch. 4.

1

Defending the faith: evangelicalism and anti-Catholicism

In November 1853, the Unitarian minister Andrew McIntyre visited the Belfast neighbourhood of Sandy Row for the first time. A Dubliner newly arrived in the industrial north, McIntyre was the sole missionary of the fledgling Belfast Domestic Mission, an organisation founded a few months earlier 'to afford moral and religious instruction to the neglected and destitute classes of the inhabitants'.[1] After visiting several of the worst slums in the centre of the city, where the population seemed to live in ignorance of any religious principles and rarely, if ever, attended church, McIntyre was unprepared for what he encountered in the fiercely, self-consciously Protestant Sandy Row. 'Many of the people I met with in this district seem to know well and greatly pride themselves in the fact that they are Protestants,' he wrote in his diary, 'yet it appeared to me that they do not know much of their Bibles.'[2] The paradox was an unsettling one for McIntyre, who, like many evangelicals, believed that part of what distinguished Protestants from members of less enlightened faiths was precisely their familiarity with the Bible. On a subsequent visit McIntyre was astonished to learn that three girls he saw 'bulking marbles' and 'conducting themselves very rudely' were regular attenders at two of the area's Sunday schools. 'I observed that they do not seem to be much refined by any instructions they have got', McIntyre sniffed.[3]

What instructions the Protestants of Sandy Row got, as McIntyre discovered, came primarily from Dr Thomas Drew, a Church of Ireland minister who, as rector of nearby Christ Church, exercised tremendous influence among the Anglicans (or simply 'Protestants', as they were often called to distinguish them from Presbyterians and other Dissenters) in the neighbourhood. Like McIntyre, Drew was committed to strengthening the Protestant character of Belfast, but his ideas were rather different from McIntyre's. Where McIntyre looked for Protestantism in personal morality, knowledge of the Bible and social 'refinement', Drew's ideal Protestant was one who worked to defend the faith from its enemies, most especially the Roman Catholic Church. Popery and the Papacy –

terms denoting the theological and political aspects of Catholicism, respectively – were '[t]he most subtle, fierce, and predominant foe, with which the Protestant has to contend', Drew explained to a Sandy Row audience in 1857.[4] For Drew, Catholicism was a 'blood-stained religion', an idolatry, a propagator of the 'doctrines of demons' and a subverter of 'laws human and divine', and it was the task of the bold and honest Protestant workers of Belfast to deliver Ireland from its clutches.[5] Once memorably (if uncharitably) described by the Liberal Protestant *Northern Whig* as an 'Evangelical acrobat who collects crowds while he tumbles from this to the other world, swallows (Kentish) fire, balances Jacob's ladder, juggles Church and State about, and otherwise amuses himself in a holy manner', Drew was considerably less 'refined' in his approach than McIntyre would have liked, but it resonated with the people of Sandy Row in a way that McIntyre's own moralising strictures never could.[6]

With their differing attitudes towards working-class Protestants, McIntyre and Drew neatly embodied the dual nature of middle-class evangelicalism in Victorian Belfast. In a crude sense, theirs was the difference between moral evangelicalism, concerned with promoting individual faith and bourgeois codes of conduct, and political evangelicalism, which sought to mobilise working-class Protestants to defend 'Protestant liberties' from papal machinations. Neat dichotomies of this sort are rarely found in nature, however, and in many ways the two men were driven by an overlapping set of assumptions that all Belfast evangelicals shared. Both, for instance, believed Protestantism to be under threat, either from the corrosive squalor of the Belfast slums or from the Catholic Church. To save Protestantism, both turned to the poorer classes of the city, seeking to bolster the faith of the slums through tracts, sermons, home visitations and material relief. Both, moreover, were animated by a strong dose of anti-Catholic prejudice: Drew had built a career upon denouncing Popery, of course, but even McIntyre, who decried the 'party feeling' of Sandy Row, found occasion to deride individual Catholics for being 'as bigoted as they are ignorant'.[7] In all this, both men reflected the evangelical spirit of their age, not only in Belfast but in many British cities besides; indeed, neither would have been out of place roving the streets or pounding the pulpits of London, Manchester or Glasgow.

Belfast, however, was not a British city in any ordinary sense, and, at a time when Catholics made up one-third of the city's population and Catholicism in the rest of Ireland seemed not just strong but getting stronger, the public evangelicalism of McIntyre and Drew had the potential to become deeply polarising. Historians have long recognised the overwhelming economic and political dominance enjoyed by Protestants in mid-Victorian Belfast, but few have examined the important role played by religious belief and institutions in shaping Protestant–Catholic relations.[8] This neglect stems, in part, from a widespread reluctance to see communal conflict in Belfast as in any way motivated by religion – something that many contemporaries, haughtily denying that there could be anything 'religious' about sectarian rioting, also believed.[9] But to ignore religious forces is to ignore what was one of the most powerful components of collective identity in the city, even if, as McIntyre discovered in Sandy Row, a group's religious affiliation was sometimes more apparent in its communal solidarity than in any particular form of spirituality.

In this chapter and the next, I shall examine how the social networks associated with religious belief provided much of the raw material out of which each community forged its urban identity. It is not my intention to argue that religion was somehow what both sides were 'fighting about', but rather to show how social networks based upon shared religious beliefs and backgrounds informed people's relationships with each other and with the city itself. The most powerful force shaping these relationships was Protestant evangelicalism, an elite-driven movement with which both working-class Protestants and Catholics had to come to terms. For Protestants, as this chapter will show, evangelicalism was both a stabilising and a cohesive force, offering workers and elites a common language through which to articulate their beliefs and aspirations, even if they did so in somewhat different ways. For Catholics, meanwhile, evangelicalism had the opposite effect, creating a set of practices and institutions that were often openly hostile to their presence in the city and instilling a sense of collective insecurity that their own elites were unable to allay. The Catholic response to evangelicalism will be the subject of Chapter 2.

I begin this chapter with a brief discussion of the nature of Ulster evangelicalism and the catalysts behind the major burst of evangelical mobilisation that took place in Belfast during the 1850s. I then chart the two primary forms of this evangelical onslaught, which I have already categorised as moral and political evangelicalism. Next I discuss the issue of proselytism, the point at which evangelicalism overflowed from the Protestant neighbourhoods and began directly influencing relations between Protestants and Catholics. The chapter concludes with a discussion of open-air preaching, which concentrated all the strands of evangelicalism into a potent – and ultimately unstable – mixture of working-class outreach, proselytism and anti-Catholicism.

Evangelicalism and the city

By the time Andrew McIntyre made his first tentative expeditions into the wilds of Sandy Row, evangelicalism had already been a powerful force in Ulster society for a hundred years. It had come from England in the 1740s with John Wesley and other itinerant preachers, shock troops of a wider awakening that stretched 'from the Urals in the east to the Appalachians in the west'.[10] As its geographic breadth suggests, this was a movement that cannot be narrowly or easily defined. D. W. Bebbington captures something of its essence by proposing a 'quadrilateral of priorities': '*conversionism*, the belief that lives need to be changed; *activism*, the expression of the gospel in effort; *biblicism*, a particular regard for the Bible; and what may be called *crucicentrism*, a stress on the sacrifice of Christ on the cross'.[11] In the specific context of Ulster, evangelicalism offered an exciting blend of spiritual intensity and grassroots energy that was much more attractive, for many, than the staid complacency of the gentry-dominated Anglican Church.[12] At the same time, the new movement fitted easily within the dominant settler ideology of Ulster Protestants, infusing a certain missionary zeal into a group already convinced that they had a civilising duty among the Catholic Irish – that they were, as Drew once put it, 'as a city set on a hill'.[13] In addition to Bebbington's 'quadrilateral', then, we might well add a fifth priority for evangelicalism as practised in Ulster: anti-Catholicism.[14] Asserting that those who had found the true path to God were also those who were most endangered by dark, anti-Christian forces, evangelicalism offered its adherents both the promise of spiritual righteousness and a sense of embattlement. As an explanatory model, it perfectly captured the convictions and fears of Ulster Protestants, becoming especially powerful after the late eighteenth century as Protestant privileges began rapidly to be eroded and Catholics began demanding (and receiving) ever more civil and political rights.

The Presbyterian Church was among the quickest to embrace the movement. As a decentralised but tightly knit body defined by a strong Scottish-Calvinist heritage and an adversarial relationship with the Anglican Church, Presbyterians were especially receptive to a movement advertising unmediated interaction with God and preaching a stern, activist lifestyle. By the early nineteenth century, evangelicals had come to dominate the Presbyterian Church, sealing their hegemony when the arch-conservative Henry Cooke purged the Synod of Ulster of liberals, who favoured an unorthodox theology of the Trinity.[15] The spread of evangelicalism among Anglicans was more uneven: the hierarchy generally sought to incorporate and defuse, rather than embrace, its evangelical enthusiasts, and the movement never came to dominate the church as a whole. In fact, it was Belfast evangelicals like Drew (who began his career in Belfast in 1833) who provided most of the evangelical energy within the Church of Ireland, sometimes to the embarrassment of their more urbane superiors.[16] For all that it embodied a grassroots, oppositional form of religion, however, the peculiar circumstances of Ulster Protestantism made the movement considerably more conservative than was the case in Britain, where it was often identified with liberal and even radical politics. In the hands of men like Cooke and Drew, evangelicalism became a tool not so much for stimulating spiritual and social change as for restoring Protestants' disappearing privileges and preserving their faith from papal depredations.[17]

By the early nineteenth century, Belfast had become the evangelical cockpit of Ulster. As the headquarters of the Presbyterian Church and a proliferation of smaller sects such as the Methodists, Baptists and Quakers, Belfast had a religious life which was much more heterogeneous was the case in than most other parts of Ulster, where Anglicans predominated.[18] Competition among these sects for the souls of the working classes – whose members often abandoned the routines of formalised religion when they migrated to the city – was correspondingly fierce. The city's teeming slums offered vast missionary fields for intrepid evangelicals of all stripes, and as the city grew evangelical organisers busily set about creating home missions, charities and prayer meetings to attract and succour the churchless poor. Such initiatives were already well under way before 1850, but they were given a tremendous boost by the massive social, economic and cultural changes that followed the famine of 1845–49, and it was in this later period that Belfast evangelicals began building a truly all-embracing religious infrastructure in the city.

Two developments forced evangelicals on to the offensive at this time. The first was the emergence of a more strident attitude within the Catholic Church, which began taking steps to tighten papal authority in England and Ireland and to counteract the conciliating tendencies that had long governed the Catholic clergy's relations with Protestants. The opening salvo came in September 1850, when Pope Pius IX restored to the English clergy the ecclesiastical titles that had been stripped from them during the Reformation. This 'papal aggression' sent shockwaves throughout Britain, strengthening Protestant fears of the Pope's political power and provoking considerable anti-Catholic chest-thumping in the press, pulpits and streets of British cities. In Ireland, evangelicals detected elements of a similar plot – or, more accurately, a second prong of the same plot – in the appointment that very year of Paul Cullen as Primate of Armagh (he became Archbishop of Dublin in 1852). As the most powerful bishop in

Ireland and an Apostolic Delegate serving as the Pope's representative in Ireland, Cullen introduced a range of reforms designed to strengthen the papacy's role in church governance and to bring Irish devotional practices more in line with official teachings. Among other things, this entailed a massive increase in the number of priests, nuns, churches and Catholic schools throughout Ireland, and it also meant a less conciliatory attitude towards Protestantism. Although these institutional changes were rather slow in coming to Belfast itself (as we will see in Chapter 2), many Belfast evangelicals sensed a general revival of the old 'intolerance' of the Inquisition in Cullen's reforms, and they began girding themselves for a fight.[19]

The second major development that spurred evangelical organising in the immediate post-famine period was the tremendous growth of Belfast itself. Agricultural restructuring in the countryside, the mechanisation of linen weaving in the city and the emergence of new industries such as shipbuilding all propelled migration to Belfast on a massive scale, transforming the busy town of 70,000 in 1841 into a bustling metropolis of 122,000 in 1861, with more arriving every year.[20] As had happened in Britain a generation earlier, evangelical anxieties about the religious condition of the poor increased greatly during these years, and, beginning in the early 1850s, the moral state of Belfast's workers became a topic of grave concern among the well-to-do. Many poor people, lacking the time, inclination or proper clothing to attend church, were held to have fallen into a state of 'practical heathenism', as the *Belfast Newsletter* put it.[21] The everyday squalor in which the people lived, brought to light in a series of missionary reports, scientific inquiries and literary works, horrified many wealthy Protestants and convinced them that moral decay must inevitably accompany such physical degradation. The most famous account was W. M. O'Hanlon's *Walks among the Poor in Belfast*, which luridly described not only the poor housing and sanitation endured by the poor, but also the foul temptations to which they were subjected, from drinking and gambling to prostitution and sexual promiscuity.[22] If the 'dangerous and perishing classes' were to be saved from such evil influences, warned the city's evangelical fathers – indeed, if Protestant Belfast itself was to be saved – the wealthy people of Belfast had to fight back with every ounce of spiritual and physical charity at their disposal.[23]

By almost any measure, conditions were indeed grim for the Belfast poor. According to an 1852 report, Belfast's annual mortality rate was one in thirty-five, significantly greater than the United Kingdom average of one in fifty. The proportion of deaths due to fever was 16.2%, more than double the Irish average of 6%. Four-room houses that could scarcely hold ten people frequently housed eighteen to twenty, and sewers and open drains made cholera and other diseases a persistent problem, even in the newer districts of west Belfast.[24] The extent to which church attendance was a priority among people living in such conditions is uncertain, but, as Hempton and Hill point out, 'social distinctions, seating patterns, and the cultural assumptions of those in control of the content of public worship, reinforced a sense of alienation' that probably kept most slum-dwellers away from church.[25] On the other hand, an 1852 census of the Christ Church district conducted by ministers of Drew's church found that of the 1,374 Anglican families in Sandy Row, some 886 attended church, a respectable rate of 64%. Moreover, nearly half owned Bibles and 40% owned prayer books.[26] From an evangelical perspective, however, such figures were more likely to be a source of concern than of reassurance: the glass, after all, was little more than half full.

There was another facet of urbanisation that was even more troubling for Belfast evangelicals. This was the presence among the working classes of large numbers of Catholics (they were 34% of the total population in 1861), whose supposed loyalty to a foreign monarch made them even more worrisome than the most unrepentant Protestant heathen. An early instance of this anxiety could be seen in Belfast evangelicals' response to the sectarian riot that broke out in Birkenhead, outside Liverpool, in 1850. The riot had arisen when Irish Catholics attempted to interrupt a Protestant meeting condemning the 'papal aggression' and were repulsed by the police. Birkenhead Catholics later accused the police of acting with partiality and brutality, but in Belfast the lesson to be drawn from this event was quite different. The *Newsletter*, easily the most conservative and anti-Catholic paper in the city, saw in the riot clear evidence 'that the minds of the ignorant Roman Catholic masses are being gradually prepared for an illegal defence of the present Papal usurpation by their priests'.[27] Henry Cooke, the Presbyterian minister whose conservative politics had helped shape the evangelicalism of his own church, likewise alleged that the Catholics at Birkenhead had been acting 'in support of the Pope' and ominously warned that 'there is not a town in the empire, where some Roman Catholics would not be willing to set agoing a like work'.[28] In this atmosphere of suspicion and fear, Belfast's Catholics seemed to present a threat to Belfast Protestantism that was out of all proportion to their actual size and influence.

Defending Protestantism: moral evangelicalism

After 1850, the most prominent and far-reaching evangelical organisations were those that sought to provide moral instruction to the working classes. The most visible manifestation of this moral evangelicalism was the tremendous push for church construction that animated all major Protestant denominations during this period. Church construction was a uniquely communal activity, mobilising Protestants of all social classes to raise money for buildings that were often designated especially for the poor. Among the most important working-class churches built during these years were the Berry Street Presbyterian Church, founded in 1852 and given to the young firebrand Hugh Hanna (whom we shall meet below), and the Albert Street Presbyterian Church, founded in 1854 in a part of west Belfast where young people were 'exposed to many temptations'.[29] All told, the Presbyterians built twenty new churches in the city between 1800 and 1857, and by 1861 they could boast twenty-four churches, not counting three Unitarian Presbyterian meeting houses, one United Presbyterian congregation and two Covenanting meeting houses.[30] The Anglicans fared only slightly worse with fourteen churches in 1864, and many of these, such as Christ Church, expanded greatly during this time.[31] Meanwhile even the Methodists, never a dominant group in the city, could claim twelve churches for their various divisions in 1864. This meant there was roughly one Protestant church for every 1,300 Protestant inhabitants, while Catholics, who had only four churches at this time, had just one for every 10,300.[32]

Despite the large number of churches, many evangelicals worried that thousands of workers still remained untouched by the institutions of religion.[33] For these there was a growing stable of domestic missionaries ready to bring religious instruction directly into the working-class neighbourhoods. In addition to the Belfast Town Mission, founded in 1827 by an interdenominational group of evangelicals, there now existed the Church Mission (Anglican, founded in 1843), the Belfast Domestic Mission (Unitarian, founded in 1853), the Belfast Parochial Mission (Anglican, founded in 1856) and the Belfast Female Mission (non-denominational, founded in 1862), all treading the same streets and knocking on many of the same doors.[34] According to their own figures, in 1853 agents of the Belfast Town Mission made 33,171 visits to individual families, conducted 1,669 prayer meetings (with a total attendance of 103,119), and distributed some 49,099 tracts.[35] In a city of roughly 90,000 inhabitants – and even allowing for some overlap within these figures – it is clear that the Town Mission and its counterparts touched the lives of a tremendous number of Belfast's inhabitants.

In addition to its domestic missions and churches, mid-Victorian Belfast also hosted a multitude of young men's associations, intellectual improvement societies, working-class reading rooms, Sunday schools and temperance societies.[36] Many charities too were under the influence of evangelicals. Groups such as the Ulster Female Penitentiary, the

Magdalen Asylum and the Seamen's Friend Society were dominated by evangelicals, and several evangelical leaders also sat on the boards of the Poor Law Union and General Hospital.[37] Catholics, meanwhile, were neither welcome nor especially eager to join the governing boards of those charities most identified with Protestants, although before the Catholic Church built up its own alternative institutions many poor Catholics were forced to rely upon them for material assistance.[38] At a time when local government provided few social services for the poor and the Catholic Church was still too weak to provide its own services, evangelicals had both the energy and the resources to become a significant, even essential force within the city's expanding public institutions.

It is difficult to measure the extent to which these groups engaged in overt efforts to convert Catholics. Certainly, as we will see in the next chapter, the potential for proselytism within Belfast's public bodies was a real concern among the Catholic clergy, and there is some evidence that missionary groups did seek out poor Catholics for conversion.[39] Nevertheless, individual missionaries rarely strayed into exclusively Catholic districts or visited Catholic homes, and some, such as Andrew McIntyre, tended to focus on the temporal relief of those Catholics whom they did encounter rather than engaging in any outright proselytism.[40] The chief importance of this first set of evangelical organisations lies, therefore, not in their direct effect upon Catholics but in the relationships they created between the Protestant working classes and the evangelical elite. Of course, many workers were suspicious of the moralising strictures of these self-appointed moral reformers, and sometimes suspicion became outright hostility when wealthy evangelicals began interfering with the more 'intemperate' and 'rough' amusements of the Belfast slums. But although, as Hempton and Hill suggest, a large 'cultural gap' did exist between poor Protestants and middle-class evangelicals, it was also the case that many of these groups offered recreation, charity and community for those willing to partake of it, and clearly many did so.[41] Middle-class evangelicals may not have succeeded in instilling Protestantism on their own, strictly bourgeois terms, but they did help to reinforce a type of Protestant identity that was defined not simply as opposition to Catholicism but also as a set of distinct religious practices and beliefs. More than anything, their initiatives showed that Protestantism enjoyed a central place in Belfast's emerging urban culture, a place that was not shared by Catholics.

Defending Protestantism: political evangelicalism and the Orange Order

While domestic missions, churches, temperance campaigns and Sunday schools occupied most of Belfast's evangelical energies during the 1850s, a vocal and influential minority were not content simply to strengthen Protestantism from within. For clergymen like Henry Cooke and Thomas Drew, the fight had also to be taken to the enemy itself, specifically to the Catholic Church and those within the British state who indulged its 'aggressions'. Die-hard conservatives and enthusiastic imperialists, these men believed Ulster to be on the front line in a worldwide struggle against the forces of darkness, and in their sermons and political campaigns they sought to spread this global perspective among all Protestants, from the wealthiest linen magnate to the poorest labourer. Although they also advocated strict personal morality and religious devotion, their popularity derived largely from the skill with which they tapped into the raw sectarianism that underlay Ulster society. For the Protestant working classes, in particular, they helped to imagine the Catholic Church as a sort of unifying enemy, a nebulous entity on to which poor Protestants could project many of their fears and anxieties about urban life. This enemy had the virtue of being simultaneously global and local, a shadowy force creeping forth from Rome yet also something that one could find just down the street, in faces one passed every day.

The Presbyterian Henry Cooke created the template for Belfast's distinctive brand of political evangelicalism in the 1830s and 1840s, pioneering the role of the Protestant minister as public intellectual and political power-broker – 'the archetypal Ulster protestant political parson', in the alliterative words of his biographer.[42] Cooke's most famous triumph had come in 1841, when he roused Belfast Protestants to repulse the 'invasion' of Ulster by Daniel O'Connell, whose campaign to repeal the Act of Union and establish an autonomous Irish parliament was then in full swing. On arriving in Belfast O'Connell was met by such angry crowds that he was forced to deliver a truncated address from his hotel and to flee the city under police protection the next day, while Protestant rioters wrecked the homes of Catholic priests and O'Connell supporters.[43] What Cooke seems to have grasped, and what others came to recognise as well, was that in order to counteract the rising tide of Catholic self-assertion they had to mobilise Protestants *en masse*. As O'Connell himself had shown in his earlier campaign to secure political rights for Catholics, Irish people could successfully wrest change from the British state if large numbers of them mobilised around a specific cause: the implicit threat of violent unrest that hovered above such mass movements had a remarkable power to focus British policymakers on Irish demands. It was something of a double game, this O'Connellite strategy of playing at respectable politics while recruiting an army with which to overawe the state, and it was a dangerous one, too – the people, once roused, could not always be controlled – but it was one that Cooke and his evangelical progeny played with considerable skill.

Cooke's influence had peaked in the decades before the famine; by the early 1850s, it was Thomas Drew who was most clearly Belfast's premier political parson. As rector of Christ Church, an Anglican church located on the fault line between Sandy Row and the Pound, Drew waged his war from the very centre of Belfast's sectarian rivalries. His congregation consisted chiefly of the millworkers, servants and petty artisans of west Belfast, among whom he enjoyed considerable popularity not just for his fiery sermons but for the host of educational and philanthropic services his church provided.[44] In addition to his pastoral duties, Drew frequently delivered public lectures in which he offered a distinctly evangelical interpretation of world events, following in the tradition of evangelical thought that David Miller has called 'prophetic' and what others might define as 'interventionist' or 'fundamentalist'.[45] For Drew, Good and Evil were actual physical presences in the world, and the ongoing struggle between Protestantism and Catholicism was the earthly embodiment of a cosmic battle with apocalyptic implications. Any advance for Romanism was therefore not simply a geopolitical or strategic setback, but quite literally a triumph of Evil over Good. Whatever the issue, whether it was Catholics appointed to high political office in Dublin, the expansion of the British Empire or the conflict between Turkey and Russia in the Crimea, Drew had a biblical explanation for it, and a suitably biblical remedy, which invariably called for Protestants to stand up for their faith against their enemies.[46]

In 1854 Drew founded the Christ Church Protestant Association, a body designed to involve working-class Protestants in the great political campaigns of the day through education and political mobilisation. Among the group's stated goals were 'to aim at the recovery of all ground, lost in the struggle for <u>Protestant Ascendancy,</u> of truth above error, and of freedom over superstition, aggression, and ecclesiastical tyranny', and, more concretely, 'to aim at the <u>repealing</u> of the <u>Act of 1829,</u> by which Romanists have been permitted to legislate . . .'.[47] All Protestants were eligible to become members of the group, and, although most members were working-class, several prominent politicians, evangelical ministers and industrialists lent it their patronage.[48] At the group's popular quarterly meetings in the Music Hall, members and non-members gathered to hear Drew and other speakers discuss the religious and political tenets of Protestantism while expostulating on the major events of the day. The body also sent petitions to Parliament in support of Protestant causes, and it expressed its organisers' interest in imperial and military affairs by drafting letters of congratulation and condolence to British army officers and nobles in the Crimea and elsewhere.[49]

It is uncertain how successful the Christ Church Protestant Association and similar groups were in spreading political awareness or evangelical conviction among ordinary Protestants. Many Belfast Protestants undoubtedly came to Drew's lectures primarily to watch the famous preacher work himself into an exhilarating oratorical lather; after all, basking in such rhetorical pyrotechnics was a free form of entertainment at a time when few workers had much disposable income. At the same time, given the heavy working-class presence at most evangelical events during these years, it is worth considering whether there was also some-thing in the evangelicals' message that might have appealed to poor Protestants. Unfortunately, we lack any direct sources from poor Protes-tants about what they thought of these events, but we might well imagine that one lesson that was likely to strike a chord with them was the simple message that Catholicism – whether embodied in the Pope, Jesuits, priests or their own Catholic neighbours – was in some way responsible for the profound insecurities of life in the city. It is often forgotten that, although Protestants as a group were in a position of undoubted superiority in Victorian Belfast, many poor Protestants endured precisely the same disruptions – the uprooting from tight-knit rural communities, the de-skilling, the hazards of life in working-class slums – that affected migrant groups everywhere during the Industrial Revolution. For many Belfast Protestants, the anti-Catholic harangues of Drew and his cohort may have been relevant precisely insofar as they offered an explanation for their own rather attenuated urban existences. This hypothesis gains some support when we consider the most important Protestant organisation of the period, the Orange Order.

The Orange Order was an exclusively Protestant fraternity founded in 1795 with the aim of preventing the erosion of Irish Protestants' political, cultural and economic power. Primarily an organisation of the lower classes, the Order had a complicated relationship with the state and the Protestant gentry, both of whom oscillated between tacit support and open disavowal of Orangeism, depending upon the political expediencies of the day.[50] In the immediate post-famine years, after a brief period of official favour during the Young Ireland rebellion of 1848, the Order was under-going a period of introspection and declining membership. After a terrible fight at an Orange procession at Dolly's Brae, County Down, in 1849, the government banned all 'party' processions, undermining an important component of Orangeism's popular appeal and leading many influential patrons to distance themselves from the group.[51] While overall membership began to decline, however, the movement enjoyed a surge of activity in Belfast itself. Between 1853 and 1861, the number of official Orange lodges in the city rose from thirty to ninety, while the total number of Orangemen jumped from just 1,335 in 1851 to 4,000 in 1870.[52] This expansion was undoubtedly driven by the rapid influx of Protestant migrants from the Ulster countryside, where Orangeism was traditionally strongest, and, as we will see in Chapter 3, it helped to perpetuate many of the patterns of conflict that had afflicted rural Ulster for generations.

Although clergymen such as Drew, Cooke and T. F. Miller (the Anglican vicar of Belfast) were all publicly associated with Orangeism to one degree or another, and although the Order was actively courted by many of the city's political rulers, Orangeism in Belfast was a much more organically working-class phenomenon than the evangelical organisations discussed thus far. To be sure, the most prominent Orange leaders in Belfast, like Orange leaders elsewhere, tended to come from the upper ranks of Protestant society, and, as David Miller suggests, this probably helped preserve (in a modified form) the 'special relationship' between Protestant elites and lower-class Protestants that had existed in the countryside.[53] But, contrary to recent speculations by Kerby Miller, the Orange Order in Belfast was not at this time dominated by 'small gentry, clergymen, or ... middle-, lower-middle-, or quasi-middle-class men' whose status and reputations formed 'vital linkages of authority and dependence' between elite and working-class Protestants.[54] Instead, it appears that most Orange leaders in Belfast were artisans, sea captains and men of even lower social status.[55] This does not rule out the possibility that the Orange Order acted as a conduit for elite Protestant 'hegemony' and 'unionism', as Kerby Miller suggests, but it should caution us against seeing Orangeism as a mere device for top-down 'social control'. As Henry Patterson and others have noted, working-class Protestants retained a fierce independence in Victorian Belfast that frequently led them into conflict with their elite patrons.[56] This independence did not manifest itself in any sustained labour movement against the capitalist elite (which is the kind of thing Kerby Miller is looking for), but, rather, in the 'rowdy' popular culture and disdain for 'respectability' that animated plebeian Protestantism during these years, especially within the Orange Order.

Instead of seeing mid-Victorian Belfast Orangeism as the embryo of the cross-class unionist alliance that developed in the later nineteenth century, then, it is probably more helpful to think of it as a forum in which elite evangelicalism commingled with popular Protestant culture, and where both groups' anti-Catholic beliefs found reinforcement and focus. From the point of view of Drew and his evangelical colleagues, the Order offered an ideal way to educate working-class Protestants about the threats they faced from organised Catholicism. In one of Drew's Orange pamphlets, entitled 'Twenty Reasons for Being an Orangeman', fully half of the reasons had to do with opposition to the Catholic Church. Reason number nine was typical: 'Because I learn by the doctrines, history, and daily practices of the Church of Rome, that the lives of Protestants are endangered, the laws of England set at nought, and the crown of England subordinated to the dictation of an Italian bishop.'[57] To the Orange leadership, a working-class rank and file imbued with such anti-Catholic principles offered an ideal fund of loyal Protestant manpower for their various political campaigns, and they did not hesitate to draw upon that fund in times of crisis. During the uproar over the 'papal aggression', for example, the Order's Grand Lodge sent a memorial to Queen Victoria promising '1,800 lodges of loyal Orangemen' to defend 'our common religion and liberties' should the necessity arise.[58] In addition, those Orangemen favoured with the franchise were repeatedly implored to vote for candidates who could be trusted to defend Protestant causes in Parliament.[59] Orangemen without political rights (and this was most of them) could also participate in the political process, albeit informally, by helping to pack political meetings, hooting or jeering selected candidates and occasionally – though this was discountenanced by 'respectable' Orangemen – taking part in election riots.[60]

Aside from these political activities, there is little evidence that working-class Orangemen took an active role in the religious elements of evangelicalism. Although missionary bodies periodically asked the Order for donations, the Orange lodges do not themselves appear to have undertaken any proselytising or domestic missionary initiatives. This aloofness was partly due to the suspicion with which many Dissenting evangelicals tended to regard Orangeism, which they continued to identify with the Established Church and the Anglican aristocracy.[61] It was also a result of the moralising tone that many of these evangelicals adopted in their dealings with the lower classes, especially since Orangemen, with their 'rough' culture of pageantry and violence, were precisely the sorts of lost souls whom many bourgeois evangelicals were seeking to reform. Eventually, Orange lodges espousing evangelical principals such as temperance did appear in Belfast, but during this early period it appears that the moral reform agenda of the evangelicals made little headway within most Orange lodges.

Far more important to the average Orangeman than the political or religious agendas of the Protestant elite were the social and economic

benefits that came with lodge membership. As one official Orange historian has put it, 'what mattered to the ordinary man was to be able to feel
that his own position and living, and those of his family, were secure'.[62]
Like the Orange lodges that took root among immigrant communities in
Britain and North America, Orangeism in Belfast provided an important
measure of social cohesion and stability for Protestant migrants.[63] Among
its other functions, Orangeism appears to have acted in Belfast as a sort
of friendly society, offering incoming migrants a ready-made social
network through which to obtain jobs, housing, and other material advantages.[64] Orange lodges also served as social venues in which Protestant
men could escape from the disorienting bustle and diversity of the city
and forge social ties with fellow Protestants across the social spectrum.
Inside the lodge, they got to know their Protestant neighbours by drinking with them, singing Protestant songs and participating in secret
Protestant rituals. 'There is nothing so peaceful, so quieting, or that
rendered a community more peaceable and orderly than that of having a
proper place where they can utter their sentiments', remarked one Orange
leader at the opening of a Sandy Row lodge in 1868.[65] Outside the lodges,
Orangeism played a similar function, allowing working-class Protestant
men to proclaim their communal loyalties by attending Orange demonstrations, wearing Orange scarves and lilies and occasionally (although it
was illegal) taking part in Orange processions. All this was bound up in
an ethical system more acceptable than that preached by evangelical moral
reformers, a system that prescribed (in Drew's words) 'vigilance, energy,
and witness-ship for God' alongside 'loyalty, patience, firmness, and
brotherly love'.[66]

   More than anything, to become an Orangeman in post-famine Belfast
was to adopt an identity that could shield one from the uncertainties of
urban life. For Orangeism took off in Belfast during a period of profound
disruption in the world of the working-class Protestant male, a moment
when the mechanisation of linen manufacturing forced formerly independent weavers to abandon their traditional livelihoods.[67] These men
often found themselves submitting to the galling necessity of taking on
unskilled wage labour, forced for the first time to become dependent on
impersonal ties with employers and landlords and, what was more, watching as their wives and children undertook much the same sort of work. It
was a deeply emasculating experience for many Protestant men, but
Orangeism offered them a way to reassert some measure of control over
their social and political worlds.[68] As Peter Gibbon suggests, Orangeism
offered Protestant men an essentially '*martial*' identity, promoting the
virtues of 'stoutness-sturdyness, readiness, openness, boldness and
redoubtability-indomitability', and, of course, 'personalistic loyalty' to

one's brethren.[69] It was a deeply conservative identity as well, not only in its politics but also in its paternal ideal of the Protestant male as the physical and moral guardian of his wife, his children and the larger Protestant community.[70] Against this idealised conception of Protestant masculinity Orangeism imagined an effeminate Catholic 'other' that was neither manly nor independent, but cowardly, underhanded and easily led by priests. By defining themselves against this stereotype, Orangemen were able to construct a set of monochromatic certainties about themselves, their Catholic opponents and each group's relative place in the city. Together with the social and economic benefits of Orangeism, these certainties helped to overcome some of the more troubling realities of industrialised life.

Evangelical offensive: missionaries and controversialism

Reason number five of Thomas Drew's 'Twenty Reasons for Being an Orangeman' stated that among the duties of an Orangeman was to 'deliver Romanists from mental perversion and spiritual slavery'.[71] While there is no evidence that working-class Orangemen, either individually or collectively, seriously took up this challenge, the goal of converting Catholics to Protestantism was a powerful impulse among many other Protestant groups in Victorian Belfast. Evangelicalism is by definition a missionary movement, of course, and in Ireland it derived much of its vitality from a utopian vision of a country cleansed of Popery and basking in the millennial glow of pure faith unmediated by priests and popes. This proselytising impulse was motivated by a mixture of altruism and political calculation: while many evangelicals genuinely desired to save Catholic souls, many also recognised that in so doing they were robbing the Pope of a potential fifth column that might be mobilised to carry out Rome's aggressions. Proselytising initiatives were therefore capable of showing evangelicalism at its most charitable as well as its most paranoid and sectarian, and, while it is certainly right to classify all such initiatives as anti-Catholic, it is also important to note that that not all forms of anti-Catholicism are the same.[72] In Belfast, a diverse group of Protestants heeded the evangelical directive to 'cause them to come in', and their methods ranged from the quietly persuasive to the openly confrontational. Although successful conversions were probably rare, the strength and popularity of these proselytising measures helped to reinforce notions of Protestant exceptionalism at the same time as they fuelled Catholic feelings of vulnerability.

Evangelical proselytism was a matter of considerable public debate throughout Victorian Ireland. The famine, which killed roughly a million

people and forced another million to emigrate, had been interpreted by
many evangelicals as a 'visitation from God' and a sign that Catholicism
was causing the ruin of the Irish people.[73] Numerous evangelical groups
from Ulster and Britain had therefore sent missions to famine-ravaged
Connaught to relieve physical distress and to bring about the conversion
of Catholics. Belfast evangelicals were at the centre of many of these
famine missions, and during and after the famine missionary activity
gained popularity among a broad segment of the Protestant middle class.
The major figure in this movement was John Edgar, a Presbyterian minister with ironclad evangelical credentials stretching back to his days as an
antislavery agitator and temperance reformer in the 1820s and 1830s.[74]
Edgar's most famous sermon, 'The Cry from Connaught', galvanised the
Belfast missionary movement in 1846 with a moving depiction of his
recent visit to the west of Ireland.[75] Couched in conciliatory language
calculated to pluck at middle-class consciences, Edgar articulated an
eminently respectable form of evangelicalism that seemed worlds away
from the bilious harangues of Thomas Drew. 'I advocate no proselytism
in a bad sense,' he said, 'no bribery, but I desire to impress on all minds
that it is not by formal dogmatic theology or regular systematic preaching, that we are to commend ourselves to the understandings and hearts
of our unenlightened countrymen; neither is it by a fierce onset of controversial war.' Urging Protestants to 'send prudent, experienced men, of
sweet and homely spirit, kind and generous souls, into the bosom of
Roman Catholic families', Edgar distributed some 26,000 copies of the
pamphlet 'The Cry from Connaught'.[76]

Largely because of Edgar's skill at publicising the cause, Belfast soon
became a leading centre of evangelical proselytism within Ireland and
around the world. Edgar himself helped organise the Ladies' Relief Association, which sought to introduce muslin weaving to Connaught, as well
as the Presbyterian Church's Mission to the Catholics of Dublin, the Presbyterian Students' Mission to Connaught and the Presbyterian Home
Mission.[77] By 1861 the Presbyterians could also boast a Foreign Mission,
a Jewish Mission, a Colonial and Continental Mission, and an Indian
Mission, while a somewhat smaller number of missionary groups populated the Anglican side of the aisle.[78] Such groups offered the Protestant
middle classes an important outlet for their philanthropic impulses, and
they contributed to Belfast's growing reputation as the centre of Irish
Protestantism and, in the eyes of its practitioners, the fountainhead of a
uniquely favoured and virtuous evangelical faith.

None of this directly impacted on Catholics living in Belfast, of course,
although Catholic leaders did frequently condemn the Connaught
'soupers' for their predatory tactics.[79] More directly polarising within

Belfast was a practice known as controversialism, which, as its name suggests, was a somewhat more confrontational form of proselytism than Edgar advocated. Controversialism had been practised in Ireland since before the famine, and it generally took two forms: printed sermons, pamphlets or periodicals attacking Catholic doctrine; and public meetings challenging Catholics to debate the errors of Catholicism with an evangelical preacher.[80] Controversialists believed that, because of the tyranny of their priests, Catholics had no knowledge of or access to the Word of God. Once they were exposed to the undeniable truth of the controversialist's point of view, however, conversion would naturally follow. Some sought to accomplish this by means of rational persuasion, others by emotive tirades against the errors of Popery. Often their pamphlets and lectures were simply excuses to wage public assaults on the Catholic Church rather than genuine attempts at conversion, but it would be a mistake to assume that these men were not sincere in their desire to spread the faith. If abusing Catholicism was their only goal, there were plenty of other avenues through which to do so.

The leading controversialist in Belfast during the post-famine period was undoubtedly William McIlwaine, Anglican incumbent of St George's Church. Since 1841 McIlwaine had built a reputation in Belfast as a fearless opponent of Catholic error, and large crowds flocked to his lectures. At a typical lecture in 1853, he ridiculed the Catholic practice of saying masses 'to cure sick cows, restore rotten potatoes, and contribute to success in catching fish', argued that the Catholic Missal was 'unscriptural', and dared Catholic priests 'to meet him and prove that he was wrong'.[81] Priests rarely, if ever, accepted such invitations, and the usual effect of McIlwaine's lectures was not so much to promote interfaith dialogue as to arouse sectarian passions. In May 1856, for instance, violence broke out at a characteristically tendentious lecture in the Victoria Hall when a handful of Catholics interrupted McIlwaine's address and were chased from the hall by angry Protestants.[82] Around the same time a letter appeared in the Catholic newspaper the *Ulsterman* (which diligently denounced McIlwaine throughout this period) alleging that Protestants ('ragamuffins', 'bogtrotters', 'factory girls' and 'rif-raff') were assembling nightly before McIlwaine's house and, to the 'very great annoyance of his neighbours', playing party tunes on fifes and drums. The writer threatened to gather together 'an opposing band' of Catholics to counteract McIlwaine's supporters, but nothing more seems to have come of the dispute.[83]

Another Belfast controversialist making his reputation in the early 1850s was the Presbyterian minister Hugh Hanna. Hanna's later career as an anti-Catholic agitator and politician is relatively well documented, and we shall find him playing a leading part in Belfast's sectarian battles from the 1857 riots onwards. What is less well known, however, is that much of Hanna's early career was devoted to converting working-class Catholics; indeed, this was a duty that was central to his evangelical mission throughout the 1850s. After his appointment to Belfast's Berry Street Presbyterian Church in 1852, one of Hanna's first initiatives was to create a Mission to Romanists to complement his broader mission to churchless Presbyterians. 'We love our Roman Catholic countrymen, but we abhor their errors', he wrote in his first annual report,

> we love their souls – we labour and pray for their salvation. They are in darkness denser than that of Egypt – we hold up the torch of truth, and seek to lead them out of Rome's dungeons into open day, that they may breathe the pure atmosphere of Heaven, and rejoice in the matchless splendour of the Sun of Righteousness.[84]

Following established controversialist practice, Hanna gave a series of lectures in 1852 on 'the Rule of Faith, Papal Supremacy, Infallibility, and Purgatory', all of which, he claimed, attracted 'large numbers' of Catholics. He also conducted informal meetings with Catholics, including open discussions 'on the peculiarities of their Church' at which Catholics were encouraged to debate religious questions with Hanna and members of the congregation.[85]

It is unclear how many Catholics attended these meetings. Hanna claimed that he attracted several hundred in the first year alone, although this is probably an exaggeration.[86] What does seem to have been the case is that these 'anti-Romish lectures', in the words of a sympathetic biographer, excited 'immense interest' among both Protestants and Catholics in the neighbourhood. 'It often happened that the church was crowded to the doors, the grounds around the church were crowded, and the assembly extended over the public thoroughfare outside, vainly hoping to effect an entrance. The excitement among the mill population was intense.'[87] In his own account, Hanna highlighted the anger his mission inspired among Catholic priests, claiming that, while many initially looked upon his activities with indifference, they soon became alarmed by his success. 'No company of cursing priests can prevent the people from attending,' he declared. 'Though they keep guard upon my gates, armed with scourge of scorpions, when I preach Popery, I'll engage to have Romanists in my audience.'[88] The following year he expanded his Mission to Romanists by publishing a series of short tracts for those Catholics who could not attend his meetings in person, the first of which was entitled 'Purgatory and Priestcraft Exposed'.[89]

Hanna's determination to convert Catholics stayed with him until at least the end of the decade. In 1859, when his church became the centre of an evangelical revival sweeping through Belfast, Hanna tried vigorously to spread the 'revival spirit' among poor Catholics, often over the objections of their priests and neighbours.[90] During this time the evangelical press ran numerous stories of Catholic conversions, particularly among mill girls who attended prayer meetings at Hanna's church.[91] It is difficult to know how seriously to take these accounts of Catholic conversion – they probably reveal more about the aspirations of the evangelicals themselves than about any permanent conversions among Catholics – but it does appear that these proselytising efforts aroused considerable hostility from priests, neighbours and family members of the converts.

On the whole, the number of conversions among Catholics during this period was probably quite small, but the overall impact of these proselytising initiatives was nevertheless significant, for they served to advertise and endorse the essential anti-Catholicism of the entire evangelical project. Domestic missions, churches, Sunday schools, reading rooms and even Thomas Drew's political organisations were designed principally to shore up Protestantism from within, and, although they were all fuelled by anti-Catholic assumptions, their attitude was rarely directly confrontational. The proselytising initiatives of McIlwaine, Hanna and even Edgar crossed that threshold, however, taking the battle directly to the Catholics in what was usually interpreted by them as an insult and a threat. As such, these initiatives blurred the lines between benign and malicious forms of evangelicalism, making it exceedingly difficult for outsiders to distinguish between the two and encouraging Catholics, in particular, to view most forms of evangelicalism as part of a monolithic threat. 'Week after week,' observed the *Ulsterman* in 1854,

> the walls of Belfast and our Northern towns are covered with placards announcing to the ignorant crowd, that some peripatetic preacher will hold forth on the 'abominations of Popery.' And week after week, in church or meeting house, some one of these firebrands raves by the hour on the inexhaustible theme ... His howlings are accepted as inspired eloquence by ignorant crowds; his statements, mad and wicked as they are, are believed as truths; and the hearers go forth with bitter hatred nursing in their hearts against their countrymen who worship at the altars where their fathers bowed and prayed long centuries ago.[92]

In this atmosphere of generalised suspicion, even the relatively benign Belfast Town Mission, which rarely sought out Catholics for conversion, found itself accused of being a 'wolf among the sheep' – that is, of luring unsuspecting Catholics into its grasp only to poach their souls.[93] The next chapter explores in more detail the Catholic response to evangelical proselytism; here, it is important simply to observe how easily Catholics could interpret the widely varying strands of Belfast evangelicalism as part of a unified anti-Catholic conspiracy.

Open-air preaching

The most public face of evangelicalism in mid-Victorian Belfast was undoubtedly open-air preaching, a form of working-class outreach held by many to be the most effective method of reaching large numbers of churchless urban dwellers. The practice fell into disrepute when Hugh Hanna held an open-air service near the Custom House in September 1857 that sparked a week of rioting, an event we shall explore more fully in Chapter 3. With the recent exception of Janice Holmes, most historians have interpreted Hanna's actions as an attempt to claim Belfast as a 'Protestant city' by using a rabble-rousing anti-Catholic lecture to pursue what was essentially a 'political' goal.[94] However, such an interpretation fails to account for the hidden depths of emotion and belief that were stimulated by the open-air preaching crisis of 1857. To appreciate this, it is necessary to examine open-air preaching within the context of the larger evangelical tradition of which it was a part and, in particular, to understand that this was a form of evangelicalism that was intimately connected – in both Catholic and Protestant minds – with proselytism.

Open-air preaching, as its nineteenth-century practitioners liked to point out, had a pedigree stretching back to biblical times. Jesus himself had preached in the open air during the Sermon on the Mount, they observed, and in later centuries those Protestants who were persecuted for their beliefs had held services under 'the canopy of nature . . . a far nobler amphitheatre than any work of art'.[95] The practice of holding religious services outdoors appears to have come to Ireland with John Wesley in the 1740s and 1750s, and, as Wesley himself discovered, it was a style of evangelicalism that could easily arouse the hostility of Irish Catholics.[96] Despite its dangers, or perhaps because of them, open-air preaching continued to be a favoured evangelical device for British itinerant preachers travelling around Ireland in the nineteenth century, particularly during the great evangelical offensives in the second quarter of the century. For these men, not only was open-air preaching a divinely sanctioned apostolic practice, but it also had the practical benefit of reaching Catholics directly, without the interference of their priests. Once exposed to the truth of God's grace, these preachers felt, Catholics would surely renounce their own erroneous doctrines.

Few, if any, of these British itinerants ever came to Belfast; their missions were concentrated mainly in the Catholic counties of the south and west, and occasionally in southern Ulster counties like Cavan. Nevertheless, the activities of these preachers greatly influenced the way open-air preaching was understood in Belfast, and the hostility they aroused in other parts of Ireland demonstrated the divisive potential of this uniquely public form of evangelicalism. In the immediate post-famine period, the largest British initiative was probably that coordinated by the Evangelical Alliance in the summer of 1853. Convinced that 'the real cause of the unhappy and afflicted condition of Ireland is its deficiency in that pure and vital godliness taught in Scripture', this London-based coalition dispatched a hundred English and Scottish ministers to preach in the streets of dozens of Irish towns and villages.[97] On Sundays and market days the preachers drew large crowds of curious onlookers in places like Limerick, Clonmel and Kilkenny, but curiosity often turned to anger when the preachers began insulting their audiences' faith. In Limerick one preacher was hurled from his platform when he 'began to assure those who were about him that they were buried in the abyss of sin and misery – that they possessed no faith – that their religion was a mockery, their doctrine a snare, their priesthood a delusion, their worship idolatry'.[98] In Clonmel a group of Catholics attacked six preachers, throwing one down a flight of steps and chasing another into the home of a Protestant, while in Nenagh crowds threw mud and manure baskets at the hapless missionaries.[99] All summer the Catholic press relentlessly ridiculed the missionaries as 'barrel preachers' and the 'Dirty Hundred'. Local magistrates, policemen and other authorities blamed the men for causing wanton breaches of the peace, and in Limerick the mayor himself ordered the missionaries to leave town.[100]

More disturbances followed. In 1855 the Irish Church Missionary Society, another British organisation, sent yet another batch of a hundred missionaries to Ireland. Between September 1855 and April 1856, some sixteen assaults took place in Kilkenny alone, leading one policeman to note that 'ill-feeling has been excited and stirred up between two classes of Her Majesty's subjects previously living in harmony and cordiality together . . .'.[101] This observation echoed the remarks of a Limerick Protestant three years earlier, who alleged that the preachers 'have caused more disunion and injury than can be contemplated, previous to which the members of every religious persuasion were uniting in brotherly love'.[102]

In Belfast, the Catholic and Protestant papers followed these events with intense interest. Condemning the missions in Kilkenny and the Glens of Antrim as 'one of the vilest, basest, and audacious frauds that ever disgraced Christianity or disturbed the peace of a country', the *Ulsterman* warned that any such preaching in Belfast would be met with less forbearance than it received elsewhere.[103] The ultra-Protestant *Newsletter*, meanwhile, decried 'the vile treatment received by the Protestant missionaries at the hands of their Romish persecutors' and ominously warned, 'this is a battle which cannot much longer continue without results so serious that we are almost afraid to contemplate them'.[104] Both of these arguments prefigured those that would be made during Belfast's own open-air preaching crisis in 1857. At issue was, on the one hand, the right of Catholics to be free of 'nuisance' and 'annoyance' from those who deliberately insulted their faith and, on the other, the 'Protestant liberty' of free religious expression and the particular right to spread the Protestant faith via public evangelism. By the time the open-air preaching controversy migrated to Belfast itself, these arguments would be well rehearsed.

Belfast did host its own open-air evangelical services in the years before 1857, but the nature of the movement was substantially different from that which was inflaming tempers in Kilkenny and Limerick. In 1851 the Presbyterian minister William Johnston, inspired by his father's open-air services in the nearby village of Tullylish, began holding public services in the lanes and entries of Belfast's working-class slums. For Johnston, open-air preaching was an ideal way to reach the city's poor. Not only did it bring the Gospel directly to the people, reaching those who might not otherwise invite a domestic missionary into their home or send their children to Sunday school, but it also overcame the resistance of people who would not attend church for want of suitable clothing.[105] Excited by this new technique, dozens of evangelical ministers soon began holding their own open-air services. Methodists, whose faith had spread principally through open-air services in the previous century, proved especially enthusiastic, as did Johnston's fellow Presbyterians, who established a 'Committee on Open-Air Preaching' to coordinate their efforts. Between 1851 and 1856, the number of Presbyterian ministers engaged in open-air preaching throughout Ulster rose from eight to sixty, and the total number of services grew from fifty to 280. Meanwhile, the estimated number of attenders expanded from 1,300 to 65,215.[106]

Few of these services were explicitly anti-Catholic; preachers were more likely to fulminate against drinking and other forms of immorality than against the intoxicating effects of Popery. Moreover, the vast majority of open-air services were held in predominately Protestant parts of town, and, as a result, most passed without any significant disturbance. On the rare occasions when preachers strayed into mixed or Catholic districts, however, violence could erupt. In 1853 Johnston was attacked during a service in Pinkerton's Row, one of the mixed-religion inner-city slums, and forced to flee from a hostile crowd. The following week a Methodist minister named McKay was attacked in a vacant lot on the Falls

Road, an area that was slowly becoming populated by Catholics.[107] Two years later, in the midst of an otherwise glowing report of his open-air services, Johnston complained that 'Satan has sometimes stirred his slaves to intimidate or disturb' his audiences in Belfast. These disturbances probably happened in the Catholic neighbourhood of Smithfield, where Johnston had recently been preaching.[108]

In order to understand what drove Johnston and others to endanger life and limb by holding evangelical services in Catholic areas, it is necessary to recall the latent anti-Catholicism of the entire evangelical project. While most ministers prudently confined their services to Protestant areas, there was a powerful impulse within the open-air movement to utilise this evangelising tool among those who were even more in need of God's saving grace than churchless Protestants. The Presbyterian General Assembly's endorsement of open-air preaching in 1853 hinted at this impulse when it proclaimed the necessity of 'bringing the Gospel before the minds of many who attend to no place of worship, *or none where they hear the truth'*.[109] The following year, when the General Assembly established a 'Committee on Popery' devoted to 'opposing the arrogant claims of Rome, and resisting her persecuting spirit and deeds', William Johnston was among its first members, alongside such anti-Catholic luminaries as Hanna and Edgar.[110] For men like Johnston, the temptation to use open-air preaching for such sectarian purposes was undoubtedly strong, even if it risked provoking Catholic anger. Given that it had long been used as a proselytising tool elsewhere in Ireland, it is unsurprising that open-air preaching should occasionally have been turned to that purpose in Protestant-dominated Belfast.

Conclusion

The open-air preaching movement neatly embodied the different strands of post-famine evangelicalism in Belfast. Fuelled by bourgeois anxieties about working-class irreligion, committed to providing unmediated access to God's grace, powered by an overwhelming missionary zeal and spiced with a dose of anti-Catholicism that could be adjusted according to taste, open-air preaching, like evangelicalism generally, was a complex concoction. From the outside, its practitioners were often judged solely by the activities of their most fanatical colleagues. Fine distinctions within the movement were inconsequential to anyone who viewed the whole evangelical project as a chauvinistic insult to the religion of the majority of the Irish people. Viewed from within, however, the practice of open-air preaching was open to as many different shades of opinion as could fit within the evangelical tent, and if all were complicit in the movement's essential anti-Catholicism, not all drew the same conclusions as to how those anti-Catholic principles should be enacted. Most were content to strengthen Protestantism from within; some, however, were determined to go on the offensive.

This chapter has explored the different avenues that evangelicals took in post-famine Belfast to build up the Protestant faith in the face of the twin challenges of urbanisation and Catholic advance. The ideologies and assumptions driving their initiatives were important in themselves, of course, but equally important were the social relationships that came out of these beliefs. Although deep divisions separated the Protestant working classes from their middle-class counterparts, many of the evangelical and political organisations that took root during these years helped to forge some tenuous links between the two. While most working-class people had little time for the condescension of their self-appointed evangelical saviours and many turned a deaf ear to the preachers who appeared in their neighbourhoods every summer, many others undoubtedly appreciated the material and moral succour that these elite groups provided. Moreover, the centrality of evangelicalism to Belfast's civic culture – the prominence of its charities, the political influence of its ministers, the dense network of reading rooms and Sunday schools and young men's organisations it provided – created an unmistakable sense that Belfast was an indubitably Protestant city, and one, moreover, in which working-class Protestants enjoyed a special place. That much of this evangelical culture was avowedly anti-Catholic added another layer to the city's Protestant identity, and it was here, in the mingling of working-class and evangelical attitudes towards Catholics, that both groups found their sturdiest common ground. During moments of communal crisis the divisions within Protestantism did not dissolve, but the networks of association between the different classes could easily be set into motion, enabling those Protestants with violent intentions to act with the knowledge that many of their social superiors condoned anti-Catholic behaviour. Neither class was a simple receptacle for the beliefs of the other, but where their beliefs overlapped, both found strength.

Notes

1 The Belfast Almanac 1864 (Belfast: Alexander Mayne, 1864), 87.
2 A. McIntyre, diary, 21 Nov. 1853, PRONI, D/1558/2/3.
3 *Ibid.*, June 1855.
4 *Report of the Commissioners of Inquiry into the Origin and Character of the Riots in Belfast, in July and September, 1857; together with Minutes of Evidence and Appendix*, HC 1857–58 (2309) XXVI (hereafter, *1857 Belfast Riots Inquiry*), Appendix 1, 250–1.

5 *Ibid.* See also Thomas Drew, *A Sermon, Preached in Christ Church, Belfast, on the evening of November 5, 1856, being the Anniversary of the Deliverance from the Popish Gunpowder Plot, and also of the Arrival of William III., Prince of Orange, before the Assembled Orangemen of Belfast* (Belfast: A. Welsh, 1856).

6 *Northern Whig*, 27 Aug., 1857.

7 A. McIntyre, diary, 5 Sept. 1853, PRONI, D/1558/2/3.

8 One important exception is David Hempton and Myrtle Hill, *Evangelical Protestantism in Ulster Society, 1740–1890* (New York: Routledge, 1992), 121–8.

9 See e.g. *1857 Belfast Riots Inquiry*, 2.

10 Hempton and Hill, *Evangelical*, xii.

11 D. W. Bebbington, *Evangelicalism in Modern Britain: A History from the 1730s to the 1980s* (Winchester, Mass.: Allen & Unwin, 1989), 2–3. Italics in original.

12 Hempton and Hill, *Evangelical*, 3–19.

13 *1857 Belfast Riots Inquiry*, Appendix 1, 251.

14 Hempton and Hill, *Evangelical*, 47–61, 123–4; David Hempton, 'Belfast: The Unique City?', in *European Religion in the Age of the Great Cities, 1830–1930*, ed. Hugh McLeod (London: Routledge, 1995), 145–64.

15 This was the Arian party led by Henry Montgomery. See Hempton and Hill, *Evangelical*, 69–76; and Peter Brooke, *Ulster Presbyterianism: The Historical Perspective, 1810–1970* (Belfast: Athol Books, 1994), 121–8.

16 Hempton and Hill, *Evangelical*, 63–9; S. Peter Kerr, 'Voluntaryism within the Established Church in Nineteenth Century Belfast', in *Voluntary Religion: Papers Read at the 1985 Summer Meeting and the 1986 Winter Meeting of the Ecclesiastical History Society*, ed. W. J. Shiels and Diana Wood (Oxford: Basil Blackwell, 1986), 347–62; Desmond Bowen, *The Protestant Crusade in Ireland, 1800–70: A Study of Protestant–Catholic Relations between the Act of Union and Disestablishment* (Dublin: Gill and Macmillan, 1978), 61–80.

17 Hempton and Hill, *Evangelical*, 43–4, 79–80; Myrtle Hill, *The Time of the End: Millenarian Beliefs in Ulster* (Belfast: The Belfast Society, 2001), 17–31.

18 The census of 1861 provides some idea of the diversity within Belfast Protestantism. In a total population of 120,777, Presbyterians numbered 42,229 (35%); Anglicans, 29,832 (24.7%); Methodists, 4,949 (4.1%); Baptists, 227; and Quakers, 202. *The Census of Ireland for the year 1861. Part IV. Report and Tables relating to the Religious Professions, Education, and Occupations of the People*, HC 1863 (3204–III) LIX, vol. 1, 10–12.

19 On the Protestant response to Cullen's reforms, see Desmond Bowen, *History and the Shaping of Irish Protestantism* (New York: Peter Land, 1995), 269–315.

20 Ian Budge and Cornelius O'Leary, *Belfast: Approach to Crisis* (London: Macmillan, 1973), 28.

21 *Belfast Newsletter*, 18 June 1857.

22 Rev. W. M. O'Hanlon, *Walks Among the Poor of Belfast, and Suggestions for Their Improvement* (Belfast: Henry Greer, 1853).

23 John Edgar, *The Dangerous and Perishing Classes. A paper read before the Statistical Section of the British Association, at Belfast, September 3, 1852* (Belfast: Belfast Social Inquiry Society, 1852).

24 A. G. Malcolm, *The Sanitary State of Belfast, With Suggestions for its Improvement, a Paper Read before the Statistical Section of the British Association, at Belfast, September 7, 1852* (Belfast, Henry Greer, 1852), 8–14, 26.

25 Hempton and Hill, *Evangelical*, 112.

26 Census of Christ Church, 1852, PRONI, CR/1/13D/1.

27 *Belfast Newsletter*, 3 Dec. 1850.

28 Henry Cooke, *The Papal Aggression! Lecture by the Rev. H. Cooke, D.D., LL.D., on the Present Aspect and Future Prospects of Popery*, 2nd ed. (Belfast: William McComb, 1851), 22–3.

29 Presbyterian Church of Ireland, *Reports of the Berry Street Congregation* (Belfast: Banner of Ulster Office, 1853), 3. Albert Street Presbyterian Church Records, Minutes of Committee, PRONI, MIC/1P/16/1–2.

30 James Morgan, 'The Presbyterian Churches of Belfast', *The Irish Presbyterian* (June 1857), 141–4.

31 The number of baptisms in Christ Church more than doubled between 1852 and 1857, jumping from 134 to 313 per year. Annals of Christ Church, PRONI, T/2159/1, 137 and 232.

32 Church numbers come from *Belfast Almanac 1864*, 88–9. Ratios are derived using 1861 census figures. Chapter 2 below discusses the Catholic churches in more detail.

33 James Morgan ('Presbyterian Churches') estimated in 1857 that there were some 10,000 Presbyterians who did not belong to any congregation.

34 R. M. Sibbett, *For Christ and Crown: The Story of a* Mission (Belfast: 'The Witness' Office, 1926), 76; *Belfast Almanac 1864*, 85–7; *1857 Belfast Riots Inquiry*, Appendix 7, 255–6.

35 'Belfast Town Mission', *The Irish Presbyterian* (Nov. 1854), 301.

36 Hempton and Hill, Evangelical, 113–21.

37 *Henderson's Belfast Directory, 1861* (Belfast: News-Letter Office, 1861).

38 Alison Jordan, *Who Cared? Charity in Victorian and Edwardian Belfast* (Belfast: Queen's University Institute of Irish Studies, 1993), 191–4.

39 See e.g. the report of a Belfast Town Mission meeting in *Banner of Ulster*, 29 Oct. 1857.

40 A. McIntyre, diary, PRONI, D/1558/2/3.

41 Hempton and Hill, *Evangelical*, 116.

42 Finlay Holmes, *Henry Cooke* (Belfast: Christian Journals Limited, 1981), 208.

43 Catherine Hirst, *Religion, Politics and Violence in Nineteenth-Century Belfast: The Pound and Sandy Row*, Four Courts Press, 2002), 49–50; William McComb, *The Repealer Repulsed*, ed. Patrick Maume (Dublin: University College Dublin Press, 2003).

44 Christ Church records, 1835–65, PRONI, MIC/583/23–25; Census of

Christ Church 1852, PRONI, CR/1/13D/1; Hempton and Hill, *Evangelical*, 112; Hirst, *Religion*, 44–5; Peter Kerr, 'Voluntaryism', 347–62.

45 David W. Miller, 'Presbyterianism and "Modernization" in Ulster', *Past and Present*, 80 (Aug. 1978), 85; see also Boyd Hilton's discussion of the difference between 'moderate' and 'extremist' evangelicalism in the early nineteenth century in *The Age of Atonement* (Oxford: Clarendon Press, 1988), 7–26.

46 See e.g. the reports of Drew's sermons on the 'Turko-Russian Question', given in Christ Church in December 1853, in *Belfast Weekly Mail*, 16 and 23 Dec. 1853.

47 Annals of Christ Church, PRONI, T/2159/1, 161–2. Underlining in original. The 'Act of 1829' was the Catholic Emancipation Act, which granted political rights to Catholics.

48 Besides Drew, Richard Davison, one of Belfast's two Conservative MPs, was an honorary vice-president, as were the Anglican ministers Theophilus Campbell and Tresham Gregg, along with the prominent Orangeman W. J. Gwynne. Among the committee members were the foundry owners Francis and William Coates (the latter was also a JP). Annals of Christ Church, PRONI, T/2159/1, 161–2.

49 Annals of Christ Church, 197–9; *Belfast Newsletter*, 14 May 1857.

50 On the early years of the Orange Order, see Hereward Senior, *Orangeism in Ireland and Britain, 1795–1836* (London: Routledge and Kegan Paul, 1966).

51 On Dolly's Brae, see Chapter 3.

52 Belfast County Grand Lodge, *Centenary Official History, 1863–1963* (Newtownabbey: Universal Publishing Company, 1963), 15, 27; Budge and O'Leary, *Belfast*, 92–3. The Orange Order's Registry of Warrants (held at the Grand Orange Lodge of Ireland, Belfast) for the year 1856 shows forty-one warrants for lodges in the Belfast district. The membership of each lodge varied, but at least one lodge in 1857 is known to have had some ninety members. See Thomas Ward's evidence, *1857 Belfast Riots Inquiry*, 186.

53 David Miller, *Queen's Rebels: Ulster Loyalism in Historical Perspective* (Dublin: Gill and Macmillan, 1978), 56–64.

54 Kerby A. Miller, 'Belfast's First Bomb, 28 February 1816: Class Conflict and the Origins of Ulster Unionist Hegemony', *Eire-Ireland*, 39 (Spring–Summer 2004), 262–80.

55 Comparing the Orange Registry of Warrants for the Belfast district in 1856 (held at the GOLI in Belfast) with *The Belfast and Province of Ulster Directory for 1858–9 vol. iv.* (Belfast: James Alexander Henderson, 1858), vol. 4, reveals the overwhelmingly proletarian character of Orangeism during these years. Although only thirty-four names of individual lodge masters are listed in the registry (and not those of the members of the lodges), it is apparent that only a handful of these men were members of the upper or middle class, while most of them were either members of the skilled working classes or did not have enough social status to be listed in the street directory at all. Of the lodge masters who can be identified with

any degree of certainty, the representatives of the middle and upper classes
are: Francis Hull, of Hull Brothers Flax Spinning Mill, 1 and 3 Falls Road,
living at 2 Northumberland St, off the Falls Rd; James McFerran, coal
merchant; Andrew Clogher (an uncommon surname), sexton of St Anne's
Church, 29 Academy St; Wm Mortimer, possibly of W & J Mortimer, shoemakers, 2 Church Lane; James Gardner, listed as a gentleman, 3 Canning
St; William Hamilton (two people of that name are listed in the directory),
cork manufacturer or merchant; and John Hamilton (two listed), starch
works owner or starch manufacturer. The rest of the identifiable lodge
masters seem to have come from the 'respectable' working classes, while
fifteen lodge masters were not listed in the street directory at all, a circumstance that usually signifies low social status.

56 Henry Patterson, *Class Conflict and Sectarianism: The Protestant Working
    Class and the Belfast Labour Movement, 1868–1920* (Belfast: Blackstaff
    Press, 1980); Frank Wright, 'Protestant Ideology and Politics in Ulster',
    European Journal of Sociology, 14 (1973), 213–80. In the present study, see
    esp. Chapters 4 and 5.
57 Quoted in the *Ulster Observer*, 17 Dec. 1863.
58 Quoted in R. M. Sibbett, *Orangeism in Ireland and Throughout the Empire*,
    vol. 2 (London: Thynne & Co., 1914), 395.
59 See e.g. the address by the Grand Lodge during the General Election of
    1857, *Belfast Daily Mercury*, 7 Feb. 1857; and K. Theodore Hoppen, *Elec-
    tions, Politics, and Society in Ireland, 1832–1885* (Oxford: Clarendon Press,
    1984), 319–25.
60 *Ulsterman*, 1 Apr. 1857; *Belfast Newsletter*, 1 and 2 Apr. 1857; James
    Barnett's evidence, *1857 Belfast Riots Inquiry*, 210; Thomas Boyle John-
    ston's evidence, *ibid.*, 233–4.
60 *Ulsterman*, 17 July and 12 Sept. 1857; Hoppen, *Elections*, 387–8.
61 J. Brown, 'Part 2: From the Diamond to Home Rule, 1795–1886', in M.
    W. Dewar, John Brown and S. E. Long, *Orangeism: A New Historical
    Appreciation* (Belfast: Grand Orange Lodge of Ireland, 1967), 139–40.
62 J. Brown, 'Part 2', 118.
63 K. Miller, 'First Bomb', 274–5, discusses the social function of Orangeism
    during the first decades of the nineteenth century. On Scotland, see Elaine
    McFarland, *Protestants First: Orangeism in Nineteenth Century Scotland*
    (Edinburgh: Edinburgh University Press, 1990), 88–91. On Liverpool, see
    Frank Neal, *Sectarian Violence: The Liverpool Experience, 1819–1914*
    (Manchester: Manchester University Press, 1988), 31–2 and 170–1. On
    Canada, see Hereward Senior, *Orangeism: The Canadian Phase* (Toronto:
    McGraw-Hill Ryerson Limited, 1972), 7–9 and 72–3.
64 Patterson (*Class Conflict*, pp. xiv–xv) has argued against the view that
    Orangeism drew its strength in Belfast from its ability to monopolise the skilled
    trades, but he does acknowledge that Orangeism 'accentuated an existing mech-
    anism of exclusion' of Catholics from certain economic sectors and was
    probably especially useful to unskilled Protestants arriving in the city.
65 Stewart Blacker quoted in Wright, 'Protestant Ideology', 248.

66 'Twenty Reasons for Being an Orangeman', quoted in the *Ulster Observer*, 17 Dec. 1863.

67 Peter Gibbon, *The Origins of Ulster Unionism: The Formation of Popular Protestant Politics and Ideology in Nineteenth-Century Ireland* (Manchester: Manchester University Press, 1975), 55–6.

68 D. Miller, *Queen's Rebels*, 64.

69 Gibbon, *Origins*, 80. Italics in original.

70 Some indication of the ways in which Orangeism helped enforce a plebeian code of conduct among Protestants may be gleaned from rules against theft, marrying 'Papists', 'offending against religion and morality', 'drunkenness', 'defying lodge authority' and 'seducing an Orangeman's sister', to name some of the reasons for which members of the Orange Order were expelled by the Grand Lodge during its meetings in 1857 and 1858. The minutes of these meetings are held at the NLI. The gender roles prescribed by nineteenth-century Orangeism and its influence on personal and familial religiosity and 'morality' have never adequately been explored by historians, but such a study might begin with the gender rhetoric employed by Grand Lodge memorials and Twelfth of July speeches delivered to Orange audiences.

71 'Twenty Reasons for Being an Orangeman', quoted in the *Ulster Observer*, 17 Dec. 1863.

72 John D. Brewer with Gareth Higgins, *Anticatholicism in Northern Ireland, 1600–1998: The Mote and the Beam* (London: Macmillan Press, 1998), 133.

73 Peter Gray, *Famine, Land and Politics: British Government and Irish Society, 1843–1850* (Dublin: Irish Academic Press, 1999), 96–106; Robert Dunlop, 'The Famine Crisis: Theological Interpretations and Implications', in *'Fearful Realities': New Perspectives on the Famine*, ed. Chris Morash and Richard Hayes (Dublin: Irish Academic Press, 1996), 164–74.

74 W. D. Killen, *Memoir of John Edgar, D.D., LL.D.* (Belfast: William Mullan, 1869), 2–43.

75 Killen, *Memoir*, 227–52; Christine Kinealy and Gerard MacAtasney, *The Hidden Famine: Poverty, Hunger, and Sectarianism in Belfast, 1845–1850* (London: Pluto Press, 2000), 127.

76 John Edgar, 'The Cry from Connaught', in *Select Works of John Edgar, D.D., LL.D* (Belfast: n.p., 1868), 488–9.

77 Hamilton Magee, *Fifty Years in 'The Irish Mission'* (Belfast: Religious Tract and Book Depot, 1905), 42–3; Killen, *Edgar*, 227–52, 292; *Report of the Belfast Students' Missionary Association, for the year ending 31st January, 1857* (Belfast: Banner of Ulster Office, 1857); LHL, *Minutes of the Proceedings of the General Assembly of the Presbyterian Church in Ireland*, vol. 2.

78 *Henderson's Belfast Directory, 1861*.

79 See e.g. *Ulsterman*, 4 Dec. 1852 and Kinealy and MacAtasney, *Hidden Famine*, 10. 'Souperism' referred to the alleged practice of bribing starving peasants with soup in exchange for conversion.

80 Bowen, *History*, 213–15.
81 *Belfast Weekly Mail,* 25 Feb. 1853.
82 *Ulsterman,* 6 May 1856.
83 *Ibid.,* 2 May 1856.
84 Presbyterian Church of Ireland, *Berry Street*, 27.
85 *Ibid.*
86 *Ibid.* Another sympathetic source reported of one meeting that 'the atten-
    dance was above six hundred, a large proportion being Roman Catholic'.
    Belfast Newsletter, 2 Dec. 1852.
87 'Nemo' [F. S. Gordon], *St Enoch's Church, Belfast, and Rev. Dr. Hanna.
    Historical Sketch* (Belfast: Whiffin & Hart, 1890), 15.
88 Presbyterian Church of Ireland, *Berry Street*, 27.
89 *Belfast Weekly Mail,* 17 June 1853.
90 See Hanna's letters in John Weir, *The Ulster Awakening: Its Origin,
    Progress, and Fruit. With notes of a tour of personal observation and
    inquiry* (London: Arthur Hall, Virtue, & Co., 1860), 43 and 123–4.
91 *Banner of Ulster*, 4, 7, 18 and 21 June; 5 July; and 9 Aug. 1859. See Mark
    Doyle, 'Visible Differences: The 1859 Revival and Communal Identity in
    Belfast', in *Irish Protestant Identities*, ed. Mervyn Busteed, Frank Neal and
    John Tonge (Manchester: Manchester University Press, 2008).
92 *Ulsterman*, 13 Sept. 1854.
93 *Ulsterman*, 5 Nov. 1856.
94 Janice Holmes, 'The Role of Open-Air Preaching in the Belfast Riots of
    1857', *Proceedings of the Royal Irish Academy*, 102C (2002), 47–66.
    Holmes is the first to explain the importance of open-air preaching as an
    evangelical tool, but she fails to discuss its intrinsic proselytising tendencies
    or the ways in which it evoked fears of 'souperism' among Belfast Catholics.
    She also fails to notice the opposition that these open-air services periodi-
    cally provoked in Belfast prior to 1857.
95 'Open-Air Preaching', *The Irish Presbyterian* (1 Oct. 1857), 259–60.
96   David Hempton, 'Evangelicalism in English and Irish Society, 1780–1840',
    in *Evangelicalism: Comparative Studies of Popular Protestantism in North
    America, the British Isles, and Beyond, 1700–1990*, ed. Mark A. Noll,
    David W. Bebbington and George A. Rawlyk (Oxford: Oxford University
    Press, 1994), 164–5.
97 Memorial of the Committee of the Executive Council of the British Organ-
    isation of the Evangelical Alliance to Lord Palmerston, 8 Sept. 1853, TNA,
    Home Office Records, HO45/5129A/12–15.
98 *Limerick Reporter and Tipperary Vindicator*, 2 Aug. 1853.
99 *Ibid.*; 'British Evangelical Mission to Ireland', *The Irish Presbyterian* (Sept.
    1853), 132–6.
100 Emmet Larkin and Herman Freudenberger, eds., *A Redemptorist Mission-
    ary in Ireland, 1851–1854: Memoirs by Joseph Prost, C. Ss. R.* (Cork: Cork
    University Press, 1998), 47–8.
101 *Returns of the number of convictions for assaults on the agents of the Irish
    Church Missionary Society, in the city of Kilkenny, for the last twelve*

months; of the number of additional police force lately introduced into Kilkenny; Copies of reports and correspondence on the subject of the increased police force; and resolutions of the grand jury to the Lord Lieutenant, and his Excellency's reply, HC 1856 (517) LIII, 5.

102 Letter from 'A Protestant', *Limerick Reporter and Tipperary Vindicator*, 5 Aug. 1853.

103 *Ulsterman*, 11 Aug. 1856.

104 *Belfast Newsletter*, 24 July 1856.

105 'Open Air Preaching', *The Irish Presbyterian* (1 May 1856), 121–3.

106 *Banner of Ulster*, 8 Oct. 1857.

107 *Belfast Weekly Mail*, 19 and 26 Aug. 1853.

108 'Open-air Preaching', *The Irish Presbyterian* (Jan. 1855), 19–22.

109 *Minutes of the Proceedings of the General Assembly of the Presbyterian Church in Ireland*, vol. 2, 204. Italics added.

110 *Ibid.*, 295–6.

2

Belfast Catholics: 'a mere incohesive heap'

At the commission of inquiry into Belfast's 1857 riots, an attorney asked Bernard Hughes, a wealthy Catholic bakery owner, whether Belfast was 'governed by Protestants or Catholics'. 'I think', replied Hughes, 'this town is governed by Protestants, but the bone and sinew of the town is Roman Catholic. What I mean by that is, that it is a Roman Catholic town, and that it is governed by Protestants in every department.' Hughes then explained how Catholics were excluded from economic and political power in Belfast. Although they comprised the bulk of the workforce in the textile mills, he said, Catholics could not attain higher positions in the Protestant-owned mills, as Hughes had learned when his own son was repeatedly denied apprenticeships in favour of Protestants. Although there were some 150 wealthy Catholics qualified to be magistrates, he noted, nearly all the city's magistrates were Protestants, and the local police force, though theoretically open to Catholics, was filled almost completely by Protestants appointed by the Town Council. The Town Council, moreover, was wholly Protestant except for Hughes himself, who had been elected two years previously as the city's first Catholic town councillor. When asked if he had personally suffered because of his religion, Hughes told of hostile Protestants who had tried to ruin his business by spreading damaging rumours about his bread and of a group of evangelical moral reformers, appointed by the police, who had persecuted him for violating Sunday trading laws. 'I have had thirty years' experience in Belfast,' Hughes said, 'and I say the Roman Catholics have been harshly governed.'[1]

As the best-known Catholic businessman and politician in the city, Hughes knew better than most the difficulties that Catholics faced in Belfast. His very success had made him a uniquely threatening figure in this Protestant-dominated city, for in his public persona he embodied many virtues – hard work, moderation, moral uprightness, respectability – that many Protestant partisans imagined to be solely Protestant virtues. It is unsurprising, therefore, that his remarks at the riots commission –

particularly his comment that Catholics were the city's 'bone and sinew' – came in for immediate and scathing ridicule by Protestant propagandists. Shortly after his testimony, a group calling itself the United Protestant Committee published a table listing the relative economic and social standings of Protestants and Catholics in Belfast. Using an 1856 street directory, records of public institutions, several unnamed 'authentic and reliable sources' and, apparently, the rather unscientific method of judging a person's religion by his or her surname, the table professed to demonstrate who were the real 'bone and sinew' of the city. The verdict was not in the Catholics' favour. Among the 'professionals and tradesmen' there were some 1,598 Protestants but only 156 Catholics. Among those belonging to 'public bodies' (managers or members of charities, town councillors, Poor Law Guardians, jurors, electors, etc.) there were 17,384 Protestant names but only 2,973 Catholic ones. Even the number of skilled labourers suggested a distinct Protestant advantage: 3,121 Protestants compared with only 878 Catholics.[2] There was little information on the number of unskilled labourers in the city, and it had been Hughes's contention that it was here that the bulk of the Catholic 'bone and sinew' could be found, but there seemed to be little doubt that most of the city's wealth and influence was in the hands of Protestants.

The United Protestant Committee's report is, regrettably, not very reliable, published as it was for purely partisan purposes and using inexact statistical methods, but its main points are substantially corroborated by other sources. Workhouse and census records show that Catholics were more likely to be impoverished and illiterate than their Protestant counterparts, while information submitted to the riots commission of 1864 showed that Catholics owned just 10% of the city's rated (i.e. taxable) property.[3] The impression that Catholics comprised a minority of the city's skilled labour is supported by the analysis of A. C. Hepburn, who argues that many Protestant employers felt compelled by their Protestant workers to keep Catholics out of skilled or supervisory positions.[4] This meant that Catholics remained confined to the unskilled sectors of the textile industry, working alongside unskilled Protestants in many cases but, as the period progressed, increasingly employed in their own, entirely 'Catholic' mills. To be sure, there was also a significant underclass of poor Protestants at this time, and, especially in the riotous districts of the Pound and Sandy Row, many Catholics and Protestants had roughly the same social and economic standing, but it is undoubtedly also true that, in the city as a whole, Catholics were in a position of quite pronounced economic weakness.[5]

In terms of political power, Hughes's claim that Belfast was 'governed by Protestants' is also impossible to dispute. Both of Belfast's parliamentary seats had always been held by Protestants, and, as was the case for most of the 1850s, these were usually men closely associated with the ultra-Protestant elements in the city.[6] At the local level, there was only one Catholic magistrate out of thirty-two in the entire borough, with most appointments going to wealthy Protestant industrialists and merchants.[7] As noted above, Hughes was himself the first Catholic elected to the Town Council (and only one of three Catholics to hold office there before 1897), and other municipal bodies, such as the Harbour Commissioners, Water Commissioners and Poor Law Guardians, were similarly dominated by Protestants. This meant that municipal employees such as market inspectors, customs officials and, crucially, police officers also tended to be Protestants. In the case of the local police force, which answered to the Town Council, there were only six or seven Catholics among the 160 men serving in 1857, and by 1864 this number had dropped to five.[8]

Economic and political powerlessness is a common experience for migrant populations in industrialising cities, of course, and in many ways the experiences of Catholics in Belfast resembled those of Irish Catholic enclaves in Britain and North America; they were the 'Irish in Belfast', in Hepburn's evocative phrase, '. . . a minority group in an industrial society seeking to establish itself in more or less hostile territory'.[9] Like their counterparts abroad, Belfast Catholics would take several decades to develop the sorts of religious, social, economic and political institutions they needed to promote a sense of communal confidence and identity. In the meantime, the massive numbers of Catholics who arrived in Belfast during the 1840s and 1850s (their numbers jumped from an estimated 19,712 in 1834 to some 41,406 in 1861) found themselves struggling for a foothold in an alien urban environment in which their presence was, at best, grudgingly tolerated by the host population and, and worst, actively resisted. As a result, the Catholic communal networks that emerged during this period were substantially weaker than those enjoyed by their Protestant rivals. In the previous chapter, I suggested that Protestants' communal networks tended to encourage sectarian behaviour; here, we shall see how Catholics' own communal networks failed to restrain it.

In what follows, I first examine the institutional role of the Catholic Church, which, under the leadership of Bishop Cornelius Denvir, failed to adapt to the massive influx of poor Catholics with anything like the energy or boldness that so characterised the evangelical groups of the period. Next, I discuss the tiny band of middle-class Catholics who struggled to construct their own version of communal identity while attempting, without much success, to fill the institutional void left by the church among the Catholic poor. The final section of the chapter explores the obscure but influential role played by the so-called Ribbon societies, which, unconstrained by the church hierarchy or meddlesome middle-class laymen, developed their own, distinctly plebeian response to the challenges of urbanisation and evangelicalism.

The 'spirit timoris' of Bishop Denvir

In most of the industrial cities where Irish Catholics found themselves after the famine – Liverpool, Glasgow, London, New York, Boston – the Catholic Church, and especially the local parish priest, played a vital role in easing the traumas of migration and urbanisation. Most immigrants came from conservative rural backgrounds in which the church was the central political, social and cultural institution, and so in their new urban homes many turned instinctively – if, at times, unenthusiastically – to that same institution to provide a communal focal point and a sense of conti-nuity with the past. Often the church, with its creaky institutional machinery, was slow to adapt to the influx, and in a number of places national or class rivalries prevented it from becoming an effective pres-ence for very many years. But in all of these places the church eventually managed to expand to meet the demands of the Irish poor, not only by building new churches and providing new priests, but also by undertaking many of the same domestic missionary and charity activities as its Protestant rivals. In most places this process had begun well before the famine – New York City, for example, already had a Roman Catholic orphan asylum, a Roman Catholic benevolent society and an asylum for girls by the 1820s[10] – so that by the 1840s and 1850s, as waves of Irish immigrants poured into these cities, the church was generally able to accommodate the newcomers' spiritual and temporal needs. Wherever it expanded in this way the Catholic Church managed both to preserve a distinctive (and often assertive) Irish Catholic identity among these immi-grants and also to delay, for a time, the immigrants' assimilation into the broader community.[11]

The pattern was the same with the 'Irish in Belfast'. An initial state of atrophy, in which incoming Catholics remained virtually untouched by the institutions of religion, was eventually overtaken by a period of self-confident expansion that helped to seal off Catholics from the dominant Protestant culture and give them a certain parity and security in their own communal institutions.[12] However, all this happened much later in Belfast than it did in other cities, partly because Belfast's great industrial takeoff happened later (in the middle of the nineteenth century rather than at the beginning) and partly because, in absolute terms, the number of Catholics living in Belfast was much smaller than that in London, New York and elsewhere. This meant that the period of the Catholic Church's atrophy –

which lasted until about 1865 – happened at precisely that moment when the evangelical Protestant churches were experiencing their most signal successes. So while the Catholic Church in London, for example, was able to respond to the mid-Victorian evangelical challenge by developing its own systems of 'district visiting, ragged schools, self-help societies and bread and soup charities', nothing of the sort materialised in Belfast.[13] This meant, first, that those cross-class bonds (however strained at times) that played such a crucial role in forging a strong and self-assured working-class Protestant identity did not develop between elite and working-class Catholics during this period. It also meant that Catholic leaders, feeling their own institutional weakness, were unusually sensitive to the ubiquitous threat of Protestant proselytism among the Catholic poor. Finally, this period of institutional atrophy meant that it was left to other portions of the Catholic population, often more radical than the ecclesiastical authorities, to mount a response to the evangelical onslaught, and many did so with rather more violence than the church would have liked.

Much of the Catholic Church's indirection during this period can be traced to the peculiarly timorous leadership of Belfast's bishop, Cornelius Denvir. In the early part of his career Denvir had been a vigorous and energetic administrator, heavily promoting Bible reading in the diocese, for example, and raising money for the construction of St Malachy's Church in 1844. As communal relations deteriorated during and after the famine, however, Denvir shied away from any initiative that might antagonise Protestants, and 'his increasing nervousness and timidity in the face of politico-religious bitterness turned him more and more into a recluse'.[14] In 1851 he declined a request from a Catholic revivalist (probably one of the Jesuit or Redemptorist fathers travelling around the country at this time) to bring his mission to Belfast on the grounds that it might cause trouble with local Protestants.[15] He also refused to provide Catholic lay organisations such as the St Vincent de Paul Society (which arrived in Belfast in 1850) or the affiliated Ladies' Charitable Society with any official hierarchical support, leaving them dependent upon the scattered and unreliable contributions of individual donors and unable to compete with the much wealthier Protestant charities.[16]

The most striking evidence of Denvir's failure to respond to the challenges of urbanisation can be seen in the area of church construction. In the previous chapter, I pointed out that a major priority for Belfast's evangelical Protestants was to build and expand churches for the poor: by 1864 the Methodists had twelve churches, the Anglicans fourteen and the Presbyterians upwards of twenty-four. The Catholics, meanwhile, had but three – St Malachy's, St Patrick's and St Mary's – plus one small chapel across the river in Ballymacarrett. No new Catholic churches were constructed during this entire period, from 1844 to 1866, to accommodate a group comprising roughly a third of Belfast's population. St Mary's, the church attended by the largest proportion of working-class Catholics, was so crowded that Sunday masses overflowed into the street, 'and even the early-comers and the physically forceful had often to be content with standing room in the aisles and porch.'[17] Plans for a new Catholic cathedral, St Peter's, were drawn up in 1858 after Bernard Hughes donated a large parcel of land near the Pound, but the project was almost entirely dependent upon private contributions, and, without the support of the diocese, construction became bogged down in debt and delays for eight years. It did not open until 1866, after Denvir retired.[18]

Just as serious as the lack of church accommodation was Denvir's unwillingness or inability to expand the number of priests in the city.[19] In 1852 the Primate of Ireland, Joseph Dixon, complained to Rome that there were only four priests in all of Belfast. With such a small number, he wrote, it was impossible to baptise even half the city's Catholics, while probably a third of them never attended any of the sacraments.[20] The following year one of Denvir's most vocal critics, the merchant James Canning, noted that there had been only two confirmations in the last seventeen years and that Denvir himself was rarely seen inside the churches, while 'thousands of souls are permitted to go astray'.[21] Concerns about the number of priests even exercised Rome, where, by 1857, the Pope and the propaganda office were becoming 'particularly anxious' that Denvir appoint more priests in the parish.[22] By that year, the number of priests had inched upwards to nine.[23]

In a certain respect, Denvir was something of an anachronism. While his diffidence was partly dictated by temperament and ill health, it also stemmed from a conviction, common among clergymen of his generation, that Catholics should maintain a low profile and avoid confrontation with Protestants. In the post-famine dispensation of Paul Cullen, however, the current was flowing strongly in the opposite direction. As Primate of Armagh and, after, 1852, Archbishop of Dublin, Cullen instituted a series of sweeping reforms meant to discipline and reinvigorate the church. With the assistance of an enthusiastic crop of young clergymen educated in Rome and the new Catholic college in Maynooth, he oversaw a phenomenal 'devotional revolution' that involved, among other things, greatly increasing the number of clergymen; founding dozens of new schools, hospitals and charitable missions; and giving the church a greater role in nationalist politics.[24] This was a much more assertive brand of Catholicism than Ireland had seen in some time, and it entailed, in part, a less conciliar attitude toward Protestants. No longer would Catholics meekly submit to Protestant domination: under Cullen's dispensation, Catholics would boldly and unashamedly proclaim their faith, defending it from all enemies. To say the least, Denvir's refusal to combat Protestant aggression in Belfast fitted poorly with this new spirit. 'Dr. Denvir is a man of very good intentions,' wrote Primate Dixon to Rome, 'but the "spirit timoris" as regards the Orangemen among whom he lives so predominates in him that he is utterly unfit to be left in the administration of the church in Belfast. Indeed it may be said that to a great extent Dr. Denvir's administration has ruined Belfast.'[25] In 1860 Denvir was given a coadjutor, an enthusiastic Cullenite named Patrick Dorrian, whose job it was to energise the diocese and to nudge the old man towards retirement. It took another five years before Denvir gave up his post, however, and it was only after he was gone that Dorrian was able to implement any meaningful reforms.[26]

One of the most troubling consequences of Denvir's diffidence, from his superiors' point of view, was that it left Belfast Catholics vulnerable to the predations of Protestant proselytisers. This was most apparent in the schools, where the Cullenites feared that Catholic children were being exposed to dangerous Protestant doctrines while remaining ignorant of their own faith. Denvir did promote some Catholic schools in the diocese – he brought the Sisters of Mercy to the city in 1854, for example – but his general preference was for secular, state-run education. In 1848, he supported the creation of the new Queen's University in Belfast as part of a projected nondenominational Queen's College system, and he also served as a commissioner of the National Schools system, a network of nondenominational state schools which, in principle, Presbyterians, Anglicans and Catholics could all attend. Both positions were unpopular with Cullen and the rest of the hierarchy, however, who insisted that Catholics be educated in their own, separate institutions.[27] Under pressure from his superiors, Denvir resigned his post as National Schools Commissioner in 1857 and began half-heartedly to promote Catholic education. But he failed to create enough new schools to appease his critics, and in 1863 Dorrian complained to Archbishop Dixon that, of some 12,000 Catholic children in the city, only 2,370 were enrolled in Catholic schools, while the remainder 'are not attending any, but, no doubt a very large number of these – many hundreds – are going to Protestant N[ational] Schools, or even worse'.[28] It was not only in the National Schools that Denvir's critics detected proselytising threats, of course. 'What opposition we have to deal with', wrote Dorrian in 1863, 'may be surmised from the large swarm of dissenting ministers, Bible-readers &c. that abound here, and who have the bulk of the wealth of the town in their hands.'[29] Two years later, Dorrian estimated that the church in Belfast was losing 1,000 Catholics a year to Protestant proselytism, and had been doing so since around 1840.[30]

When Denvir finally stepped down in 1865, Dorrian, long frustrated in his efforts to promote a more vigorous ecclesiastical presence in Belfast, lost little time in starting a number of projects to strengthen the Catholics' position *vis-à-vis* the Protestants while also reinforcing the authority of the church hierarchy. One of his first accomplishments was the opening of St Peter's Cathedral in 1866 with a spectacular high mass, and in the twenty years that followed he oversaw a tremendous revival of Belfast Catholicism through new missions, schools, churches, priests, nuns, orphanages and other services, along with a 'less craven subservience to government, the Belfast corporation and the Protestant community'.[31] Dorrian's was a more aggressive administration for a more polarised age, but it came after an unusually weak period for the church that left a strong imprint on the traditions and cultures of ordinary Catholics. For the generation of Catholic migrants who arrived in the city between 1850 and 1865, being a Catholic in Belfast was not associated with the institutions of the church – priests, sacraments, social and charitable associations – so much as it was with being a disadvantaged minority in an alien urban environment. This fact not only informed the way Catholics thought about their own place in the city, which was clearly subordinate to that of Protestants, but also instilled in many a violent sort of anti-Protestantism that was unrestrained by any ecclesiastical counter-measures.

The Catholic bourgeoisie

One group that sought to find a way around the atrophy of the Denvir years was the small band of prosperous laymen who comprised Belfast's Catholic elite. Men like Bernard Hughes, the wine merchant Daniel Rogan Brannigan, the *Ulsterman* editor Denis Holland and the landlord and merchant William Watson were among the most energetic members of this tiny group that tried, in a number of different ways, to build a united, self-confident and above all respectable Catholic presence in Belfast. Predominantly merchants and professionals, with a particularly heavy representation in the drinks trade, these Catholics were not, on the whole, industrialists, nor were many of them involved in the burgeoning shipbuilding sector.[32] This meant that, while some of them were quite wealthy, they had a relatively small stake in the city's main economic activities, and their influence over the great commercial and industrial bodies in the city – the Chamber of Commerce, the banks, the railroad boards and so forth – was rather limited. Since they employed relatively few workers, especially compared with the vast workforces employed by the textile magnates, their contact with and influence over the Catholic working classes was also rather limited, even if, as Hempton suggests, they were more dependent on their 'poorer co-religionists' than were their Protest-ant counterparts.[33] Partly for this reason, they never quite succeeded in moulding Belfast Catholics into the unified and assertive social bloc that they desired.

For most of the 1850s it was anti-Catholicism that brought Belfast's Catholic elite together: when they met, it was usually to oppose some new 'aggressive' measure coming from local evangelicals or other Protestant partisans. A typical gathering occurred in May 1854, when Catholic leaders held a public meeting to oppose a bill requiring the inspection of convents operating under the National Schools system. In a packed theatre, speaker after speaker spoke of the threat such inspections posed to Catholic women and derided the anti-Catholic prejudice under-lying the measure. The meeting was dominated by the leading lights of Catholic respectability: Hughes, Watson, Holland, Doctors Henry Murney and Alexander Harkin, the merchants Terence O'Brien and Joseph Magill, the distiller Peter Keegan, and many others forcefully denounced the proposal, insisting on their rights as British subjects and urging the government to reconsider the proposal. Yet this was no insur-rection. An air of genuine yet restrained indignation informed the proceedings, typified by Watson's declaration that the Catholics of Belfast 'are always anxious and have ever evinced a desire to live in peace and harmony with all our fellow-townsmen of every creed and denomination' and his challenge to Protestants 'to bring forward a single instance in which any one of our revered clergymen have . . . ever offered one unkind or unchristian word respecting them, or any other denomination of worshippers whatever'.[34] To a large extent, this noncombative tone fitted well with the accommodationist stance of Bishop Denvir, who, in fact, frequently lent his support to such initiatives. For these Catholics the goal was not to overturn the rules, which, after all, were set by a group much larger and wealthier than themselves, but rather to prove themselves worthy of the same civil and religious liberties enjoyed by Protestants.

But accommodation did not necessarily mean assimilation. At the same time as they sought to prove their own respectability to the Protestant elite, middle-class Catholics also worked to foster a distinctive identity of their own. One way in which they hoped to do so was by holding St Patrick's Day banquets, the first of which took place in 1853. These were usually small, genteel soirees, gathering together the upper crust of the Catholic bourgeoisie along with a handful of clergymen.[35] In 1853 the banquet was held at Kearns's hotel in Donegall Place, where a group of a hundred Catholic dignitaries, including two priests from Ballymacarrett and Ballymena, gathered to dine, listen to some 'excellent airs' performed on a harp and a violin and make speeches and toasts. Among those toasted were Pope Pius IX, Daniel O'Connell, the prelate and priests of Ireland, St Patrick and Queen Victoria. It was, in all, a modest affair, the speakers praising the progress of Catholics in Belfast and expressing some moderate nationalist sentiments but avoiding any intemperate language that might alienate Protestants. Watson, the chairman of the soiree, emphasised that in toasting the Pope they 'owed no allegiance to the prince of a Roman state ... but spiritually to the Vicar of Christ', and pointed out that 'the spiritual allegiance which we owe the Pope ... is by no means antagonistic to that which we owe and willingly pay to our good and amiable Queen'. Belfast Catholics, he insisted, 'are as loyal, faithful, and sincere in their temporal allegiance to her majesty as any other portion of her subjects'. Nevertheless, several speakers, including a surgeon named McElheran and the *Ulsterman* editor Denis Holland, expressed their deep antipathy towards British landlords, lawmakers and those who would divide the Irish people, while praising the distinctive virtues and long-suffering patience of Irish Catholics. Calling for greater unity among Ulster Catholics, Holland declared 'that there were better men nowhere, and they needed only thorough union, and harmony of action, to learn their own worth and assert their own dignity'. Remarking upon the banquet afterwards, Holland's newspaper expressed its hope that 'the banquet of Patrick's day in 1853 [may] be the first of a long series creating a new era in our social politics, and testifying to the growing intelligence, independence, and harmony of all classes of the people'.[36] Through such communal events, the Catholic bourgeoisie sought to define Belfast Catholicism as dignified, loyal and worthy of respect, and they hoped that the rest of Catholic Belfast – particularly the weavers and labourers crowded into west Belfast – would follow their example.

This was easier said than done. The church, which might have been the bourgeoisie's natural ally in promoting Catholic unity and respectability, was weak and disorganised. The lower classes themselves, like lower-class people everywhere, were suspicious of bourgeois reformers, and, in any case, they travelled in rather different social orbits. Soon it was clear that St Patrick's Day banquets alone would not do the trick: by 1856 the *Ulsterman* was complaining that Belfast Catholics seemed to care little for St Patrick's Day, and in the years to come that holiday failed to become the unifying event that Catholic leaders hoped it would.[37] Surveying the state of Belfast Catholicism in his last leader before the *Ulsterman* folded in January 1859, Holland concluded that 'Outside the institutions devoted specially to the ministry of religion ... there is not in Belfast any one intellectual or social institution from which a stranger might gain a clue to the existence here of so vast a number of intelligent human beings professing the olden Christian faith of your Irish forefathers!' While other religious groups in Belfast had their 'concentration[s] of strength' and 'machinery of power', Holland wrote, 'the fifty thousand Catholics, or more, are, for all purposes of mutual, social, moral, and intellectual good, a mere incohesive heap, without form or life'.[38] The contrast with their Protestant counterparts was obvious.

By this time the Catholic bourgeoisie had come to realise that leading by example was not enough. If they were to promote 'intelligence, independence, and harmony' among Belfast Catholics, then they had to reach out to the working classes directly and provide them with the sorts of moral and intellectual improvement activities that Protestants enjoyed. This was the impetus behind the Catholic bourgeoisie's greatest initiative of the period, the Catholic Institute, which was founded in 1859 by a partnership of wealthy Catholics who purchased a large building on Hercules Street, in the centre of town, and equipped it with a library, a reading room, a lecture hall and meeting facilities. Holland, who anticipated the foundation of the Institute in his final *Ulsterman* leader, said that its founders hoped that the working classes would use it as a place for the 'education and cultivation of mind and morals' and an alternative to the 'the saloon and the "free-and-easy."'[39] Especially promising was the role the Institute might play in counteracting the evil influence of secret Ribbon societies. As Watson, the Institute's first president, explained, 'By promoting order, [the Catholic Institute] will use all the means in its power for the suppression of secret societies. By that means the young men of this community will not be deceived by the designs of base and unprincipled informers, who would traffic upon the life-blood of their fellow men.'[40] The Institute's artistic, scientific and religious lectures would serve the same purpose, helping to 'improve' the working classes while simultaneously instilling a sense of common interest and identity among all classes of Catholics.[41]

For a while the Institute managed to fulfil some of these lofty expectations, holding well-attended lectures, hosting important meetings and acting as a communal headquarters during times of crisis. Its obviously respectable leadership and its willingness to work with the church hierarchy (one of its intended functions was to act as a boarding house for visiting priests) meant that it generally enjoyed the support of the ecclesiastical authorities, and in 1862, when it founded its own newspaper, the *Ulster Observer*, it did so with the explicit approval of the Armagh bishops and installed fifteen priests and four bishops on the paper's board of directors.[42] Through the *Observer* and its editor, A. J. McKenna, the

Catholic middle classes propagated a forceful but non-sectarian brand of Belfast Catholicism, frequently championing specifically Catholic causes but also urging unity between Catholics and Protestants in the name of their common Irishness. As McKenna explained in the paper's first number, Ulster Catholics 'are still an enslaved people' held down by a Protestant Ascendancy whose 'annihilation' the *Observer* would work avidly to effect, but this did not mean Protestants and Catholics could not bury the past and work together in 'the cause of a common country, destined to be great and powerful, and which is still mutely appealing to her children to make her so'.[43]

Despite its initial success, two problems quickly surfaced that the Catholic Institute was ultimately unable to overcome. The first was the indifference with which ordinary Catholics regarded it. In 1863 the board of directors complained, 'Our Catholic population do not appear to know or appreciate the advantages which they possess in the Institute. Its reading-room and library, and its spacious lecture halls should assuredly be turned to better purposes than what they have hitherto been.'[44] It is likely that the Institute – situated as it was in a grand building right in the commercial heart of the city – failed to attract much working-class participation because it never brought its improving mission directly into the working-class neighbourhoods, as so many Protestant bodies did. As Hugh Hanna and Thomas Drew could attest, the promise of a wholesome intellectual and moral education was in itself unlikely to coax the working classes away from the 'saloon and the "free-and-easy"'; if one were to reach the Catholic poor, one had to travel to the places where they lived and worked, and this was not something the Catholic elite managed to do.

The second thing that killed the Catholic Institute was its inability to overcome the tensions between the laity and hierarchy that were increasingly dividing respectable Catholic society. Despite their early support for, and even participation in, the Institute and the *Observer*, Denvir and Dorrian always worried that these bodies might fall into the hands of secret societies or start promoting anti-clerical or revolutionary doctrines. This was especially true of Dorrian, who, as a Cullenite and an ultramontanist, was much more jealous of ecclesiastical authority than Denvir. Following an 1864 papal encyclical demanding 'increased vigilance against all possible dangers to Catholicism, whether through the press, education or any anti-clerical forms of association', Dorrian became increasingly insistent that the clergy maintain direct control over any body claiming to act in the name of Catholics.[45] When he took over from Denvir in 1865, he immediately provoked a property dispute with the Institute's directors that provided him with an excuse to demand full ecclesiastical control over the body.[46] The directors, facing possible excommunication, refused to hand over their investment and instead dissolved the Institute. The *Ulster Observer* continued to be published for three more years, but it did so under ever-tighter ecclesiastical scrutiny. Eventually, when the paper began tacking too closely towards an endorsement of violent nationalism, Dorrian pulled the plug on it, too – but not before a series of very public and acrimonious exchanges between the bishop and the newspaper's editor, which were gleefully reported in the Protestant press.[47]

Long before this moment, however, the organising momentum among Catholics had begun to shift from middle-class laymen to a reinvigorated church hierarchy, and the effect was to give Belfast Catholicism a decidedly sacerdotal air in the later decades of the century. The respectable, accommodationist vision of Belfast Catholicism that the bourgeoisie had been promoting had proved neither ecclesiastical enough for the church authorities nor accessible enough to the bulk of the Catholic working classes to have any lasting effect. And as the city became more polarised, their desire for accommodation with Protestant society seemed, like Denvir's quietude, to be dangerously anachronistic. Instead of seeking accommodation, Catholics increasingly embraced one of the two competing versions of Catholic insularity on offer: the institutional kind advanced by the bishops and the violent kind pursued by underground associations and Catholic rioters.[48] Neither side had much time for the respectable Catholicism advanced by the middle classes, who found themselves after 1865 stranded between two equally hostile shores.

Ribbonism

While the Catholic bourgeoisie were trying and failing to create a unified Catholic community in Belfast, the growing number of poor Catholics living in neighbourhoods like the Pound and Smithfield were developing their own, largely autonomous urban culture. Most of them were migrants from rural Ulster, unskilled, uprooted and often illiterate, and in this they actually differed very little from their Protestant counterparts. But while poor Protestants were steadily being brought into the fold of elite evangelicalism, most working-class Catholics had very little contact with institutionalised Catholicism in any form. Just as importantly, these Catholics also lacked anything that might serve as a Catholic equivalent to the Orange Order. As the previous chapter suggested, Orangeism provided Protestant men with an important social network that both promoted elite–worker interaction and offered a way to demonstrate their manliness by acting as defenders of the Protestant community. Nothing in the Catholic community could match this. The Catholic Church under

Denvir was determined not to answer Orange 'aggression' with any antagonistic initiative of its own, and the Catholic middle classes were reluctant
to imitate bellicose evangelicals by playing to the sectarian prejudices of
their own coreligionists. Above all, both the Catholic hierarchy and the
Catholic bourgeoisie were deeply suspicious of any sign of autonomous,
grassroots organising from within the working classes. For this reason,
working-class Catholics who wanted to answer Orangeism on their own
terms had to be much more secretive – that is, much less public and
performative – than their Orange rivals.

Instead of a Catholic version of Orangeism, then, what emerged in
Belfast was a series of loosely affiliated, pub-based secret societies known
to contemporaries as Ribbon societies, from the green and white ribbons
that their members supposedly wore. Unlike Orangeism, which has always
been more or less visible, Ribbonism was a shadowy phenomenon about
which there has been considerable confusion among historians as well as
contemporary observers. Many contemporaries believed Ribbonism to be
a vast, interlocking revolutionary conspiracy encompassing all of Ireland
and a good portion of the Irish population of Britain, and for this reason
both the British state and the Catholic Church sought to suppress it. In
reality, it is far from clear that Ribbonism was as centralised, organised
or widespread a phenomenon as its enemies alleged, but the confusion
over what constituted Ribbonism has persisted, and historians have
applied the label to groups as radically diverse as the conservative agrarian movements of Munster and the armed sectarian organisations of rural
Ulster.[49]

The most successful investigations of Ribbonism, and the ones that I
shall follow in discussing the groups that existed in Belfast, are those by
the historians Tom Garvin and Michael Beames, who have defined
Ribbonism as an Ulster- and north-Leinster-based confederation of secret
societies that grew out of the nationalist, quasi-revolutionary Defender
societies of the late eighteenth century.[50] According to this interpretation,
Ribbonism in the first half of the nineteenth century had a formal organisational structure made up of lodge, parish, county, provincial and
national levels encompassing Ireland as well as British cities such as
Manchester, Liverpool and Glasgow.[51] All these groups used similar passwords, signs and initiation ceremonies, but the degree of communication
and coordination between the lodges was probably minimal. As the years
passed and the Ribbon societies drifted away from the Defenders' ideology of insurrectionary nationalism, the various branches became
embroiled in all sorts of internal divisions and petty rivalries, troubles
that were exacerbated by the ubiquitous government informers who infil-
trated the groups. By the 1850s Ribbonism seems to have been a system

in crisis, formally retaining its nationalist principles and organisational hierarchy but increasingly fractured, localised and hunted, its activities becoming ever more sectarian and, in many cases, criminal.

As with Ribbon history generally, it is very difficult to piece together details about the origins and nature of Ribbonism in Belfast. Catherine Hirst has shown that it existed in Belfast from at least the 1830s, when a local barrister estimated that there were some fifty-three 'companies' of Ribbonmen operating in the city, and by 1845 Ribbonism was widespread enough that the moderate nationalist Belfast Repeal Association forced its members to take an oath denouncing it.[52] After this period information about Ribbonism in Belfast becomes extraordinarily hard to come by, but there were three episodes during the 1850s that shed some dim light on the continuing operations of the group. The first was the 1854 trial of an alleged Ribbon 'county delegate' named James Hagan, who was found guilty of membership of an illegal society and transported for four years, principally on the strength of documentary evidence linking him to other Ribbonmen. The second episode was the parliamentary inquiry into the 1857 Belfast riots, during which magistrates and policemen offered some partial evidence about the size and shape of Ribbonism in the city. The third and most enlightening episode came in 1859, with the sensational arrest and trial of twenty-three alleged Ribbonmen in Belfast. The evidence presented during the 1859 trial came almost entirely from two informers who claimed to have been members of the Ribbon society in Belfast, and, as this was uncorroborated by any more reliable evidence, it failed – as it must, according to British law at the time – to secure the men's conviction, and they were released on bail after eight months in prison. These three episodes will form the backbone of the following discussion, but it is important to emphasise that most of what is known about Ribbonism in Belfast comes either from informers who were usually offered cash or promised lenient sentences for their testimony, or from hostile policemen with little direct knowledge of the groups. Nothing that follows, therefore, should be taken as conclusive proof about the nature or extent of Ribbonism in Belfast during the 1850s. It is, at best, a series of informed speculations about an area of working-class Catholic life that must always remain more or less obscured by shadows.

The breadth of Belfast Ribbonism in the 1850s is perhaps the most difficult thing to establish. During the 1857 riots inquiry, Resident Magistrate William Tracy stated that he believed Ribbonism had been 'nearly snuffed out' in recent years, although he immediately conceded that 'there may be something of it here yet'.[53] George Stewart Hill, a former constable who had helped secure James Hagan's conviction in 1854, offered slightly more precise information, telling the 1857 inquiry that Ribbonmen were still quite active in the city and that he had himself recently been approached by a prospective informer offering to give information about the group.[54] Most other state officials questioned in 1857, however, maintained that Ribbonism was a relatively minor force in the city, and the inquiry commissioners concluded that there was little truth to Protestants' allegations that it was widespread in Belfast.[55] On the other hand, the arrest of the twenty-three suspected Ribbonmen in 1859 seemed to suggest that the extent of Belfast Ribbonism was much larger than many had suspected, especially if, as one informer testified, there were in fact some twenty Ribbon lodges in Belfast.[56] If this was true, it could mean that there were as many as 720 Ribbonmen in Belfast at this time, a significant number but still a tiny percentage of the roughly 40,000 Catholics in the city.[57] In the absence of any evidence to the contrary, it seems safe to conclude that only a slim minority of Belfast Catholics were active Ribbonmen in the 1850s.

More significant than the size of the Ribbon movement was the social position of its adherents, which allowed them to exercise a disproportionate degree of power within their neighbourhoods. Beames and Garvin have demonstrated that, in Ireland generally, Ribbon societies drew their members from the lower middle classes (publicans, clerks, shopkeepers and the like), the more 'respectable' working classes (artisans such as tailors, smiths and shoemakers) and the rural farming classes. 'Essentially,' writes Beames, 'the bulk of the membership were persons in regular employment with some limited amount of disposable income.'[58] In this respect, it is significant that several accused Ribbonmen in Belfast were publicans, a group of men who, by virtue of the central place they held in the social world of the working-class male, often enjoyed considerable influence among their neighbours.[59] Other Belfast Ribbonmen tended to come from similar social ranks: James Hagan, the man transported for Ribbonism in 1854, was a petty trader in the Smithfield market,[60] and, of the identifiable individuals arrested in 1859, there were, besides two publicans, one nail maker, a dairy seller, a greengrocer, a tailor, a former legal clerk, a bakery overseer and a butcher – all people in positions with the potential to exercise considerable influence among the lower classes.[61] The remaining men of this group appear mostly to have been lodgers residing in the Cromac area of the city, a mixed-religion working-class neighbourhood far from the millworker areas of the Pound and Sandy Row. They seem to have been single, mobile men who had likely belonged to similar groups in the countryside, and many were probably navvies (another group especially prone to Ribbonism) employed in work on the new canals, docks and other improvement projects of the period.[62]

All this is significant, for it indicates that Ribbonism in Belfast was not something that was especially widespread among the riotous millworkers of the Pound (who hardly fitted Beames' criterion of having 'some little amount of disposable income'), but it may very well have been common among their immediate social superiors, men who would have exercised some influence over poorer Catholics. Evidence of positive support for Ribbonism among non-members is rare, but during the 1859 trials sizeable crowds did gather outside the courthouse to express solidarity with the accused. On the men's release from jail in April, crowds of supporters greeted them with expressions of 'the wildest joy' and, amid shouts of encouragement and support, formed a massive procession from the Crumlin Road courthouse to the Donegall Street home of their solicitor, John Rea. The celebrations continued into the evening with the lighting of two tar barrels in Hercules Street and sustained cheering for the men and their attorneys.[63] This sort of popular enthusiasm might simply reflect a belief among some Catholics that the men had been unjustly accused or 'sold out' by the informers, but it seems also to suggest that Ribbonism, or at least individual Ribbonmen, could elicit some degree of support within the wider Catholic population.

Looking at all this, it seems as though Ribbonism in Belfast was both a minority movement involving a narrow stratum of locally influential Catholics and a movement that, under certain circumstances, could count upon the vocal support of a somewhat wider constituency. What was it, then, that these Ribbonmen actually *did*? This was a question about which there was considerable confusion at the time, and no clear answer has emerged in the intervening years. At the simplest level, being a Ribbonman in Belfast consisted primarily of attending monthly meetings, usually held at a pub, to which one gained entry by providing a password.[64] At these meetings new passwords were sometimes established, delegates to other regional meetings possibly assigned, and the initiation of new members carried out. Beyond this, it is difficult to know what, precisely, went on. Certainly some drink was imbibed (many Ribbon oaths included a provision against becoming intoxicated at meetings so as to avoid divulging the secrets of the body), and conditions were undoubtedly ideal for the fostering of some sort of male camaraderie. For some Ribbonmen, this social function may very well have been the most important benefit of Ribbon membership.

So was Ribbonism nothing more than an overblown Catholic men's club? Most outsiders were of the firm opinion that it was not. Instead, many believed that Ribbon meetings were primarily concerned with plotting a violent revolution to overthrow the state, or worse. 'Ribbonism seeks a disruption of the empire, subversion of order, the downfall of the

Protestant religion, destruction of both throne and altar, and the massacre or extermination of Protestants', declared a typical Orange pamphlet of the period.[65] Other observers, more sympathetic to Catholics and to the cause of Irish nationalism, similarly assumed that Ribbonmen were violent nationalists. 'Secret societies have never helped, and will never help, in working out the salvation of Ireland', warned the *Ulsterman*, which urged its readers to have nothing to do with 'these fatal germs of our country's lowliness and prostration'.[66] The secretive, oath-bound and exclusively Catholic nature of the groups lent some plausibility to these allegations, and it was on the strength of such beliefs that Daniel O'Connell and other constitutional nationalists had condemned Ribbonism since the 1820s. A similar belief animated the police and the courts, who treated Ribbonmen as traitorous conspirators and frequently punished them with transportation. Whether the authorities still considered Ribbonism to be a serious nationalist threat by the 1850s is unclear, but at least one frantic Louth magistrate felt it necessary in 1857 to warn Dublin Castle that the local Ribbonmen were planning to take advantage of the Indian 'insurrection' of that year to attempt to 'rescue Ireland from British control and [achieve the] total extirpation of Protestantism'.[67]

By this period, however, such fears were clearly overblown. Whatever the revolutionary ideals of the Ribbon societies in the early part of the nineteenth century, these had almost entirely faded by the 1850s. Leaving aside (for the moment) the anti-Protestant agenda of Ribbonism, it is abundantly clear that in the post-famine period the 'nationalism' of the Ribbon societies was little more than an ornamental veneer. Ribbon passwords and signs often retained superficially political or nationalist references, but these were usually confused or anachronistic phrases without any immediate revolutionary currency, and two of the Ribbon oaths discussed at the 1854 and 1859 trials actually included allegiance to Queen Victoria as one of their provisions – hardly something to which insurrectionary nationalists would swear.[68] Furthermore, no witness, informer or prosecutor alleged in either Belfast trial that what was afoot among the Ribbonmen was any sort of insurrectionary activity, and in fact many went out of their way to avoid discussing the issue. Thus, for example, the prosecutors in the Hagan case felt it necessary to remind the jury that the Crown did not need to prove that the secret society to which Hagan belonged was a treasonous one; it had only to prove that he belonged to an oath-bound society, which was an illegal offence in itself.[69] If the prosecution had had any evidence of treasonous plotting by Hagan, one imagines they would surely have presented it.

The absence of any nationalist plotting by Ribbonmen does not mean that these societies were not politicised, of course, nor that they did not harbour some sort of nationalist ideals, but, as R. V. Comerford has shown with regard to the later Fenian conspirators, men sometimes joined nationalist societies for reasons other than (or in addition to) an immediate desire to stage a nationalist revolt.[70] In the case of Ribbonism, one of the ancillary functions of these groups seems to have been to act as 'a form of "friendly" or mutual aid society as well as a body committed in some degree to insurrection'.[71] Among the practical benefits one obtained by becoming a member were the so-called 'travelling tickets' that allowed members to travel freely throughout Ireland and Britain and to call upon the support of fellow members along the way. Some Ribbon groups also supplied needy members with financial assistance and helped them obtain jobs.[72] A Ribbon oath from Longford, presented at one of the Belfast trials, suggests that another membership benefit was 'first preference in dealing and trade' from fellow Ribbonmen, a provision that would have been especially appealing to publicans.[73]

Mutual aid societies were themselves completely legal, however, and if this had been the extent of Ribbonism's functions then its members would have had no need to incur the wrath of the authorities and of their own priests by taking Ribbon oaths. For it was the oaths that made Ribbonism illegal in the eyes of the state and anathema to the church, and it was the oaths that distinguished it from other lower-class organisations, including the Orange Order. But if, as I have been arguing, Ribbonism was not primarily an insurrectionary movement during this period, then why did its members feel the need to take these illegal oaths? The judge in Hagan's 1854 trial, after perusing the mountains of documentary evidence presented to him, speculated about the real purpose behind the oaths:

> The members have been bound together by oaths and obligations, and those who took the oaths and obligations had no kind of control over their own actions, for they considered themselves entirely bound by the wicked mandates of their superiors in that society ... It was a society not without its functions – that is, not without the means of punishing those who disobeyed its wicked orders. Disobedience to its mandates were often resisted by violence on persons, and human life has been taken in order to satisfy its bloody vengeance. It appears that it has had too many adherents; many of them undoubtedly from inclination and sympathy, but I believe many joined it from fear ... It is not alone those crimes, but you have also to answer for the many victims which you and your associates have made of the young and unwary dupes that fell within your snares.[74]

Ribbon oaths, in this interpretation, were little more than a means of compelling individuals' silence about the illegal activities of the group. Other evidence supports the idea that some Ribbonmen, at least, were coerced into swearing allegiance to the group. At the 1857 riots inquiry

George Stewart Hill told of two men who had been beaten near Bally-mena, County Antrim, for not joining the Belfast group, while Garvin, looking at Ribbonism as a whole, has found that the groups often perpe-trated 'horrifying beatings and murders to ensure conformity' and levied subscriptions '*in terrorem*' on reluctant individuals.[75] If this is true, then provisions such as the following, taken from the same Longford oath mentioned above, would have had an especially coercive effect on reluc-tant members:

> I, Hugh Masterson, with the sign of the cross, do declare and promise, in the name and through the assistance of the Blessed Trinity, that I will endeavour to keep inviolately all the secrets of the Ribbon Society from all but those whom I know to be members of the same society; that I will endeavour to extend it in town and country, as far as possible, amongst as many of my friends and acquaintances as I consider to be worthy of it ... and that I will never stand by to see a member of the society ill-treated without aiding and assisting him.[76]

Such an oath, once sworn, would be broken only with great reluctance by cowed individuals who might very well have been involuntary parties to the 'Ribbon conspiracy'.

By the 1850s this 'seedy and possibly criminal' side of Ribbonism seems to have been in the ascendant: by then, says Garvin, the groups' nationalist and insurrectionary origins had given way almost entirely to unsavoury activities like setting up mafia-style 'protection rackets' to extort money from shopkeepers, publicans and others.[77] There is also evidence from this period that Ribbonmen violently intimidated jurors during Ribbon trials and extracted forced contributions from working-class Catholics to offset their legal costs.[78] The most important illegal Ribbon activity of the period, however, was to act as a sort of sectarian fighting club for lower-class Catholics. This was another legacy of the late eighteenth century, arising from the superheated sectarian rivalries of rural Inner Ulster that had sustained the old Defender organisations, and it was a function that Ribbonism seems to have performed more and more frequently as the century progressed.[79] Like Orangemen, Ribbonmen often presented themselves as a defensive body established to fend off the attacks of the other side, and many of the Ribbon societies' activities – the collection of money for the legal defence of rioters, the passing around of so-called 'quarrelling' words to help members identify each other during a fight and possibly even the provision of firearms to Ribbonmen and their families – were designed specifically to aid Catholics during sectarian clashes with Protestants. When John Kelly, one of the informers in the 1859 Belfast trial, asked prior to his own initiation about the purpose of the group, he was told that it was 'to oppose Orangeism'.[80] He then swore that he would 'take part in any quarrel where a brother should be engaged'.[81]

Just how important the Ribbon societies were during the Belfast riots of this period is unclear. As mentioned above, most officials questioned about the role of Ribbonism during the 1857 riots insisted that the group's presence in Belfast was negligible, and the riots commissioners themselves found that there was very little evidence of an organised 'Ribbon conspiracy' in the city. Only one official, the former constable George Stewart Hill, suggested that Ribbonmen were active during the riots, claiming that he had seen a known Ribbonman among a crowd of Catholics 'walking in procession with insignia on him, and carrying a pistol'.[82] This is the only such incident mentioned by Hill (who seems to have been on familiar terms with several Ribbonmen), and the most it suggests is that individual Ribbonmen participated in, but were not necessarily responsible for, the riots.

On the other hand, it remains distinctly possible that Ribbon societies provided the organisational skeleton for the Catholic side of the rioting, as was perhaps the case with Orangemen on the Protestant side. As the next chapter will demonstrate, much of the violence during Belfast's riots was carried out by a relatively small group of committed extremists, who, at times, seemed to be acting 'in concert'. The Ribbon societies would certainly have been an ideal conduit through which these extremists could act, forming a sort of sectarian hard core that managed to keep up the violence when others would have let matters rest. The intimidation and coercion that these groups were known to have practised, along with their powerful social status within the Catholic community, would have been enough to ensure that the extremists were able to act with a certain degree of impunity as well as with the support, coerced or otherwise, of a good portion of their Catholic neighbours. As we will see, the practice of extorting 'black mail' from non-combatants during outbreaks of rioting closely resembled the Ribbon 'protection rackets' described by Garvin. It is also noteworthy that at least one of the accused Ribbonmen of 1859 (John Hacket, an overseer at Bernard Hughes's bakery) played a major role in organising the Catholic Gun Club, a group that came together publicly after the riots in July 1857 to help working-class Catholics purchase guns.[83] It was to be expected that the hostile Protestant press would refer to this group as the 'Ribbon Gun Club', but there is a real possibility that there was some truth in the allegation.[84]

It is, then, quite difficult to assess the importance of Ribbonism to the development of communal violence or Catholic identity in Belfast during the 1850s. The evidence, such as it is, allows for a number of characterisations of Belfast Ribbonism that range from the relatively benign to the darkly sinister. Vaguely nationalist, geared towards providing mutual aid, coercive of its own members and undoubtedly sectarian, Ribbonism had many different faces in the working-class neighbourhoods of Catholic Belfast. The role it played for an individual Catholic probably depended upon her or his own relationship with the body and its members, but it is clear, by way of comparison, what Ribbonism was not. It was not a group with a clear political or religious agenda; it did not have an open, public presence within the Catholic community; and it was not supported or even tolerated by the Catholic elite. All this made Ribbon societies profoundly dissimilar to the Orange Order, even if the two movements mirrored one another in other ways. Far from bolstering the Catholic community's identity or profile in the city, Ribbonism seems instead to have fractured and demoralised it, alienating the middle classes and clergy from the Catholic masses and sounding a note of cynical and coercive violence from within the working-class Catholic neighbourhoods themselves.

In the end, perhaps Ribbonism's greatest significance was rhetorical: in much the same way that Orangeism was becoming a repository for all sorts of Catholic fears about organised Protestant conspiracies, so did Ribbonism, periodically uncovered during investigations such as those examined here, come to embody the (remarkably similar) fears of Protestants. In 1849 the *Belfast Newsletter* had described Ribbonism as a conspiracy that was 'haunting us by the wayside, penetrating into our homes, poisoning our meals, and invading our sleep'.[85] Drawing on such fears, Orange witnesses at the 1857 riots inquiry argued repeatedly that the threat of Ribbonism required the maintenance of their own loyal, defensive and perfectly legal confederation.[86] These fears were probably unwarranted, but they nevertheless indicated the ways in which both sides could impute the most nefarious and conspiratorial motives to their religious opponents. It was a way of thinking that naturally helped justify one's own conspiracies.

Conclusion

Ribbonism took root in the working-class Catholic neighbourhoods largely because it had few competitors. Churches were few, Catholic charities and missionary groups largely nonexistent, and 'respectable' fraternal organisations that might have been accepted by the church or the middle classes had yet to emerge. At the risk of adopting the bourgeois assumptions of the Catholic elite, it does appear that Ribbonism and other sectarian groups were able to flourish in these neighbourhoods largely because wealthier Catholics failed to restrain them. However, as Chapter 1 demonstrated, elite groups can foster sectarian tendencies just as well as they can dampen them; indeed, later chapters will show the Catholic elite periodically abandoning their quest for respectability and egging on Catholic rioters during moments of crisis. It was not simply the absence of cross-class networks among Belfast Catholics that promoted violence, therefore, but also the peculiar circumstances of Catholic life in the city – specifically, their economic, political and social powerlessness among a hostile host population. This circumstance bred a deep sense of vulnerability that pervaded all levels of Catholic society, prompting Bishop Denvir to keep his head down, leading the middle classes to strive for acceptance and compelling the working classes to devise their own ways of defending and asserting themselves. If this last group fell under the sway of an extremist minority, it was because of their own profound demoralisation as well as the skill with which that minority mobilised and magnified their fears. This was especially true during outbreaks of rioting, as we shall shortly see.

Notes

1 Bernard Hughes's evidence, *Report of the Commissioners of Inquiry into the Origin and Character of the Riots in Belfast, in July and September, 1857; together with Minutes of Evidence and Appendix*, HC 1857–58 (2309) XXVI (hereafter, *1857 Belfast Riots Inquiry*), 240–3.
2 Report of the United Protestant Committee, *Banner of Ulster*, 27 Oct. 1857.
3 Catholics comprised 43% of workhouse inmates in 1853, although they were only one-third of the population, while the illiteracy rate among Catholics over the age of five was 30.2%, compared with just 10.6% for Protestants. Sybil Baker, 'Orange and Green: Belfast, 1832–1912', in *The Victorian City: Images and Realities*, ed. H. J. Dyos and M. Wolff (London: Routledge & Kegan Paul, 1973), vol. 2, 802; *The Census of Ireland for the year 1861. Part IV. Report and Tables relating to the Religious Professions, Education, and Occupations of the People*, HC 1863 (3204–III) LIX, vol. 1, 39; *Report of the Commissioners of Inquiry, 1864, respecting the Magisterial and Police Jurisdiction Arrangements and Establishment of the Borough of Belfast*, HC 1865 (3466) XXVIII (hereafter, *1864 Belfast Riots Inquiry*), Abstract of Appendices F and G, 364.
4 A. C. Hepburn, *A Past Apart: Studies in the History of Catholic Belfast, 1850–1950* (Belfast: Ulster Historical Foundation, 1996), 126–7.
5 Catherine Hirst, *Religion, Politics and Violence in Nineteenth-Century Belfast: The Pound and Sandy Row* (Dublin: Four Courts Press, 2002), 14–18.
6 From 1852 to the end of the decade Belfast's two MPs were Hugh McCalmont Cairns and Richard Davison, both Anglicans with significant support within the local Tory party and Orange Order.
7 *Ulsterman*, 14 Nov. 1856.

8   *1857 Belfast Riots Inquiry*, 4–5; *1864 Belfast Riots Inquiry*, 5.

9   Hepburn, *Past Apart*, 8.

10   Kevin Kenny, *The American Irish: A History* (New York: Longman, 2000), 77.

11   J. A. Jackson, *The Irish in Britain* (London: Routledge and Kegan Paul, 1963), 135–51; Callum G. Brown, *The Social History of Religion in Scotland since 1730* (London: Methuen, 1987), 61–4; W. M. Walker, 'Irish Immigrants in Scotland: Their Priests, Politics and Parochial Life', *The Historical Journal*, 15 (1972), 649–67; Kenny, *American Irish*, 71–80; Jay P. Dolan, *The Immigrant Church: New York's Irish and German Catholics, 1815–1865* (Baltimore: Johns Hopkins University Press, 1975), esp. ch. 3; Ryan Dye, 'Catholic Protectionism or Irish Nationalism? Religion and Politics in Liverpool, 1829–1845', *The Journal of British Studies*, 40 (July 2001), 357–40.

12   Ambrose Macaulay, *Patrick Dorrian: Bishop of Down and Connor, 1865–85* (Dublin: Irish Academic Press, 1987); Marianne Elliott, *The Catholics of Ulster: A History* (London: Penguin Books, 2000), 283–4, 296; Desmond Bowen, *History and the Shaping of Irish Protestantism* (New York: Peter Land, 1995), 311–12.

13   Sheridan Gilley, 'Protestant London, No Popery, and the Irish Poor: II (1850–1860)', *Recusant History*, 11 (Jan. 1971), 35; see also Sheridan Gilley, 'Catholic Faith of the Irish Slums: London, 1840–70', in *The Victorian City*, ed. Dyos and Wolff, (vol. 2), 837–53.

14   Macaulay, *Patrick Dorrian*, 56. See also P. Rogers, *St. Peter's Pro-Cathedral, 1866–1966* (Belfast: Howard Publications, 1966), 15. For a more charitable assessment of Denvir's career in Belfast, which applauds Denvir's desire to promote cooperation between Protestants and Catholics but ignores his failure to expand the church, see Desmond Bowen, *Paul Cardinal Cullen and the Shaping of Modern Irish Catholicism* (Dublin: Gill and Macmillan, 1983), 185–9.

15   Father Ignatius of St Paul to Cornelius Denvir, 19 Feb. 1851, DDC, Denvir Papers, D.51/4.

16   Both organisations were continually plagued by financial difficulties into the mid-1860s. In 1864, for example, the St Vincent de Paul Society reported that it had accrued only £300 in the past year, with one-third of that sum coming from the society's members themselves. *Ulster Observer*, 12 Jan. 1864. Macaulay (*Patrick Dorrian*, 107) cites a letter from Dorrian to Dixon in which the former relates Denvir's hostile attitude towards both the St Vincent de Paul Society and the Sisters of Mercy, whose impoverished schools Denvir refused to support with parish funds.

17   Rogers, *St. Peter's*, 16–17.

18   *Ibid.*, 18. See also articles on St Peter's in the *Ulster Observer*, 14 Apr. 1862 and 11 Feb. 1864.

19   Macaulay, *Patrick Dorrian*, 88.

20   Quoted *ibid.*, 92. Archbishop Cullen passed these complaints on to Rome. See Emmet Larkin, *The Making of the Roman Catholic Church in Ireland,*

1850–1860 (Chapel Hill, NC: University of North Carolina Press, 1980), 150.

21 James Canning to Rev. Joseph Dixon, 5 Oct. 1853, Cardinal Tomás O Fiaich Library, Armagh, Down and Connor file, Archbishop Joseph Dixon papers. According to Bowen (*Cullen*, 187) Canning was a wealthy merchant who had 'contributed handsomely to the Catholic University'.

22 Archbishop Paul Cullen to Cornelius Denvir, 14 Mar. 1857, DDC, Denvir Papers, D.57/4.

23 Hepburn, *Past Apart*, 129.

24 Emmet Larkin, 'The Devotional Revolution in Ireland, 1850–75', *The American Historical Review*, 77 (June 1972), 625–52; Larkin, *Making*; Bowen, *Cullen*; Elliott, *Catholics*, 269–90.

25 Quoted in Rogers, *St. Peter's*, 10.

26 Macaulay, *Patrick Dorrian*, 102–8.

27 *Ibid.*, 55–6 and 89. On Cullen's opposition to mixed education in Ireland, see E. R. Norman, *The Catholic Church and Ireland in the Age of Rebellion, 1859–1873* (Ithaca, NY: Cornell University Press, 1965), 23–5 and 33–85; and Larkin, *Making, passim.*

28 Patrick Dorrian to Archbishop Joseph Dixon, 8 Sept. 1863, Cardinal Tomás O Fiaich Library, Armagh, Down and Connor file, Archbishop Joseph Dixon papers. See also *Ulsterman*, 10 Dec. 1856.

29 *Ulsterman*, 10 Dec. 1856.

30 Macaulay, *Patrick Dorrian*, 49.

31 David Hempton, 'Belfast: The Unique City?', in *European Religion in the Age of the Great Cities, 1830–1930*, ed. Hugh McLeod (London: Routledge, 1995), 151. See also Rogers, *St. Peter's*, 18; Macaulay, *Patrick Dorrian*, 117–19; Bowen, *History*, 311–12.

32 According to the 1857 report of the United Protestant Committee, cited in note 2 above, Catholics owned only three of the fifty-five textile mills in the city, but they did constitute some 10% of Belfast's doctors and lawyers. See also Hepburn, *Past Apart*, 123.

33 Hempton, 'Belfast', 147.

34 *Ulsterman*, 10 May 1854.

35 On the history of St Patrick's Day celebrations in pre-famine Ireland and their association with genteel society – especially the Anglo-Irish elite and Dublin Castle – see Mike Cronin and Daryl Adair, *The Wearing of the Green: A History of St. Patrick's Day* (London: Routledge, 2002), 1–7.

36 *Ulsterman*, 19 Mar. 1853.

37 *Ibid.*, 19 Mar. 1856.

38 *Ibid.*, 24 Jan. 1859.

39 *Ibid.*

40 *Belfast Morning News*, 15 July 1859.

41 Macaulay, *Patrick Dorrian*, 140–1; Jack Magee, *Barney: Bernard Hughes of Belfast, 1808–1878* (Belfast: Ulster Historical Foundation, 2001), 113–21.

42 Magee, *Barney,* 116; Macaulay, *Patrick Dorrian*, 193.

43 *Ulster Observer*, 1 July 1862.

44 *Ibid.*, 27 June 1863.
45 Magee, *Barney*, 114; Macaulay, *Patrick Dorrian*, 141.
46 Magee, *Barney*, 116.
47 *Ibid.*, 118–20, 130–1; Macaulay, *Patrick Dorrian*, 193–7.
48 The two main Catholic newspapers of the era reflected this rift. One, the *Ulster Examiner*, was controlled by Dorrian and the hierarchy and espoused a moderate form of church-led constitutional nationalism, while the other, A. J. McKenna's *Northern Star*, promoted a more revolutionary agenda.
49 Tom Garvin, 'Defenders, Ribbonmen and Others: Underground Political Networks in Pre-Famine Ireland', *Past and Present*, 96 (Aug. 1982), 154; A. C. Murray, 'Agrarian Violence and Nationalism in Nineteenth-Century Ireland: The Myth of Ribbonism', *Irish Economic and Social History*, 13 (1986), 56–73. A recent example of this sort of semantic confusion can be seen in J. Lee, 'The Ribbonmen', in *Secret Societies in Ireland*, ed. T. D. Williams (Dublin: Gill and Macmillan, 1973), 75–91, in which Lee, following contemporary sources, applies the term to parochial agrarian societies operating primarily in Munster.
50 Garvin, 'Defenders', 133–55; M. R. Beames, 'The Ribbon Societies: Lower-Class Nationalism in Pre-Famine Ireland', *Past and Present*, 97 (Nov. 1982), 128–43.
51 On Ribbonism in England, see Donald M. MacRaild, '"Abandon Hibernicisation": Priests, Ribbonmen and an Irish Street Fight in the North-East of England in 1858', *Historical Research*, 194 (Nov. 2003), 557–73; and John Belchem, 'Ribbonism, Nationalism and the Irish Pub', in John Belchem, *Merseypride: Essays in Liverpool Exceptionalism* (Liverpool: Liverpool University Press, 2000), 67–100.
52 Hirst, *Religion*, 22–3 and 59–60. Hirst uncritically accepts an 1845 estimate by the Catholic *Vindicator* newspaper that there were 1,000 Ribbonmen in the city at this time, but a report from the city's resident magistrate in 1842 suggested that the number of active Ribbonmen was probably closer to 130, not counting seventeen men singled out by the magistrate as known organisers. The addresses given for these seventeen men suggest that many of them lived in or near the Pound. Resident Magistrate of Belfast to Dublin Castle, 31 Jan. 1842, Colonial Office records on Ribbonism, PRONI, MIC/448/3/70–71.
53 William Tracy's evidence, *1857 Belfast Riots Inquiry*, 30.
54 George Stewart Hill's evidence, *ibid*, 155.
55 *1857 Belfast Riots Inquiry*, 10–11.
56 *Northern Whig*, 15 Jan. 1859; *Belfast Weekly News*, 5 Mar. 1859.
57 Beames, 'Ribbon Societies', 132, states that an earlier rule capped each lodge at thirty-six members. This may be an exaggerated figure, however, as both informers in the 1859 trials repeatedly claimed that the meetings they attended had consisted of only about twenty men.
58 *Ibid.*, 131. See also Garvin, 'Defenders', 149.
59 *Northern Whig*, 4 Jan. 1859. The public house was also a common meeting place for Ribbon societies, and it is significant that the Belfast arrests in

1858 and 1859 took place almost solely in public houses. On pub-based Ribbonism in Liverpool, see Belchem, 'Ribbonism'.

60 *Northern Whig*, 16 Aug. 1853. In 1864, David Ruddle, a Protestant trader in Smithfield, told the Riots Commission of his acquaintance with a man who had been arrested for Ribbonism and who, on his return four years later, was able to reassume his place in the market with Ruddle's help. It is likely that this man was James Hagan. David Ruddle's evidence, *1864 Belfast Riots Inquiry*, 341.

61 The names and addresses of the first sixteen men arrested appear in the *Belfast Weekly News*, 12 Dec. 1858, which described the men as 'respectable-looking persons'. This information has been checked against *The Belfast and Province of Ulster Directory for 1858–9* (Belfast: James Alexander Henderson, News-Letter Office, 1858), vol. 4. Other information on the occupations of those arrested comes from Assize records and testimony reported in the *Northern Whig*, 4 and 15 Jan., 1 Apr. and 19 July 1858; and the *Belfast Weekly News*, 28 May 1859.

62 *Belfast Weekly News*, 5 Mar. 1859; Hugh Carolin's evidence, report of Spring Assizes, *Northern Whig*, 1 Apr. 1859; and George Stewart Hill's evidence, *1857 Belfast Riots Inquiry*, 157. One of the passwords reportedly used in Belfast was 'Let each man fill his station', to which the reply was, 'The navvies are making preparation.' *Northern Whig*, 15 Jan. 1859. See also Garvin, 'Defenders', 149; and Baker, 'Orange and Green', 795.

63 *Northern Whig*, 8 Apr. 1859; *Belfast Weekly News*, 16 Apr. 1859.

64 Hugh Carolin's evidence, *Northern Whig*, 15 Jan. 1859.

65 Sagitarius, *Orangeism Versus Ribbonism: A Statement on behalf of the Orange Institution* (Dublin: Roe and Brierley, 1852), 8.

66 *Ulsterman*, 15 Feb. 1854. See also remarks in the Liberal Protestant *Northern Whig*, 17 Jan. and 3 Aug. 1859.

67 Louth magistrate to Thomas Larcom, Colonial Office records on Ribbonism, 1842–67, PRONI, MIC/448/3/376–7.

68 Report of the Spring Assizes, *Ulsterman*, 25 Mar. 25 1854; John Kelly's evidence, report of the Spring Assizes, *Northern Whig*, 1 Apr. 1859.

69 Attorney General's opening statement, report of the Spring Assizes, *Ulsterman*, 25 Mar. 1854.

70 R. V. Comerford, *The Fenians in Context* (Dublin: Wolfhound Press, 1985), 111–16; and 'Patriotism as Pastime: the appeal of Fenianism in the mid-1860s', *Irish Historical Studies*, 22 (Mar. 1981), 239–50.

71 Beames, 'Ribbon Societies', 135. See also Garvin, 'Defenders', 140.

72 Beames, 'Ribbon Societies', 135 and 140.

73 Report of the Spring Assizes, *Ulsterman*, 25 Mar. 1854.

74 *Ibid.*

75 George Stewart Hill's evidence, *1857 Belfast Riots Inquiry*, 155–7; Garvin, 'Defenders', 151, italics in original.

76 Report of the Spring Assizes, *Ulsterman*, 25 Mar. 1854.

77 Garvin, 'Defenders', 151, 154.

78 Memorial from the magistrates of Armagh, Louth and Monaghan to Sir

George Grey, Home Secretary, 24 Feb. 1852, NAGB, HO45/4530/2.

79 Beames, 'Ribbon Societies', 139–40; Garvin, 'Defenders', 142.

80 John Kelly's evidence, report of the Spring Assizes, *Northern Whig*, 1 Apr. 1859.

81 John Kelly's evidence, *Northern Whig*, 15 Jan. 1859.

82 George Stewart Hill's evidence, *1857 Belfast Riots Inquiry*, 153.

83 John Hacket's evidence, *1857 Belfast Riots Inquiry*, 134–8. This group will be discussed in more detail in Chapter 4.

84 *Belfast Weekly News*, 5 Sept. and 10 Oct. 1857; *Belfast Newsletter*, 12 Sept. 1857.

85 *Belfast Newsletter*, 24 July 1849.

86 James Gwynne's evidence and Earl of Enniskillen's evidence, *1857 Belfast Riots Inquiry*, 176–83.

3

An unenviable notoriety: the 1857 riots

On 12 July 1857 a young man named John Loughran decided to celebrate the anniversary of the Battle of the Boyne in a rather peculiar way. The anniversary, often known in Ulster simply as 'the Twelfth', was traditionally celebrated by Protestants as the victory of Protestantism over Catholicism during the Williamite wars of the 1690s, and the usual way in which they marked the occasion was with processions, music, sermons and soirees held under the auspices of the Orange Order. But John Loughran was no Protestant. The son of a respected Catholic merchant in Belfast, he was a stranger both to the Protestant inhabitants of Sandy Row and to the working-class Catholics of the nearby Pound, and so when he arrived in the former neighbourhood on the afternoon of the Twelfth offering to buy an orange lily from a stranger named James Bell, nobody could say what, exactly, he had in mind. Loughran paid half a crown for the lily, and, as the two men went into a pub to share a bottle of porter, he told Bell that he intended to wear the lily on one side of his hat while on the other he would place a green shamrock, the symbol of the Catholics. 'It was only a flower,' explained Loughran, mentioning that he was himself a Catholic. 'We did not ask you what was your religion,' replied Bell, 'we do not care for a man's religion, but for his principle.' Finishing his drink, Loughran bought Bell's pipe for a shilling, left the pub, and climbed onto a cart headed over the Saltwater Bridge, down Durham Street, and into the Pound.[1]

Meanwhile, in the Pound, a large crowd of Catholics had come out to watch the Sandy Row Orangemen march into Thomas Drew's Christ Church, a building that stood directly between the two neighbourhoods. Several years earlier the government had outlawed all 'party processions', so the Orangemen were forced to march without the usual emblems, flags, banners, music or orange lilies, but the procession was large enough to attract the attention of the Pound Catholics, many of whom remembered previous riots on the Twelfth and were ready to defend their neighbourhood from invasion. Instead of invading, however, the Orangemen filed

Map 3.1 Principal sites of the 1857 riots

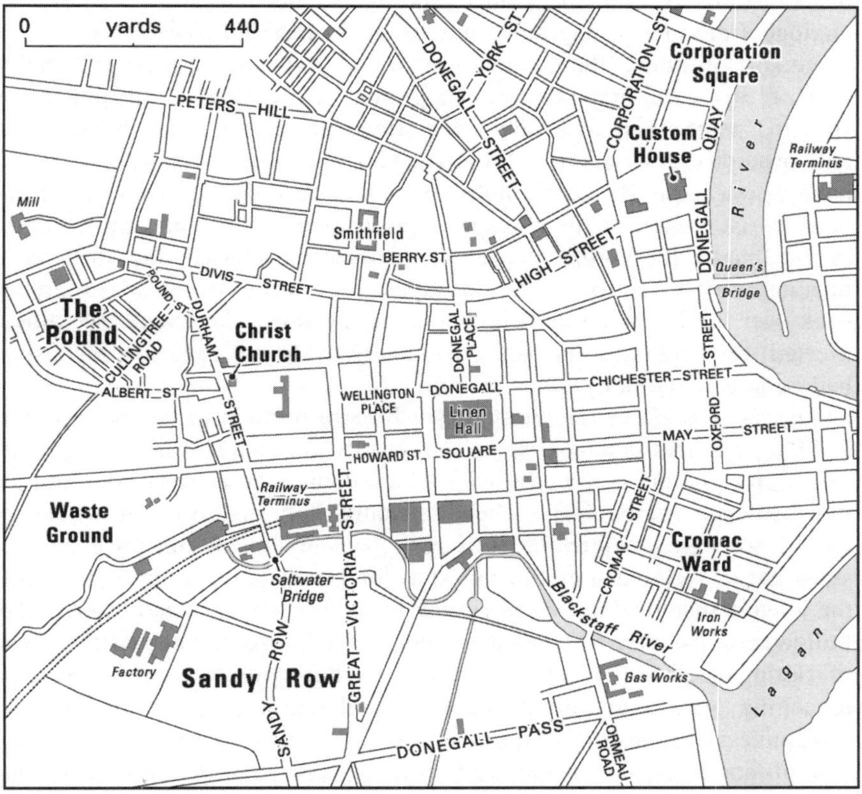

peacefully into the church, donned the orange scarves that they had hidden under their bowler hats, and settled in to listen to Drew's sermon about the threats Protestants faced from an unscrupulous, anti-Christian conspiracy emanating from the Church of Rome.

While Drew harangued the Orangemen with lurid tales of papal intrigue, Loughran, sporting his orange lily and slightly the worse for drink, bounded over the bridge and found himself amid a crowd of anxious Catholics. Imagining him to be a hostile Protestant mounting some sort of attack, the Catholics surrounded the young stranger, hauled him off his cart, and began beating him mercilessly. Some policemen standing nearby rushed to the scene, freed Loughran from his attackers, and promptly arrested him for disturbing the peace. As Loughran was hauled away, the Pound Catholics returned to their defensive positions near Christ Church while a group of policemen watched and waited nervously. Finally the Orangemen emerged from the church, but, instead of turning north to confront the Catholics, they turned south and marched back over the bridge to their homes in Sandy Row. The danger seemingly averted, the Catholics also returned slowly to their homes. For Belfast, it had been a remarkably quiet Twelfth.[2]

The story of John Loughran was a bizarre prelude to the Belfast riots of 1857, one that demonstrated the carefully guarded sectarian geography of the city as well as the ease with which communal anxiety could topple into violence, particularly when outsiders were involved. It would be another two days before the riots really got underway, but once the two sides began fighting they did not stop for nearly a week, by which time the longest sustained period of rioting in Belfast's history had taken place. Following these July riots, an even more widespread and destructive week of rioting occurred in early September, after a dispute about open-air preaching once again upset the territorial equilibrium of the city. So disruptive were these riots that the government sent a rare parliamentary commission to Belfast to inquire into their cause, and the city itself, long a source of pride for its wealthy inhabitants, began to acquire a reputation for religious violence that was giving it, in the words of one observer, 'a very unenviable notoriety' throughout the United Kingdom.[3]

The parliamentary inquiry found that the 'originating cause' of the rioting in July was the 'Orange party's' celebration of the Twelfth, 'a festival which is used to remind one party of the triumph of their ancestors over those of the other, and to inculcate the feeling of Protestant superiority over their Roman Catholic neighbours'.[4] The inquiry came to a similar conclusion about the open-air preaching riots in September, laying blame at the feet of evangelical orators whose provocative displays had drawn predictably violent responses from insulted Catholics.[5] Protestant provocation followed by Catholic retaliation: the same pattern characterised both periods of rioting, according to the commissioners. The British press agreed, ridiculing 'Roaring' Hugh Hanna, the minister whose open-air service sparked the September riots, and suggesting that the only thing motivating the 'Belfast Evangelizers' was a desire to 'gall the Roman Catholics'.[6] While nothing could excuse the actions of the Catholic rioters, the newspapers argued, the ultimate responsibility for the rioting lay with Protestant demagogues who deliberately insulted Catholics for their own petty ends.

That explanation of the 1857 riots has remained essentially unaltered. In 1969 Andrew Boyd, looking for the historical roots of Northern Ireland's emerging 'Troubles', identified these riots as an important stage in the rise of evangelical 'bigots' in Belfast politics, a process that culminated in Boyd's own day with the movement surrounding the Rev. Ian Paisley.[7] Other historians have followed Boyd's analysis, highlighting the roles played by Drew and Hanna in setting fire to a tightly packed powder keg of sectarian hatred as part of a deliberate and successful attempt to stir popular anger for their own gratification.[8] Catherine Hirst, the most recent historian to investigate these riots, has argued that 'the Orange ministers . . . cannot be credited with implanting extremism amongst the Protestant mob', but the ministers nevertheless 'legitimised their actions and gave them a cause to fight for which attracted wide support among Protestants' – a position virtually identical to that of Boyd.[9] Others, such as David Miller, have taken a broader view, suggesting that these riots and others were essentially about territory, the consequences of 'an escalating series of gestures by which each side overstepped the accepted physical boundaries or committed some novel "aggressive" act in a ritual of provocation and retaliation that ended in violence'.[10] The actions of the evangelicals in 1857 fitted neatly into this pattern, says Miller, for they took place on or near 'contested' areas in the city – in Drew's case at the intersection of the Pound and Sandy Row, and in Hanna's at the religiously neutral riverbank, near the Custom House – thereby provoking violence from Catholics who were offended by evangelical attempts to 'claim' these areas as Protestant.

The reality was somewhat more complex. While it is certainly true that Orange and evangelical demonstrations provoked the initial violence of July and September, the rioting that ensued was propelled not by disagreements about the particular transgressions of Drew and Hanna, but by the social relationships that existed within and between working-class neighbourhoods. For this reason, the nature of the violence often seemed to be a disproportionate response to the events that had provoked it. Other factors, such as people's earlier experiences of rioting, longstanding rivalries among neighbours and co-workers and each side's emotional responses to violence itself, transformed what began as a conflict over public evangelicalism into something much more diffuse, and much less easily defined. The provocative actions of Drew and Hanna, in other words, were embedded within a larger set of ideological and social structures governing the city as a whole, and the shape of the violence depended upon how those structures interacted during times of crisis. 'Sectarianism' was not a nebulous force that simply lay dormant until some evangelical minister came along to activate it; it was a way of thinking and acting that was rooted in each group's social relationships and shaped by the city itself.[11]

The previous chapters have gone some way towards elucidating those relationships by examining the networks that bound different social groups together in mid-Victorian Belfast. In this chapter, I shall examine the specific patterns of violence that emerged during the 1857 riots, discussing the deep forces shaping the violence as well as the way in which violence itself helped to accelerate communal polarisation. This investigation takes us into the working-class neighbourhoods themselves to explore the complex relationships between combatants and non-combatants, the gendered divisions of labour that emerged during the riots, the remarkably ritualised nature of some types of fighting and the invasive and tragically polarising nature of others. To begin the discussion, I first examine the rural antecedents of Belfast's riots in order to uncover the sorts of communal violence with which the city's migrant population would have been familiar. I then demonstrate the essentially rural character of the riots as they developed in Belfast in July of 1857, before concluding with a broader discussion of the much more destructive, and much more illuminating, riots in September.

The rural antecedents

To a large extent, Belfast's earliest riots reproduced the patterns of conflict that had been common in the Ulster countryside for generations. This is hardly surprising, for it was migrants from rural Ulster – especially from the sectarian battlegrounds of Counties Antrim and Down – who formed much of the labour force in Belfast's burgeoning industries.[12] The folk memories, traditions and predispositions that these migrants brought with them necessarily shaped the communal development of Belfast itself, providing a template for communal interaction that would be transformed over the years by the urban geography of city. In rural areas, particularly in places where Protestants and Catholics were roughly equal in number, violence had accompanied struggles over land, resources and political power since the Plantation of Ulster in the early seventeenth century. Starting in the 1780s, rural rioting had become both more vicious and more frequent as Catholics, growing in assertiveness as well as numbers, began to challenge the structures of Protestant dominance. This challenge from below was coupled with a series of legislative assaults from above that began with the removal of the Penal Laws in the late eighteenth century and culminated in 1829 with the Catholic Emancipation Act, a measure granting Catholics full political rights. These measures drove Protestants increasingly on to the defensive, and, as their formal power eroded, poor rural Protestants relied more and more upon violence to maintain their dominance.[13] The Orange Order, which was formed after a particularly brutal riot in rural Armagh in 1795, was itself a product of this intensified sectarian atmosphere, and, along with its Ribbon counterparts, it was to play an important role in much of the rural violence that followed.

What elements characterised these rural Ulster riots? First, as Sean Farrell has demonstrated, most rural riots were highly ritualised.[14] They tended to follow a widely recognised pattern of provocation and retaliation, usually revolving around an Orange procession either through territory that was understood to be 'Catholic' or through areas where the sectarian geography was contested. These processions were carefully choreographed displays of plebeian Protestant power, employing instantly recognisable 'party' tunes, emblems, flags, banners and regalia – items symbolic, for Protestants, of their loyalty to the British Crown and its defence of the Protestant religion.[15] The processions usually passed off peacefully, but, as Farrell has demonstrated, during times of unusual political excitement (such as the Catholic Emancipation agitation of the 1820s) they often degenerated into violence.[16] Such procession-based riots were not spontaneous outbursts, therefore, but predictable and, to an extent, policeable events that often involved some degree of premeditation and planning on both sides.

The style of violence that characterised these riots was also quite ritualised. Most riots consisted of what Farrell calls 'set-piece confrontations' in which both sides met over large expanses of ground and fired shots at one another from well-concealed positions. The goal of such encounters was not primarily to kill or injure the other side, but rather to prove each side's strength.[17] Since many riots were battles over territory, they often took the form of an 'invasion' by one side or another, frequently becoming demonstrations of power wherein each side sought to convince the other that it had enough guns, fortitude and 'manliness' to defend its patch of territory. To be sure, many of the fights did end in terrible destruction and loss of life, but deliberate injury was often secondary, from the point of view of the rioters, to demonstrating one's willingness and ability to defend one's group from the attacks of the other.

A second characteristic of rural violence was that Catholics often found themselves at a disadvantage as regards the local administration of justice. The Orange Order had enjoyed the patronage of Protestant landowners from the early days of its existence, and, since most landlords were also magistrates, these outbreaks frequently saw the authorities acting with clear partiality in arresting, trying and sentencing rioters.[18] One especially egregious example occurred during the notorious battle at Dolly's Brae in 1849, when two local magistrates, William and Francis Beers, led an Orange procession into a ferocious battle with Catholics living along a contested patch of road near Castlewellan, County Down.[19] A subsequent investigation condemned 'the union of the two characters of magistrate and Orangeman in the same person' and recommended that the Beers brothers, along with the local Orange leader Lord Roden, lose their magisterial commissions.[20] Although the inquiry also recommended that Orangemen no longer be permitted to become magistrates, no systematic attempt to eradicate Orangeism from the magistracy was undertaken at this time, and Catholics would continue to complain that, in many parts of Ulster, their Protestant opponents enjoyed the tacit – and often explicit – support of local law enforcement.

A third element common to rural riots was the practice of 'wrecking', a type of attack in which rioters destroyed houses and property, and sometimes assaulted non-combatants, either to force the inhabitants to move away or simply to demonstrate their group's dominance over an area. As far back as the so-called 'Armagh Troubles' of the 1780s and 1790s, and probably earlier, 'wreckings' had played an important role in shaping the sectarian geography of rural Ulster, violently enforcing residential and occupational segregation in what was essentially a primitive form of ethnic cleansing.[21] At Dolly's Brae, Orange rioters indulged in an especially ugly form of 'wrecking', setting several Catholic homes aflame and invading and murdering the inhabitants of others. Some thirty Catholics, many of them non-combatants, died in what was an unusually brutal attack, victims including a ten-year-old boy shot while running across a field, a seventy-year-old woman and an 'idiot' whose skull was crushed with musket butts.

'Wreckings' often expanded the sphere of violence beyond the initial group of combatants to the community at large. Individuals who bore no grudge against their communal opposites before a riot often feared and despised them by the time the riot was over. Because these rural battles were usually short-lived and sporadic, however, the personal grievances evoked by them usually had time to fade (except, perhaps, after extraordinarily violent clashes such as that at Dolly's Brae). Moreover (and, again, with the exception of Dolly's Brae), because rural riots took place out in the open and not in some confined urban space, non-combatants often had opportunities to avoid the violence altogether, and so to avoid being drawn into whatever conflict was exciting the extremists. On the whole, ample space (between people) and time (between riots) helped to lessen the impact of rural violence for most ordinary people.

The July riots

In the first half of the nineteenth century most of the riots in Belfast had been virtually indistinguishable from rural forms of violence. They were usually short-lived, procession-based outbursts, following familiar patterns of provocation and retaliation and sparking some expulsionist-style 'wrecking' that helped to create the segregated neighbourhoods of the Pound and Sandy Row. The earliest of these riots occurred in 1813, when a crowd of Catholics assaulted an Orange procession returning to Belfast from Lisburn, and in the three decades that followed similar fights broke out with some frequency.[22] In the post-famine years, as Belfast's industries expanded and the population lunged towards 120,000 people, these rural patterns were to prove surprisingly resilient. The July riots of 1857, in particular, demonstrate the lingering influence of rural violence on the city's working-class neighbourhoods. Indeed, to see the riots as essentially rural riots in an urban setting is not too wide of the mark. At the same time, however, the city was slowly beginning to exert some influence on the nature of sectarian rioting. In the 1850s the most significant influence was public evangelicalism, a movement that was certainly not unique to Belfast but which, in the densely crowded streets of the city, played a more important role in shaping communal identities than it had in the countryside. The shift was both subtle and profound: whereas rural rioting was often sparked by conflicts over territory and characterised by demonstrations of strength, rioting in Belfast was increasingly framed by different styles of religious worship and informed by uncompromising religious attitudes that often cast communal rivalries in a somewhat cosmic, not to say apocalyptic, light. These increasingly rigid communal identities were reinforced by an equally rigid sectarian geography determined by the urban landscape itself, a landscape that allowed for much less fluidity – both physically and ideologically – than had existed during rural conflicts. At this early stage Belfast's urban landscape was still exerting only a limited influence over the patterns of working-class violence, but its importance would grow steadily in the coming years, as we will see.

The emerging relationship between evangelicalism and a more severe type of communal identity becomes apparent when we consider the origins of the riots in July. Thomas Drew, whom I introduced in Chapter 1 as an important practitioner of 'political' evangelicalism, was not just a fiery orator and political gadfly; he was also a Deputy Grand Chaplain of the Orange Order, and it was in this capacity that he addressed the Orange gathering at Christ Church on the Twelfth of July. At a time when Orange processions were illegal, Drew's church acted as a sort of makeshift Orange lodge, a space where Orangemen could don their regalia, socialise with their brethren and listen to Drew's stirring sermons, the topic of which on this day was Matthew 5:13–16: 'Ye are the salt of the earth.' Drew began by praising the virtues of tolerance. 'The Sermon on the Mount is an everlasting rebuke to all intolerance', he told his listeners, 'and all legislative and ecclesiastical cruelty.' This was not a plea for harmonious relations between Protestants and Catholics, however, but an attack on the Catholic Church, which was, according to Drew, at the root of all intolerance. 'Of old time,' he continued, 'lords of high degree, with their own hands, strained, on the rack, the delicate limbs of Protestant women; prelates dabbled in the gore of helpless victims; and the cells of the Pope's prisons were paved with the calcined bones of men and cemented with gore and human hair!'[23] This sordid history of Romish intolerance demanded eternal vigilance from all Protestants, but of late the British government had been failing to defend Protestants' 'liberties' from such abominations. Catholics were now to be found in 'the chief places of justice, and the many offices in the state, customs, and excise and foreign departments'. They could even be seen carrying on their 'Jesuit intrigues' within 'our Protestant universities'.[24] In the outer reaches of the Empire, the government was 'anticipat[ing] the demands of Rome' by conciliating Catholicism at every turn, when 'their mission is, or ought to be, unmistakable; to aim at the Protestantizing of the world!' If the state was not up to that challenge, Drew said, then the Protestants of Ireland would have to take up the task themselves.[25]

What sorts of relations, if any, should Protestants cultivate with individual Catholics? On this subject Drew was curiously mute. Aside from a passing reference to 'the tried and oppressed ones in Rome's bondage-lands', by which he meant the Italian nationalists currently resisting papal rule, he made no direct reference to individual Catholics as such.[26] This was unusual for an evangelical address in this period. Anti-Catholic orators usually inserted a disclaimer into their speeches in which they insisted that their objection was to the Church of Rome, not to its misguided adherants, and they often enjoined Protestants to treat their Catholic neighbors with civility, lest their own un-Christian conduct should become cause for reproach. Hugh Hanna would make such claims during the open-air preaching controversy in September, but here Drew made no distinction between the sin and the sinners. He seems instead to have been content with informing his listeners of the perilous state of Protestantism, assigning Orangemen a special role in defending their faith and leaving them to draw whatever further conclusions they chose.

The Catholics of the Pound, of course, heard none of this, but the excitement aroused in the Pound by the procession to Drew's church, and the impact of his sermon upon the thinking of the Sandy Row Orangemen – they could rest assured, at least, that they had a powerful patron behind them, even if the finer points of Drew's religio-political doctrines were somewhat murky – set in motion a series of escalating confrontations that developed slowly over the next two days. Each evening after work, large crowds gathered in the streets and began yelling, cheering and firing guns into the air to warn potential invaders that they were ready to defend themselves. When no invasion occurred, both neighbourhoods started making more concrete 'preparations for war'.[27] In Sandy Row, Protestants strung orange arches made of lilies across the street, chimney to chimney, to delineate their territory. They also created sniper posts in several half-built buildings by removing loose bricks, a practice known as 'loopholing'. In the Pound, Catholic women and children tore cobbles out of the streets and piled them near doorways to provide ready ammunition for their husbands and fathers. Children, perched atop their fathers' shoulders, broke the gas lamps that lit the Pound in order to hinder any policeman or Protestant invasion force that might enter the neighbourhood's narrow, torn-up streets.[28] Every member of the community, regardless of age or gender, had a role to play in these preparations, for each had a stake in the conflict that was brewing. An invasion, if it came, would probably be led by a small band from the other side, and all were prepared to defend themselves if they had to.

The battle began on Tuesday 14 July, after the mills closed for the day. As men and women returned home from work, some of them assembled in the streets of Sandy Row and the Pound armed with stones, clubs and firearms, waiting for night to fall so that they could fight without attracting police attention. While they waited, gangs on both sides attacked the homes of people in their own neighbourhoods who were known to belong to the opposite faith, throwing stones and firing shots through windows to indicate that they were no longer welcome.[29] When dusk descended about nine o'clock, several hundred people – mostly young men – confronted each other across a stretch of waste ground that separated the two neighbourhoods, near the cottage of a Catholic widow named Betty Donahue. This field, Donahue later testified, was a popular fighting spot for the 'young boys' of the district.[30] It was unclear who threw the first stone, but the battle that ensued – 'frightful to look at and dangerous to be near', according to the *Ulsterman*'s reporter – principally comprised ritualised, long-distance combat. Paving stones and bricks flew across the field and over the heads of the screaming youths, the occasional missile finding its target and wounding a rioter on one side or the other. Along with these heavy, jagged projectiles, the combatants had also brought brickbats and sticks, in case the fighting moved to closer quarters.[31]

Soon the constabulary, led by Sub-Inspector Harris Bindon, rushed into the fray to separate the parties, but with little immediate effect except for exposing their own members to danger. During the entire fight they managed to arrest only three Protestants and two Catholics. When three local policemen chased a group of Catholics into the Pound, they quickly became disorientated in the darkened streets and found themselves ambushed by an angry crowd. The men fled into the shop of a man named Heyburn, who, on refusing to hand the men over to the mob, watched helplessly as rioters stormed into his shop and dragged the policemen out, looting some of his goods along the way. The rioters then beat the policemen so severely that when Resident Magistrate William Tracy found them some time later his first thought was that they were dead. Someone brought out a candle, and it became clear that the men were still alive, if only just. They were immediately rushed to the hospital, where all three eventually recovered.[32]

The next few days followed a similar pattern. Indeed, what is striking about these riots is the remarkably consistent, almost languorous rhythm they acquired over the course of that week. Day after day Protestants and Catholics would go off to work in the morning, put in a full day's labour (which was occasionally accompanied by conflict inside the textile mills – see below), and generally go about their daily routines, leaving the streets mostly quiet and giving the police ample time to recuperate. But at night, when the mills closed, large crowds would linger in the streets and yell, cheer, and fire 'bravado' shots into the air, demonstrating to the other side their numbers as well as their strength of arms. Then, some time between eight and ten o'clock, a few rioters would use the looming darkness to stake out positions on Widow Donahue's waste ground and begin throwing stones and firing shots at each other. Here is how the *Newsletter* described these scenes:

> ... on every successive evening, the course pursued by the rioters has been invariably the same. A number of them from the notorious locality of 'The Pound' meet together in an adjacent field – if possible, behind a ditch or embankment – having previously supplied themselves copiously with munitions, in the shape of brick-bats, 'pavers,' and some with more genteel, but

more deadly weapons – pistols and guns. Another party is then organised, who move out into the open field, or, if they can, take up a sheltered position, like their opponents. A regular, or rather irregular, hedge-fire is now commenced by both parties under cover. Brick-bats, stones, and bullets whiz indiscriminately through the air, but without, so far as we have been able to learn, much effect on either side; and it continues for only a few minutes, for a black body of constabulary and local police, under their different leaders, is immediately seen to approach them at 'double quick.' In an instant, the formerly opposing and apparently irreconcilable parties co-mingle and take to mutual flight or shelter, which, if they can, they hold, until a favourable opportunity presents itself. They renew the attack, but this time it is upon the policemen, whom they pelt right and left . . .[33]

During the entire period of the July riots only three gunshot wounds were reported, and these may have been accidental.[34] While there might very well have been many more unreported injuries and even some deaths, it seems that the primary purpose of these confrontations was not so much to inflict physical harm as to assert territorial dominance, principally by intimidating the other side enough to prevent an invasion.

The battles remained entirely confined to the Pound, Sandy Row and the waste ground connecting them – the 'disturbed districts', as newspaper reporters were coming to call them. This fact is significant, for it meant, first, that no other part of the city was touched by the violence, making it 'quite possible that a considerable portion of the inhabitants of Belfast knew very little of the state of things actually existing in their own town'.[35] Second, the suburban character of these neighbourhoods offered rioters space to act out their rituals of provocation and retaliation in much the same way and with much the same freedom as if they were taking place in the countryside, a fact remarked upon by William Tracy during the trial of a group of rioters who deliberately 'went away to a remote part of the town where there was room to wreak their evil passions on each other'.[36] In fact, the only element of their urban environment that the rioters utilised at all was the closely built system of lanes, alleys and entries within their respective neighbourhoods, which they quite smartly turned to their own advantage when escaping from the police, for in these instances the rioters' knowledge of the terrain far exceeded that of their pursuers. As one policeman put it, 'We looked on the place as a rabbit warren, for the moment we came forward the people went into the houses, and when we had passed they pelted us with stones.'[37]

Aside from the long-range battles, the other element that characterised the July riots was a significant amount of 'wrecking'. The most notorious incident was a Protestant attack upon buildings belonging to the Catholic businessman William Watson. Watson had deliberately rented out most of his rooms to Protestants in the belief that, as he put it, 'they would keep down the disturbance'. Albert Crescent, where the buildings were located, 'was a kind of battle-ground for both parties, and I was under the impression that the Catholics never were the assailing party, and that the Orangemen would not attack Protestants'.[38] Watson's impression was mistaken: for the crime of giving money to a Catholic landlord, his Protestant tenants found themselves targeted by the Sandy Row rioters, some two or three hundred of whom descended upon the buildings during the afternoon of 18 July. While several local policemen and constables looked on, the crowd smashed the windows, tore off the doors and shutters, piled the debris in the street, and set it all on fire. By the time the military arrived to disperse the rioters and extinguish the bonfire, a large number of people had gathered in the Pound to mount a counteroffensive, but none took place. This outbreak of 'wrecking' was but one of several in July, but it was the clearest example of the communal code of conduct that the more violent elements within the Protestant party were seeking to enforce. It was also, according to the riots commissioners, one that afforded substantial evidence of the ineptitude, and perhaps even partisanship, of the local police force.[39]

The fighting finally petered out on Sunday 19 July. An early-morning burst of rioting and sniper attacks was quelled by the constabulary, who, along with a detachment of military and magistrates, remained posted on the streets all day. And although Sunday could potentially have been the most violent and prolonged period of the riots – this was, after all, the day when the mills closed and the workers enjoyed their single day of leisure – the overwhelming force on the streets kept the rioters from getting at each other. The authorities had finally hit upon the tactic of posting groups of policemen and soldiers at strategic spots between the two groups, effectively cordoning one neighbourhood off from the other at places like the notorious Saltwater Bridge – a spot now becoming known as the 'Boyne Bridge' in recognition of its importance as a communal battleground.[40] A recent announcement that the constabulary would fire upon any crowd from which gunshots were heard may also have persuaded the rioters to curb their attacks.[41] Whatever the reason, the major battles had come to an end in the 'disturbed districts' for the moment, although small skirmishes continued throughout July and August and into September.

The September riots

On 12 July, the very day on which Thomas Drew delivered his Orange sermon in Christ Church, the Belfast Town Mission dispatched a group of ten ministers to the poor areas of town to conduct open-air services. The ministers stuck chiefly to the Protestant neighbourhoods, amassing large crowds that numbered some 2,800 in all and attracting little in the way of violence.[42] Open-air services were by now a familiar part of the Belfast summer, and, as I noted in Chapter 1, they rarely caused much excitement so long as the preachers stayed away from Catholic or mixed areas. The preachers seem to have adhered to this rule that July, and, after the rioting erupted on 14 July, most of them wisely postponed their open-air services until tempers cooled; violence, they felt, would only be a distraction and a hindrance to their mission, and few had any interest in becoming martyrs.

Hardly had the riots ceased, however, before the Belfast Parochial Mission, a new Anglican body without much experience of open-air preaching, decided to go ahead with a planned series of outdoor services on the steps of the new Custom House.[43] The spot was ideal for evangelical ministers to reach a large number of souls: situated along the banks of the river, the Custom House looked out upon Donegall Quay, a popular summer promenade for working-class families, especially on Sundays.[44] In the superheated sectarian atmosphere of 1857, however, a Protestant sermon at this spot was bound to attract opposition from Catholics, who, even during quiet periods, objected to open-air services in mixed areas. Adding to the potential for violence was the fact that the inaugural service was to be held by none other than William McIlwaine, the notorious anti-Catholic controversialist who, as recently as the previous Easter, had aroused Catholic anger with his annual series of 'Lent Lectures on Popery', which had been devoted this year to the question 'Is Popery Christianity?'[45] No matter that the proposed Custom House services were to be strictly non-controversial worship events: any public manifestation of evangelicalism in such a manner and at such a time was certain to stir Catholic anger.

The magistrates naturally feared the worst. 'Mr. McIlwaine is a very zealous minister,' William Tracy, the Resident Magistrate, wrote to Dublin, 'but he wants judgment, and has made himself so unpopular with the Roman Catholic party by his eternal controversies, that I am certain the peace of the Town will be seriously endangered by his appearance as a street preacher.'[46] Appealing to the minister's better judgement, Tracy and his colleagues persuaded McIlwaine to postpone his service until tempers had cooled, and so it was not until 9 August, three weeks later than scheduled, that McIlwaine held his Custom House service. No interruption took place on that first day; according to McIlwaine, the crowd at the Custom House was 'a most orderly congregation' that even included 'several Roman Catholics'.[47] A second service the following week, conducted by Charles Seaver, passed off in a similarly quiet manner, except that a handful of boys made a 'slight noise' during the sermon.[48] But on 23 August, when it was Thomas Roe's turn on the Custom House steps, persistent interruptions led the police, stationed in great numbers in and around the Custom House, to read the Riot Act and arrest a number of the 'most prominent' hecklers. After Roe, with difficulty, managed to complete his service, some of the rowdier elements in the crowd turned and attacked another preacher working nearby, a man named John Mateer, who was well known for his regular Sunday sermons preached from a Harbour Office shed.[49]

While the violence at the Custom House escalated, an intense debate arose in the Belfast papers over the 'open-air preaching controversy'. As we saw in Chapter 1, this was a subject that had aroused passions for the past several years, and all sides were well prepared with their arguments. For defenders of the Anglican ministers, the recent disturbances offered yet more evidence of the ways in which Catholics routinely persecuted Christ's ministers. The Presbyterian *Banner of Ulster*, long a champion of the open-air movement, decried the 'sectarian bigotry and intolerance' of those Catholics who had interrupted the services and warned them against 'rousing the indignation of the men who have never yet quailed, when called on, to struggle either for civil or religious independence'.[50] The Anglican-Tory *Belfast Newsletter* saw something even more sinister afoot. Borrowing a page from Drew's Twelfth of July sermon, it claimed that the recent attacks were part of a broader Catholic conspiracy to wipe out Protestantism. The 'papal aggression' of 1850, the propping up of the Papacy by French troops in Rome, the false allegations of souperism emanating from western Ireland and the ultramontane reforms of Archbishop Cullen were all of a piece with the recent actions of the Catholic mobs at the Custom House, who, the *Newsletter* warned, were clearly acting as part of 'a more regularly concerted scheme than belongs to the skill of mobs to institute'.[51]

Not all Protestants interpreted the matter in such apocalyptic terms, however. Interestingly, the preachers whose services had been interrupted explained their own actions not in terms of the worldwide struggle against Popery but simply as an evangelical effort to stem the tide of irreligion among the poor. In successive letters to the *Newsletter* in early September, two of the ministers who had recently preached along the quays, John Mateer and Charles Seaver, made it clear that their goals were simply to reach out to the churchless, not to defend some abstract right of public religious expression. They would happily preach indoors, they claimed, should the wealthier citizens of Belfast provide them with a space in which to do so.[52] Other ministers, including those Presbyterians who had pioneered the open-air movement, also expressed concern that their mission of compassion was being twisted into something political and potentially dangerous to the peace of the city, and they urged those ministers leading the current agitation to practise restraint.

But by this time the issue had grown beyond the mere question of reaching out to churchless working-class families. For an increasing number of Protestants, to oppose open-air preaching was to oppose civil and religious liberties, to 'persecute', to practise 'bigotry' and 'intolerance'. To succumb to such assaults would be to take the first step toward the eradication of Protestantism from the city. 'Allow them to stop your preaching in the streets,' Henry Cooke told a hastily gathered crowd at the Donegall Square Wesleyan Church on 31 August, '[and] they will soon stop it in the churches.'[53] Other Protestant leaders soon took up the cause, and before long there had emerged, in the words of the *Newsletter*, a widespread movement 'for upholding the religious liberty of the town, and for effectually ridding Belfast of the disgrace of being at the mercy of a Romish mob'.[54] Open-air preaching, the *Newsletter* explained, was a vital component of the city's Protestant identity; it was what distinguished Belfast from Kilkenny, Limerick, Cork and other cities in the 'Romish South', where 'priests are regnant, and their mobs omnipotent, and the authorities bow to their behests'.[55] If Belfast were to preserve its Protestant identity, open-air preaching must be defended.

On the other side of the debate, many Catholics saw the recent sermons at the Custom House as deliberate insults to their faith.[56] Coming as they did just after the riots of July, and associated as they were with a prominent anti-Catholic agitator like McIlwaine, the open-air services became 'almost necessarily in the public mind connected with the celebration of the last 12th of July festival, and as a new means for its further celebration'.[57] One Catholic wrote to the *Ulsterman* urging his co-religionists to respond to the open-air preachers with 'counter demonstrations', as this was the only effective way 'of banishing Souperism from the land'.[58] The *Ulsterman* endorsed this idea, stating that 'measures must be taken to protect the faith of Catholics from slander and their feelings from outrage'.[59] The paper printed similar arguments over the next few days, including one letter urging the magistrates to silence the 'brazen-tongued fanatics' by commanding them to 'move on and not disturb the peace with their croakings and howlings'. The newspaper's editors did urge their readers to 'keep away from these miserable, fanatic, and blasphemous displays', and the clergy, too, warned their congregations to avoid the preachers, but for many Catholics what was going on at the quays looked like an insult that, for the sake of Catholic honour, had to be answered.[60]

Worried about the escalating violence, the Parochial Mission decided in late August to suspend its services until a more peaceful atmosphere prevailed. And there the matter might have rested, had not the Presbyterian minister Hugh Hanna decided to take up the cause. At a meeting of the Belfast Presbytery on 1 September, Hanna suggested that he hold his own open-air services on the following Sunday to 'vindicate' the Protestant liberties that were being threatened by Catholic mobs. Most of his colleagues opposed the idea, but Hanna, who had never been involved in the open-air preaching movement before, was adamant.[61] Over the next few days he made it known throughout the city that he would hold his own Custom House service on 6 September, come what opposition there may. He later admitted that he expected to attract Catholic hostility, but, unlike many of his colleagues, he welcomed the idea, seeing it as a unique opportunity to strengthen Protestantism through conflict. 'Our most valuable rights have been obtained by conflict,' he explained, 'and if we cannot maintain them without that, we must submit to the necessity.'[62]

Sunday 6 September began as a typical Sunday in the city. Working-class men and women of all faiths passed their day of leisure in the usual fashion, walking along the riverbank, watching the ships docked in the bustling port and pausing to inspect the two cannons, recently captured in the Crimea during the siege of Sebastopol, on display in front of the Custom House.[63] Early in the afternoon some observers reported seeing a group of men, apparently acting together but trying hard to avoid any appearance of cooperation, arrive on the quays and post themselves at strategic locations near the Custom House.[64] Whether these men were members of a Ribbon society is unknown, but it would certainly be consistent with what we know about Ribbonism if some of them were. What they were planning could be gleaned from a placard that had appeared on the dead walls of the city overnight:

> Down with open-air preaching! Down with fanatic Drew, the squinting divine; the enemy of tranquility and peace! Gather to the Custom-house, on Sunday, the 6th instant, at 3 o'clock, and give the Orange bigot such a check that he will not attempt open-air preaching again. Catholics of Belfast, Down, and Antrim, we see by the public placards that our religion is again to be assailed, our public walks obstructed by that low and ruffianly fanaticism which has been lately got up by our Evangelical neighbours for the sole purpose of creating a quarrel, and perhaps for the purpose of shedding Catholic blood. Since they have got our worthy member, Mr Cairns, installed with the high honour of the ranter's badge, we therefore call upon all our Catholic neighbours and brethren to come and defend their rights as loyal subjects and peaceable citizens; and we have not the slightest doubt but we shall compel these disturbers of the public peace to respect the feelings of those who differ from them in religion – who, whilst they are never the aggressors, know how to defend themselves when attacked.[65]

It later emerged that this placard had been printed at the office of the *Ulsterman* (though the newspaper's editor, Denis Holland, denied all knowledge of it), and a hundred copies had been pasted around town before the authorities were able to remove them.[66]

To understand what it was these Catholics thought they were opposing, it is helpful to examine the placard in some detail. The most obvious point is that it clearly confuses Hugh Hanna with Thomas Drew, erroneously claiming that it was the latter who was to preach that day. Drew, in fact, had never been associated with the open-air movement, but since July his name had been repeatedly invoked by the *Ulsterman* as a symbol of all that was threatening about militant Protestantism. As a leader of the Orange Order and a key figure in the evangelical resurgence, Drew neatly combined the twin threats of evangelical Protestantism: theological anti-Catholicism (often understood by Catholics to mean proselytism or 'souperism') and the supposed political alliance between the Orange Order and the local Belfast government. By conflating Drew with Hanna, the placard hinted at the ways in which any manifestation of evangelical Protestantism could become absorbed in Catholic minds into a monolithic 'Orange conspiracy' that included Anglicans, Presbyterians, Orangemen and Tory politicians. The second thing to note about the placard is that it appealed to the rights of Catholics as 'loyal subjects' to 'defend themselves when attacked'. This suggests a degree of conservatism, or at least a lack of overt nationalism, among Hanna's opponents that many later commentators have failed to recognise. Opposing Hanna was not presented here as an act of political rebellion, but rather as a way of ensuring that extreme Protestantism (the power of which was here signified by the recent election of Hugh Cairns to Parliament) did not continue to dominate the city's politics. Thirdly, the placard presents the evangelical ministers as 'disturbers of the public peace' and the Catholics who oppose them as 'peaceable citizens'. This was consistent with the stance that both sides usually adopted during these riots: it was always one's opponents who were guilty of the transgressions, while one's own community acted exclusively in self-defence. Finally, there is an assumption here that any public display of evangelicalism was a deliberate insult to Catholics. This was the argument that the *Ulsterman* had been making for the past several weeks, and it is further proof of just how far public religious expression had become a polarising force in the city.

And so, acting on the ideas expressed in the placard, the group of Catholic men on the quays waited for the minister to appear. At the last minute, however, Hanna decided to relocate his service to Corporation Square, a site 420 yards from the Custom House and not within the latter's direct line of sight.[67] What prompted this change of venue is unclear, unless perhaps Hanna was seized by a belated desire to claim the moral high ground by appearing to take extra steps to avoid a riot. Whatever his intentions, when he ascended the platform to begin his service Hanna was stopped by two local magistrates, John Clarke and William Coates, who urged him not to proceed. He refused to yield, insisting on his constitutional right to preach in the open air and claiming the protection of the magistracy and police in the discharge of that right, and, armed with Psalm 119, a few hymns and the text of Hebrews 1:3 – 'How shall we escape if we neglect so great salvation?' – he mounted the platform.[68]

Accounts of how the riot started inevitably vary according to the sympathies of the source. Either, as the *Newsletter* claimed, 'thousands' of Catholics stormed the crowd as soon as they discovered that Hanna had moved to Corporation Square or, as the *Ulsterman* had it, a small group of 'little boys' attempted to interrupt the services only to be sharply rebuked by some adult Catholics standing nearby.[69] Whatever the initial provocation, some forty or fifty Protestant shipyard workers, whom Hanna had specially recruited to defend his 'congregation', turned upon the Catholic hecklers and drove them back towards the docks.[70] While Hanna continued his service, a running battle broke out along the quays as Catholic and Protestant men chased each other up and down the crowded riverbank with stones, staves and bludgeons. Several bystanders became caught up in the melee, including a man who fled from a band of marauding shipcarpenters by hiding inside a ship and another who jumped into the river to escape attack.[71] In all, the Catholics seem to have got the worst of this initial engagement, but it was not long before other parts of the city, hearing of the commotion on the docks, erupted into angry scenes of fighting and wrecking in support of the rioters. In Millfield, a group of constables fired on a Catholic crowd after a reading of the Riot Act failed to disperse them. And in Donegall Place, Donegall Square, Rosemary Street and other areas in the normally tranquil heart of the city, rioters broke windows and attacked pedestrians in a series of seemingly random attacks.[72]

The violence kept up for over a week. As in July, the fighting was centred on the Pound and Sandy Row, where combatants once again staged nightly, ritualised battles across empty fields. But this time other neighbourhoods were beginning to join the fight. One particularly disturbed area was the Cromac district, east of the city centre, where gangs of rioters wrecked the homes of several Protestant and Catholic families. On Thursday night rumours circulated among the Catholics of this area that nearby St Malachy's Church was going to be attacked, and hundreds rushed to occupy the building and its grounds. No attack materialised, but Catholic efforts to defend this church from wrecking mobs would become an increasingly important feature of riots in the area. On the same night shots were reported in the direction of Donegall Pass, a mostly Protestant neighbourhood to the south of the city centre that had rarely seen rioting before. 'From the state of the town generally,' the *Belfast Daily Mercury* reported, 'it may be fairly asserted that life was not quite secure in Belfast, on Thursday night, in a very extensive district.'[73]

If these riots were becoming more widespread than those of July, they were also more often characterised by 'wreckings' and expulsions. Sometimes the expulsions consisted simply of gangs of rioters throwing stones at windows, shutters and doors in order to terrify the inhabitants into abandoning their homes. Sometimes, however, the confrontations were more invasive, as when Hugh Kenny, a Catholic resident of Sandy Row, had his cooking utensils and furniture smashed by a crowd who stormed into his house. A similar thing happened to a musician named Davison, who watched as a crowd threw his piano and fiddle into the street, and to a Mr Taylor, who was hauled out of his Massereene Street home and beaten until a group of women rescued him.[74] Usually these attacks were made upon people who happened to be of the 'wrong' religion for the neighbourhood, but there is also evidence that the rioters targeted people they knew to hold political views at odds with their own. On 12 September the *Mercury* reported that a crowd of Protestants had 'visited the houses of persons who were at all suspected of having a tendency toward Liberalism, which means a "leaning to Rome" in the vocabulary of Sandy-row', and it gave the example of a Protestant man – a stranger to Belfast and 'not in any way connected with politics' – who was forced to flee his home because he had 'committed the grievous sin' of marrying a Catholic. Such episodes, the *Mercury* claimed, were common on both sides.[75]

These expulsions had several important ramifications. First, and most obviously, they violently reinforced a form of communal segregation that was already being informally maintained throughout much of the city.[76] Even before the riots residential mixing had been minimal in certain parts of the city, but after 1857 violent expulsions became an increasingly common way of ensuring that this communal segregation remained intact. As we shall see, future expulsionist outbursts were often centred upon the newer, as yet unsegregated suburbs that grew up on the edges of the city – the places, in other words, where new migrants settled who had not yet been initiated to the city's peculiar sectarian geography. Just as important as the residential segregation they enforced, however, was the impact that the expulsions had on communal identity itself. By their very nature, expulsions of this sort blurred the lines between combatants and non-combatants, binding each community together in shared feelings of resentment, suspicion and fear, and drawing every member of a community – not just the minority who were actively involved in the rioting – into a pattern of conflict and retaliation. This development secured for the most violent elements within each community a level of support in their neighbourhoods that they would not normally have commanded, and it helped to embed communal divisions in uniquely powerful ways.[77]

That the expulsions were often carried out by minority groups within each neighbourhood is apparent from the testimony of those who came before the riots inquiry in September.[78] Several witnesses claimed to have got on well with their neighbours before the rioting began, and some, such as the Catholic widow Betty Donahue, told of how sympathetic neighbours – in her case, a friend of her late husband's – warned them that the rioters were planning to wreck their homes unless they abandoned them by a specified date.[79] What these reports suggest is that it was often not the neighbours themselves who were forcing out people with whom they had often coexisted peaceably for months or years, but rather small bands of vigilantes who had decided to impose their own vision of communal uniformity upon their neighbourhoods. Indeed, as Donahue's daughter testified, in some cases the wreckers even punished members of their own community for not taking a more active part in the rioting. Such was the fate of John Russell, a Protestant living near the Donahues who had his furniture pulled from his home and destroyed in the street 'because he would not join among the rest of them'.[80]

The impression that the 'wreckings' were conducted by small groups of extremists is also supported by the records of those tried before the Belfast Police Court in July and September, where the names of the same people and families recur frequently as ringleaders of riotous gangs. One ringleader was a Catholic named Francis Brownlee, who was arrested in July after police observed him leading Catholic rioters over the course of four days.[81] Another prominent rioter was Joseph Brown, a Protestant millworker who lived on the Crumlin Road and was arrested on 6 September for wrecking Catholic homes on nearby Mitchell's Row. Brown had been arrested for a similar offence in July, and he was probably the same Joseph Brown who had been arrested back in 1854 for assaulting Catholic millworkers at Mitchell's Mill, which was in the same area.[82] Often these gangs included several members of the same family, such as Alexander and James McGrogan, two Catholic brothers who attacked several Protestant homes in September, and John Dawson and his wife Ann, who were accused of wrecking Catholic homes on Mitchell's Row at about the same time.[83]

How did many moderate, peaceful people come to acquiesce in this expulsionist violence? Certainly some residents were directly threatened by the rioters on their 'own' side, but such incidents seem to have been rare. Frank Wright offers another possible explanation: 'It takes few people to start an expulsionist crisis ... and any disapproval their efforts meet from their neighbors ... loses its effect once their "own" expulsionists can point to the work of the ones on the other side.'[84] Violence carried out by the other side, in other words, automatically justified violence by one's own. Moreover, as Peter Shirlow has suggested with respect to Belfast's more recent conflicts, simple fear – fear of the extremist elements in one's own community, fear of potential enemies in one's midst, fear of invasion from the other side – can easily lead otherwise peaceful people to acquiesce in their 'own' rioters' actions.[85] It is a dynamic that has been seen frequently in our own time in places like Bosnia, Iraq, India and Sri Lanka: mutual fear, generated by the actions of extremists, can play a powerful role in shaping incoherent communal affiliations into concrete, sharply bounded communal identities. In these circumstances, only people of great courage are able to stand up to the violent extremists acting in their name.

But to understand fully the potential of this sort of violence to draw entire neighbourhoods into a conflict, it is important also to understand the ways in which expulsionist violence transgressed the boundaries between public and private space. To watch as rioters entered one's home, dragged furniture, cooking utensils and other personal items into the streets, and set them aflame was a profoundly traumatising, even radicalising experience for those not yet actively committed to the rivalries of their communities. It was, as the riots commissioners pointed out, a cyclical form of violence, likely to arouse 'personal animosity' between perpetrators and victims and slowly 'extending the number of the parties between whom individual hatreds exist'.[86] It was, above all, a uniquely domestic form of violence that brought the abstract political and religious conflicts between Protestants and Catholics into the homes of many – young and old, male and female – who might not otherwise have given much thought to the cosmic and eternal struggle between Ireland's two great religious traditions. Whatever the religio-political principles originally at stake, expulsionist violence transformed the conflict into a poisonous web of deeply personal bitterness and hatred among all sorts of people.

This helps, in part, to explain the prominence of women rioters in Belfast, something that has been noted before but never adequately explained.[87] Women were not usually parties to the initial conflicts – no source mentions women among the rioters at Hanna's service on 6 September, for example, and among the fifty-two people arrested for rioting in July, all were male[88] – but as the violence spread to individual neighbourhoods, and as women increasingly became the victims of 'wreckings' and the anxieties that these produced, they took on important roles in support of the male combatants. This was nothing new: at Dolly's Brae and other rural riots women routinely marched alongside men in Orange processions or, on the Catholic side, hurled insults at Orange processionists and policemen alike. But in Belfast what was emerging was a more carefully defined, gendered division of labour whereby women, in addition to shouting abuse at their enemies, directly aided the combatants by supplying them with ammunition and acting as lookouts to warn of approaching policemen or soldiers. On the first day of rioting in September, the *Mercury* reported, 'the women, as usual, were busy breaking bricks and carrying stones into the streets', and on 11 September they were seen 'using the most abominable language towards each other, and aggravating, by their conduct and demeanour, the evil passions of their husbands and brothers already too much inflamed'.[89] Women also appeared in the crowds of 'wreckers' seeking the removal of undesirable elements from their neighbourhoods; on one occasion, remarked the *Mercury*, they were even more 'clamorous' than the men 'for the expulsion of the obnoxious individuals'.[90]

One place where women played an especially prominent role was in the textile mills. In 1857 many mills still maintained religiously mixed workforces, most employers calculating that keeping the machinery running was more important than enforcing religious uniformity among their employees. John Boyd's mill was one such integrated establishment, and it was here in September that a Catholic worker accused Eliza Lawson and several other Protestant women of assaulting her with bobbins while she was on her way to breakfast. Boyd himself gave evidence in the case, and he used the opportunity to deny rumours that he and other Protestant mill owners were deliberately dismissing all their Catholic employees, although he did know of a few instances where this had taken place. Rather, he said, what was happening was that his Protestant workers were attempting, 'by beating and threats, to drive them (the Roman Catholics) out of the work'. So bad was the situation in his mill, Boyd said, that a number of the machines had had to be shut down for lack of workers. In other mills things were even worse. According to one of the solicitors at the trial, some 150 Catholic girls had been forced out of Murphy's mill in Tea Lane, near Sandy Row, and some of them were 'actually starving'.[91]

Intimidation of this sort was also common outside the mills. 'Numbers of the boys and girls engaged in mills are afraid to go to work lest they should be beaten, as has occurred to several', reported the correspondent for the Dublin-based *Freeman's Journal*; 'Catholics employed in a mill in the Sandy-row district, have ceased to go there, as they would be assaulted on their way home.'[92] One such Catholic was Mary Jane McDowell, a girl who had to pass through Sandy Row on her way to work in Tea Lane. She told the riots inquiry how she and about fifty other Catholic women were assaulted on their way home one night by a crowd of women and children who threw stones at them, yelling, 'Pull the Papist entrails out of them, for bloody Papish whores.' When McDowell asked a policeman standing nearby for help, he told her 'to be off home'.[93] Longstanding rivalries between mills also erupted during the riots. In September the streets around the Crumlin Road, north of the Pound and Sandy Row, saw intense fighting between the Protestant employees of Johnston & Carlisle's mill and the Catholics of Mitchell's mill.[94]

This female rioting was crucial in solidifying of communal divisions in both communities, for it meant that male rioters could count on the support of large numbers of their female neighbours in their ritualised, territorial conflicts. And as the sphere of violence expanded, these conflicts inevitably took on a significance that went well beyond the initial disputes over public evangelicalism. Rioting, in a sense, became detached from any 'underlying cause' and entered a self-perpetuating cycle of reprisal and retaliation in which every member of the community had a stake. Along the way, distinctions between combatants and non-combatants were vanishing. Indeed, many people who did not participate in the actual fighting were beginning to support the cause in other ways. On 8 September a retired schoolteacher wrote to the Lord Lieutenant complaining that incarcerated rioters were having their fines paid by people who themselves never engaged in any actual violence. 'There are behind these rioters', he wrote, 'a class of persons who are superior to them in condition, & who contribute money to get them (the rioters) out of their difficulties.'[95] In July the *Mercury* alleged that the rioters' fines were 'almost always paid' by subscriptions collected among 'the lower orders of the town', a practice that the newspaper felt demonstrated the 'general sympathy that exists for such criminals'.[96] In the Police Court on 14 July the forty-shilling fine imposed on a fish seller named Thomson was promptly paid by a man who rushed down from the gallery, exclaiming that he 'would not let his brother fisherman go to jail'. On seeing this, Tracy remarked, 'There, now, the fine is paid, as if there were other parties behind the work', to which one of the attorneys quipped, 'Oh, your Worship, you do not know what purses these fishermen have.'[97]

Those sympathetic to the rioters could show their support in other ways. One correspondent suggested to the *Newsletter* that the 'antidote to the intolerance and impudence of the Belfast Roman Catholics' was to 'punish the entire body for twelve months to come, by withholding from them, as far as possible, all custom, countenance, and support'. The writer claimed that this system of 'exclusive dealing' (the term 'boycott' had not yet been coined) was already widely practised among Catholics, and, since Protestants controlled most of the city's capital, the system should soon have an effect upon Catholic tradesmen, who would then use their influence to restrain their riotous co-religionists.[98] Such proposals appear to have been widespread at this time, for even the normally reticent *Belfast Mercantile Journal* was moved to run a rare leader denouncing any system of commercial segregation as dangerous to the prosperity of the city.[99]

All this contributed to the polarisation of the two communities around their most extreme elements. A report in the *Mercury* recognised the ways in which this minority-driven violence was rending the social fabric of the entire city:

> What would seem to be the fact is, that a comparatively few violent char-
> acters have been industriously engaged in keeping up an agitation since the
> Twelfth of July last and that, as ample grounds of irritation existed, their
> inflammatory appeals and addresses have resulted in the state of things that
> so unhappily exists in the town ... [I]rritation and rioting fast tended to
> anarchy and a state of civil strife which it will be fortunate if they do not
> leave indelible impressions of hostility on the minds even of those who
> formerly bore the character of peaceable and well-disposed citizens.[100]

By the time the rioting died down the following week, after an abortive attempt by Hanna to host another open-air service, Belfast's rival communities were more segregated and embittered than ever.

Conclusion

In the coming years Hugh Hanna would frequently boast about his success-ful 'vindication' of the right of open-air preaching in 1857. Almost thirty years later, during the cataclysmic riots of 1886 (in which Hanna and his followers played no small part), Hanna still proudly recalled his defiant actions in September 1857, remarking, 'there has been no event in my life that I regard with greater satisfaction'.[101] By his own reckoning Hanna had won a great victory that September: never again would the right to preach in the open air be held hostage by Belfast's 'Popish mobs', and in later years the Custom House itself would become famous as a platform for evangelical speakers – 'Belfast's version of Speakers' Corner', as A. T. Q. Stewart put it.[102] But this victory had come at a steep price. After 1857 Belfast's commu-nal polarisation would accelerate considerably, fuelled by the resentments and rivalries that had accumulated during the riots and perpetuated by the residential segregation that was now being violently enforced by an extremist minority. The power of these extremists would grow with the years, and each fresh outburst, whatever its origins, only strengthened their grip. What had begun as a disagreement about the rights of religious expression, fought according to the rules of sectarian battles in rural Ulster, had been transformed in the working-class streets into something that was much less easily categorised, and much less easily resolved. Whole neighbourhoods had been drawn into a conflict in which many inhabitants had had no previous interest, and violence had convulsed parts of the city where rioting had rarely been known before. Slowly, Belfast's riots were losing that binary simplicity that characterised so many Orange–Ribbon fights in the countryside. In their variety and complexity, Belfast's patterns of violence were becoming identifiably urban.

Notes

1 James Bell's testimony, *Report of the Commissioners of Inquiry into the Origin and Character of the Riots in Belfast, in July and September, 1857; together with Minutes of Evidence and Appendix.* HC 1857–58 (2309) XXVI (hereafter, *1857 Belfast Riots Inquiry*), 189. See also Dr Alexander Harkan's evidence, *ibid.*, 224.

2 *1857 Belfast Riots Inquiry*, 2–4.

3 James MacAdam, diary, 16 Sept. 1857, PRONI, D/2930/7/7.

4 *1857 Belfast Riots Inquiry*, 8.

5 *Ibid.*, 13.

6 *Times* (London), 9 Sept. 1857. 'The Ballad of Roaring Hanna' appeared in *Punch*, 26 Sept. 1857.

7 Andrew Boyd, *Holy War in Belfast* (Tralee: Anvil Books, 1969), 10–44.

8 Ian Budge and Cornelius O'Leary, *Belfast: Approach to Crisis* (London: Macmillan, 1973), 79–80; Sybil Baker, 'Orange and Green: Belfast, 1832–1912', in *The Victorian City: Images and Realities*, ed. H. J. Dyos and M. Wolff (London: Routledge & Kegan Paul, 1973), vol. 2, 803; Sean Farrell, *Rituals and Riots: Sectarian Violence and Political Culture in Ulster, 1784–1886* (Lexington, Ky.: University Press of Kentucky, 2000), 143–50; Marianne Elliott, *The Catholics of Ulster: A History* (London: Penguin Books, 2000), 353–6.

9 Catherine Hirst, *Religion, Politics, and Violence in Nineteenth-Century Belfast: The Pound and Sandy Row* (Dublin: Four Courts Press, 2002), 164. Hirst also follows Boyd in peppering her discussion with numerous factual mistakes, such as her assumption that Hanna was an Orangeman, her assertion that Drew was one of the preachers who was assaulted on the steps of the Custom House in August and an erroneous chronology of the September riots that has them starting at least a week later than they actually did.

10 David Miller, *Queen's Rebels: Ulster Loyalism in Historical Perspective*

(Dublin: Gill and Macmillan, 1978), 69.

11 For a similar analysis of another part of the British Empire, see Patricia A. Gossman, *Riots and Victims: violence and the construction of communal identity among Bengali Muslims, 1905–1947* (Boulder, Colo.: Westview Press, 1999).

12 Solid information on the backgrounds of Belfast's inhabitants in 1857 is difficult to establish, but, according to the census of 1861, 75.2% of the city's population were born in Counties Antrim and Down (including Belfast) while 15.8% came from the other seven counties of Ulster, 5.14% were born in England, Wales or Scotland, and 0.57% hailed from abroad. Only 3.3% of the city's population were born in Ireland outside of Ulster. See Budge and O'Leary, *Belfast*, 30.

13 For more on this dynamic, see Chapter 5.

14 Farrell, *Rituals*, esp. chs. 2 and 4. See also Peter Gibbon, *The Origins of Ulster Unionism: The Formation of Popular Protestant Politics and Ideology in nineteenth-Century Ireland* (Manchester: Manchester University Press, 1975), 37–8.

15 Neil Jarman, *Material Conflicts: Parades and Visual Displays in Northern Ireland* (New York: Berg, 1997), 53–8; Farrell, *Rituals*, 108–17.

16 Farrell, *Rituals*, 83–101.

17 *Ibid.*, 52–3.

18 On the role of the landed gentry in patronising the Orange order in the early stages of its development, see Hereward Senior, *Orangeism in Ireland and Britain, 1795–1836* (London: Routledge and Kegan Paul, 1966). On the continued problem of Orange-sympathising magistrates well into the 1880s, see James Loughlin, 'Parades and Politics: Governments and the Orange Order, 1880–86', in *The Irish Parading Tradition: Following the Drum*, ed. T. G. Fraser (New York: St Martin's Press, 2000), 33–4.

19 For a full narrative of the Dolly's Brae riot, see Farrell, *Rituals*, 1–4. The discussion that follows draws upon Farrell's narrative as well as evidence found in a parliamentary report, *Papers relating to an Investigation Held at Castlewellan into the occurrences at Dolly's Brae, on the 12th July, 1849*, HC 1850 (331) LI (hereafter, *Dolly's Brae Investigation*), 11–12.

20 *Dolly's Brae Investigation*, 11–12.

21 On the 'Armagh Troubles' see Farrell, *Rituals*, 10–31; Gibbon, *Origins*, 22–40; Senior, *Orangeism*, 29–41; David W. Miller, 'The Armagh Troubles, 1784–95', in *Irish Peasants: Violence and Political Unrest, 1780–1914*, ed. Samuel Clark and James S. Donnelly, Jr. (Dublin: Gill and Macmillan, 1983), 155–91; and David W. Miller, ed., *Peep O'Day Boys and Defenders: Selected Documents on the Disturbances in County Armagh, 1784–1796* (Belfast: Public Record Office of Northern Ireland, 1990), 113–29.

22 Hirst, *Religion*, 19–34; Budge and O'Leary, *Belfast*, 75–7; Baker, 'Orange and Green', 790–6.

23 *1857 Belfast Riots Inquiry*, Appendix 1, 248. This sermon was first published in the *Downshire Protestant*, edited by Drew's friend and fellow Orangeman William Johnston of Ballykilbeg, on 17 July 1857.

24 *1857 Belfast Riots Inquiry*, Appendix 1, 250.
25 *Ibid.*
26 *Ibid.*
27 *Ibid*, 4–5.
28 *Ibid.*, 5. The description of children climbing atop men's shoulders to extinguish street lamps comes from William Tracy's testimony about one such incident on 14 July, *ibid.*, 21.
29 *Ibid.*, 5.
30 Betty Donahue's evidence, *ibid.*, 86–9. See also Mary Anne Donahue's evidence, *ibid.*, 90.
31 *Ulsterman*, 17 July 1857.
32 William Tracy's evidence, *1857 Belfast Riots Inquiry*, 22, 29. See also Harris Bindon's evidence, *ibid.*, 52.
33 *Belfast Newsletter*, 18 July 1857. A similar report appears in the *Belfast Daily Mercury*, 16 July 1857. See also William Tracy's evidence, *1857 Belfast Riots Inquiry*, 23.
34 Two Catholic boys, Patrick Murphy and Adam Ward, were shot by the Sandy Row rioters while playing marbles, and Mary Anne Tynan, a young Catholic millworker, was shot in the eye. Ward subsequently had his leg amputated. Catholics, including Tynan in her testimony before the riots inquiry, alleged that these attacks were deliberate. Protestants insisted that they were accidental.
35 *1857 Belfast Riots Inquiry*, 8.
36 Report of the Police Court, *Belfast Daily Mercury*, 16 July 1857.
37 *Ibid.*, 21 July 1857.
38 William Watson's evidence, *1857 Belfast Riots Inquiry,* 127.
39 *1857 Belfast Riots Inquiry*, 6–7. A subsequent investigation found that similar allegations against the constabulary, as distinct from the local police, were without foundation. See *Report to the Lord Lieutenant of Ireland by Messrs. Fitzmaurice and Goold, with the Minutes of the Evidence taken by them at the Inquiry into the Conduct of the Constabulary during the Disturbances at Belfast in July and September, 1857*, HC 1857–58 (333) XLVII. The question of the partisanship of these forces will be discussed in more detail in Chapters 4, 5, and 6 below.
40 *Ulsterman*, 20 July 1857.
41 *Belfast Daily Mercury*, 20 July 1857; *Banner of Ulster*, 21 July 1857.
42 *Banner of Ulster*, 14 July 1857.
43 This body's list of patrons was a virtual 'who's who' of Belfast's civic leadership, providing a neat illustration of the degree to which evangelical Protestantism had penetrated the civic culture of the city. It included, in addition to William McIlwaine and Thomas Drew, the vicar of Belfast, Thomas Miller (who was also an Orangeman); both of Belfast's MPs, Richard Davison and Hugh Cairns; the mill owners J. J. Murphy, John Boyd and William Ewart; the local magistrates Dr J. G. McGee, W. T. B. Lyons, Robert Thomson, William Coates and Charles Lanyon (the prolific architect who, among other things, was responsible for designing the Custom House

and Queen's College); the former superintendent of police and Orangeman Adam Hill; and Resident Magistrate William Tracy. Many of these were the very men who would be charged with policing the city during the coming riots. *1857 Belfast Riots Inquiry*, Appendix 7, 255–6.

44 Hirst (*Religion*, 162) mistakenly claims that 'non-controversial ministers had been preaching at the customs house for years without disturbance', when in fact the building had been completed just a few months before the September riots.

45 *1857 Belfast Riots Inquiry*, Appendix 6, 254–5.

46 William Tracy to Thomas Larcom, 26 July 1857, NAI, CSORP (1857) *6324*.

47 William McIlwaine's evidence, *1857 Belfast Riots Inquiry*, 74.

48 *Belfast Daily Mercury,* 17 Aug. 1857.

49 *Banner of Ulster*, 25 Aug. 1857.

50 *Ibid.*, 3 Sept. 1857.

51 *Belfast Newsletter*, 27 Aug. 1857.

52 *Ibid.*, 3 and 4 Sept. 1857.

53 *Banner of Ulster*, 1 Sept. 1857.

54 *Ibid.*

55 *Belfast Newsletter*, 5 Sept. 1857.

56 Janice Holmes, 'The Role of Open-Air Preaching in the Belfast Riots of 1857', *Proceedings of the Royal Irish Academy*, 102C (2002), 63–5.

57 *1857 Belfast Riots Inquiry*, 11.

58 *Ulsterman*, 19 Aug. 1857.

59 *Ibid.*

60 *Ibid.*, 26 Aug. 1857.

61 Report of Belfast Presbytery meeting, *Banner of Ulster*, 3 Sept. 1857.

62 Hugh Hanna's evidence, *1857 Belfast Riots Inquiry*, 167.

63 The Crimean cannons were mentioned by John Rea during his examination of Chief Constable Thomas Green, *1857 Belfast Riots Inquiry*, 67.

64 *Belfast Daily Mercury*, 7 Sept. 1857.

65 *Ibid.*

66 Charles Hunt to Thomas Larcom, 8 Sept. 1857, NAI, CSORP (1857) 7559; *Ulsterman*, 9 Sept. 1857.

67 Hugh Hanna's evidence, *1857 Belfast Riots Inquiry*, 166–7.

68 *Belfast Daily Mercury*, 7 Sept. 1857; *Belfast Newsletter*, 7 Sept. 1857.

69 *Belfast Newsletter*, 7 Sept. 1857; *Ulsterman*, 7 Sept. 1857. The *Belfast Daily Mercury* provided probably the most consistently reliable account of the riots, for it was willing to criticise the actions of both sides while maintaining a strictly liberal, middle-class perspective that opposed all violence by the lower orders of any faith whatever. Even this perspective was not without its problems – there was a tendency, for example, to overstate the severity of violent outbreaks and to present the forces of the state in a favourable manner – but the reports in the *Mercury* provide probably the least slanted view of the events of the riots. It is on these, therefore, that I principally rely in the narrative that follows.

70   Hugh Hanna's evidence, *1857 Belfast Riots Inquiry*, 167.

71   *Ulsterman*, 7 Sept. 1857.

72   *Belfast Daily Mercury*, 7 Sept. 1857.

73   *Ibid.*, 12 Sept. 1857.

74   All three incidents happened on the same evening. *Ibid.*, 10 Sept. 1857.

75   *Ibid.*, 12 Sept. 1857.

76   A. C. Hepburn, *A Past Apart: Studies in the History of Catholic Belfast, 1850–1950* (Belfast: Ulster Historical Foundation, 1996), 122–3.

77   This is the essence of what Frank Wright calls 'communal deterrence'. See the Introduction above.

78   Frank Wright, *Two Lands on One Soil: Ulster Politics before Home Rule* (Dublin: Gill and Macmillan, 1996), 156–7.

79   Betty Donahue's evidence, *1857 Belfast Riots Inquiry*, 86–9. See also the evidence of Biddy Burke, *ibid.*, 124–5; John Smith, *ibid.*, 134; Ellen Grant, *ibid.*, 138–9; and Sarah Anne Charlwood, *ibid.*, 198–9.

80   Mary Anne Donahue's evidence, *1857 Belfast Riots Inquiry*, 89.

81   Report of the Quarter Sessions, *Belfast Daily Mercury*, 29 Oct. 1857.

82   Reports of the Police Court, *Ulsterman*, 11 Sept. 1857, and *Belfast Daily Mercury*, 11 Sept. 1857; Report of the Assizes, *Ulsterman*, 23 Sept. 1854.

83   Reports of the Police Court, *Belfast Daily Mercury*, 10 and 11 Sept. 1857.

84   Wright, *Two Lands*, 257; see also Farrell, *Rituals*, 149–50.

85   Peter Shirlow, '"Who Fears to Speak": Fear, Mobility, and Ethno-Sectarianism in the Two "Ardoynes",' *The Global Review of Ethnopolitics*, 3 (Sept. 2003), 76–91; Peter Shirlow, 'Ethno-Sectarianism and the Repro-duction of Fear in Belfast', *Capital and Class*, 80 (Summer 2003), 77–94.

86   *1857 Belfast Riots Inquiry*, 2.

87   Gibbon, *Origins*, 70–1.

88   *1857 Belfast Riots Inquiry*, Appendix 15, 296. The absence of women here may be explained partly by a reluctance on the part of the police to arrest women rioters. William Tracy, for one, felt that women and children comprised at least two-thirds of the riotous crowds in July, a fact that he used to explain his reluctance to fire upon the crowds. See William Tracy's evidence, *ibid.*, 25; and Report of the Assizes, *Belfast Daily Mercury,* 24 July 1857. Nevertheless, a careful examination of the available evidence reveals that, apart from the cases of violence between female millworkers, which I shall discuss below, very few women were formally accused of acting as belligerents during the riots of July and September.

89   *Belfast Daily Mercury*, 7 and 12 Sept. 1857.

90   *Ibid.*

91   Report of Police Court, *ibid*, 12 Sept. 1857.

92   *Freeman's Journal*, 12 Sept. 1857.

93   Mary Jane McDowell's evidence, *1857 Belfast Riots Inquiry*, 123–4; see also Elizabeth Coyle's evidence, *ibid.*, 142–3, for an account of a similar occurrence in July.

94   Report of the Police Court, *Ulsterman*, 11 Sept. 1857. This area had long been the scene of violence between Protestant and Catholic millworkers. See

reports in the *Ulsterman* from September 1854 for the rivalry between Protestants working in Ewart's mill, another mill in the area, and the Catholics employed by Mitchell.

95 Thomas Dixon to Lord Lieutenant Carlisle, 8 Sept. 1857, NAI, CSORP (1857) 7802.
96 *Belfast Daily Mercury*, 21 July 1857.
97 *Ibid.*, 15 July 1857.
98 *Belfast Newsletter*, 11 Sept. 1857.
99 *Belfast Mercantile Journal*, 29 Sept. 1857.
100 *Belfast Daily Mercury*, 15 Sept. 1857.
101 *Times* (London), 6 Sept. 1886.
102 A. T. Q. Stewart, *The Narrow Ground: Aspects of Ulster, 1609–1969* (London: Faber, 1997), 146.

4

Local government and Catholic alienation

In late July 1857, during a lull in the summer's fighting, a mysterious invitation began circulating among the Catholic workers of the Pound and Smithfield:

> Belfast, 31st July, 1857.
>   Sir, – You are most earnestly requested to attend a preliminary meeting, in the large room, No. 47, West side of Smithfield, on Thursday evening, the 6th day of August next, to consider the best means of defence against the aggression and violence of the Orangemen in this district, and to adopt such measures as the meeting may approve of for carrying the same into execution.
> Chair to be taken at half-past seven precisely.
>   This Circular to be presented at the door. – Admission 1*d*.[1]

Those who arrived, penny in hand, at the small theatre at No. 47 Smithfield on that Thursday evening found the place packed with some six or seven hundred of their neighbours. As they waited in the crowded room for the meeting to begin (despite the circular's promise, no one took the chair at half-past seven) these Catholic working men undoubtedly discussed the riots that had recently convulsed their neighbourhoods. The clear superiority in arms enjoyed by the Protestants, the outbreaks of home wrecking, the rumours of collusion between the police force and the Protestants – the stories would all have been repeated and embellished dozens of times by the time the meeting began an hour later. Finally John Hacket, an overseer at Bernard Hughes's Falls Road bakery and (so it was rumoured) a Ribbonman, came to the chair.[2] He began by reading the circular of 31 July aloud, adding only that the Catholics of Belfast must also pledge to protect their co-religionists in other districts. 'Down with them, if the government does not', yelled a voice from the audience.[3]

The next speaker, John Hughes, introduced a resolution that explained the meeting's purpose.

> That it being the undisputed right and privilege of every free and loyal subject of the British constitution, to keep and possess firearms; that, in

consequence of repeated and unprovoked outrages and destruction of property committed by the Orangemen in certain districts, and the great want of
protection afforded us by the constituted authorities; we, the Catholics of
Belfast, in public meeting assembled, consider it not only our privilege, but
also our duty to provide ourselves with arms for our protection and defence,
and we, therefore, proceed at once to the formation of a gun-club whereby
every worthy and intelligent man may be furnished with some means of
protection and self-defence.

J. Fitzsimons then rose to address the meeting. He had just as much right,
he said, to arm himself with a gun as to 'buy his old woman a petticoat'.
At a mere sixpence per week, the club's subscription rate would, it was
true, 'keep half a pint of whiskey out of the whiskey shop', but this was
a small price to pay to arm the Catholics 'by the time this row might again
commence'. The longest speech of the evening came from Denis Holland,
editor of the *Ulsterman*, who praised these men's determination but
warned them that they must act only on the defensive. Perhaps, said
Holland, the existence of this club would force the Irish Executive finally
to take notice of the appalling state of law enforcement in Belfast and to
provide some substantive reforms. After a few formalities thanking the
various speakers, the men filed out of the theatre and returned to their
homes, confident that they and their neighbours were finally going to
acquire the arms that would place them on an even footing with their
enemies.[4]

The records of this first meeting of the Catholic Gun Club reveal two
things about Catholic attitudes towards Belfast's local government. The
first, most obvious one is that many Catholics, convinced that they could
not look to the local authorities for protection, were determined to take
the defence of their homes and neighbourhoods into their own hands. The
Liberal Protestant *Northern Whig*, conceding that there were some
grounds for Catholics' fears, compared the group to the 'vigilance
committees' of the American frontier, in which common citizens took to
enforcing the law where no army or police yet existed to protect them.
Such things might be necessary in America, remarked the *Whig*, but it
was scandalous that such a group should exist 'in commercial, manufacturing, well-settled, largely-policed, considerably-garrisoned Belfast'.[5]
Plebeian Catholic vigilantism of this sort was not without historical precedent in Ireland, however. The Defender movement of the late eighteenth
century had arisen from similar circumstances, when widespread alienation from the local authorities had led rural Catholics to take up arms
against their landlords and their plebeian Protestant rivals.[6] The Gun
Club's emphasis on arming Catholics also evoked powerful memories of
the time, not so very long ago, when Catholics were legally barred from

possessing arms (the ban was lifted in 1793).[7] Note that the above resolution appealed to 'the undisputed right and privilege of every free and loyal subject of the British constitution, to keep and possess firearms': arming oneself was a badge of citizenship, a declaration of one's right to equal treatment before the law, and for these Catholics the Gun Club signified their determination to claim that right.

The second thing the meeting illustrated was the balancing act that the Catholic elite was trying to perform with respect to working-class vigilantism. By speaking at the meeting and publicising its activities in the *Ulsterman*, Holland was both endorsing this extra-legal display of force and hoping to rein it in. In particular, he hoped the Gun Club would demonstrate the extent of Catholics' distrust of the local authorities and thereby shock the central government into implementing some reforms. This was consistent with the strategy that Catholic leaders usually adopted in seeking to bring change to Belfast: aware that the local government was unlikely to implement reforms on its own, they often appealed to officials in London and Dublin to force change from above. This had been the case in 1856, for example, when wealthy Catholics petitioned the government to create more Catholic magistrates in the city, and it was also what prompted Catholic leaders to embrace the 1857 and 1864 riots inquiries, which many local Protestants regarded with suspicion.[8] But until now most wealthy Catholics had disavowed outright violence, urging poor Catholics not to respond to Protestant 'aggression' with violence of their own. The *Ulsterman*'s endorsement of the Catholic Gun Club suggested that this attitude was beginning to change.

The Catholic Gun Club enjoyed only a brief and unspectacular existence before it disbanded in October 1857. An early effort to buy guns from a local dealer was quashed when Thomas Lindsay, chief constable of the local police, got wind of the deal and pressured the seller to withdraw. When rioting resumed in early September the Gun Club still had not managed to acquire any guns, though by this time it could count some 263 dues-paying members.[9] Many Protestants, ignorant of the workings of the group and fearful of what it portended, assumed that it was behind the rioting of September, but there is little evidence that the Gun Club, operating as such, was involved in the fighting.[10] In early October the club disbanded after Holland convinced the organisers that the recent riots inquiry would bring about substantial reforms to the local government, and after this date nothing more was heard from the group.[11] As it happened, however, no police reform was forthcoming at this time, and it is likely that similar vigilante groups continued to exist, on a more secretive scale, for some time to come.[12]

This chapter examines the roots of this profound, occasionally violent anti-state alienation that took hold among Belfast Catholics in the 1850s and 1860s. It begins by describing the nature of the city's local government, which was controlled by a savvy and unscrupulous clutch of Tory politicians who exploited Protestants' sectarian prejudices with great skill while excluding Catholics from the levers of power. It then considers the mutually hostile relationship that developed between the Catholic working classes and that arm of the local government with which they had the most frequent contact, the local police. It was this hostility, combined with a broader distrust of the local government generally, that promoted the sort of Catholic vigilantism embodied by the Gun Club and that became, in the long run, a vital component of Belfast Catholics' images of themselves and their place in the city.

The Tory faction

Government in nineteenth-century Belfast was primarily a local affair. Nearly all of the activities of the state with which the inhabitants had any contact – from tax collection to market inspection, from the courts to the police force – were controlled locally, by men who jealously guarded their power against the encroachments of the central government. In this, Belfast resembled many other Victorian cities, where political power lay predominately with the municipal corporations, the magistracy and the wealthy men who staffed them, rather than with the national elite in London.[13] Unlike the local governments of England and Scotland, however, Belfast's local government was the remnant of a colonial settlement regime, an ethnic and religious enclave in which power (and wealth) lay in the hands of the Protestant descendants of Protestant settlers.[14] In a sense, Belfast's government was one of the last remaining outposts of the old Protestant Ascendancy, its power resting upon its ability to exclude Catholics while maintaining the special status of Protestants.[15] It was also an inherently unstable regime: vulnerable to the vicissitudes of central government policy and to Catholics' ever-increasing demands for equality, it was a chauvinist anachronism in an age of centralisation and reform. All this meant that Belfast's local government did not enjoy the same legitimacy in the eyes of the populace that its British counterparts enjoyed, and it also meant that the tenor of local politics here was more openly sectarian than was the case in all but the most reactionary of British municipalities.

Like many other towns in Ulster, Belfast had always been under the effective control of Conservative adherents to the Church of Ireland. In the eighteenth and early nineteenth centuries, the town had been dominated by the Donegall family, 'unimaginative "Church and King" Tories' who owned most of the town's land and wielded power through the Belfast Corporation, which they carefully packed with family members and political cronies.[16] In the 1820s the family's hold on the town began to slip, the mounting debt of the spendthrift Second Marquis forcing him to sell off much of his Belfast property to tenants and speculators. As the Donegalls declined, a new batch of urban Tories, with heavy investments in the town's burgeoning commercial and manufacturing interests, emerged in their place. These new Tories were considerably more attuned to the needs of the growing town than the Donegalls had been, and during these early years they embarked upon ambitious and much-needed improvement projects such as paving the roads and setting up a professional police force. They were also rather more adept than the Donegalls at overcoming the political challenges of the day, which, after the Catholic Emancipation Act of 1829 and the Reform Act of 1832, threatened to open up the political playing field to Liberal Protestants (a dwindling but still vibrant group composed largely of Presbyterians and other Dissenters) and Catholics.[17] Guided by their election agent John Bates, the Tories exploited legal loopholes to pad the electoral register with their own supporters, sometimes by leaving the names of deceased voters on the rolls, sometimes by sending policemen to overvalue the dwellings of their supporters and thereby to enfranchise them. In this way Bates and company managed to weather the tide of political reform with considerable ease, successfully fending off challenges both from the Donegalls and from the Liberals over the coming years.[18]

In 1842 the old Belfast Corporation was replaced by a new, ostensibly more representative Town Council, but Bates, holding tightly to the city's electoral machinery, managed to fill all forty seats on the new body with members of his own party. He also installed himself as Town Clerk, from which position he directed Belfast's political affairs without interruption for thirteen years. During that time not a single Liberal or Catholic won election to the Town Council, even though these groups comprised perhaps as much as a third of the electorate.[19] The Liberals were temporarily more successful at winning parliamentary seats, but after 1852 these, too, were almost always held by Tories.

Bates and the Tories governed Belfast in a manner that combined a genuine impulse towards urban reform with an opportunistic political chauvinism, blending the reformist principles of the great British municipalities with the exclusionary principles of the Protestant Ascendancy. Three elements of the Tory dispensation stand out. The first is the party's extensive electoral corruption, something that, while certainly not unusual in nineteenth-century Ireland, was striking for its ingenuity. In addition to packing the electoral rolls with their own (real or imaginary) supporters,

after 1842 the Tories adopted an intricate method of disenfranchising
Liberal voters (Protestant and Catholic) by way of the local tax collector.
According to the electoral laws, voting privileges (which belonged to all
£10 male householders) were contingent upon one's ability to pay the
various local rates collected throughout the year, and anyone failing to pay
these rates could find himself turned away from the polls on election day.
Since the Town Council appointed most of the rate collectors, it was an
easy matter for the Tories to ensure that some rates were simply not
collected from Liberal electors.[20] Between 1843 and 1857, according to
documents submitted to an 1858 inquiry, 'the number of those rejected
for non-payment of the various municipal imposts ranged from *twice*
the total electorate in 1843 to nearly half the number registered in
1857'.[21] Such a system made it extremely unlikely, barring some sort of
catastrophe, that the Liberals would dislodge the Tories by means of
normal electoral politics.

The second notable element of Tory rule was the openly sectarian style
of the party's politics. 'I have ever been at my post to support the interests of the Established Churches of these kingdoms', ran a typical Tory
election address during the 1857 general election campaign, 'and to maintain the rights of the Presbyterians of Ulster; and, for the future, as during
the past, my first care shall be the promotion and protection of the
Reformed religion, as it is cherished by every denomination of Protestants.'[22] Dominated by Anglicans and buttressed by a growing number of
Anglican-friendly Presbyterians, the Tories consistently presented themselves as *the* Protestant party in Belfast, the party whose job it was to
defend Protestants from the threats of organised Catholicism. This was
politics in the old Ascendancy mode: the Tories derived their legitimacy
not from their ability to secure equal protection before the law for all religious groups, but rather from their willingness to protect the special
status of Protestants against the claims of Catholics. As we will see in the
next chapter, such a conception of state legitimacy had long since disappeared from official thinking in Dublin and London, but this simply made
the Tory establishment in Belfast all the more determined to hold their
ground.

The Tories' 'No Popery' politics was most evident in their alliance with
the forces of popular anti-Catholicism in the city. They forged these bonds
in a number of ways. First, the party cultivated close relationships with
clerical power-brokers such as Henry Cooke and Thomas Drew, who
happily made time among their other theological duties to campaign for
Tory candidates at the hustings and from the pulpit. Second, the party
worked closely with the leaders of the Orange Order, who encouraged the
brethren, enfranchised or not, to come out in support of Tory candidates

on election day. A few prominent Tory politicians were also members of the Orange Order, although the extent of Orangeism on the Belfast Town Council during these years is still unclear.[23] A third tactic that boosted the Tories' pan-Protestant credibility was their active support for Belfast's many evangelical organisations. During the great evangelical resurgence of the 1850s everything from young men's societies to missionary groups boasted Tory town councillors, magistrates and MPs among their officers.[24] Indeed, perhaps the most public iteration of the Tory faction's 'Protestantness' was its practice of attending and presiding over evangelical and anti-Catholic meetings. When, for example, Mayor William McGee came before the Presbyterian Students' Missionary Association in 1853 to introduce the Rev. J. A. Wylie's lecture on 'Rome, and the Workings of Romanism', he was doing something little different from what many of his predecessors had done over the years. And when the Rev. Wylie told the cheering audience how 'our island alone stands erect, free and independent; and will do so, if we make no compromise with Popery ... if we be men, and not sit in apathy, till we be dragged like sheep to the slaughter', Mayor McGee – sitting alongside Henry Cooke, John Edgar and John Potts, chairman of the Town Council's Police Committee – was leaving little doubt as to where his party stood in the global struggle against Catholicism.[25]

The Tories' pan-Protestant politics were a natural complement to the almost total absence of Catholics from political office and municipal appointments that I discussed in Chapter 2. This exclusion was the result of several factors, including deliberate discrimination against Catholics practised by some Tory leaders; the systematic disenfranchisement of Liberals, among whom were most of the city's Catholic voters; and the natural tendency of a ruling party to hand out municipal jobs to its own supporters. This made the entire structure of municipal government, and not just the Town Council, an important bulwark against the erosion of Protestant power, and it was looked upon as such by those Protestants who feared Catholic encroachment. This circumstance naturally fuelled Catholic alienation from the local government, and the Catholics' denunciations of the 'bigoted, inefficient cabal' that 'treats us with scorn, and ... does not allow members of our creed to hold office under it' were becoming increasingly angry as the years passed.[26]

The third notable element of Tory rule in Belfast, apart from the party's electoral corruption and anti-Catholicism, was its vigorous promotion of development projects designed to encourage economic growth and social 'improvement'. Activities such as lighting and widening the streets, establishing new markets and expanding the docks proved enormously beneficial to the business interests of the town, and they earned the Tories the support of a large portion of the rising capitalist classes. The party's social record was more mixed. Despite several undoubted accomplishments, such as implementing a ten-hour working day and creating new parks and wash-houses, the Tories failed to relieve many of the city's most pressing problems, particularly its abysmal housing and the grossly polluted Blackstaff River.[27] But if we judge them according to their own 'desire to emulate and outstrip' the great British industrial cities, as Cornelius O'Leary puts it, the Belfast Tories' record compares quite favourably with those of their municipal contemporaries, most of whom were likewise concerned more with economic expansion than with social amelioration.[28] Unusually for an urban party that consisted of manufacturers, merchants and professionals, moreover, the Belfast Tories also worked closely with their counterparts among the rural Protestant gentry, always making sure that their improvement projects would benefit rural as well as urban interests.[29] Indeed, it was by acting as a bridge between the reactionary, pan-Protestant world of the gentry and the modernising needs of the rapidly growing city that the Belfast Tories found their greatest strength. An old-fashioned 'Church and King' party decked out in reformist garb, the Tory faction offered something to just about every Protestant interest in Belfast and beyond.

All this made Belfast something of an anomaly among its industrial peers in Britain, for in places such as Birmingham, Leeds, Bradford, Manchester and many other cities it was Liberals, not Tories, who ruled. There it was Liberals who had swept into power following the 1832 Reform Act and who by the middle of the nineteenth century were presiding over their cities' industrial prosperity with such skill, while the Tories languished in obscurity on their country estates.[30] Moreover, because it was Liberals and not Tories who dominated in the great British cities, local politics tended to revolve not around issues of 'Church and King' conservatism but around questions of class, as the interests of Capital (as represented by the Liberals) contended with the demands of Labour (as represented by the unions, among others) in that most paradigmatic of modern struggles. This broad framework (and I confess that this is a very crude rendering of a complex subject) applied even in a city like Glasgow, where massive Irish immigration created a religiously and ethnically mixed workforce that nevertheless managed to forge a remarkably vigorous labour movement in the nineteenth century.[31]

The only significant British exception to this trend was Liverpool, another city of high Irish immigration in the early and mid-Victorian years. As Liverpool historians have long recognised, the peculiarly sectarian tone of that city's local politics, which was likewise dominated by an openly anti-Catholic Tory clique, helped fracture the working classes along religious lines, preventing the emergence of an independent labour movement and fostering bloody sectarian riots that occasionally rivalled those of Belfast itself.[32] Indeed, of all the great British cities it was Victorian Liverpool that most closely resembled Belfast in the sectarianism of its politics and the bitterness of its communal violence, and it therefore bears asking whether, as in Liverpool, the simple fact that Belfast was ruled by Tories helps to explain its unusually vicious record of sectarian violence.

The answer is a qualified yes. As with their Liverpool counterparts, there is little doubt that the Belfast Tories helped shift the political discourse away from questions of class and towards issues of religious identity and political loyalty. This was not difficult to do, of course, and in many respects the Tories simply exploited the sectarian animosities that already predominated in Belfast. But the party's peculiar mixture of urban reformism and 'No Popery' politics also helped to narrow the terms of political debate in the city, making it very difficult for their opponents to challenge the status quo without also appealing to people's religious identities. This was because, in strictly material terms, the Tories seemed to be doing an admirable job running the city – the roads were being paved, the lamps were being lit, business was booming – and so the only real stick with which the Liberal opposition could beat the Tories was their sectarianism. In so doing, however, the Liberals risked becoming themselves just another sectarian party. In such circumstances, class politics along the lines of the British model simply failed to develop.[33]

On the other hand, as we will see in the next chapter, the Belfast Tories were somewhat more constricted in their actions than were their Liverpool counterparts. In order to get Protestant workers on their side, they often had to pander to a certain vulgar anti-Catholicism that many officials in Dublin and London found distasteful, for it undermined the position of detached impartiality that the Irish Executive was trying to cultivate. During periods of social peace the Tories were generally free to play the Orange card as much as they liked, but when the party's sectarianism seemed to be fostering that most dreaded of Irish maladies, social disorder, officials in Dublin Castle tended to react swiftly and sharply. This sort of central-government interventionism was much less common in Britain itself, and as a result no similar governmental oversight seems to have constrained the Liverpool Tories in their own sectarian career. In essence, what made Belfast distinct from Liverpool was that Belfast had two versions of the state competing for legitimacy – the local, represented by the Town Council, and the central, represented by Dublin Castle – and because of this fracturing neither Catholics nor Protestants felt they could fully trust the state to look after their interests. This made Belfast much less stable, and its sectarian rivalries much more volatile, than even the most polarised British cities, and for this the local Tory party was only partly to blame.

The local police

During the Victorian era local governments across the United Kingdom extended their reach in a number of different directions. As cities industrialised, trade expanded, and social life generally became more complex, municipal corporations began assessing, surveying, inspecting and regulating an ever-greater swathe of their citizens' affairs, often professionalising tasks that had formerly been undertaken by volunteers. Belfast was no exception to this trend, and as the city grew the Town Council and its associated bodies amassed a sizeable army of market inspectors, lamplighters, clerks, customs officials and other agents to help them govern the city. Most of the time the behaviour of these state employees was uncontroversial; even in a city saturated with sectarian attitudes, the lighting of the lamps and the inspecting of linen shipments remained largely neutral activities. But there were times when even the most innocuous activities could incite storms of protest over the alleged partisanship or sectarianism of the state's agents. Ongoing clashes between publicans, many of them Catholics, and overseers appointed by the Town Council (at the behest of evangelical leaders) to enforce Sunday trading laws resulted in a series of sensational courtroom confrontations that riveted the city for months in 1853.[34] The following year Liberals, led by the fiery Presbyterian solicitor John Rea, launched a blistering assault on Tory-appointed rate collectors and others responsible for disenfranchising Liberals through the local rates. Rea's anti-Tory campaign was a protracted and bruising struggle that the Liberals eventually lost, but for a time he and his allies succeeded in obstructing nearly every government meeting in town; from Easter vestries to Town Council sessions, rare was the meeting in 1854 or 1855 that succeeded in conducting any municipal business at all.[35]

As far as most working people were concerned, the most visible agents of the state were undoubtedly the local police. Until 1865 Belfast actually had two police forces: the Irish Constabulary, which had roughly fifty officers posted in the city in 1857, and the local or 'Town Council' police, with a combined night and day force of 160. The next chapter discusses the constabulary in some detail; here it is necessary to note only that this centrally controlled, semi-military force normally patrolled Belfast only during periods of unrest, its everyday duties being confined mainly to the outlying areas. All regular policing duties within the 'watched and lighted' districts, including night patrols, surveillance, removing obstructions from thoroughfares and apprehending criminals, were performed by the blue-coated local police, commonly (and derisively) known as the 'Bulkies'. This force was unarmed (except for truncheons or walking sticks), resident in civilian houses (unlike the constabulary, who lived in barracks) and almost entirely Protestant – there were only six or seven Catholics on the force in 1857, five in 1864.[36]

Like other Victorian police forces, the Belfast men were expected to perform two separate but complementary functions. The first was the narrow one of preventing ordinary crime and disorder, of which the unruly lanes and courts of Belfast offered more than their share.[37] Their second duty, which in many respects was an extension of the first, was to 'improve' the morals of the working classes by combating the 'rough' street culture of pubs, brothels and other popular amusements deemed offensive to middle-class respectability. Robert Storch, writing about policing in northern England, has described the Victorian policeman as a sort of 'domestic missionary' whose job was to journey to the dark reaches of the working-class slums to spread the gospel of sobriety, work discipline and moral righteousness.[38] Like conventional missionaries, policemen encountered considerable popular opposition in the discharge of this duty, their reception made none the friendlier by their status as '*ex-workingmen*' who, as Stanley Palmer points out, 'were seen not to labor at a task but only to walk and watch, ceaselessly'.[39] In his recent study of the Belfast police, Brian Griffin finds widespread working-class hostility to the 'Bulkies', particularly when they interfered with cherished popular amusements like badger baiting, prize fighting, playing at 'bullets' or 'road bowls' and the ubiquitous drunken brawling. Verbal abuse, physical assault and even mass attacks by hundreds of men and women trying to rescue an unlucky neighbour from police custody were common occupational hazards for the Belfast police.[40] 'It was a characteristic of a Belfast mob', sighed Resident Magistrate William Tracy after one such incident, 'that it would join the Russians in an onslaught against the police.'[41] Nor was this sort of violence confined to one religious group or the other. 'There is absolutely no evidence', says Griffin, 'to suggest that a Protestant drunk was in any way more inclined to go quietly to the police office than a Catholic drunk.'[42] In most ordinary, everyday cases, assaulting the police was something in which Protestants and Catholics indulged with equal gusto.

Ecumenical attacks on policemen were also common during riots. 'They seemed to have forgotten their hostility to each other', recounted Tracy of a battle he and the police broke up during the riots of 1857, 'and appeared ready to assail the magistrates and police, against whom they threw stones indiscriminately, with the most perfect impartiality.'[43] Whatever else they were, these riots were a vital component of Belfast's working-class culture, and the policemen who interfered with them were treated no more charitably than those who interfered with workers' more secular pursuits. This was true not only of members of the local force but also of constables, soldiers and magistrates. In July 1857 rioters threw stones at the mayor himself when he tried to disperse a crowd in the Pound, and in late May 1858, after a Catholic funeral procession sparked violence near Sandy Row, the warring crowds stoned the constabulary and magistrates with such abandon that Tracy nearly ordered the constables to fire into the crowd.[44] For their part, the unarmed local police usually tagged along with the military or constabulary during these riots, most competent observers agreeing that the local men lacked the training, equipment or discipline to handle rioters on their own.[45] 'The local police are of little or no use in cases of popular commotion,' Tracy informed Dublin Castle in 1858. 'They fear the Catholics too much, and regard the Orange party too highly to permit them to act efficiently against either.'[46]

The second part of Tracy's statement conveys the other essential truth about policing in mid-Victorian Belfast: while neither working-class group had any particular affection for the police, the 'Bulkies' were especially despised among Catholics. The reasons are not hard to find. Protestant almost to a man, the local police were inevitably associated in Catholic minds with their Tory masters on the Town Council, and the force's reputation suffered as a result. Griffin maintains that the Town Council practised deliberate 'discrimination against Catholics in its police appointments', although if this was so it did not imply a total ban on Catholics, a handful of whom served on the force throughout the 1850s and into the 1860s.[47] What is more likely is that, as the 1864 riots inquiry heard, the method of recruiting policemen was inherently biased towards Protestants. Job openings, when they came up, were posted only in the police office, and the natural tendency was for serving policemen to pass on the news of these openings to their own friends and family.[48] Despite repeated claims by town councillors that they never asked an applicant's religion, however, it does seem that in most cases the men's religion was known before recruitment, since many applicants were sponsored by their clergymen or by members of the Town Council itself.[49] The social backgrounds of the men also lent credibility to Catholics' distrust. Most were the sons of small farmers from Belfast's hinterland, and before joining the force many had worked as labourers, weavers and petty artisans – precisely that class among whom Orangeism thrived.[50]

Given these circumstances, many Catholics drew the natural conclusion that the local police could not be trusted. But several factors amplified this distrust into a profound alienation from the entire structure of local government in Belfast. One of these factors was the Liberal politician and solicitor John Rea, who, as part of his wider anti-Tory campaign, made frequent, high-profile allegations of Orangeism in the police force. As a solicitor, he had many opportunities to publicise his allegations in court, mostly by cross-examining policemen (who were often called upon to testify in criminal cases) as if they actually were Orangemen. A typical examination occurred during the 1854 trial of two Catholic men accused of stabbing a Protestant during a Twelfth of July fight. Rea, acting for the Catholics, questioned the arresting officer, Detective-Constable McIlroy, about a man named Dawson who had witnessed the altercation.

Rea: Is Dawson one of the brethren?
McIlroy: I don't know.
R: Are you one?
M: No.
R: Were you at any time?
M: I was.
R: What was the number of your lodge?
M: I belonged to No. 40.
R: Where was that situated?
M: We used to meet in a house in Waring Street.
R: When did you cease to be connected with No. 40 – as you joined, you should never have left it?
M: Four or five years ago.
R: That is, you gave in a nominal resignation when you became a Town Council official?
M: Yes.
. . .
R: You ought to wear your scarf; you would have a more official look.
M: I wore it before now.
R: Very good; and perhaps will again, too?
M: No, I will not.
R: Was Mr. Bates there?
M: I did not see him. (Laughter, in which the bench joined.)
R: It is a pity he was not there; but he prefers to get others to do his business for him. (Renewed laughter.)[51]

Sometimes, as here, Rea elicited a confession from a serving policeman about former membership of the Orange Order, but just as often these accusations met with flat denials.[52] In such cases he still managed to get his point across, however, as during the 1854 trial of three Protestant policemen charged with beating an elderly Catholic named Patrick Hughes. 'Did Pat not give you the sign that he was an Orangeman?' asked

Rea of one of the policemen. Then, without waiting for an answer, he continued: 'Did you not make an attack on every party who did not prove himself an Orangeman to your satisfaction? Did you not break down the Catholic power with your sticks, because they did not give the sign? Did you beat a Brother, or a former Brother, at riots?' 'I can't tell,' came the policeman's feeble reply.[53]

These scenes had a reliable echo chamber in the *Ulsterman*, which highlighted Rea's courtroom accusations for its Catholic readers.

> Here are men confessedly members of a secret society – a society which has sown disorder and hatred broad-cast through the province – and for years held its anniversary of riot and bloodshed. Upon these men the Corporation fixes its choice, as the guardians of the peace, among a portion of the population whom, from childhood, they have been taught to hate and detest ... We cannot waste words on the wretched ignorant men who so outrage law, and justice; but with all our power we denounce and stigmatise the scandalous and infamous conduct of those who, holding the highest civic posts in the community, violate their duty, and disgrace themselves by appointing such men as the guardians of the peace and order of the town.[54]

'Orange constables', 'Orange peace preservers' and the more suggestive 'Town Council police' were the *Ulsterman*'s favourite epithets for the local policemen, and it used them any time a whiff of partisanship could be discerned in the force's actions.[55] Instances of policemen intervening to protect Catholics – as happened in 1855 when a group of drunken Protestants stabbed two Catholics in a Christmas Eve brawl on Durham Street – tended, on the other hand, to pass unnoticed.[56]

It is unclear whether any serving policemen actually were Orangemen. The force prohibited policemen from belonging to the Orange Order, and in his study Griffin has not found 'a single instance in which John Rea proved [current] Orange membership on the part of serving policemen'.[57] On the other hand, as Griffin himself acknowledges, such repeated accusations undoubtedly influenced Catholic perceptions of the police, and perceptions were what mattered. In an important sense, the accusations of Rea and the *Ulsterman* helped to politicise Catholic perceptions of the police: by linking the police so prominently to the demonstrably anti-Catholic Town Council, their allegations encouraged Catholics to understand their antagonism towards the police in religio-political, rather than class, terms. If relations were poor between police and people in the Catholic neighbourhoods, Rea and the *Ulsterman* suggested, this was not because the police were attempting to impose an alien form of bourgeois morality upon the people's rowdy plebeian culture, but because they were sent there by the Town Council with deliberate instructions to oppress Catholics. The force's supposed 'Orangeness' was of vital importance here, for it brought the weight of half a century's collusion between rank-and-file Orangemen and the local Protestant establishment (landlords, magistrates and clergymen) to bear on Catholics' perceptions of the police. To an insecure Catholic population fearful of Protestant aggression, the idea that Protestant politicians, policemen and rioters were all leagued together in 'foul conspiracies' hatched in the 'dark dens' of the Orange lodges, as one Catholic put it, was, once articulated, difficult to shake.[58]

We can only conjecture, of course, about the extent to which working-class Catholics took the accusations of Rea and the *Ulsterman* seriously, but we obtain a more direct glimpse of their attitudes when we examine the riots themselves. As noted above, the local police were generally felt to be useless during outbreaks of rioting. Because of their poor discipline and lack of firearms, the men often stood by in mute impotence when faced with riotous crowds – when, that is, they were not clambering over walls or retreating under a hail of stones.[59] Where others might have seen simple ineptness, however, many of the working-class Catholics who testified before the 1857 inquiry instead saw evidence of partisanship, and many told of policemen deliberately refusing to interfere with Protestant rioters as they assaulted innocent Catholics.[60] Hopewell Kelly, whose five-month-old child died, she said, as a result of exposure suffered when rioters attacked her home, told the inquiry that five local policemen and a magistrate had done nothing while her home was wrecked by some two or three hundred people.[61] James Carolan, a Catholic employee of the *Ulsterman*, claimed to have seen several policemen helping a Protestant crowd erect an orange arch.[62] And Margaret Jane McDowell, a young millworker, said that when she asked a policeman for protection from Protestant rioters, 'he told me to be off home, and to raise no disturbance, or he would take me to the police office if I gave him any more insolence'.[63] That some Protestants told similar stories of police inaction is significant, however, for it suggests that in some cases, at least, the idea of police partisanship was in the eye of the beholder.[64]

Catholic hostility towards the police was probably fuelled by the riot reporting of the *Ulsterman*, which Tracy and others accused of pandering to the prejudices of the 'lower order' of Catholics with its sensational denunciations of the police.[65] 'It is plain,' ran a typical leader in 1857,

> perfectly plain ... that the Orangemen are not interfered with when they outrage Catholics even in the presence of the police; that the Orangemen count upon a sort of sanction to their lawless aggressions; and it is only too evident, too painfully true, that Catholics do not meet with that protection which they have a right to get.[66]

The newspaper's reports were peppered with stories suggesting an alliance between 'Orange' rioters (as the Protestants were invariably called) and the police. One told of a member of the Harbour Police opening a gate for Protestant rioters during Hugh Hanna's open-air service so that they could get weapons from a shipyard.[67] Another incident occurred in Brown Square, where Protestant rioters were seen whispering to a group of local policemen shortly before the police turned away and abandoned the streets to the expulsionist crowds.[68] In one of its gloomier moods, the *Ulsterman* gauged the state of feeling among the 'humbler Catholics' and, ignoring the impact its own reporting must have had on Catholic attitudes, concluded ruefully that 'for some time to come at least that portion of the population will look with suspicion on and will refuse all confidence to, the local magistracy, and specially to the municipal police, whose real or supposed partisanship has filled them with the bitterest feelings'. Instead of entrusting their security to the magistrates and police, the paper speculated, the Catholics would henceforth trust '*to their own* right arms, to their own physical strength' for protection from 'Orange' mobs.[69]

Adding to the Catholics' sense of persecution was the peculiar topography of the Pound, which, with its dark, narrow streets, demanded considerably more police attention than the wider thoroughfares of Sandy Row. Local policemen's palpable sense of unease on entering the Pound, and the markedly less hostile reception they received in Sandy Row, only strengthened Catholics' convictions that the men's sympathies were with the Protestants.[70] 'The constables (night and day)', wrote a priest to Bishop Denvir in 1857 during a riot in the Pound, reflecting the popular mood there, 'are nearly all Orangemen and they drag the poor Catholic off to the police court for nothing.'[71] In the fevered atmosphere of these riots, Catholics' natural suspicions of the police fed into a frightening sense that the forces of law and order were actively seeking to injure them. Given the working-class origins of the police (many of whom actually lived in Sandy Row), the fact that some of them were indeed former Orangemen and several undisputed cases of police partisanship uncovered during the riots commissions of 1857 and 1864, such fears were probably justified.

Conclusion

The founding of the short-lived Catholic Gun Club in 1857, which I described at the beginning of this chapter, was but the most visible expression of the profound anti-state alienation that gripped Belfast Catholics during this period. This alienation had its roots in the 'No Popery' politics of the local Tory establishment and in the sectarianism, real and perceived, of the local Belfast police force, whose reputation among poor Catholics plummeted with every fresh outbreak of rioting. It is probable, though impossible to say for certain, that public bodies like the Gun Club overlapped considerably with the underground Ribbon societies described in Chapter 2, strengthening and legitimising the 'defensive' activities of such groups in the Catholic neighbourhoods. Whatever their precise nature, however, Catholic vigilantism of this sort proved greatly destabilising, for not only did it push the forces of the state off to the margins in the Catholic neighbourhoods, but it also helped to justify similar vigilante initiatives among working-class Protestants, perpetuating a cycle of conflict and reprisal in which the most violent individuals on each side came to exercise disproportionate power among their neighbours. This parallel, and in some ways even more severe, crisis of state legitimacy among working-class Protestants is the subject of the next chapter.

Notes

1 *Report of the Commissioners of Inquiry into the Origin and Character of the Riots in Belfast, in July and September, 1857; together with Minutes of Evidence and Appendix*, HC 1857–58 (2309) XXVI (hereafter, *1857 Belfast Riots Inquiry*), Appendix 10, 266.
2 As noted in Chapter 2, Hacket (or Hackett) was one of the men arrested for Ribbonism in 1859. Like the other accused Ribbonmen, he was released on bail after the prosecution failed to present any evidence against him other than that supplied by two informers.
3 *Ulsterman*, 7 Aug. 1857.
4 *Ibid.*
5 *Northern Whig*, 8 Aug. 1857.
6 David Miller, 'The Armagh Troubles, 1784–95', in *Irish Peasants: Violence and Political Unrest, 1780–1914*, ed. Samuel Clark and James S. Donnelly, Jr. (Dublin: Gill and Macmillan, 1983), 170; Nancy J. Curtin, *The United Irishmen: Popular Politics in Ulster and Dublin, 1791–1798* (Oxford: Clarendon Press, 1994), 148–50.
7 Allan Blackstock, '"The Invincible Mass": Loyal Crowds in Mid Ulster, 1795–96', in *Crowds in Ireland, c. 1720–1920*, ed. Peter Jupp and Eoin Magennis (New York: St Martin's Press, 2000), 90; Sean Farrell, *Rituals and Riots: Sectarian Violence and Political Culture in Ulster, 1784–1886* (Lexington, Ky.: University Press of Kentucky, 2000), 30.
8 On the magistrates question, see *Ulsterman*, 14 Nov. 1856. On Catholic attitudes toward the riots inquiries, see *ibid.*, 11 and 16 Sept. 1857; and *Ulster Observer*, 15 Nov. and 10 Dec. 1864. On Protestant attitudes to the inquiries, see *Banner of Ulster*, 19 Nov. 1864; and *Belfast Newsletter*, 10, 16, 21 and 22 Nov. 1864.

9 John Hacket's evidence, *1857 Belfast Riots Inquiry*, 136. See also *1857 Belfast Riots Inquiry*, Appendix 10, 266, as well as reports in the *Ulsterman*, 7, 12 and 19 Aug. and 9 Oct. 1857.

10 See, e.g. *Belfast Newsletter*, 11 and 12 Sept. 1857; and *Banner of Ulster*, 12 Sept. 1857.

11 *Ulsterman*, 9 Oct. 1857.

12 In fact, the Gun Club does not seem to have been the first such vigilante group set up by Catholics. In his evidence before the 1857 riots inquiry, John McLaughlin, proprietor of the *Ulsterman*, stated that a similar group had existed in Millfield prior to the 1857 riots and that this had been grafted on to the latter. John McLaughlin's evidence, *1857 Belfast Riots Inquiry*, 112.

13 Richard Price, *British Society, 1680–1880: Dynamism, Containment and Change* (Cambridge: Cambridge University Press, 1999), 175–85; Derek Fraser, *Power and Authority in the Victorian City* (New York: St Martin's Press, 1979); John Garrard, *Leadership and Power in Victorian Industrial Towns, 1830–80* (Manchester: Manchester University Press, 1983).

14 Frank Wright, *Two Lands on One Soil: Ulster Politics before Home Rule* (Dublin: Gill and Macmillan, 1996), 11–20.

15 The first use of the term 'Protestant Ascendancy' to signify Protestant social, economic and political domination in Ireland appeared in the late eighteenth century, when the legal basis of that domination was being undermined by reforms granting political and civil rights to Catholics. Prior to this, Catholics had been legally barred from voting or holding office, openly practising their religion, owning guns or inheriting land, to name a few of the provisions of the so-called Penal Laws. Presbyterians and other Dissenters faced restrictions as well, making for an elite class of Anglican landowners in whom nearly all of the formal power in the country was vested. On the history of the term 'Protestant Ascendancy', see Jacqueline Hill, 'The Meaning and Significance of "Protestant Ascendancy", 1787–1840', in *Ireland after the Union: Proceedings of the Second Joint Meeting of the Royal Irish Academy and the British Academy, London, 1986* (Oxford: Oxford University Press, 1989), 1–22.

16 Ian Budge and Cornelius O'Leary, *Belfast: Approach to Crisis* (London: Macmillan, 1973), 7. On the Donegall family, see W. A. Maguire, 'Lords and Landlords: The Donegall family', in *Belfast: The Origin and Growth of an Industrial City*, ed. J. C. Beckett and R. E. Glasscock (London: British Broadcasting Corp., 1967), 27–40.

17 On the impact of these and other reforms on the Irish electorate as a whole, see K. Theodore Hoppen, *Elections, Politics, and Society in Ireland, 1832–85* (Oxford: Clarendon Press, 1984), 1–33.

18 Budge and O'Leary, *Belfast*, 41–8.

19 Wright, *Two Lands*, 222 n.57; *Report of the Commissioners of Inquiry, 1864, respecting the Magisterial and Police Jurisdiction Arrangements and Establishment of the Borough of Belfast*, HC 1865 (3466) XXVIII (hereafter, *1864 Belfast Riots Inquiry*), Appendix B, 363, Table E.

20 *Belfast Politics and Parliamentary Elections* (Belfast: Banner of Ulster Office, 1865), 98–9; Jack Magee, *Barney: Bernard Hughes of Belfast, 1808–1878* (Belfast: Ulster Historical Foundation, 2001), 67–9.
21 Budge and O'Leary, *Belfast*, 64. Italics in original. Details of this scheme can be found in *Belfast Politics and Parliamentary Elections*, 104.
22 Election address of Richard Davison, *Ulsterman*, 25 Mar. 1857 (special edition).
23 A partial survey of the available evidence indicates that, in addition to the vicar of Belfast, T. F. Miller, and the superintendent of the local police force, Adam Hill, at least three Belfast town councillors of the period were Orangemen: William John Johnson, John Preston and John Oulton, listed as town councillors in *The Belfast and Province of Ulster Directory for 1858–9* (Belfast: James Alexander Henderson, News-Letter Office, 1858) and as attenders at Grand Orange Lodge meetings in 1862 and 1863 (reports held in the NLI). On Miller, see e.g. *Belfast Newsletter*, 14 July 1849. On Adam Hill, see his evidence in *1857 Belfast Riots Inquiry*, 234–9.
24 In addition to those groups noted in earlier chapters, local evangelical bodies with Tory patrons included the Presbyterian Young Men's Association, whose meetings were frequently chaired by Belfast's 1857 mayor, S. G. Getty (*Banner of Ulster*, 5 Feb. 1857); the Belfast Female Mission, patronised by John Lytle (who was mayor for several years during the 1860s) and other town councillors (*ibid.*, 7 Jan. 1864); and the Young Men's Christian Association, which counted several prominent town councillors among its members in 1853 (*Belfast Weekly Mail*, 28 Jan. 1853).
25 *Belfast Weekly Mail*, 4 Feb. 1853. Potts would shortly become a member of the Presbyterian General Assembly's 'Committee on Popery', founded in 1854. *Minutes of the Proceedings of the General Assembly of the Presbyterian Church in Ireland,* vol. 2, 295–6.
26 *Ulsterman*, 3 June 1854; see also *ibid.*, 3 Feb. 1855.
27 Budge and O'Leary, *Belfast*, 54–7.
28 Cornelius O'Leary, 'Belfast Urban Government in the Age of Reform', in *The Town in Ireland: Papers Read before the Irish Conference of Historians, Belfast, 10 May – 2 June 1979*, ed. David Harkness and Mary O'Dowd (Belfast: Appletree Press, 1981), 201. For a more critical assessment, see Sybil Baker, 'Orange and Green: Belfast, 1832–1912', in *The Victorian City: Images and Realities*, ed. H. J. Dyos and M. Wolff (London: Routledge & Kegan Paul, 1973), vol. 2, 804.
29 Wright, *Two Lands*, 161–3 and 221–2.
30 For an overview, see Fraser, *Power*.
31 See Chapter 7.
32 Frank Neal, *Sectarian Violence: The Liverpool Experience, 1819–1914* (Manchester: Manchester University Press, 1988); P. J. Waller, *Democracy and Sectarianism: A Political and Social History of Liverpool, 1868–1939* (Liverpool: Liverpool University Press, 1981); Joan Smith, 'Labour Tradition in Glasgow and Liverpool', *History Workshop*, 17 (Spring: 1984), 32–56. A similar dynamic seems to have also been in place in south

Lancashire and north Cheshire. See Neville Kirk, 'Ethnicity, Class and Popular Toryism, 1850–1870', in *Hosts, Immigrants and Minorities: Historical Responses to Newcomers in British Society 1870–1914*, ed. Kenneth Lunn (New York: St Martin's Press, 1980), 64–106.

33 The most insightful discussion of Ulster politics during this period, with an especial focus on the failure of Ulster's Liberals to counteract the polarising tendencies of the age, is Wright, *Two Lands*. See also Peter Gibbon, *The Origins of Ulster Unionism: The Formation of Popular Protestant and Ideology in Nineteenth-Century Ireland* (Manchester: Manchester University Press, 1975); Henry Patterson, *Class Conflict and Sectarianism: The Protestant Working Class and the Belfast Labour Movement, 1868–1920* (Belfast: Blackstaff Press, 1980); and Mark Doyle, 'Fighting like the Devil for the Sake of God: Protestants, Catholics, and the Origins of Violence in Belfast, 1850–1865' (Ph.D. thesis, Boston College, 2006), 202–25.

34 *Belfast Weekly Mail*, 1 and 22 Apr., 20 May, 3 and 17 June and 2, 9 and 23 Sept. 1853; *Belfast Newsletter*, 23 Sept. 1853; *Ulsterman*, 10 and 24 Sept. 1853; and Brian Griffin, *The Bulkies: Police and Crime in Belfast, 1800–1865* (Dublin: Irish Academic Press, 1997), 102–3. The Catholic bakery owner Bernard Hughes likewise complained that Town Council-appointed overseers had persecuted him for 'setting the sponges' in his bakery on Sunday, in violation of the Sunday trading laws. Bernard Hughes's evidence, *1857 Belfast Riots Inquiry*, 240–3.

35 On John Rea's anti-Tory crusade, which entailed, among other things, bringing a suit against the Town Council in the Court of Chancery on the basis of alleged financial irregularities, see Doyle, 'Fighting', 208–25; Magee, *Barney*, 67–72, 133–43; Budge and O'Leary, *Belfast*, 60–3; *The Town Council in Chancery. The case of the Attorney General at the relation of John Rea, Esq., v. the Belfast Municipal Corporation heard before the Lord Chancellor of Ireland, June, 1855* (Belfast: Northern Whig Office, 1855); and *Report of the Commissioners Appointed to Inquire into the State of the Municipal Affairs of the Borough of Belfast, in Ireland, with Appendices and Minutes of Evidence*, HC 1859, session 1 (2470) XII.

36 *1857 Belfast Riots Inquiry*, 4; *1864 Belfast Riots Inquiry*, 5.

37 Griffin, *Bulkies*, 58–88.

38 Robert Storch, 'The Policeman as Domestic Missionary: Urban Discipline and Popular Culture in Northern England, 1850–1880', *Journal of Social History*, 9 (Summer 1976), 481. See also Storch, 'The Plague of Blue Locusts: Police Reform and Popular Resistance in Northern England, 1840–1857', *International Review of Social History*, 20 (1975), 61–90.

39 Stanley H. Palmer, *Police and Protest in England and Ireland, 1780–1850* (Cambridge: Cambridge University Press, 1988), 450. Italics in original.

40 Griffin, *Bulkies*, 99–115.

41 Report of the Police Court, *Ulsterman*, 5 May 1855.

42 Griffin, *Bulkies*, 110.

43 William Tracy's evidence, *1857 Belfast Riots Inquiry*, 23. See also *Belfast Daily Mercury*, 18 July 1857 and *Banner of Ulster*, 18 July 1857.

44 *1857 Belfast Riots Inquiry*, 6; *Belfast Newsletter*, 31 May 1858.
45 *Belfast Daily Mercury,* 30 Sept. 1857; William Tracy's evidence and John Thompson's evidence, *1857 Belfast Riots Inquiry*, 29 and 217; *1864 Belfast Riots Inquiry*, 5–7; Major Thomas Esmonde's report to Dublin Castle, 31 Aug. 1864, NLI, Esmonde Papers, MS.5931.
46 William Tracy to Thomas Larcom, 4 June 1858, NLI, Larcom Papers, 7624/102.
47 Griffin, *Bulkies*, 127.
48 *Banner of Ulster*, 10 Dec. 1864; *1864 Belfast Riots Inquiry*, 6.
49 Griffin, *Bulkies*, 125–7. In *1857 Belfast Riots Inquiry*, see Bernard Hughes's evidence, 240. In *1864 Belfast Riots Inquiry*, see Samuel Black's evidence, 122–7; Robert Thomas McGeagh's evidence, 208–13; and David Taylor's Evidence, 132–40.
50 Griffin, *Bulkies*, 122–4; *1864 Belfast Riots Inquiry*, Appendix B, 359–61, Table A.
51 Report of the Police Court, *Ulsterman*, 19 July 1854.
52 For other successful identifications of former Orangemen among the local police, see the Report of the Quarter Sessions, *Belfast Daily Mercury*, 29 Oct. 1857; Robert Blair's evidence, *1857 Belfast Riots Inquiry*, 162–4; and Samuel Donaldson's and John McClean's evidence, *ibid.*, 244–7.
53 *Ulsterman*, 19 Aug. 1854.
54 *Ibid.*
55 Pre-1857 examples can be found *ibid.*, 18 July and 23 Aug. 1854; 17 and 20 Jan. and 13 July 1855; and 14 Mar. 1856.
56 *Ibid.*, 19 and 21 Mar. 1856. During the fracas massive crowds of onlookers attacked the local policemen as they tried to arrest the Protestant combatants, but although the *Ulsterman* carried reports of the rioters' trial at the Spring Assizes, no editorial mention of the event was deemed necessary.
57 Griffin, *Bulkies*, 131.
58 Letters from 'Observer', *Ulsterman*, 12 Nov. and 26 Dec. 1856.
59 *Banner of Ulster*, 18 July 1857; *Ulsterman,* 20 July 1857; *Belfast Daily Mercury*, 16, 18 and 20 July, 7, 8, 10 and 12 Sept. 1857.
60 In *1857 Belfast Riots Inquiry*, see Hopewell Kelly's evidence, 93–5; James Carolan's evidence, 96–8; Margaret Jane McDowell's evidence, 123–4.
61 Hopewell Kelly's evidence, *1857 Belfast Riots Inquiry*, 93–5.
62 James Carolan's evidence, *1857 Belfast Riots Inquiry*, 96–8.
63 Margaret Jane McDowell's evidence, *1857 Belfast Riots Inquiry*, 123–4. Also in the *1857 Belfast Riots Inquiry*, see the evidence of William Murphy, 125; Anne Sharpe, 128; Ellen Grant, 138–9; Elizabeth Coyle, 142–3; Mary Anne Connolly, 143; Patrick McGiveny, 224–8; James McIntyre, 228–30; and Bernard Hughes, 240.
64 Sarah Anne Charlewood's evidence, *1857 Belfast Riots Inquiry*, 198–9.
65 William Tracy to Thomas Larcom, 12 Aug. 1857, NAI, CSORP (1857) 6808.
66 *Ulsterman*, 11 Sept. 1857.
67 *Ibid.*, 7 Sept. 1857.

68 *Ibid.*, 14 Sept. 1857.

69 *Ibid.*, 22 July 1857. Italics in original.

70 *1857 Belfast Riots Inquiry*, 4 and 7; William Tracy's evidence, *ibid.*, 27 and
    29; William Tracy to Thomas Larcom, 16 July 1857, NLI, Larcom Papers,
    7624/3; *Belfast Newsletter*, 4 June 1858; James McCance's evidence, *1864
    Belfast Riots Inquiry*, 145.

71 S. Conway to Denvir, 19 July 1857, NLI, Larcom Papers, 7624/5.

5

The idea of order: Dublin Castle and Belfast Protestants

On 10 September 1857 a small item appeared in the advertising columns of the *Belfast Newsletter*. Three days earlier a thousand Sandy Row Protestants had gathered in a building on Grosvenor Street to discuss the open-air preaching riots that had just broken out, and this was one of the resolutions they had approved that day. Declaring that 'the peaceable, industrious, and loyal inhabitants of Durham Street and Sandy Row' had for years been 'the constant objects of Popish violence . . . for no other reason, except their being generally Protestants', the resolution described the riots as 'part of a uniform and universal design for the extermination of Protestantism and the destruction of Civil and Religious Liberty'. Therefore, it continued, it was the duty of Protestants 'to unite ourselves in a bond of brotherly union, for the purpose of self-preservation, the preservation of the public peace, and the maintenance of our Civil and Religious Rights . . .'.[1] Soon a new group, the Protestant Defence Association, came into being to carry out these goals. To outsiders it looked like a mirror image of the Catholic Gun Club that had been formed in July, and in many ways the comparison was apt. Like the Gun Club, the Protestant Defence Association was an extra-legal effort to pool the communal resources of one working-class group against the threats – or perceived threats – coming from the other. Also like the Gun Club, it was a momentary response to an immediate crisis: once the controversy over open-air preaching passed, the Protestant Defence Association was reabsorbed into the nebulous substructures of working-class life, and its members faded once more into obscurity.[2]

But there the similarity ends. In the previous chapter we saw how the Catholics of the Gun Club had pledged to 'provide ourselves with arms for our protection and defence' in a way that echoed the Catholic self-defence bodies of the previous century. Here, in contrast, were working-class Protestants pledging to undertake not only their own 'self-preservation' but also 'the preservation of the public peace, and the maintenance of our Civil and Religious Rights'. This was a far more ambitious project than that of the Catholics, for it cast Protestants as defenders not simply of their own homes and families, but of public order generally. Like the Catholic doctrine of self-defence, the Protestants' desire to preserve order had deep historical roots. Ever since the Plantation of Ulster in the seventeenth century, when English and Scottish Protestants had arrived in Ireland as a religiously outnumbered but politically favoured settler class, a powerful tradition of Protestant self-reliance had developed. In the following years, and especially in the last turbulent decades of the eighteenth century, numerous Protestant 'peace-keeping associations' had emerged as a sort of plebeian complement to the Protestant elite's formal mechanisms of control.[3] Over time, the notion that Protestants were the rightful guardians of order – and that Catholics represented a threat to order – took hold among all classes of Protestants, becoming a central component of the Ulster Protestant identity.

By 1857, however, most of the old Ascendancy structures of rule had begun to crumble, their old protector, the British state, having decided to abandon the Protestant garrison in favour of a more rationalised and centralised form of government. The Protestant Defence Association and bodies like it represented a refusal on the part of some Belfast Protestants to accept these changes. David Miller has noted that 'Protestant rioters regarded their actions not as violations of public order, but as measures to defend and restore it where the government was unwilling to do so.'[4] This chapter traces the origins of this Protestant vigilantism, which, I shall argue, was driven largely by Protestants' refusal to accept the legitimacy of the central government's intervention in Belfast's local affairs. While this tension between Belfast Protestants and officials in Dublin and London helps to explain much of the city's violence during these years, a secondary argument here will be that the government's own increasingly repressive policing practices significantly exacerbated the violence, and would continue to do so for years to come. The two problems were related, for they both stemmed from the essentially imperial relationship that existed between Britain and Ireland.

This is a contentious claim. Whether, and to what extent, nineteenth-century Ireland should be considered a British colony has been a topic of much debate in recent years.[5] Yet most historians agree that how one answers this question depends upon one's focus and perspective. An Indian witness to the Amritsar massacre of 1919, when the Irish-born Brigadier-General Reginald Dyer ordered his troops to fire on an unarmed crowd, killing several hundred, might understandably equate the Irish with imperial repression.[6] On the other hand, that same Indian, traumatised by the brutality of British imperialism, might well turn to the writings of Irish nationalists such as Arthur Griffith, Padraig Pearse or

Thomas Davis for inspiration.[7] With respect to sectarian violence in Ulster, an Indian observer might also note some similarities with Hindu–Muslim violence in northern India, and he or she might even suspect that they both sprang from similar causes – most probably this would be attributed to the imperial policy of 'divide and rule'. In this last instance our Indian observer would be only partly right, for, as we will see, the British state's objective in nineteenth-century Ireland was not to exploit pre-existing divisions between two indigenous religious groups, but to transfer power from an ineffective and illegitimate Protestant garrison to its own centralised institutions. But this project was necessary only because of Ireland's own colonial past, its history of settlement by Protestants at the behest of British statesmen who used them to rule the country until the emergence of popular politics forced a change. Even more importantly – and here the comparison with India and other colonies is most appropriate – the state's response to violence in Belfast laid bare the fact that British rule here rested not on consent but on coercion. This was apparent not only in the severe crisis of legitimacy that the state suffered as it began pulling the rug out from under the Ascendancy, but also in the attitudes of British officials themselves, whose response to the problem of disorder in Belfast was increasingly to brush aside the rule of law and to overwhelm the city with military force. It was a way of handling violence that would have been unacceptable in Britain itself, but it would have been quite familiar to Reginald O'Dwyer in Amritsar. In this respect, at least, nineteenth-century Ireland does look very much like a colony indeed.

I begin with an examination of the political context behind the Protestants' alienation from central authority, looking at the ways in which the British state sought to create a new, impartial regime in Ireland that took power away from Protestants and placed it in the hands of the Irish Executive in Dublin Castle. I then consider the impact of this policy in Belfast, highlighting three aspects of the government's response to the 1857 riots as evidence of the Executive's increasingly interventionist attitude toward the city. I conclude with an analysis of the great Protestant demonstration in Belfast's Botanic Gardens in 1862, which illustrated, both in itself and in its violent aftermath, Belfast Protestants' rejection of the Executive's reforming agenda.

The Irish Executive and the ideal of impartiality

The British state's project of creating a rationalised, impartial dispensation in Ireland had been underway for decades. The tremendous violence of the last years of the previous century (especially the cataclysmic rebellion of 1798) had revealed the fundamental weakness of the Protestant garrison, which neither commanded the loyalty of the Catholic majority nor seemed able (or willing) to curb the violence of lower-class Protestants. Ongoing nationalist agitation after the Act of Union in 1801, along with recurring agrarian violence that many in Britain interpreted (inaccurately) as politically motivated, only strengthened the desire to find some way of curbing Irish unrest. From the start, reformers had sought to do so chiefly by enhancing the police power of the Irish Executive based at Dublin Castle, but before 1829 such reforms had been fitful and incomplete.[8] The passage of the Catholic Emancipation Act that year, which granted formal political equality to Catholics, changed the equation substantially. With the admission of Catholics into the political nation, the idea of a privileged Protestant garrison ruling Ireland along the old chauvinist lines had become untenable, and state officials, worried that widespread Catholic disaffection might make the country ungovernable, found themselves forced to rethink the entire basis of British rule in Ireland. Beginning in the 1830s, then, a series of Whig administrations, fired by an intense reforming zeal and allied with Daniel O'Connell's Irish party, adopted a series of reforms designed to undermine the mechanisms of Protestant power and to replace them with a new set of centralised institutions directly answerable to Parliament. That the central government could govern more effectively and impartially than local Protestants was taken for granted, and the changes that the reformers introduced reflected the optimism and self-confidence of men utterly convinced of the rationalising power of the state.[9]

Two features characterised the state's reforming programme, which historians usually describe as a two-pronged policy of conciliation and coercion.[10] The conciliation prong sought to give Catholics a greater role in running the country through such measures as appointing Catholics to high office, allowing greater Catholic participation in local government and granting government support to Catholic institutions. The idea, as a pragmatic Robert Peel put it, was to try 'detaching (if it be possible) from the ranks of repeal, agitation and disaffection a considerable portion of the respectable and influential classes of the Roman Catholic Population'.[11] Although the Conservative Peel was one of the most vigorous of the Irish reformers, it was usually Whigs who implemented these changes; the hostility that Peel provoked within his own party when he attempted to create a permanent state grant for the Catholic seminary at Maynooth was a fair measure of the extent to which British Tories still resisted any concessions to Irish Popery.[12] Partly because of this entrenched opposition within Britain, most of the reformers' conciliatory gestures remained largely symbolic during this period, few substantive reforms being undertaken until the late 1860s. But the symbolic power of the Maynooth grant or (especially during Whig governments) the appointment of Catholics to state offices as judges, magistrates and Crown solicitors must not be underestimated.[13] As would soon happen elsewhere in the Empire, Britain was enlisting the natives as partners in government, hoping to ease popular disaffection by replacing the old structures of settler domination with a new, more collaborative dispensation.[14] From a Whig perspective this made good, practical sense, but from the point of view of the Irish Protestant elite and their British allies it was a course fraught with danger. For not only were Protestants being stripped of their traditional privileges, but they were also being threatened with the prospect of a new 'Catholic Ascendancy' that would, they feared, have catastrophic consequences for both the prosperity and the liberties of Irish Protestantism.

The second prong of the state's reforming programme was the creation of a more centralised system of coercion and control in the country. These reforms were by far the most visible evidence of its abandonment of the Ascendancy, for they extended the reach of the central government into even the most remote and jealously guarded Protestant strongholds. The intrusion was most keenly felt in the area of policing. Before the 1820s policing in Ireland was a local matter, conducted by town watches, militias and yeomen who, especially in Ulster, were often controlled by Protestant landowners or their agents. The Irish Constabulary, created in 1822 and substantially reorganised in 1836, put an end to most of this. Introduced as a counterinsurgency force at a time of widespread political agitation and agrarian unrest – which often blended together, in British minds, into one monolithic picture of Irish disorder – the Irish Constabulary was a semi-military force that answered directly to Dublin Castle. Unlike the traditional forces, whose members had strong local ties, Irish constables were normally stationed far from home and rotated frequently from district to district. They lived in separate barracks, were forbidden to marry, and were drilled according to military principles, often under commanders who were themselves former military men.[15] Consistent with the government's policy of employing more Catholics in state positions, at least two-thirds of all constables between 1851 and 1870 were Catholic, and many of those stationed in Ulster were easily identified as such by their southern brogues.[16] The most striking thing about the Irish Constabulary, and the thing that set it apart even from other police forces within the United Kingdom, was its firearms. Equipped with pistols, rifles and bayonets, the Irish Constabulary was the sort of force that would scarcely have been tolerated in England, where traditional fears of standing armies dictated that policemen remain unarmed. But in Ireland, where preventing disorder was the state's overriding objective, any such scruples were quietly dismissed – as, indeed, they were elsewhere in the Empire, where the coercive style of policing pioneered by the Irish Constabulary greatly influenced the formation of other colonial police forces.[17]

Another sinew of the state's power was the Stipendiary or Resident Magistracy, whose members acted as the chief judicial officials in their districts. Paid and appointed by the Chief Secretary's office in Dublin, Resident Magistrates were the eyes and ears of the Irish Executive in the provinces, sending monthly reports on the state of their districts to Dublin Castle and taking command of the military and constabulary during popular disturbances. Their chief duty was to sit on the bench at Petty Sessions, where they presided alongside members of the traditional local magistracy over ordinary criminal cases. But unlike the local magistracy, whose members were mostly large landowners or (in the cities) wealthy industrialists, Resident Magistrates were professionals with few local attachments. To ensure their independence they were paid the respectable sum of £500 per annum, and, like the constabulary, they were frequently rotated from one place to another. Traditional magistrates often resented these outsiders; among their most common complaints was that Resident Magistrates acted with undue favour towards Catholics, a charge that was unlikely to have arisen against magistrates under the old Ascendancy system.[18] For their part, however, the central authorities generally exhibited great faith in the Resident Magistrates, trusting them, along with the constabulary, to administer and enforce the law impartially, even if this put them at odds with local Protestant grandees.

Presiding over this expanding police apparatus was an Irish administration headed by a Lord Lieutenant – a viceroy whose duties were becoming largely ceremonial – and a Chief Secretary – a political appointee, frequently absent in London. Most of the day-to-day administration of the country was overseen by the Under-Secretary, a civil servant who, among many other duties, maintained regular contact with Dublin Castle's network of Resident Magistrates, constabulary inspectors, military officers and informers. Between 1853 and 1869 this office was held by Thomas Askew Larcom, an Englishman by birth and an engineer by training who had spent much of his early career measuring, mapping and studying Ireland with the Ordnance Survey, the Board of Works and various famine relief organisations.[19] Like many statesmen of his generation, Larcom was a strict utilitarian and empiricist, and when it came to handling Ireland's internal conflicts his attitude was pragmatic, forceful and scrupulously impartial. In the words of Montagu Burrows, 'Larcom ... undertook to govern all parties alike with even-handed justice, to remove abuses, and to prevent disorder, not only by systematic vigilance, but by disseminating a belief in the ubiquity of the government's power.'[20]

This assessment is borne out in Larcom's voluminous correspondence, held at the National Library of Ireland and Trinity College, Dublin, which conveys a strong conviction that the central government, if allowed to act uninhibited by inefficient and sectarian local officials, was capable of maintaining order without favouring one religious group over another. We will see ample evidence of this conviction below.

With utilitarian reformers like Larcom setting the tone in Dublin, then, and with an increasingly centralised police structure at their disposal, policymakers in London and Dublin tried several different measures to ease Irish unrest. In the turbulent 1830s these consisted primarily of emergency measures that suspended due process and gave law-enforcement officials a free hand in quelling violence. In the immediate post-famine years, as agrarian violence began to fade in the south and west, extraordinary measures of this sort became less common. But sectarian violence remained a problem in Ulster, and it was at this time that Parliament passed two controversial laws meant to remove the imme-diate causes of sectarian strife. The Party Processions Act of 1850 and its sister act, the Party Emblems Act of 1860, both appeared in the wake of unusually bloody sectarian clashes in rural Ulster. The first, enacted after the Dolly's Brae fracas of 1849, prohibited any procession accompanied by firearms, 'party' music or 'any banner, emblem, flag, or symbol, the display whereof may be calculated or tend to provoke animosity between different classes of Her Majesty's subjects'.[21] The second measure, passed in response to a clash between Orange marchers and Catholics in the Armagh village of Derrymacash, extended the ban to include the display of provocative party symbols from buildings or other places.

These measures tell us a lot about how the British state had decided to position itself with regard to Ulster's internal conflicts. Approaching the problem from an essentially pragmatic perspective, the Party Processions Acts sought to suppress Catholic and Orange displays equally, without regard to the specific colour of the 'party emblems' on display. They also entrusted the enforcement of the ban to the Resident Magistrates and constabulary, empowering them to disperse crowds, remove arches from roadways and enter buildings to remove offensive banners or flags.[22] That these centralised forces were more trustworthy than local forces was taken for granted: one had only to look at the role of the magistrates at Dolly's Brae to see that local officials were often themselves deeply entangled in the conflicts. By focusing on the outward displays of sectarianism, more-over, state officials had an objective, empirically verifiable set of criteria for judging whether a procession was or was not a 'party procession'. The underlying motives of the processionists, or indeed any speculation as to how observers might interpret a procession that lacked the proscribed party emblems, was not part of the equation.

In practice, the enforcement of the Party Processions Acts was anything but straightforward, for it relied heavily upon the discretion of individual magistrates. If no actual disturbance was expected, magistrates often found it more prudent to allow a procession than to suppress it. Even in those cases where a clear violation of the law occurred, they were less likely to disperse assemblies than to take down the names of the participants and prosecute them afterwards.[23] And even then, as one Resident Magistrate in Armagh pointed out, there was no guarantee that the offenders would be convicted at trial. Until the ban was accepted by 'public opinion', the magistrate warned, 'agitation, accompanied by strife, & bitterness, must be expected'.[24] Indeed, as we will see, this murkiness in the law's enforcement would give Protestant partisans plenty of reasons to believe that the ban was being enforced in a one-sided manner. Furthermore, like the proposals that periodically surfaced for the outright abolition of the Orange Order, the ban on party processions failed to address the fundamental problem of sectarianism in Ulster, which went much deeper than a few indiscreetly displayed ribbons and banners. It was, in short, a blunt instrument unsuited to the delicate problem it was meant to address. Indeed, the same might be said of the entire bundle of reforms introduced during these years: in seeking to empower Catholics, centralise authority and take control away from Protestants, the Irish Executive caused resentment among Protestants while failing fully to appease Catholics. As several historians have noted, this predicament would become more acute as the nineteenth century progressed, until finally the entire apparatus of British rule in Ireland began to fall apart.[25]

Dublin Castle and Belfast

In Belfast these developments followed a somewhat different trajectory from that in the rest of Ireland. Unlike many of their Irish counterparts, Belfast's Protestant elite had remained largely immune to government interference throughout the 1830s and 1840s and into the post-famine era, wielding power not only through the Belfast Town Council but also through the Harbour Commissioners, the Poor Law Commissioners and associated bodies. Dublin Castle had managed to plant one Resident Magistrate in Belfast, but this official was legally subordinate to the mayor, who remained the borough's chief magistrate.[26] There were also more than thirty local Justices of the Peace with whom the Resident Magistrate had to cooperate, and, in a district that by 1857 contained roughly 150,000 inhabitants (including residents of the outskirts), some such cooperation was often necessary.[27] The constabulary presence in

Belfast was also quite limited. Belfast was one of only three cities in Ireland to have its own police force in the 1850s (the others were Dublin and Londonderry), and against the local force's 160 men there were only fifty constables permanently stationed in the city, their chief job being to patrol the unlit outskirts and to assist the magistrates during outbreaks of rioting. As we have seen, the conduct of the local police did not inspire much Catholic confidence in the local administration of justice, but for many Belfast Protestants the relative autonomy of their city from the bureaucrats and reformers in Dublin Castle was a source of considerable pride.

Nevertheless, by the 1850s the balance of power in Belfast was beginning to shift, and what tipped the scales was the local authorities' manifest inability to quell sectarian violence. Although Dublin Castle normally treated Catholic allegations of an 'Orange conspiracy' in Belfast with caution, it was fast becoming clear that, whether they were partisan or not, the Belfast authorities were incapable of preventing or suppressing riots on their own. This assessment led Dublin Castle to test new, more 'impartial' and repressive policing strategies that necessarily gave the central government a larger profile in the city. At first its intervention was welcomed by harried local authorities and Protestant partisans alike, but over time many began to chafe at Dublin's repeated interference in their city.

Order v. liberty during the open-air preaching crisis

In Chapter 3 I described how Hugh Hanna's open-air service in Corporation Square plunged Belfast into a protracted period of rioting in September 1857. The controversy over open-air preaching, we saw, had been driven by the insistence of Hanna and his followers upon vindicating their abstract 'civil and religious liberty' to worship outdoors, which many Catholics took to be a calculated insult to their faith. What I did not examine in any depth, however, was the response of central and local officials to this crisis, but here, too, Hanna's actions inspired markedly different responses. For both groups Hanna's insistence on preaching in the open air created tension between the government's duty to guarantee free religious expression and its duty to preserve the public peace. Faced with such a dilemma, the central authorities were inclined to prefer order over liberty, and as the crisis persisted they showed that they were prepared to abridge the latter if it meant preserving the former. Local officials, meanwhile, were much more interested in the ideological conflict that underlay Hanna's actions, and, although they also sought to preserve order, they were sometimes prepared to tolerate a little disorder for the sake of a higher principle.

At the start of the controversy, both the central and the local officials appeared to be of the same mind. In a letter of July 1857 to William McIl-waine, whose open-air mission at the Custom House was the catalyst for the controversy, four local magistrates and the Resident Magistrate, William Tracy, affirmed McIlwaine's right 'to preach in the open air, as elsewhere', but pleaded with the minister to postpone his services, 'for the sake of peace, order, and religion itself'.[28] This initial appeal to McIl-waine worked, and many hoped that the crisis would resolve itself without the authorities having to take a firm position on the matter. Weeks later, when it became clear that the open-air controversy was not going away, and that, indeed, it was beginning to cause significant strife in the city, central and local officials still refused to prohibit the services outright. A Dublin Castle law advisor studying the case wrote in early August, 'If the Rev. Mr McIlwaine will insist on preaching in the open air, when such dangerous consequences are anticipated, & contrary to the strong remon-strance of the several magistrates, I know of no law to prevent him.'[29] A few weeks later a local Tory magistrate, Thomas Verner, forcibly criti-cised the preachers and urged them to move their services indoors, but he, too, resisted prohibiting the services altogether.[30] This official attitude prevailed right up to Hanna's performance on 6 September, when, in a last-ditch effort to dissuade him from ascending the platform, two local magistrates approached him and asked him to reconsider. Hanna, insist-ing on his 'constitutional right' to preach outdoors, indignantly refused, and the magistrates let him proceed.[31]

It was only after the rioting broke out that the conflicting priorities of the central and local officials became apparent. One difference lay in the degree of willingness and ability of each group to deploy large bodies of police. On the day of Hanna's service the local authorities had posted only a handful of policemen near Corporation Square – in order, they said, to avoid sending any signal that a riot was expected. When the fight-ing started, so small and underequipped was this local force that the policemen had to send to the nearest constabulary barracks for reinforce-ments before they could confront the rioters.[32] This minimalist policing strategy stood in sharp contrast to the response of Dublin Castle, which dispatched a highly visible and repressive force of 150 armed constables to Belfast within days of the initial outbreak. By the end of the first week of rioting Dublin Castle had sent 350 constables and soldiers to Belfast along with 245 reserve men, and the Lord Lieutenant had 'proclaimed' Belfast under the provisions of the Crime and Outrage Act, making it illegal for any civilian to possess firearms and empowering the magis-trates to search for arms in private homes.[33] This was a marked change even from Dublin Castle's response to the rioting of the previous July, when it had waited eight days before sending in its own forces, and it suggested that, in future, its officials would be much less hesitant to send large forces to Belfast to restore order.[34]

Evidence that Dublin Castle was concerned more with preserving order than with supporting Hanna's abstract right to public expression came on 21 September, two weeks after the initial flare-up in Corporation Square. Not content with the 'victory' for Protestant liberties that he had won two weeks earlier, Hanna had begun to gather forces for another, even grander demonstration that would (he promised) attract 10,000 Protestants from all over Ulster. By now, however, the central authorities had dropped all talk of defending Hanna's abstract right to preach, deciding instead that the time had come to silence 'that meek Divine', as Tracy mockingly called him.[35] On the morning of Hanna's grand demonstration, Lord Carlisle, the Lord Lieutenant, sent the following terse note to Larcom:

> I will call after church. It strikes me you should telegraph to the Mayor to disperse all assemblages. Yrs. ever, C.[36]

With legal niceties thus brushed aside, Larcom forwarded the order to Belfast, where the mayor, a handful of magistrates and a large contingent of soldiers and policemen obligingly broke up the demonstration. When Hanna pleaded with the magistrates not to interfere with the free exercise of his liberties, the mayor replied that he did not, on his own account, expect any violence from Hanna's gathering, but since he was a magistrate he had to enforce the orders of the central government. After some further discussion, followed by a brief scuffle between the policemen and the crowd, the gathering dispersed, and no further disturbance took place.[37]

Years later, Larcom would remind Lord Carlisle of this 'famous telegram' of 1857, whose 'epic simplicity and unreserve ... the Chancellor confirmed the next day by saying that it was exactly the right thing for the Lord Lieutenant to do, though certainly what no lawyer could have advised!'[38] In the immediate context of the 1857 riots, it was also something more than the local authorities were prepared to accept without protest. 'I have made up my mind not to act magisterially any more', the mayor of Belfast, S. G. Getty, told Tracy. 'I have already acted unconstitutionally, in preventing open-air preaching, when, instead of doing so, I should have thrown up my commission, and I will now do so if I receive any similar orders on the subject.' Other magistrates, reported Tracy, were beginning to express similar opinions.[39] The ultra-Protestant *Belfast Newsletter* was no less upset, denouncing Carlisle's order as 'downright and positively, distinctly, actually, and indeed, *illegal*, without warrant in the law or the Constitution of England' and threatening to bring to account every constable and magistrate who colluded in this '*coup d'etat*'.[40] As it happened, Hanna attempted no further open-air demonstration that year, so whether the mayor and the other magistrates were prepared to follow through on their threats is unknown. But the Lord Lieutenant's blithe disregard for 'Protestant liberties' had clearly angered them, and in the years to come Dublin's meddling in Belfast's local affairs would provoke increasingly hostile responses from the city's Protestant leaders.

The Orange Order and state legitimacy

If the open-air preaching controversy had exposed one area of tension between Dublin Castle and the Belfast Tories, the debate over Orangeism that took place in the aftermath of the 1857 riots exposed another. The Orange Order, of course, was a central pillar of the Tories' 'No Popery' politics in the 1850s, so statements such as the following, from the government commissioners investigating the 1857 riots, tended to rankle somewhat: 'The Orange system seems to us now to have no other practical result than as a means of keeping up the Orange festivals, and celebrating them, leading as they do to violence, outrage, religious animosities, hatred between classes, and, too often, bloodshed and loss of life.'[41] The commissioners recommended the wholesale disbandment of the Orange Order, but before their report was issued the Whig Lord Chancellor in Ireland, W. Maziere Brady, decided upon a more immediate step to undermine the Order. In an open letter to the Marquis of Londonderry in October 1857, Brady declared that known members of the Orange Order would no longer be appointed to the local magistracy. 'It is manifest that the existence of this society,' wrote Brady, 'and the conduct of many of those who belong to it, tend to keep up, through large districts of the north, a spirit of bitter and factious hostility among large classes of her Majesty's subjects, and to provoke violent animosity and aggression.' For this reason, he said, it was undesirable for any person charged with preserving the public peace to be associated with that body.[42]

This was not the first time that Dublin Castle had taken aim at Orange magistrates. Thomas Drummond, who served as Irish Under-Secretary in the 1830s, had also tried to purge Orangemen from the magistracy, but he had been unable to do so by the time of his death in 1840.[43] Since then other Whig administrators had also exhibited broadly anti-Orange tendencies – Lord Carlisle, who as Lord Lieutenant often displayed a striking ignorance of Irish realities, was shocked in 1857 to learn that there were any Orange Lodges left in Ireland at all[44] – but no one had yet attempted to revive Drummond's assault on Orange magistrates. Brady's proclamation was neither unprecedented nor revolutionary, therefore, although the fact that he was a Catholic (one of the few ever appointed to the post of Lord Chancellor) gave an extra bit of flavour to the ensuing controversy. All the same, the state's attitude towards the Order had been far from consistent in recent years. As recently as 1848 Lord Clarendon, also a Whig, had approved the clandestine arming of Dublin Orangemen in order to fend off the nationalist threat presented by the Young Ireland conspiracy, and other instances of official patronage of the Order had occurred within living memory.[45] Now, in 1857, many Orangemen regarded Brady's proclamation as yet one more instance of Whig 'treachery' springing from a misguided policy of conciliating Catholics.

From the perspective of the Order's defenders, Brady's assault on Orange magistrates seemed a disproportionate response to the recent events in Belfast, where little credible evidence of Orangeism within the local magistracy had surfaced.[46] Even before the appearance of Brady's letter, the *Belfast Weekly News* had declared that Catholics' attacks upon the local magistracy were part of 'a Papal plot to crowd our local magistrates' Bench with Romish magistrates', and now, it seemed, its worst fears were being borne out. On 17 October the paper ran a letter from an indignant Orange magistrate in County Down who insisted that 'my decisions from the Bench have never been influenced by my connection with the society' and vowed to resign his commission if the prohibition were allowed to stand.[47] Soon the balladeers were taking up the cause. In a song entitled 'No Orange Magistracy, or The "J. P." Letter', the singer imagines Chancellor Brady declaring,

> Then see in Belfast all they've done,
>   Their Orange sermons, and street preachings;
> We'll break these ties which *drew* them on,
>   To Doctor *Drew* and all his teachings

The ballad concludes with Brady expressing his earnest hope that the Prime Minister, Palmerston, will 'wink' at the Irish Executive's efforts to make 'Popery . . . Lord of all'.[48]

In November the Grand Orange Lodge drafted a letter of remonstrance to Lord Palmerston declaring the Chancellor's policy to be 'arbitrary' and 'inquisitorial', and it called upon the Orangemen of Ireland to defend their organisation from government attacks. 'Were the British Constitution in good working order,' the Grand Lodge explained in an open letter to its members, 'there should be no Orangeism. It is because it does not work well – has never worked well in Ireland – that our Institution became a necessity.'[49] In February 1858 the Orange leadership sent a delegation including Lord Enniskillen (Orange Grand Master), Hugh Cairns (MP for Belfast) and William Verner (MP for Armagh) to Palmerston's

London home to protest against the ban. Responding to a long speech by Cairns extolling the Order's honourable place in Irish society, Palmerston said that the principles guiding the Orange Order seemed, in fact, to be better suited to the Middle Ages, 'those periods of society when anarchy prevailed, and when one body of people were in the habit of arming themselves to resist some outrage or violence committed by another, and this because they felt that they could not depend upon the Government of the country for adequate protection or security'. Why, asked Palmerston, did such an organisation still need to exist 'in the present age'? 'Self defence, my lord,' said Enniskillen. 'Self defence against what?' replied Palmerston, 'I must really say that I think it is offensive as regards the government and institutions of the country, to say that the general government of the nation is not adequate to protect individuals from violence.'[50] What was at stake in this contest, to borrow from Max Weber's famous thesis, was the government's claim to monopolise the legitimate use of violence in Ireland.[51] From Palmerston's point of view, the defence of the people of Ireland was the sole prerogative of the state. From the Orange leaders' point of view, the state was clearly incapable of protecting 'loyal' Protestants in Ireland, and so they were justified in taking steps to protect themselves. It was, at bottom, a simple question of sovereignty.

Luckily for the Orangemen, the debate over Orange magistrates soon resolved itself in their favour, thanks to an Italian revolutionary named Felice Orsini. On 14 January 1858, Orsini and a handful of accomplices hurled three bombs at the French Emperor, Napoleon III, while he was on his way to the theatre in Paris, narrowly missing him. It was soon discovered that the plot had been hatched by Italian refugees living in London, and in the international outcry that followed (in which several French generals publicly threatened to invade Britain) Palmerston was forced to resign. A new Tory government under Lord Derby came to power that February, just days after Lord Enniskillen's Orange delegation met with Palmerston. In June the Tories, demonstrating their party's traditionally more indulgent attitude towards the Ascendancy, signalled that they would not follow through on the former Lord Chancellor's anti-Orange purge.[52] The members of the Orange establishment, no less relieved than Louis Napoleon at finding themselves still intact, heaved a sigh of relief, and before long Whitehall's attention had strayed to more pressing matters.

Overwhelming force: the 1858 riots

As the fate of Brady's Orange magistrate proposal suggests, the Irish Executive's centralising and rationalising policies were neither unidirectional nor monolithic. Rather, the government's approach to sectarian violence in Belfast – like its approach to most Irish issues – tended to oscillate between periods of bland disengagement and frantic, often heavy-handed efforts at crisis management. Often this shift coincided with political changes in London, as incoming governments scrapped the reforms of outgoing ones and set about pursuing their own Irish priorities. But no matter which party happened to be in power, both the Whigs and the Tories remained broadly reactive in their handling of violence in Belfast, periodically startled into action by some fresh crisis but unable to maintain their focus for very long. It was left mostly to the generals, the constabulary commanders and the Dublin Castle bureaucracy – 'Larcom and the police', as the cynics put it – to come up with ways of preserving the peace in Belfast, and these men, by their nature, were much better equipped to coerce than to conciliate. As a result, the Irish Executive's response to rioting in Belfast became markedly more repressive over the years, as concerns about the inefficiency and partisanship of the Belfast authorities led Dublin officials to rely more heavily on their own, more trustworthy forces. In giving the military and constabulary a greater role in policing Belfast's riots, Dublin officials also adopted a new strategy for dealing with rioters on the ground. Whereas earlier policing strategies had engaged directly with rioters by preventing contending factions from coming into collision or by dispersing fights already underway, now the authorities sought to pre-empt violence altogether by flooding the city with an overwhelming force that would overawe potential rioters and to keep the 'disturbed districts' under constant surveillance. This was an important change, for in a city where the motives and legitimacy of the state were matters of ongoing dispute, the increasingly coercive presence of the central government threatened to become yet another irritant in an already volatile situation.

These trends were already coming into focus in the months following the 1857 riots. The repeated outbreaks of that year had been highly embarrassing to both the local and central authorities, whose seeming inability to control the violence came in for considerable criticism in the press, in Parliament and from the riots commissioners themselves. A savage leader in the *Belfast Daily Mercury* expressed the general disgust of the 'respectable' classes with the authorities' leniency: 'The law is strong enough to put down rabble violence – and it must be put down – shot down – exterminated, if necessary, for the peace of society is not to be disturbed and endangered by giving an impunity to the scum of Belfast ruffianism.'[53] As far as the authorities were concerned, such brutal tactics were generally felt to be too extreme. At a riots trial in July, the Resident Magistrate, William Tracy, had responded to such criticism by insisting that if he had ordered his forces to fire into the crowds, he would have risked shooting women and children.[54] His position was broadly endorsed by officials in Dublin Castle, but the criticisms still stung, and some in Dublin were beginning to raise questions about the slowness of the central government's response. 'There is only one point which at all seems open to fair reproach,' Lord Lieutenant Carlisle wrote to Larcom shortly before leaving office, 'why did we let eight days of riot go on in July, without sending down fresh force[?]'[55] The incoming Tory administration, represented by Lord Eglinton as Lord Lieutenant and Lord Naas as Chief Secretary, were especially anxious to avoid a repetition of the mayhem of 1857, and as they took up their posts in February 1858 they, along with Larcom and Tracy, were prepared to use more coercive measures should Belfast's rival parties once again come to blows.

An opportunity to test the new measures soon presented itself. On 30 May 1858 a funeral procession for the daughter-in-law of John Hacket, the Catholic overseer at Bernard Hughes's bakery and erstwhile leader of the Catholic Gun Club, turned violent when it passed Sandy Row on its way toward Friar's Bush Burying Ground. Minor skirmishes between Catholic processionists and Protestant residents soon escalated into a full-blown street fight as people poured from their homes to throw stones at each other across the recently christened 'Boyne Bridge' that separated the Pound from Sandy Row. When a group of magistrates and constables arrived to read the Riot Act, someone pelted Tracy with a stone, and things almost spiralled out of control. Tracy, incensed at the assault and no doubt mindful of the criticism he had received the previous year, ordered the constabulary to fire. Before the men could pull their triggers, however, a young man appeared and persuaded them to hold fire while he talked to the crowds. Somehow this anonymous individual succeeded in persuading the parties to withdraw, and the excitement slowly subsided. But Tracy had sent a message: if violence persisted, he and his forces would not hesitate to fire upon a mob in order to protect themselves.[56]

The press applauded this show of force. 'Let us hope', said the *Newsletter*, 'that the authorities will not be as compassionate as last year – a compassion which, though laudable in itself, brought discredit upon the town.'[57] Over the coming days, as violence threatened once again to consume the city, the calls for vigorous repressive measures became louder. On the day after the brawl at the funeral, a Catholic crowd attacked two Presbyterian ministers in open daylight, forcing one to flee into a nearby house and severely injuring the other. So great was the fury among the 'lower class of Protestants', wrote an alarmed William McIlwaine to the new Lord Chancellor, Sir Joseph Napier, that he and the other Protestant ministers were powerless to restrain them. 'I have been speaking with some of these', McIlwaine assured Napier, '& I perceive a most deplorable spirit of getting up among them, to take the law into their own hands.' If the government should fail to take 'prompt & rigorous coercive measures', McIlwaine warned, 'our streets will swim with blood, and that soon.'[58]

Still the violence escalated. On 2 June the *Newsletter* declared the town to be 'in a worse state than during any period of the riots of last year' as Hughes's bakery in Fountain Lane, the offices of the *Northern Whig*, St Patrick's Catholic Church in Donegall Street and St Malachy's Catholic Church were all attacked, along with buildings and homes in the neighbourhood of Pinkerton's Row, an inner-city slum. Few of these areas had seen violence in 1857. Another funeral procession, this time a Protestant one, caused great commotion when fifty shipyard workers came out to protect the processionists as they passed through the Pound on their way to the Shankill area. The Pound Catholics let the procession pass, but a number of young boys accompanying the procession did stray into the Pound during their homeward march and attack some houses there. 'It would seem', commented the *Newsletter* presciently, 'that funerals are about to become the mainsprings in setting those riotously-disposed into motion.'[59]

By now rioting had been going on for four days, and it seemed that Dublin Castle was again failing to respond adequately. A day earlier the government had augmented Belfast's puny force of fifty constables with an additional one hundred men from surrounding counties, but this was having little appreciable impact.[60] The government's man on the spot, William Tracy, therefore decided to raise the stakes, announcing to a crowded Police Court on 2 June, 'I will, upon my own authority, desire every policeman to shoot any man who throws a stone at him, because the rabble think that they must wait till the magistrates read the proclamation [i.e. the Riot Act], and then give them time to disperse. The law requires nothing of the kind.'[61] On 3 June the authorities in Dublin were finally roused into action. In an unusually detailed letter to Larcom, the Chief Secretary, Lord Naas, ordered a regiment of cavalry and a regiment of infantry to be immediately sent to Belfast 'under the command of the most experienced officer that can be found in Ireland'. He also dispatched one hundred reserve constables and two additional Resident Magistrates to assist Tracy. 'Cavalry should alone be used in clearing the streets', Naas directed, and 'in case of stone throwing from windows any house from which a stone is thrown should be immediately occupied by the constabulary and held for some time by them.' He also ordered that magistrates should 'be always ready to adjudicate summarily on such cases as should not be deemed of sufficient importance to send for trial', and he instructed Maxwell Hamilton, the Crown Solicitor, to go immediately to Belfast to take depositions against those rioters held over for trial.[62]

Rarely had Belfast received such detailed attention from the authorities in Dublin. By 4 June there were more than 300 constables, 170 cavalry-men and 1,000 infantrymen patrolling the city streets – a force sufficient, as the Lord Lieutenant observed, 'to take the Town'.[63] That day the *Belfast Morning News* described a town under virtual military occupation: 'Wherever one moved, he saw a body of police; and in High Street the presence of the infantry with grounded arms, and the dragoons moving up and down to keep the horses in exercise, conveyed a salutary lesson to one class of the inhabitants, and gave assurance to another that the town was not, for another night, to be overrun by gangs of any class.'[64] To the authorities in Dublin this massive display of military might was a more effective and humane way of dispersing mobs than Tracy's earlier promise to fire upon rioters. To Naas's observation that shooting stone-throwing rioters was 'too horrible to think of',[65] Larcom replied, 'I do not think there is or was the least danger of Tracy firing on the people – but however well meant the bravado was ... a bravado is blank cartridge, & I do not like blank cartridge. It might also have had the effect of making the young Constab'y men do rash things without orders.'[66] Far better, these men felt, to station enough men in the city that the people would feel their every move being watched and therefore avoid the streets al-together. 'With the help of God', Naas declared, 'we'll put down these riots if it entails the necessity of garroting a policeman or a soldier in half the houses in Belfast – I have no notion of such things being allowed in our time at all events.'[67]

By 6 June, precisely one week after the initial fracas at the funeral, Belfast was quiet. 'One would imagine,' noted the *Ulsterman*, 'from the disposal of the forces, that the town was about to be attacked by an invad-ing army.'[68] Although rioting had once again persisted for days on end, the damage to life and property had been considerably less severe than during the riots of the previous year. There were no large-scale expulsions and few set-piece battles – nothing, in short, that a large force of soldiers and constabulary was not able to handle. As the riots wound down, the Lord Lieutenant indicated to Larcom that he expected to keep a 'large force' in Belfast for 'some time' and suggested that a senior military officer be sent to command the troops there.[69] There was some talk in the *Northern Whig* about enlisting special constables to keep the peace instead of the costly and overbearing government forces, but nothing came of the proposal.[70] As far as the Lord Lieutenant was concerned, an overwhelm-ing force answerable to Dublin was the best remedy for Belfast's violence. 'It is very well the people there thinking we have sent too large a force,' he told Larcom, 'but prevention is better than cure, & it will make them more anxious to put matters on a safer footing, if they have to pay for some extra police.'[71]

From Dublin's perspective, then, this new pre-emptive approach to Belfast's riots seemed to have produced admirable results, and state officials would continue to refine the strategy during future conflicts. To anyone paying close attention, however, two items arriving at Dublin Castle that week in June might have given cause for concern. The first was a letter to the Lord Chancellor from Thomas Drew, no stranger himself to the passions of Belfast crowds. Drew's letter told of an incident on 31 May when a crowd of people gathered outside his church, and, although the crowd was 'little more than what is always seen on a fine evening when the Mills are closed', suddenly 'the bugles were ordered to sound and a company of soldiers were sent running ... along the entire length of the street! This is folly indeed,' claimed Drew. 'Surely the people will come out universally at the sound of bugles and tramp of armed men. And so it was.' For his part, Drew blamed the local magistrates for this overreaction and even suggested that the way to overcome the local authorities' 'indecision and hesitation' was to appoint two or three more Resident Magistrates in Belfast who would act as 'cool & experienced men to save us from further calamities'.[72] Like other Protestant leaders in 1858, Drew had few qualms about asking Dublin Castle to increase its policing role in Belfast, although, as we shall see, this way of thinking would soon change. In the meantime, Drew had identified a potential problem with the state's new preventive measures: although sometimes effective at keeping riotous crowds from gathering, large numbers of troops and constables could also act as a lightning rod for both the idly curious and the violently disposed. In a city where the police were often believed to be aligned with one side or the other, violence against the police could potentially become just as serious as violence between rival bands of rioters.

The second item that arrived in Dublin Castle that week was a placard that had been taken down by Tracy during the riots. It read,

<u>Protestant Meeting</u>
A meeting will be held in the Wellington-hall on Tuesday evening the 8th instant at 8 o'clock for the purpose of taking into consideration the present alarming state of society in Belfast and adopting measures for the protection of the lives and property of Protestants against the ferocious attacks of organised Popish mobs.
Admission 2d to defray expenses.[73]

Whether this meeting actually took place, and what was said there if it did, is unknown.[74] It is possible that it represented an attempt to rejuvenate (or to perpetuate) the Protestant Defence Association, founded the previous autumn, although this can only be a conjecture. In any case, the placard showed that despite Dublin Castle's repressive actions, the spirit of vigilantism within the Protestant neighbourhoods was far from dead. Indeed, as the central government began augmenting its forces in Belfast over the years, some Protestants would become more attracted to vigilantism, not less. Nandini Gooptu has noted that increasingly repressive urban policing in early twentieth-century India (which, as in Belfast, was the state's primary response to a perceived upsurge in 'disorder' there) had the paradoxical effect of cultivating 'a martial culture and the adoption of quasi-military tactics' among certain segments of the urban poor.[75] Something similar, it seems, was happening among poor Belfast Protestants, who were beginning to recognise that a stronger role for Dublin Castle meant a weaker one for the local Protestant establishment.

The Botanic Gardens demonstration, 1862

Despite these warning signs, in the aftermath of the 1858 riots observers in London and Dublin looked to the future with confidence. 'The near equality [in numbers] of the rival creeds in the lower classes', Larcom told Naas, 'will be a cause of turbulence for some time to come – but it will die out at last there as it has done elsewhere.'[76] The *Times* was likewise hopeful that 'Irishmen will one day give up that bitterness of party spirit which is peculiarly their own, and learn to live together like the inhabitants of more pacific countries', although it conceded that 'this Millennium is probably still distant'. Like many British commentators, the *Times* felt that what was principally needed to keep the Irish from fighting 'like the servants of the Montagues and Capulets' was good government. 'Happy it is', the newspaper declared, 'that we have all England and Scotland determined to keep the peace in the sister island, else the more zealous of the two parties would speedily come to blows.'[77]

For a time the government's new policing strategy seemed to be justified by the results. Over the next four years large-scale violence in Belfast was almost entirely absent, even in the normally raucous summer months. 'The old "disturbed districts" were as peaceable as if Sandy Row and the Pound had shaken hands and resolved to quarrel no more', remarked an incredulous *Northern Whig* after the Twelfth of July in 1861.[78] Social peace was accompanied by an unprecedented burst of economic prosperity beginning in 1861, when the US Civil War disrupted worldwide cotton supplies and caused a surge in demand for Belfast linen. The promise of steady employment and high wages drew thousands of migrants to Belfast, most of them, as during earlier periods of expansion, coming from rural Ulster.[79] Few of these new inhabitants had any direct experience of a Belfast riot, of course, but like earlier migrants they carried with them the sectarian codes and animosities of their rural backgrounds. Sectarian tensions did not disappear during this period, therefore, but they remained at a slow simmer, as the rural predispositions of the newcomers mingled with the bitter memories and festering grudges of their urban neighbours.

Tensions rose to a boil again in September 1862, when Protestant leaders decided to hold a 'Great Protestant Demonstration' in Belfast's Botanic Gardens. The demonstration was held to protest against the government's recent decision to allow a Catholic procession in Dublin to celebrate the opening of a new Catholic university building. Coming as it did just one year after the famous McManus funeral of 1861, when thousands of Dubliners had taken to the streets to honour the remains of the Young Ireland leader Terence McManus, the Catholic university demonstration was thought by many northern Protestants to be, like the McManus funeral, 'allied with sedition and disloyalty'.[80] Such fears were not eased by the prominence of Catholic clergymen in the Dublin procession, nor by the fact that the procession occurred on a Sunday, in what seemed a calculated insult to Protestants' Sabbatarian principles. Worst of all, the Dublin procession took place at a time when Protestant processions were still legally suppressed under the Party Processions Acts. To a people already resentful over the Party Processions Acts' assault on their 'civil and religious liberties', it seemed the barest of hypocrisies that a 'disloyal' procession should be allowed in Dublin while the 'loyal' Orangemen of Ulster faced prosecution if they attempted the same thing.

On the day of the demonstration, 17 September, special excursion trains brought thousands of rural Protestants to Belfast. Drapers' shops, foreseeing a boost to their usual Wednesday business, adorned their windows with orange ribbons, placards and King William handkerchiefs.[81] The festive atmosphere and cheap train fares probably attracted many who were not as outraged over the Dublin procession as their leaders would have liked them to be, and it is likely that, in the words of the *Northern Whig*, 'They were in the Botanic Garden partly because any excuse for a holiday is agreeable, and partly to oblige "the minister" and the landlord.'[82] The demonstration itself was hampered by a number of embarrassing difficulties, the most bothersome of which was that none but those standing nearest the platform could hear the speakers. A secondary problem was that the platform itself kept collapsing, periodically sending the assembled Protestant dignitaries tumbling. To add to the difficulties a number of Irish Protestantism's leading lights, including the Ulster MPs Hugh Cairns and James Whiteside, along with most of the Orange gentry, failed to attend the meeting, sending along letters of regret that thinly masked their desire to avoid being associated with what could prove a rather disorderly demonstration.[83]

The speeches, on the whole, were classic expressions of the sort of wounded devotion that Protestant loyalists had been nursing for decades. William Verner, an Armagh Orangeman and MP, asked whether the government's one-sided enforcement of the Party Processions Acts was 'the treatment that men deserved who have come forward in the country's defence, who have always been looked on as the defenders of their country'. Henry Cooke, the doyen of evangelical pan-Protestantism, offered his usual denunciation of the Catholic Church as 'a grand attempt at universal monarchy'. Hugh Hanna, milking the notoriety he had attained in 1857, recalled how he had once been 'driven from my position ... at the point of the bayonet' while trying to preach the Gospel in Belfast. Among the meeting's many prosaic resolutions was that offered by the Rev. William Flannigan, rector of Killevan, which criticised the government for its 'studied appointment of Roman Catholics to offices of trust and emolument in Ireland, to the almost entire exclusion of Protestants'. This, according to the Newry MP Peter Quin, had resulted in the intolerable fact that twenty of Ireland's twenty-two Crown Solicitors were now Catholic.[84]

All of this was by now pretty standard fare for a Protestant indignation meeting, and the *Whig* was right to question whether 'the "studied appointment of Roman Catholics to offices of trust and emolument in Ireland" [was] a grievance very intimately affecting the small tradesmen, tenant-farmers, and day-labourers of the North'.[85] There was, however, one speaker who managed to overcome the torpor of the crowd. This was William Johnston of Ballykilbeg, a County Down landlord who was as yet largely unknown in Belfast apart from his being the first to publish (in his newspaper, the *Downshire Protestant*) Thomas Drew's famous Orange sermon of 1857.[86] Within four years, however, Johnston would become an Orange folk hero when he led a campaign of open defiance against the Party Processions Acts, a campaign that would carry him to Parliament in 1868 (over the heads of the two official Tory candidates) and ultimately bring about the repeal of the Acts in 1872. Historians point to Johnston's 1868 campaign as a key moment in the development of Ulster Unionism's potent mixture of plebeian radicalism and elite conservatism, but few have recognised that Johnston's revolt against the Party Processions Acts was already gathering steam, and followers, as early as 1862.[87] Johnston's appearance at the Botanic Gardens amounted to his Belfast debut, and his rousing oration was clearly the highlight of the day. 'I say the Orangemen of Protestant Ulster ... must go forth with the emblems of civil and religious liberty on the glorious anniversary of the battle of the Boyne,' said Johnston to tremendous cheering. 'The Maynooth grant must be repealed ... the Emblems Act and the Procession Act must be repealed ... and civil and religious liberty given to the Protestants of Ireland, for the Orangemen of Ulster will it so, and they will never surrender.'[88] Here, finally, was something the crowd could get excited about.

Years later the former *Northern Whig* editor Thomas MacKnight, recalling the fight over the disestablishment of the Church of Ireland in the 1860s, glibly summarised the political priorities of the Orange rank and file at this time: 'In comparison with the liberty to walk in procession with fifes, drums, and banners, as the Fenians south of the Boyne were doing, they cared little for "our Protestant institutions".'[89] This parochial concern with the 'the right to march' was on plain view that day in the Botanic Gardens. For more than a decade, working-class Protestants had grudgingly submitted to their leaders' orders that they comply with the Party Processions Acts, but they had never entirely acquiesced to the ban. In Belfast, petty infractions had been common since the early 1850s, with small, late-night drumming parties forming in the streets during the summer months, often to the great annoyance of Catholics. It had also become customary for Belfast Orangemen to travel outside the city to celebrate the anniversary with processions and rallies far from the magisterial gaze.[90] These demonstrations had been discouraged by an Orange leadership eager to maintain the Order's 'respectability', but they were never eradicated. When Johnston came forward with his rousing attack on the Party Processions Acts, therefore, his target was not just the government and its one-sided enforcement policies, but the Orange leadership as well. 'Why are not your Cairnses and your Whitesides on the platform?' he asked, as the crowd hooted and booed, 'Why are not the Torrenses and the Pakenhams and all the rest of them here? The fact is ... we must tell our representatives that we are not to be trifled with ... that, if we put them into Parliament, we can put them out again ... and, if they are ashamed of the Protestant cause, they are not the men for Ulster.'[91] These were the first stirrings of a working-class Protestant revolt not only against the government's ban on party processions, but against the Orange Order's 'respectable' leadership as well. It was precisely this dual alienation that gave rise to the sort of working-class Protestant vigilantism that I introduced at the beginning of this chapter. To the Protestants cheering Johnston that day in the Botanic Gardens, the state's violation of their traditional 'liberties' and their leaders' inability to stand up to this violation were sufficient reasons to begin enforcing their own, plebeian conception of 'order' in the Protestant metropolis.

One group of elites who did not avoid the Botanic Gardens demonstration consisted of Belfast's own Tory rulers. Charles Lanyon, current mayor of Belfast and architect of many of the city's most admired buildings, was there, as was S. G. Getty, the former mayor of Belfast and now one of its two MPs, who chaired the meeting. The local magistrates John Clarke, Dr Magee and David Taylor were all there, as were the vicar of St Anne's Church, Thomas Miller, and J. A. Henderson, editor of the *Belfast Newsletter*.[92] The Protestant gentry may have abandoned rank-and-file Orangemen, but important sections of the local establishment had decided to cast their lot with the Protestant working classes. Significantly, many of these men would shortly be responsible for policing the city when the rioting began.

Like earlier outbreaks, the 1862 riots built slowly. The demonstration itself was largely peaceful, the only disturbance coming from a lone heckler who interrupted Hanna's address with cries of 'to hell with Hanna!' before being chased away. But that night the Pound and Sandy Row were astir with rumours of a coming fight, and as the demonstration drew to a close people in both neighbourhoods began making the usual preparations, tearing up paving stones and putting out street lamps. No serious rioting happened that first night, but the following night tensions escalated when a group of Catholics attacked Hanna's Berry Street Church and a crowd of Protestants, gathered near Christ Church, got into a scuffle with the constabulary. It was not until two days after the Botanic Gardens demonstration, however, that the rioting got fully underway. On that day bands of rioters attacked several targets in the city centre, including Bernard Hughes's bakery, the Catholic-owned Royal Hotel, several churches, a spirit store and many wealthy residences. A group of Catholic navvies employed on the Ulster Railway caused serious commotion when, on leaving work for the evening, they marched down Durham Street in military formation, shovels propped against their shoulders and cheering defiantly. The constabulary managed to prevent them coming into collision with any Protestants, but over the next few days the navvies repeatedly marched through the city, introducing a new, volatile component to Belfast's riots that would become increasingly important in the coming years. [93]

As they had in 1858, the authorities in Dublin Castle adopted a strategy of overwhelming force to deal with the rioters, and the speed with which they dispatched troops to the city suggests that their procedures had been streamlined somewhat. By 19 September, the first full day of rioting, a force of 150 constables and 700 infantrymen had already been sent to the city, and this force was strengthened by another 200 constables and 360 soldiers over the coming days.[94] Largely because of this massive force, protracted battles between Catholic and Protestant rioters were rare. Instead, most of the violence consisted of attacks on businesses, homes and individuals, while some of the most notable clashes took place between rioters and constables. The *Newsletter* noted how large crowds would gather around the constables 'out of curiosity' and throw stones at them, 'just to see, of course, how the horses would stand fire'.[95] From the start, the ultra-Protestant *Newsletter* criticised the government for this heavy-handed policing, arguing that by sending so many men into the streets it was provoking, rather than preventing, violence. 'The chances are that there would have been no riot at all, but for the way in which Government took care to notify to the evil-disposed that a riot was anticipated.' Instead of 'pour[ing] military and police into the town in huge bodies', the *Newsletter* suggested, it would be better to 'rely rather on the sagacity of small bodies of men' to disperse the rioters.[96] This was a significant change from the *Newsletter*'s attitude in 1857, when it had criticised the government for its 'compassionate' policies and called for strong policing measures to quell the rioting. Protestant hostility to Dublin Castle's policing tactics was still its infancy, but it was slowly building into the sort of thoroughgoing anti-state sentiment that would fuel some of Belfast's most terrible violence.

Like the 1858 riots, the 1862 riots fizzled out after just seven days. During that time, according to William Tracy, 'no man, woman, or child was hurt, and the total damage that has been done could be repaired, as I am informed, for the small sum of £50'.[97] Meanwhile the central government was accumulating yet more evidence of the inefficiency of the local authorities. In a report to Larcom one of the officers commanding the forces in Belfast claimed that, while the forces normally stationed in Belfast were perfectly sufficient to suppress riots, their efficacy was undermined by the lack of 'unity' between the local police and the constabulary as well as by the want of 'decision and determination' among the local magistrates. Belfast's magistrates, the officer noted, were 'too much mixed up with trade there to act independently' and too 'jealous of the government magistrates sent to aid them' to be truly effective.[98] This was broadly consistent with the government's experience of earlier Belfast riots, and before long concrete steps would be taken to put the preservation of the peace in Belfast on a more centralised footing. But before this could happen another conflagration, far worse than anything Belfast had ever seen, would consume the city.

Conclusion

The demonstration and riots of 1862 vividly illustrated the two main difficulties with the British state's policies of conciliation and coercion in Belfast. First, they revealed the increasing resentment among Belfast Protestants towards the allegedly pro-Catholic policies of the Irish Executive, incidentally illustrating the rift between the local Tory party, which sided with the disaffected Protestant workers, and the more cautious Protestant gentry. Second, the events of 1862 demonstrated the shortcomings of the state's repressive policing tactics, which were beginning to cause resentment among Protestants while also provoking significant violence in their own right. The bass note underlying the state's anti-riot measures in Belfast had been an overwhelming concern with rationalisation and impartiality, which meant, in the logic of the reformers at Dublin Castle and successive governments in London, intervening more forcefully in the city's affairs. The conciliation of Catholics at the national level, and the undermining of Protestant authority at the local one, encouraged a radical alienation among Belfast Protestants that was substantially more robust than that of their Catholic counterparts. Where Catholics had confined themselves (at least rhetorically) to defending their own homes and families, Protestants took on the duty of preserving and restoring order throughout the whole of Belfast. This idea of order depended upon Protestants retaining a firm grip on Belfast's local affairs, and as this grip started to loosen it was the agents of the central government, just as much as their Catholic rivals, who would face the Protestants' anger. The extent of this crisis would become clear during the massive riots of 1864, to which we now turn.

Notes

1   *Belfast Newsletter*, 10 Sept. 1857.
2   *Belfast Daily Mercury*, 12 Sept. and 15 Oct. 1857; *Banner of Ulster*, 12 and 17 Sept., 15 Oct. 1857. There is some evidence that the Protestant Defence Association and the Orange Order overlapped. On 11 September the *Mercury* reported that men entering one meeting had been asked to state the name of their Orange lodge in order to gain admission.
3   See Allan Blackstock, '"The Invincible Mass": Loyal Crowds in Mid Ulster, 1795–96', in *Crowds in Ireland c. 1720–1920*, ed. Peter Jupp and Eoin Magennis (New York: St Martin's Press, 2000), 83–114.
4   David Miller, *Queen's Rebels: Ulster Loyalism in Historical Perspective* (Dublin: Gill and Macmillan, 1978), 72.
5   Terrence McDonough, ed., *Was Ireland a Colony? Economics, Politics, and Culture in Nineteenth-Century Ireland* (Dublin: Irish Academic Press, 2005); Stephen Howe, *Ireland and Empire: Colonial Legacies in Irish History and Culture* (Oxford: Oxford University Press, 2002); Kevin Kenny, ed., *Ireland and the British Empire* (Oxford: Oxford University Press, 2006); Keith Jeffery, ed., *'An Irish Empire'? Aspects of Ireland and the British Empire* (Manchester: Manchester University Press, 1996).
6   On the significant Irish presence in the nineteenth-century British Empire, see Scott B. Cook, 'The Irish Raj: Social Origins and Careers of Irishmen in the Indian Civil Service, 1855–1914', *Journal of Social History* 20/3

(Spring 1987), 507–30; Peter Karsten, 'Irish Soldiers in the British Army, 1792–1922: Suborned or Subordinate?', *Journal of Social History* 17 1 (Fall 1983), 31–64; and Kevin Kenny, 'The Irish in the Empire', in Kenny, ed., *Ireland and the British Empire*, 90–122.

7 On the connections between Irish and Indian nationalism, see e.g. Howard Brasted, 'Indian Nationalist Development and the Influence of Irish Home Rule, 1870–1886', *Modern Asian Studies* 14 (1980), 37–63; Michael Silvestri, '"The Sinn Fein of India": Irish Nationalism and the Policing of Revolutionary Terrorism in Bengal', *The Journal of British Studies* 29/4 (Oct. 2000), 454–86; Kaori Nagai, *Empire of Analogies: Kipling, India, and Ireland* (Cork: Cork University Press, 2006), ch. 6; and Tadhg Foley and Maureen O'Connor, eds., *Ireland and India: Colonies, Culture, and Empire* (Dublin: Irish Academic Press, 2006), Part VI.

8 Brian Jenkins, *Era of Emancipation: British Government of Ireland, 1812–30* (Kingston: McGill-Queen's University Press, 1988); Virginia Crossman, *Politics, Law and Order in Nineteenth-Century Ireland* (Dublin: Gill & Macmillan, 1996), 9–48.

9 Jenkins, *Era*, 302–3; Crossman, *Politics*, 49–89.

10 Elizabeth A. Muenger, *The British Military Dilemma in Ireland: Occupation Politics, 1886–1914* (Lawrence, Kan.: University Press of Kansas, 1991); Jenkins, *Era*. See also Charles Townshend, *Political Violence in Ireland: Government and Resistance since 1848* (Oxford: Clarendon Press, 1983).

11 Quoted in Crossman, *Politics*, 78.

12 On Peel's conciliatory reforms, see Donal A. Kerr, *Peel, Priests and Politics: Sir Robert Peel's Administration and the Roman Catholic Church in Ireland, 1841–1846* (Oxford: Clarendon Press, 1982), esp. chs. 3–7.

13 The highest political and administrative offices in Ireland tended to remain in the hands of Protestants, however. Between 1801 and 1909, the numbers of Catholics holding each major office were: Lord Lieutenant, none; Chief Secretary, none; Under-Secretary, three (of nineteen); Lord Chancellor, two (of eighteen). R. Barry O'Brien, *Dublin Castle and the Irish People* (London: Kegan Paul, Trench, Trübner & Co., Ltd., 1909), 10–17.

14 Virginia Crossman, 'Local Government in Nineteenth-Century Ireland', in *Was Ireland a Colony? Economics, Politics, and Culture in Nineteenth-Century Ireland*, ed. Terrence McDonough (Dublin: Irish Academic Press, 2005), 102–16; Alvin Jackson, 'Ireland, the Union, and the Empire, 1800–1960', in *Ireland and the British Empire*, ed. Kenny, 130–2; Ronald Robinson, 'Non-European Foundations of European Imperialism: Sketch for a Theory of Collaboration', in *Studies in the Theory of Imperialism,* ed. Roger Owen and Bob Sutcliffe (London: Longman, 1972), 117–42.

15 R. B. McDowell, *The Irish Administration, 1801–1914* (London: Routledge & Kegan Paul, 1964), 139–44; Muenger, *British Military Dilemma*, 82–4.

16 W. J. Lowe and E. L. Malcolm, 'The Domestication of the Royal Irish Constabulary, 1836–1922', *Irish Economic and Social History*, 19 (1992), 35.

17 Stanley H. Palmer, *Police and Protest in England and Ireland, 1780–1850* (Cambridge: Cambridge University Press, 1988), pp. xix and 542–5;

Richard Hawkins, 'The "Irish Model" and the Empire: A Case for Reassessment', in *Policing the Empire: Government, Authority, and Control, 1830–1940*, ed. David M. Anderson and David Killingray (Manchester: Manchester University Press, 1991), 18–32.

18 McDowell, *Irish Administration*, 114–15; Virginia Crossman, *Local Government in Nineteenth-Century Ireland* (Belfast: Queen's University Institute of Irish Studies, 1994), 22–3; Crossman, *Politics*, 98–101.

19 On Larcom's career, see Thomas E. Jordan, *An Imaginative Empiricist: Thomas Askew Larcom (1801–1879) and Victorian Ireland*, Irish Studies, vol. 5 (Lampeter, Wales: The Edwin Mellen Press, 2002) and W. A. Seymour, ed., *A History of the Ordnance Survey* (Folkestone, Kent: Wm. Dawson & Sons, 1980), 87–95.

20 Montagu Burrows, 'Larcom, Sir Thomas Askew, First Baronet (1801–1879)', *The Dictionary of National Biography,* vol. 11 (London: Oxford University Press, 1921–22).

21 *Bill to restrain Party Processions in Ireland*, HC 1850 (519) V.

22 *Copies of any Instructions issued to the Magistrates or Constabulary in Ireland relative to the Processions Act, between 1860 and 1864, both inclusive: – And, of the Commissions of Inquiry at Belfast in 1857 and 1864*, HC 1865 (134) XLV.

23 Thomas Larcom's report on the 1864 Belfast Riots, NLI, Larcom Papers, 7626/59.

24 NAI, CSORP (1864) 18209.

25 Crossman, *Politics*, 2; Townshend, *Political Violence.*5; Muenger, *British Military Dilemma, passim.*

26 Thomas Larcom to Robert Peel, NLI, Larcom Papers, 7627/17.

27 William Tracy's evidence, *Report of the Commissioners of Inquiry into the Origin and Character of the Riots in Belfast, in July and September, 1857; together with Minutes of Evidence and Appendix*, HC 1857–58 (2309) XXVI (hereafter, *1857 Belfast Riots Inquiry*), 19; *Ulsterman*, 14 Nov. 1856; *Ulster Observer*, 8 Nov. 1862; Edward Orme's evidence, *Report of the Commissioners of Inquiry, 1864, respecting the Magisterial and Police Jurisdiction Arrangements and Establishment of the Borough of Belfast*, HC 1865 (3466) XXVIII (hereafter, *1864 Belfast Riots Inquiry*), 8.

28 *1857 Belfast Riots Inquiry*, Appendix 26, 296.

29 NAI, CSORP (1857) 6533.

30 *Belfast Daily Mercury*, 25 Aug. 1857.

31 *Ibid.*, 7 Sept. 1857.

32 John Thompson's evidence, *1857 Belfast Riots Inquiry*, 217.

33 *Belfast Daily Mercury*, 10 and 16 Sept. 1857.

34 Harris Bindon's evidence, *1857 Belfast Riots Inquiry*, 54.

35 Tracy to Larcom, 21 Sept. 1857, NLI, Larcom Papers, 7624/39. See also Downshire to Carlisle, 24 Sept. 1857, NLI, Larcom Papers, 7624/47.

36 Carlisle to Larcom, 20 Sept. 1857, NAI, CSORP 16743 (1858).

37 *Belfast Daily Mercury*, 21 Sept. 1857; *Banner of Ulster*, 22 Sept. 1857.

38 Larcom to Carlisle, 29 Aug. 1864, NLI, Larcom Papers, 7626/64.
39 Tracy to Larcom (undated), NLI, *ibid.*, *7624/69.*
40 *Belfast Newsletter*, 21 Sept. 1857. Italics in original.
41 *1857 Belfast Riots Inquiry*, 11.
42 *Northern Whig*, 9 Oct. 1857.
43 On the earlier attempt to remove Orangemen from the magistracy, see Lord Carlisle's speech in the House of Commons on 7 June 1858, as reported *ibid.*, 10 June 1858.
44 Carlisle to Sir George Grey, Oct. 1857, NAGB, Home Office Records, HO45/6464.
45 On Clarendon's arming of Dublin Orangemen in 1848, see Frank Wright, 'Protestant Ideology and Politics in Ulster', *European Journal of Sociology*, 14 (1973), 252; Hereward Senior, 'The Early Orange Order 1795–1870', in *Secret Societies in Ireland*, ed. T. Desmond Williams (New York: Barnes and Noble, 1973), 44; and Frank Wright, *Two Lands on One Soil: Ulster Politics before Home Rule* (Dublin: Gill & Macmillan, 1996), 153.
46 *1857 Belfast Riots Inquiry*, 14–15.
47 *Belfast Weekly News*, 17 Oct. 1857.
48 William Archer, *Orange Melodies, Occasional Verses, Stanzas for Music, Notes* (Dublin: James Forrest, 1869). Italics in original.
49 Grand Orange Lodge of Ireland, *Report of the Proceedings of the Grand Orange Lodge of Ireland, at the Special Meeting, held in the General Central Committee Rooms, 45, Molesworth St., Dublin, On Tuesday, the 3rd, Wednesday, the 4th, Thursday, the 5th, and Friday, the 6th days of November, 1857; and at the Adjourned Special Meeting, Held in the Protestant Hall, Belfast, On Wednesday, the 20th, and Thursday, the 21st days of January, 1858* (Londonderry: Sentinel Office, 1858).
50 *Belfast Weekly News*, 20 Feb. 1858.
51 Max Weber, 'Politics as a Vocation', in *From Max Weber: Essays in Sociology*, trans. and ed. H. H. Gerth and C. Wright Mills (New York: Oxford University Press, 1946), 77–128.
52 *Freeman's Journal*, 1 July 1858; Crossman, *Politics*, 101–2.
53 *Belfast Daily Mercury*, 8 Sept. 1857.
54 *Ibid.*, 24 July 1857.
55 Carlisle to Larcom, 30 Nov. 1857, NLI, Larcom Papers, 7624/73.
56 *Belfast Newsletter*, 31 May 1858.
57 *Ibid.*; see also *Ulsterman*, 31 May 1858.
58 William McIlwaine to the Lord Chancellor, 2 June 1858, NLI, Larcom Papers, 7624/95. Underlining in original; *Belfast Newsletter*, 1 June 1858.
59 *Belfast Newsletter*, 3 June 1858; Harris Bindon to Inspector General of Constabulary, 3 June 1858, NLI, Mayo Papers, 11,021/12; and William Tracy to Thomas Larcom, 3 June 1858, *ibid.*, 11,021/12.
60 *Belfast Newsletter*, 2 June 1858.
61 *Belfast Daily Mercury*, 4 June 1858.
62 Naas to Larcom, 3 June 1858, NAI, CSORP (1858) 14915.

63 Eglinton to Naas, 3 and 4 June 1858, NLI, Mayo Papers, 11,031/12. Under-lining in original.

64 *Belfast Morning News*, 5 June 1857.

65 Naas to Larcom, 6 June 1858, NLI, Larcom Papers, 7624/111.

66 Larcom to Naas, 7 June 1858, *ibid.*, 7624/112.

67 Naas to Larcom, 6 June 1858, *ibid.*, 7624/111.

68 *Ulsterman*, 7 June 1858.

69 Eglinton to Larcom, 6 June 1858, NLI, Larcom Papers, 7624/107–8.

70 *Northern Whig*, 5 June 1858.

71 Eglinton to Larcom, 6 June 1858, NLI, Larcom Papers, 7624/107–8. Large forces of the military and constabulary remained in Belfast through the July holidays, the relative peacefulness of which helped convince officials of the efficacy of their new 'preventive' strategy. See *Belfast Weekly News*, 17 July 1858; *Northern Whig*, 13 July 1858; *Ulsterman*, 14 July 1858; Eglinton to Larcom, 9 July 1858, NLI, Larcom Papers, 7624/137; and Tracy to Larcom, NLI (undated), Larcom Papers, 7624/143.

72 Thomas Drew to the Lord Chancellor, 1 June 1858, NLI, Larcom Papers, 7624/94.

73 Tracy to Larcom, 8 June 1858, *ibid.*, 7624/116–17.

74 The *Northern Whig*, 9 June 1858, reported that it believed such a meeting did take place on 8 June, but it offered no further details.

75 Nandini Gooptu, *The Politics of the Urban Poor in Early Twentieth-Century India* (Cambridge: Cambridge University Press, 2001), 112.

76 Larcom to Naas, 7 June 1858, NLI, Larcom Papers, 7624/112.

77 *Times* (London), 1 July 1858.

78 *Northern Whig*, 13 July 1861.

79 By 1861 there were 121,602 people in the city, and within ten years that number would expand by 43%, to 174,412. In 1861 only 75.2% of Belfast's population had been born in Belfast or the surrounding counties of Antrim and Down. 15.8% came from elsewhere in Ulster, 3.3% from the rest of Ireland and 5.14% from England, Scotland and Wales. Ian Budge and Cornelius O'Leary, *Belfast: Approach to Crisis* (London: Macmillan, 1973), 28, 30–1.

80 Larcom's summary of the 1862 riots, NLI, Larcom Papers, 7625/10.

81 *Banner of Ulster*, 18 Sept. 1862.

82 *Northern Whig*, 18 Sept. 1862. The number of people attending the meeting is difficult to establish. The *Ulster Observer* counted no more than eight or ten thousand spectators (many of whom paid little attention to 'the very "spicy" speeching') while one of the meeting's organisers put the number at 80,000. The *Banner's* conservative estimate of 25,000 spectators is perhaps the most accurate. See *Ulster Observer*, 18 Sept. 1862; William Johnston, diary, 17 Sept. 1862, PRONI, D/880/2/14; and *Banner of Ulster*, 18 Sept. 1862.

83 *Banner of Ulster*, 18 Sept. 1862; *Northern Whig*, 18 Sept. 1862; *Ulster Observer*, 18 Sept. 1862.

84 *Ulster Observer*, 18 Sept. 1862. It is unclear whether Quin's figures were accurate.

85 *Northern Whig*, 18 Sept. 1862.

86 Johnston was married to one of Drew's daughters, and the two men were intimate friends, with letters passing between them almost daily on family, political and religious matters. See Johnston's diary entries for the late 1850s and early 1860s, PRONI, D/880/2.

87 On Johnston's later campaign, see Aiken McClelland, *William Johnston of Ballykilbeg* (Lurgan, Northern Ireland: Ulster Society (Publications) Limited, 1990); and Wright, *Two Lands*, 315–28.

88 *Banner of Ulster*, 18 Sept. 1862.

89 Thomas MacKnight, *Ulster as it Is: or, Twenty-eight Years' Experience as an Irish Editor* (London: Macmillan and Co., 1896), vol. 1. 144. See also Wright, 'Protestant Ideology', 252.

90 The summer of 1862 had been an especially active time for resistance of this sort, with numerous Orange processions taking place across Ulster, although none of these seemed to have set off any violence. See *Northern Whig*, 14 July 1862.

91 *Ibid.*, 18 Sept. 1862.

92 *Banner of Ulster*, 18 Sept. 1862; *Northern Whig*, 18 Sept. 1862.

93 *Belfast Newsletter*, 18, 19, 20 and 22 Sept. 1862; *Ulster Observer*, 18 and 20 Sept. 1862; *Banner of Ulster*, 18, 20 and 23 Sept. 1862.

94 *Belfast Newsletter*, 20 Sept. 1862; *Banner of Ulster*, 20 and 23 Sept. 1862. Those among the mounted men who were armed with pistols had instructions to use them against stone-throwing mobs, although more extensive use of firearms was not permitted. See telegraph from Charles Hunt RM to Larcom, 22 Sept. 1862, NLI, Larcom Papers, 7625/20.

95 *Belfast Newsletter*, 19 Sept. 1862.

96 *Ibid.*, 22 Sept. 1862.

97 *Ulster Observer*, 8 Nov. 1862.

98 Letter dated 30 Sept. 1862, NLI, Larcom Papers, 7625/25.

6

The city erupts: August 1864

It could have been a scene from the civil war raging in America. On 17 August 1864, nine days into the most destructive riots Belfast had ever seen, a reporter for the *Ulster Observer* visited the Belfast General Hospital. What he saw horrified him:

> Upwards of thirty men lay groaning in agony from the wounds received during the day. The limbs of some were amputated; the lives of others were ebbing away. All were moaning in bitter torture, the heat of the weather and the crowded state of the room increasing their pain. Mothers and sisters were weeping outside the doors – cursing the authors of all these brutal evils, and invoking upon them and their offspring, the blood that had been so barbarously shed. Even the surgeons, accustomed as they were to such scenes, could hardly gaze upon the mutilated sufferers who invoked their assistance, and the nurses, wearied and exhausted, bent their heads in mingled horror and pity over the beds they had to tend.[1]

Conditions outside the hospital were not much better. Poor families, forced out of their homes, were loading their few belongings on to carts or wandering about in search of shelter. Shutters on the windows of wealthier houses indicated that their inhabitants had already fled. Car drivers refused to carry people through the worst of the neighbourhoods and sometimes refused to venture out at all. Grocers' shops, if they were open, stood largely empty, for the farmers who supplied them were too frightened to bring their goods to town. Millworkers, unable to travel to work even to collect their wages, wandered the streets ragged and hungry. 'It is, indeed,' the *Northern Whig* remarked during the worst of the rioting, 'a reign of terror.'[2]

In all, at least eleven people died and 300 were wounded during ten days of rioting that August. But these were the official figures; among a people deeply suspicious of all authority, the number of unreported deaths and injuries may well have been several times higher.[3] Other figures told a similarly grim tale: £54,350 in property damage, lost business, and lost wages; 260 buildings damaged; 410 people summarily convicted or sent to trial for riotous offences such as aggravated assault, illegal arms possession and murder.[4] At the height of the riots no fewer than 4,556 soldiers, local policemen, constables and special constables were on patrol in Belfast, and at one point local officials had even asked Dublin Castle to declare martial law.[5] This, clearly, had not been the ritualised, somewhat restrained violence of earlier riots, when guns had been used as much to intimidate as to injure and the fighting had only rarely spilled out of the 'disturbed districts' of the Pound and Sandy Row. This had been rioting of an altogether higher magnitude, tearing up vast swathes of the urban landscape and calling forth a cosmopolitan array of protagonists in what had become a profoundly polarising and deadly conflict.

What had happened? In a great many ways, the riots of 1864 were the culmination of the trends we have been exploring for the previous few chapters. This was the moment when older, rural forms of violence began to fade away, and when new, distinctly urban patterns emerged that were unique to Belfast and its divided communities. The steady advance of working-class alienation from the state, the growing hegemony of violent extremists in working-class neighbourhoods, the sectarian alliance between Protestant workers and elites, the insecurity of the Catholics and, above all, the polarising effects of earlier outbreaks of violence – all the trends that had been shaping communal identities for the past decade now coalesced to create a type of rioting that was much more widespread and destructive than the party clashes of earlier years. These new forms of violence made extensive use of the city's diverse spaces, inscribing streets, buildings and landmarks with new sectarian meanings, creating communal focal points that would long outlast the riots themselves. Earlier riots had left behind them localised resentments and more or less 'pure' communal enclaves; these riots built upon that foundation to create a set of shared memories of violence that were intimately connected to the city itself, and to each side's imagined place within it.

This chapter describes this turning point in the development of Belfast's traditions of violence. It is organised around the principal stages of the riots of August 1864, each of which showed a progression towards a more thoroughly urban sort of rioting. The first stage was the most traditional, following familiar patterns of provocation and ritual that were driven by Protestants' continued frustration at being denied the 'right to march'. In the second stage, the riots expanded beyond their traditional bases in the Pound and Sandy Row and into the rest of the city, pulling in new class and occupational groups along the way. The final stage of the riots was dominated by a massive funeral procession in honour of a Protestant rioter shot dead by the Irish Constabulary, an event that vividly illustrated Protestants' mounting hostility towards the central authorities. The chapter concludes with a brief discussion of the riots' aftermath, specifically the workplace expulsions that followed in their wake and the government's decision, at long last, to abolish the Belfast police force.

8–14 August: effigies and 'mill girls'

For those who remembered the Belfast riots of 1862, the outbreak of rioting in 1864 probably came as no great surprise. As had happened two years earlier, a massive Catholic procession had been allowed to take place in Dublin, and, once again, Belfast Protestants had taken offence at what they saw as the government's uneven enforcement of the Party Processions Acts. This year's procession was held on 8 August to celebrate the erection of a monument to Daniel O'Connell in Dublin's Sackville Street, an event sponsored by the Catholic hierarchy and the moderate Catholic nationalists associated with John Gray's newspaper, the *Freeman's Journal*. As in 1862, Dublin Castle's legal advisors had determined that this demonstration did not fit the legal definition of a 'party procession', and so it had been allowed to proceed.[6] To many Belfast Protestants, however, the idea that a pro-O'Connell demonstration – especially one associated with such party men as Gray and Cardinal Cullen – could be anything other than a 'party procession' was preposterous, and once again it appeared that Dublin Castle was bowing to Catholic pressure while ignoring the 'civil and religious liberties' of loyal Protestants.

The *Belfast Newsletter* led the attack. In early August it suggested that Belfast Protestants respond to the O'Connell monument by erecting their own statue of William III, hero of the Battle of the Boyne. 'As an historical personage,' said the *Newsletter*, 'we really think that the King of England to whom under Providence, we owe civil and religious liberty in these Kingdoms, is as worthy of a statue in Belfast as O'Connell is worthy of one in Dublin.'[7] Before long contributions from local Protestants were pouring into the newspaper to fund the monument. Others, meanwhile, were advocating a more direct response. One Protestant wrote to the *Newsletter* calling for 100,000 Ulstermen to go to Dublin to defend their brother Protestants from 'the Ribbonmen of Ireland, and other enemies of our Queen and Constitution' who would take possession of the capital that day.[8] The *Newsletter* itself did not openly advocate the use of force, but it did warn the government that, should the O'Connell procession take place, 'They will arouse Protestant feeling to an extent which they can hardly anticipate, and destroy all confidence in the administration of the laws.'[9] Neither the 100,000 Protestants nor the King William monument ever materialised, but, as subsequent events would show, the anger of Belfast's Protestant partisans was quite real.

While the *Newsletter* fumed, the *Ulster Observer* was trying, without much success, to get its Catholic readers interested in the O'Connell monument. Earlier that year the *Observer*, borrowing the language of its Protestant adversaries, had confidently predicted that Ulster's contribution to the monument would be 'worthy of the historic renown of the province, and the undying adherence of its people to the principles of civil and religious liberty all over the world'.[10] The contributions, however, were slow in coming. On 30 July, less than two weeks before the Dublin procession, the *Observer* noted with regret that Belfast had not yet contributed any money to the monument fund, and a subsequent fundraising meeting at the struggling Catholic Institute was only sparsely attended.[11] A trickle of funds finally arrived the week before the procession, and before long the *Observer* had received 132 contributions totalling nearly £75, the donations ranging in size from the £5 of Bernard Hughes to the single shillings of two female servants.[12] This was hardly a sum 'worthy of the historic renown' of Ulster, though, and it suggested that the gulf between the 'respectable' nationalism of middle-class Catholics and the more prosaic concerns of working-class Catholics remained as wide as ever.

On 8 August, the day of the O'Connell procession, special excursion trains were on hand to carry people from Belfast to Dublin at reduced fares.[13] It is difficult to know precisely how many Belfast Catholics travelled to Dublin either to watch or to take part in the procession, but a good number undoubtedly did, for, amid the myriad ecclesiastical, trades and municipal bodies marching through Dublin that day, there were banners belonging to the carpenters, linen lappers, press printers and bakers of Belfast, all trades in which Catholics predominated. Some forty members of the Belfast Ancient Order of Foresters, a Catholic-friendly society, also marched alongside their Dublin brethren.[14] The procession itself was a grand affair, attracting some 30,000 people from outside Dublin to watch the Catholic elite, lay and clerical, parade in all their finery through the city's principal streets. Denounced by the *Newsletter*'s reporter as a rebellious display of Catholic power before the 'paralysed' authorities of Dublin Castle, the procession nevertheless ended peaceably – although we may doubt whether, as the Catholic *Ulster Observer* reported, the procession had been a model of religious harmony, with orange flags commingling with green and the marchers stepping lively to nationalist as well as loyalist party tunes.[15] Like his *Newsletter* counterpart, the *Observer*'s reporter would have been well practised at telling his readers what they expected to hear.

That evening, while jubilant crowds thronged the streets of Dublin, the Protestants of Sandy Row held their own procession. Aware of what was going on in Dublin, and aware, too, that some local Catholics had gone down to join the demonstration, a small band of Protestants constructed an effigy of O'Connell and paraded it through the streets. Adorned with a large wooden cross and a string of beads, and accompanied by the sound of fife and drums, the effigy drew a large crowd as it made its way past the working-class tenements and on to the bridge overlooking the railway tracks. This was the Boyne Bridge that separated Sandy Row from the Pound, and it was soon crowded with several thousand people, many of them carrying guns. Just before nine o'clock, as the train carrying the Catholic excursionists back from Dublin rumbled towards the bridge, someone set the effigy on fire. The crowd cheered and fired their guns into the air, while a small band of local policemen fanned out across the bridge to prevent them from invading the Pound. The crowd, content merely to have expressed their contempt for O'Connell and the Catholics who had travelled to honour him, dispersed without causing the police any further trouble. Whether the passengers on the train saw the burning effigy is not known.[16]

The following day the Pound and Sandy Row were largely quiet, but the excitement resumed that night when a crowd of between 1,500 and 2,000 Protestants marched out of Sandy Row and down the Botanic Road in a raucous funeral procession to bury the O'Connell effigy. At the front of the procession marched four men carrying on their shoulders a large black coffin, inside of which reposed the mortal remains of the previous night's effigy. The coffin was adorned with a crucifix, and many of the mourners who followed it likewise carried makeshift crucifixes that they had fashioned by tying short sticks horizontally near the tops of their bludgeons. While musicians played 'The Dead March in Saul', 'Kick the Pope' and other Orange standards, the mourners wound their way toward the gates of the ancient Catholic burying ground at Friar's Bush. On arriving at the sexton's house someone yelled, 'You damned ould ruffian, open the gate till we bury O'Connell!' The sexton pointed his gun at the crowd and told them to be on their way, and in the short scuffle that followed several people threw stones through the sexton's windows and damaged a stone cross inside the cemetery's gates. Reluctantly, the crowd then turned back towards Sandy Row, where they set fire to the coffin and threw it into the fetid waters of the Blackstaff River. After that a small band of Protestants, acting on rumours that the Pound Catholics were attacking Christ Church, charged north over the Boyne Bridge and nearly made it to the church (where no attack was taking place) before being intercepted by a body of constables. The frustrated men returned once more to Sandy Row, and the rest of the night passed in relative peace.[17]

It would be a few days yet before the rioting began in earnest. As often

Map 6.1 Principal sites of the 1864 riots, 8–14 August

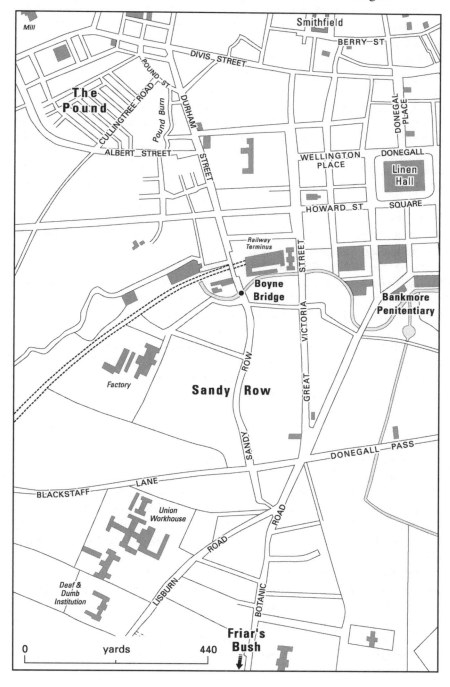

happened in Belfast, the initial provocations had not been especially violent, but they set off a cycle of rumour and suspicion that steadily escalated into open conflict. For two days after the burning of the effigy the people of the Pound and Sandy Row gathered in the streets after leaving work for the evening, astir with apprehension over what the other side was plotting. Women and children, assuming their usual roles, tore bricks and paving stones from the streets and piled them on the footpaths to serve as ready ammunition. The men stood guard against invasion, and several times bands of men tried breaking through the police cordon set up between the two neighbourhoods, but without success. Meanwhile, the authorities took the usual precaution of telegraphing Dublin for more constables, 150 of whom arrived on 10 August. Together with the 160 local policemen and the fifty constables already in the city, this force appeared sufficient to handle any outbreak that might occur.[18]

By the afternoon of 11 August, three days after the burning of the O'Connell effigy, the excitement appeared to be at an end. So calm were the 'disturbed districts' that Belfast's mayor, John Lytle, in consultation with the city's new Resident Magistrate, Edward Orme, decided it was safe to leave town for his scheduled August holiday at the Turkish baths in Harrogate, Yorkshire. Other state officials, including the Chief Secretary, the Lord Chancellor and all but one of the Lords Justice, were also on holiday, leading both the Irish and the British press subsequently to complain that the country was largely rudderless when the storm broke.[19] And, indeed, conditions began to deteriorate shortly after the mayor left. Around seven o'clock on the evening of 11 August, as men and women came home from the mills, a stone-throwing brawl broke out on Durham Street, the principal street connecting the Pound and Sandy Row. The police managed to make a few early arrests by sending some undercover operatives in among the rioters, but once the crowds caught on to this tactic they began evading the police with some skill. 'The mobs of Belfast are getting even more cowardly than ever,' remarked the *Whig* the next day, 'for their mode of warfare last night was to congregate about entries, throw volleys of stones, and then run off.'[20] With the police thus engaged, a group of Catholics set fire to an effigy of King William, subjecting the Protestant hero to the same indignities that O'Connell had suffered three nights earlier.

The fighting continued well into the morning. Around midnight it appeared that the stone throwing had ceased, but scarcely had the police returned to their quarters when, around one o'clock, a party of Catholics charged down Durham Street towards Sandy Row, wrecking houses along the way. As the weary policemen came back on to the streets, people in both neighbourhoods went from door to door, 'rapping up' their neighbours to alert them that a battle was on. About three o'clock a detachment of Protestants attacked the Bankmore Penitentiary, a Catholic home for fallen women run by the Sisters of Mercy that stood near the city centre. In retaliation, several Catholics attacked Henry Cooke's Presbyterian church in May Street, breaking the windows of Catholic and Protestant homes in the affluent Arthur Street along the way. The Protestant crowd then made a second, more violent assault on the penitentiary, followed by an attack on the home of Bishop Patrick Dorrian, who lived nearby.[21]

Apart from these isolated attacks on buildings in the city centre, most of the fighting remained within the Pound and Sandy Row. The worst attacks on the morning of 12 August took place against female millworkers heading to work at half-past five. One Catholic girl, Mary Anne Furphy, told the *Observer* how she was walking through Sandy Row on her way to Murphy's mill in Tea Lane when she came upon a group of a hundred men, women and children. 'When I came near them,' she said, 'one of them caught me by the shoulder, and shook me, and asked me where the h—l I was going. They then flung a shower of stones at me, and knocked me down. I nearly lost my senses with the blows. I cried for God's sake to let me go home.' The crowd descended on Furphy, kicking her and dragging her by the hair. They grabbed her tea can and beat her with it. They tore her shawl. Desperate for help, Furphy tried to hide behind a tall man with grey clothes walking nearby, but he pushed her back towards her attackers. She then tried to hide in a nearby house, but a woman slammed the door in her face. Finally, she managed to escape into another house. 'It was a Protestant house,' she said, 'and they treated me very kindly.'[22] Some Protestant millworkers were undoubtedly attacked in a similar manner, but over the next few days, as attacks of this sort continued, the Catholic press loudly trumpeted these assaults upon Catholic women as evidence of the unmanly actions of Protestant rioters.[23] For Catholic men, as we will see, these reports were shortly to inspire acts of violent retaliation.

Sporadic rioting continued for most of that Friday, but by Saturday morning the authorities had things more or less in hand. They were aided by the arrival of 200 more constables from Dublin on Friday evening, making a total of 400 armed constables keeping watch in the riotous areas. They were also assisted by the exertions of several priests, who went through the streets urging their people to remain indoors. By Sunday, six days after the O'Connell procession and the burning of the effigy, the Pound and Sandy Row were once again tranquil, and it looked as if the riots of 1864 would pass into history as a relatively minor footnote in the city's catalogue of sectarian clashes. A mere fifteen injuries

had been reported to the General Hospital, of which only two were
gunshot wounds, and little substantial property damage had been
sustained outside the 'disturbed districts'. By Belfast's standards, it had
been a pretty pedestrian affair.[24]

Even so, several things distinguished this early stage of the riots from
previous outbreaks in the city. As we saw in Chapter 3, a favourite spot
for communal contests in the 1850s had been the 'waste ground' at the
edge of the built-up portions of west Belfast. This open space had given
these early riots much of their rural flavour, for it had allowed the
combatants to face each other across wide distances and to act out ritualised forms of violence that rarely resulted in bloodshed. By 1864,
however, much of this open space had disappeared, swallowed up by new
houses built to accommodate the ongoing influx of migrants.[25] As a result,
rioting now had to be done within the residential confines of the Pound
and Sandy Row proper, especially in Durham Street, where rioters would
gather, hurl stones and fire shots at each other, and then disappear into
the maze of courts and entries of their respective neighbourhoods when
the police arrived. This not only made it hard for the police to locate and
arrest rioters, but it also made it difficult for the rioters to get at each
other in any great numbers or for any sustained period. They simply did
not have the space for the sort of great communal battles that had taken
place in 1857. Instead, ancillary violence such as house wreckings, flying
assaults upon policemen and public buildings and attacks on isolated individuals (such as millworkers) became the norm. This sort of violence
could be deadlier than large set-piece battles across open fields, for it
made individuals more vulnerable to random assaults by roving gangs,
and it also increased the frequency with which rioters came into contact
with well-armed and often jittery soldiers and constables. Without open
space, there also were fewer 'buffer zones' into which neutral individuals could escape.[26]

If ritual was becoming less important in structuring the violence,
however, it had clearly played a crucial role in sparking the riots. The
burning of the O'Connell effigy, the mock funeral procession and the
retaliatory burning of the King William effigy by the Catholics all
conformed to the old patterns of provocation and retaliation that the two
sides had been developing for years. The only unusual thing about these
episodes was the specific mode of provocation: effigy burning, though
common in Londonderry during Protestants' annual commemorations of
the siege of that city, was relatively rare in Belfast.[27] But in the longer
view such events were hardly unprecedented. The pope-burning processions of seventeenth-century England offer the clearest model for this sort
of symbolic violence, although another point of reference may be the

charivaris and 'rough music' common to plebeian cultures throughout early modern Europe. Like these other forms of public ritual, the Sandy Row displays acted simultaneously as communal sanctions against undesirable behaviour and as mocking, raucous popular celebrations that served to mark out patches of communal territory.[28] But we need not travel too far afield to locate the immediate purpose behind these displays. Like the *Newsletter*'s abortive plan for a King William statue, the O'Connell effigy and mock funeral were an explicit response to the O'Connell procession in Dublin, a way for Sandy Row Protestants to register their objections to the 'one-sided' enforcement of the Party Processions Acts by staging their own processions replete with 'party tunes' and ironic references to events in Dublin. In retaliation, much in the same way as Protestant cries of 'To Hell with the Pope' usually elicited a corresponding 'To Hell with King William' from west Belfast Catholics, the burning of the King William effigy served as the Catholics' answer to these insults. In this instance, it is interesting to note that Belfast Catholics were not the only ones burning King William in effigy that summer: as news of the Belfast riots spread, burnings and attempted burnings of King William effigies were reported in Dundalk, Longford, Tralee and Kilkenny.[29]

None of this is meant to suggest that the Belfast rioters were motivated by a simple tit-for-tat atavism, but rather to demonstrate the need to understand the context of a riot's precipitating events before we draw sweeping conclusions as to its 'cause'. In her recent study of this period, Catherine Hirst has argued that the burning of the O'Connell effigy helps prove that 'the causes of this riot were predominately political', an assertion that props up her broader argument that Belfast's riots were all essentially motivated by political disagreements between Protestant loyalists and Catholic nationalists.[30] As I have been arguing throughout this study, however, such a reductive explanation of communal violence is neither accurate nor especially illuminating, and in the case of the 1864 riots it can be particularly misleading. One might just as easily argue, on the basis of the prominence of crucifixes at both the O'Connell burning and the mock funeral procession, that these riots were 'predominately religious', especially since many evangelical Protestants held the crucifix to be a symbol of Catholic superstition.[31] Much more important than the spark that ignites a riot is the complex network of relationships, beliefs and communal identities that it sets in motion. The greater the riot, the more multilayered its effects, and the more we must understand not just why it started, but how and why it spread.[32]

15–17 August: navvies and shipcarpenters

In Chapters 4 and 5 we saw how working-class Protestants and Catholics were becoming radically alienated from the forces of the state in Belfast. They did so each for their own reasons – Catholics because they distrusted the Belfast Town Council and the local police, Protestants because they objected to the centralising and conciliating agenda of Dublin Castle – and these differences led them to develop somewhat asymmetrical traditions of vigilantism. Catholics, as we saw, were concerned above all with defending themselves in an alien and hostile environment, while Protestants sought to maintain a robust form of 'order' that applied to the city as a whole. During the first stage of the 1864 riots these contrasting communal goals had not been especially evident, but in the riots' second stage the different aspirations of the two groups would come into bold relief. For at this point what had begun as a localised conflict between two evenly matched opponents became a vast urban struggle that called forth the full communal resources of both sides, and suddenly the unevenness of Protestants' and Catholics' positions in Belfast became abundantly clear. The two groups who came forward to act in the name of their coreligionists during this second stage were the Catholic navvies and the Protestant shipcarpenters, men who merit a brief introduction before I resume the narrative.

The history of navvies in Belfast, like so much else having to do with working-class Catholics during this period, is obscure. 'Navvy' was a generic term, a shortened form of 'navigator', that applied to skilled and unskilled labourers employed on large construction projects such as docks, canals and railways. Navvy gangs were a common sight throughout the British Empire and North America, and they had an unsavoury reputation among 'respectable' people as drinkers and brawlers, one that was not improved by the fact that many of them were Irish Catholics, to boot.[33] The navvies of Belfast had a similarly rough reputation among middle-class Protestants, who saw them as dangerous outsiders, Catholic migrants from southern Ireland who hatched dark, anti-Protestant conspiracies in their shadowy Ribbon societies.[34] This reputation was not entirely undeserved. As I noted in Chapter 2, several navvies appear to have been among those arrested for Ribbonism in 1859, and, as we saw in Chapter 5, they had played a prominent part in the 1862 riots by marching several times through the streets in military formation. From these reports, it seems likely that some navvies did indeed form part of the sectarian hard core of Catholic rioters before 1864, but the notion that these men were necessarily outsiders to the city was inaccurate. For one thing, it is clear from the reports of the 1862 riots that many navvies lived in the Pound, not near their work at the docks, where we would expect a transient population of single men to live.[35] Moreover, we will shortly see that many of the navvies who rioted in 1864 were married or otherwise on friendly terms with the Catholic 'mill girls' who lived in west Belfast, a fact which also suggests that these men had some degree of attachment to the community. Instead of being strangers to Belfast, it is likely, as David Brooke has found in his study of railway navvies in Britain, that many navvies were recruited from among the local population or from among the ranks of unemployed agricultural labourers in the countryside.[36] In either case, Belfast's navvies were no more strangers to the city than many other working-class people in Belfast, Protestant and Catholic, even if the nature of their work was little more prestigious than that of the 'mill girls' whom they courted. In this sense, the navvies were suitable representatives of the bulk of the Catholic male workforce: largely unskilled, feared and despised by respectable Protestant opinion and existing in a fundamentally adversarial relationship with the dominant culture of a city in which they nevertheless had planted some appreciable roots.

The history of the Protestant shipcarpenters[37] during this period is also murky, but several important contrasts with the Catholic navvies can readily be drawn. First, they were probably more numerous than the navvies. In 1864 shipbuilding had yet to become a major industry in Belfast, but already the city's largest shipbuilding firm, Harland and Wolff, employed 850 workers, compared with 500 in 1860. All but fifty of them were Protestants, the Catholics among them being employed chiefly as unskilled painters, and it seems likely that these 800 Protestants outnumbered the Catholic navvies working in Belfast that summer.[38] Second, shipyard workers enjoyed higher social standing than navvies. Unlike navvy work, which was usually unskilled and dependent on the availability of construction projects, work in the shipyards was generally secure (if irregular), well remunerated and dominated by skilled workers with substantial bargaining power.[39] A third contrast is that, unlike many navvies, Protestant shipcarpenters lived far away from their coreligionists in west Belfast, congregating in the docks area to the north and east of the city centre, near the Lagan River and their work.[40] This meant that they were less immediately implicated in the periodic communal clashes between the Pound and Sandy Row, but it had not prevented them from taking sides in the past. In fact, the shipcarpenters had first appeared as a Protestant defence force back in September 1857, when Hugh Hanna recruited fifty of them to guard his 'congregation' during his open-air service in Corporation Square. After this episode, Hanna became one of the first to articulate the idea of the Protestant shipcarpenters as upholders of the law and vanguards of order when, in an open letter to the Lord Lieutenant, he sardonically suggested replacing Belfast's timid local magistrates with 'these sturdy men' who would 'maintain the tranquility of the town, and the town for their Sovereign' against Catholic attack.[41] In 1864 this image of the shipcarpenters as exemplars of loyal Protestant manhood was still being refined, but the notion that these men could preserve order more effectively than the authorities would gain substantial currency during this second stage of the riots.

Both the navvies and the shipcarpenters, then, were men whose occupational status and collective identities embodied the differences between their respective religious groups at their most stark.[42] As yet, neither group had taken much part in the 1864 riots, but this changed on Monday, 15 August, when a group of navvies wrecked a Protestant school in Brown Square. The attack was not without provocation: for several days, the Catholic press had been livid with denunciations of the Protestants assaulting Catholic 'mill girls' on their way to work in Sandy Row. On Saturday, the day after the attacks started, the *Observer* had published a direct challenge to the Catholic men of Belfast, urging its 'chivalrous' male readers to stand up for their 'sisters in blood and race' against the depredations of the 'Orangemen'.[43] Whether it took reports such as this to spur the navvies into action is uncertain, but other evidence suggests that these men did not need the *Observer* to tell them of the violence faced by Catholic women. At the riots inquiry some months later, the Resident Magistrate, Edward Orme, on prompting from a solicitor, confirmed that he had heard several Catholic men say that weekend that 'however they might bear themselves, they never would suffer their women to be beaten in the open street'. The solicitor then pointed out that many of the navvies involved in the 15 August attack 'were connected by marriage or friendly relationship' with the women who had been assaulted.[44] What happened that day seems, therefore, to have been something in the manner of a 'chivalrous' act of revenge.

As it happened, 15 August was the Feast of the Assumption or 'Lady Day', a Catholic holiday, and instead of going to work on the docks that Monday morning the navvies went to mass at nearby St Malachy's Catholic Church. As usual during periods of unrest, it is likely that the priest (or Bishop Dorrian himself) used the occasion to urge peace upon the congregation, but among the navvies any such pleas fell on deaf ears. After the services ended, between two and five hundred navvies armed with pistols, shovels and other weapons set off from St Malachy's in 'military array' through the principal streets of the town. As they marched westwards through the city centre they paused for a moment at the Corn Market and fired several shots into the air, then continued down Hercules

Street, North Street, and Millfield before finally arriving at Brown Square, a poor Protestant district north of the Pound. There they wrecked nearly every house in the square and then turned to the Brown Street National School, a predominately Presbyterian school attended by the working-class children of the area. Inside, nearly 400 children were at work on their morning exercises when a barrage of stones, bullets and other missiles suddenly crashed through the windows. Teachers ushered the frightened children into the playground to escape the shards of flying glass, but a number of children were injured before they could escape, including one child who reportedly had an eye gouged out by a large stone.[45]

The attack lasted nearly a quarter of an hour, and during that time neither the police nor any opposing band of Protestants came along to stop the destruction. The navvies then turned north, towards the Presbyterian church in Townsend Street, but before they could make it to this next target a gang of Protestant workers at the Soho foundry dropped their tools and ran out to stop them. The navvies beat a hasty retreat southward towards the Pound, where they regrouped and prepared for a second raid, this time upon Sandy Row. But the Sandy Row men were expecting an invasion, and, with the help of women and children who supplied them with stones, scythes, hatchets and swords, they easily repulsed the invaders. Once again the navvies retreated to the safety of the Pound, where they remained hidden for the rest of the day.[46]

The next morning the Protestant workers at the Queen's Island shipyards left work to search for the navvies. 'When they heard of the violence to which women and children were subjected, and especially when they became aware of the cowardly attack on a school filled with little children, they were intensely exasperated', explained the *Newsletter* in an uncharacteristic understatement.[47] Their first stop was Brown Square, where the residents, still fearful of a second attack by the navvies, cheered wildly. When it became clear that no attack was coming, the shipcarpenters and their allies marched down North Street and into High Street to look for weapons. The first place they raided was a gun shop belonging to a man named Neill, from whom they stole guns and ammunition. Next they visited Mr Currie's hardware shop, plundering knives, reaping hooks, pitchforks, shovels and anything else that might serve as a weapon. The police and military, occupied with rioters in west Belfast, were nowhere to be seen. Nor, for that matter, did any navvies come out to oppose the marauding shipcarpenters. By the time a troop of soldiers finally arrived to disperse them, the men were well armed for the impending fight.[48]

The riots commissioners later called the shipcarpenters' actions

Map 6.2 Principal sites of the 1864 riots, 15–17 August

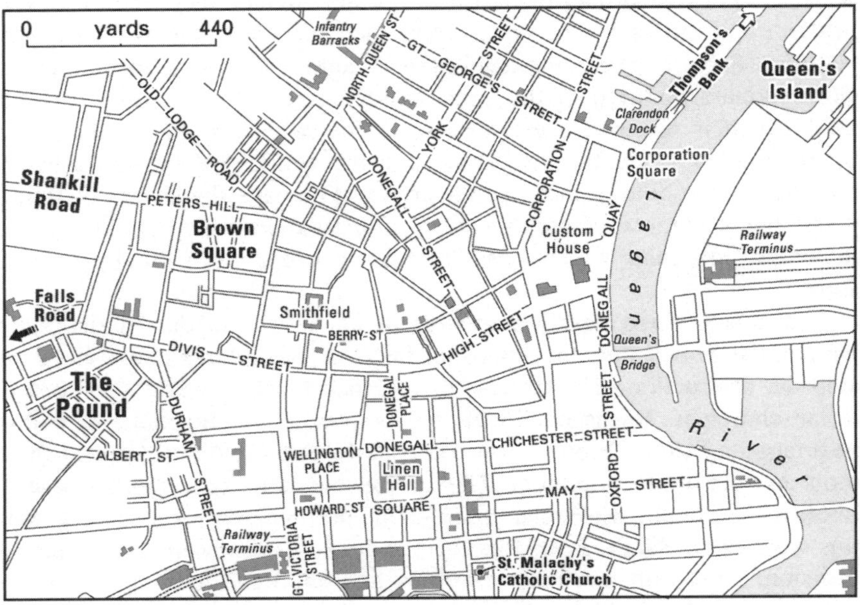

'amongst the most astonishing instances of lawless daring that have ever occurred in a civilized community', but some observers were more charitable.[49] The *Newsletter*, praising the shipcarpenters as guardians of order, justified their actions by pointing to the 'inadequacy of the peace force to cope (without resorting to measures abhorrent to most men) with the alarming difficulties which stared them in the face'. In the *Newsletter*'s version of events, the men even promised to return the stolen weapons to their owners once they had finished 'protecting' the town from the 'murdering navvies'.[50] Even the Liberal Protestant *Northern Whig*, which rarely had a kind word for rioters of either persuasion, was willing to draw a favourable contrast between the shipcarpenters and the navvies. 'They did not bludgeon and knock down unoffending people,' noted the *Whig*, 'and they did not, like the navvies, leave behind them streets wrecked systematically.'[51] The *Whig*'s somewhat favourable assessment of the shipcarpenters may have been, as Frank Wright has suggested, evidence of Liberal Protestants' increasing sympathy with Protestant rioters, but it also appears to reflect some genuine restraint on the part of the shipcarpenters themselves.[52] Unlike the 'lawless' navvies, the shipcarpenters seem to have actively cultivated an image of themselves as law-abiding citizens who were simply stepping in to restore order where the authorities had failed. 'Don't be afraid,' one shipcarpenter reportedly said as shopkeepers hastily drew their shutters, 'we are only going to protect you; we will not take a ha'pporth.'[53]

That same day, while this was going on in the city centre, the rest of Belfast was in a tremendous uproar. Earlier that morning a confrontation on the Boyne Bridge had turned deadly when the constabulary, operating according to more permissive rules of engagement than during previous riots, fired upon a stone-throwing Protestant crowd. Two Protestants – Richard Davidson, a gasfitter, and John McConnell, an employee of the Belfast gasworks – were killed.[54] This encounter set the tone for the rest of the day, the most violent day of the riots, when at least ninety-four people received serious injuries, forty of them from gunfire.[55] Factories and other large businesses stood empty, their employees unable or unwilling to come to work for fear of what might befall their homes in their absence. Gangs of men beat up passengers arriving on the Dublin train, acting on rumours that Catholic coal porters were coming from Dublin to assist the navvies.[56] That afternoon the middle-class men of the Catholic Institute held a meeting at which they repeated the old argument that the local authorities were ranged together in an anti-Catholic conspiracy, and they urged Catholics to take up arms to defend their homes and families 'from the ruthless attacks of men who are not one degree removed from savages, and who are many degrees below the level of some barbarians'.[57] Bishop Dorrian, chafing at this usurpation of his authority, issued a plea for Catholics to remain calm and insisted that this was not the time 'to speak of "manhood" or to appeal to a silly, vaunting, foolish kind of heroism', but his exhortations had little appreciable effect.[58]

On Wednesday 17 August, the riots entered their ninth day. Thus far Dublin Castle had left things more or less in the hands of the local authorities, but this was now changing. The previous night Major Thomas Esmonde, Assistant Inspector of the Constabulary and a veteran of the Crimean War, had arrived in Belfast to coordinate the government's response, and over the course of Wednesday hundreds of men streamed into the city, bringing the total number of government forces in Belfast to 974 constables, 252 cavalrymen, 1,045 infantrymen and eighty-four military officers. According to the *Whig*, such a heavy military presence was 'unprecedented in Belfast since the time of the rebellion of 1798'.[59] In one of the most perplexing (and laughably heavy-handed) policing decisions of the period, Dublin Castle also sent to Belfast two artillery pieces known as Armstrong Guns, which were pulled by six horses and manned by thirty-six artillerymen and three officers.[60] What function these guns could have performed, short of simply levelling west Belfast, is uncertain, but they were indicative of the government's new reliance on the doctrine of overwhelming force to police these riots. Meanwhile, the local magistrates had taken their own extraordinary steps to restore order, issuing a blanket prohibition on all public assemblages and empowering some 2,000 private citizens to act as special constables, an exigency that had not been resorted to in twenty years.[61]

Instead of quelling the riots, however, these measures simply displaced them into other areas. While the tramp of soldiers and the rumble of cannons filled the streets of Sandy Row and the Pound, other neighbourhoods, many of them in the newly settled streets north and west of the Pound, saw intense fighting. This was particularly true of the Falls and Shankill Roads, where rioters expelled outsiders with such thoroughness that these streets would soon become just as communally homogeneous as those of the Pound and Sandy Row. In many places there had emerged what the *Belfast Morning News* called 'a secret power or seat of authority whence certain orders are promulgated, which are rigidly enforced by its agents'.[62] In addition to forcing people from their homes (or coercing their peaceable neighbours to do so), these 'secret powers' were also issuing demands for money and guns. 'They went into a house of a tenant of my own,' the Presbyterian minister Isaac Nelson told the riots inquiry, 'and, after laying down their pistols, demanded that money should be given to them.' When asked what the purpose of this extortion was, Nelson explained, 'They said for the purpose of protecting us. They said – "Give us fire-arms and we will protect you." '[63] Threats of this sort tended to take place in the same streets where wrecking was underway, although there was at least one report of gangs demanding 'blackmail' money in the leafy middle-class suburb of Malone. On getting wind of these developments, the magistrates went around to the city's gun shops to collect any gunpowder that had not yet fallen into the rioters' hands, but their initiative seems to have come rather too late.[64]

These activities were disheartening, for they revealed once again the extent to which a violent minority could impose its will upon a cowed majority. Some people, however, refused to be intimidated by their 'own' rioters. The *Belfast Morning News* told the story of a Protestant woman who intervened to stop a Protestant crowd from wrecking a Catholic home, vowing to be the first one to prosecute the rioters if they proceeded. The newspaper also told of a group of Catholic men who stood watch for two nights over two Protestant families, most of whom were women, to protect them from the depredations of other Catholics.[65] The Presbyterian Rev. Nelson implored Protestant rioters in his neighbourhood to let the Catholics alone, and when this failed he offered his home as an 'asylum to the poor helpless people', at considerable risk to himself. He also helped displaced Catholics secure carts and horses to remove their belongings.[66]

All of this went on while the authorities remained preoccupied in the Pound and Sandy Row; indeed, it was while the police and military were searching these two neighbourhoods for guns that the greatest battle of the riots took place on the other side of town. The navvies, having spent the previous day in hiding, decided to return to work at the docks on Wednesday morning, and it was there that a group of Protestant boys found them early that afternoon. Yelling that they would not let the navvies work after what they had done to the school, the boys charged towards the docks. But the navvies were expecting trouble, and they easily repulsed their attackers with the handful of guns they had thought to bring along. The boys retreated to Coates's foundry, where they told the Protestant foundrymen of the navvies' return, and the foundrymen, in turn, sent to the Queen's Island to inform the shipcarpenters. Soon a combined force of three or four hundred foundrymen and shipcarpenters, heavily armed with their plunder from the previous day, descended upon the forty or fifty navvies at the docks. Drawing back under a hail of bullets, the navvies crouched behind walls and returned fire from their small arsenal. But the Protestants kept coming, forcing the outnumbered navvies to scramble over the docks and into the riverbed at a place called Thompson's Bank, where they soon became trapped in the reeking muck. Under a steady barrage of gunfire, the navvies tried frantically to reach solid ground, but many were wounded and unable to drag themselves through the mud. Then the tide started to come in, and the shipcarpenters, hoping to drown the navvies, began firing warning shots to pin them in place. This continued for about half an hour before the constabulary finally arrived. While several constables waded through the mud to help the struggling navvies, the shipcarpenters, flushed with victory, marched away through the cheering crowd that had gathered to watch the engagement.[67]

News of the battle spread quickly. In Sandy Row, the people rejoiced at the victory of the 'invincible shipcarpenters', who had firmly declared that they would now 'have no more nonsense'.[68] At the General Hospital, the number of wounded navvies overwhelmed the already inundated staff; several injuries were serious enough to warrant amputation, and one man, an older navvy named Neal Fagan, eventually died from his wounds.[69] Those navvies who had escaped the shipcarpenters did not return to work for several days, and it was later rumoured that many had fled to Glasgow.[70] With the defeat of the navvies the Catholics had lost their most powerful weapon against the Protestants, and for the remainder of the riots the defeated Catholics refrained from any more large-scale assaults or demonstrations.

18 August: the McConnell funeral

One of the differences between an urban riot and a rural riot is that the former, owing to the close proximity in which city dwellers live, has a much greater probability of spreading outwards from its original locations and drawing in individuals who were not parties to the originating conflict. An urban riot is therefore much more likely to attract a greater variety of protagonists, for within a city's compressed boundaries live people from a vast array of occupational, class, religious, ethnic and geographical backgrounds, any of whom may be affected by the reckless and indiscriminate attacks that accompany prolonged rioting. Where such attacks spark a desire for retribution, communal rioting resembles not so much a circle as a spiral, each new wave of attacks encompassing an ever wider geographic and social field as new groups join the fray. This is roughly what had happened in Belfast up to this point: beginning with the assaults on the millworkers on 12 August, through the navvies' assault on Brown Square on 15 August, and up to the Battle of the Navvies on 17 August, the field of combat had grown ever larger and the variety of combatants ever greater. With the disappearance of the navvies, however, the field began to contract, and it was now left to the Protestants to reassert their control over the city.

In a way it is fitting that, as the riots had begun with a procession, so, too, would they end with one. On 18 August, ten days after the O'Connell procession in Dublin and the effigy burning in Sandy Row, the Protestants of Belfast held a tremendous funeral procession for John McConnell, one of the Protestants who had been shot by the constabulary on the Boyne Bridge on 16 August. McConnell's death had been an especially poignant one: a husband and a father of five, McConnell was believed to have been an innocent bystander to the scene on the bridge, and it was also said that he had saved a Catholic from a Protestant mob just the day before.[71] He was also an Orangeman, and his death at the hands of the constabulary offered a clear illustration to many Protestants of the dangers of Dublin Castle's heavy-handed policing tactics. More importantly, the prospect of a funeral for McConnell afforded an opportunity for Orangemen and others to protest at the government's ban on party processions, to lay symbolic claim to Belfast in much the same way as the O'Connell procession had claimed Dublin for the Catholics. It was a chance to declare that Belfast was, and would remain, the capital of Protestant Ulster.

The morning of 18 August was not much different from those that had preceded it. Heavy forces of police and soldiers kept watch in the Pound and Sandy Row, escorting millworkers to the factories and trying, without much success, to disperse the crowds throwing stones and wrecking houses. Three funerals were scheduled that day for those killed during the riots: two were for Catholics, the other for McConnell. Each of the three was assigned a handful of magistrates to keep him peaceful, but while the Catholic priests were able to keep the size of their processions down, those with influence over the McConnell party (including Mayor Lytle, newly returned from his holiday in Harrogate) were not so successful. Fearing that any forcible effort to stop the McConnell funeral would end in bloodshed, the magistrates reluctantly decided to permit the procession to go ahead. The local magistrate W. T. B. Lyons, along with a large force of constables, local policemen and soldiers, escorted the procession as it set out from McConnell's home in Durham Street to the Knock burying ground across the river in Ballymacarett, a distance of about two miles from west to east.[72]

The procession got underway about three o'clock that afternoon. Its route, improvised by those in front while the police followed behind, had an unmistakable symbolic significance. Rather than taking the most direct path to Ballymacarrett, which would have skirted the southern edge of the commercial district, the procession took a northerly route, though College Square, into Wellington Street and down Donegall Place, the

Map 6.3 Approximate route of the McConnell funeral,
18 August 1864

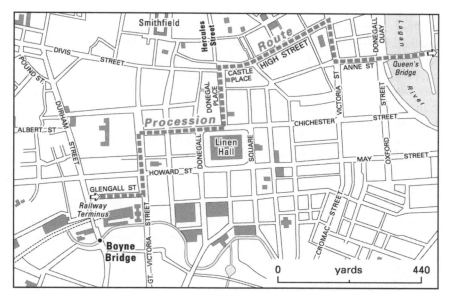

principal street in the city, before turning east down Castle Street and over the river. By marching through Belfast's wealthiest and busiest streets, the processionists were not only symbolically claiming the core of Belfast for the Protestants; they were also treading much closer to the Catholic regions of Hercules Street and Smithfield than they would otherwise have done. The potential for violence was great, therefore, and it was strengthened by the provocative nature of the procession itself. Between two and three thousand people, marching twelve to fourteen abreast and accompanied by a hearse, several carriages and not a few 'respectable'-looking people (among whom could be seen the batons of some of the newly appointed special constables), proceeded through the streets that afternoon. Many of the marchers openly brandished firearms, which they fired into the air as they rounded the corner on to Donegall Place in a deafening act of defiance. No orange banners or regalia accompanied this multitude, nor was their step enlivened by any party tunes, but this was nevertheless the grandest party procession that Belfast had seen in many years.[73]

Down Donegall Place they marched, yelling insults at Bernard Hughes's bakery while wealthy Protestants came to their windows to urge the marchers onwards. As the procession neared the corner of Hercules Street, where the Catholic Institute stood, a number of armed Catholics could be seen preparing for a confrontation. Now Lyons, hoping to avert disaster, rushed to the head of the procession with a troop of hussars. 'D—n me,' he thought (as he explained later), 'but here I am with the Queen's Hussars, attending an illegal procession, what am I to do?' The marchers, thinking Lyons was on their side, cheered and waved orange handkerchiefs as he passed.[74] It is unclear what happened next. Protestant accounts describe the Catholics of Hercules Street, aided by at least one sniper inside the Catholic Institute, opening fire on the procession before they were driven off by the hussars.[75] The *Observer*, which was published at the Catholic Institute, made no mention of a Catholic attack, claiming that the cortege had already passed before the Hercules Street men came out. Instead, the Catholic paper highlighted the apparent sanction that the procession was receiving from the local authorities. 'Mr. Lyons was in his glory, smiling at his boots, which seem to be his inamorata; and, if not gratified at the disgraceful exhibition, to which he was lending the lustre of his presence and the might of his authority, evidently indifferent to its character and the results.'[76] After this short confrontation the procession turned east, passing through Castle Street and High Street under heavy guard before finally arriving safely in Ballymacarrett, where the Rev. Hartrick, an Orangeman, performed the graveside service. The mourners returned to Sandy Row about seven o'clock, conducted thence by Lyons and the hussars, who once again intervened to prevent a clash as the procession passed Hercules Street. After that, apart from a few defiant shots fired near the constabulary at the Boyne Bridge (where McConnell had been shot), the marchers returned peaceably to their homes.[77]

Aftermath

The authorities feared that the McConnell funeral would embolden the rioters still further, but after ten days of rioting, exhaustion seems to have set in on all sides, and the violence began to dissipate that very evening. 'Our operatives had left their work, many of them', explained the local magistrate and millowner James Kennedy, 'and earned little money . . . and when the second week came in they had no money to buy food and, of course, nothing to buy powder and shot . . .'.[78] Alderman William Mullen also believed that exhaustion had a lot to do with ending the riots, noting that, throughout the riots, the people 'never slept, or worked, or left their districts'.[79] The thousands of policemen, soldiers and special constables in the city must also have had an effect, of course, as did the so-called Peace Meetings convened by middle-class leaders on both sides, whose activities I shall discuss shortly. To these causes we may add two more. First, as already noted, the Catholic navvies were either lying low or had fled the city, and few others on the Catholic side were willing to keep up the fighting. Second, the McConnell funeral had allowed the Protestants successfully to reclaim their 'right to march' and to demonstrate their continued power in the city. For those who cared about these things, further violence must have seemed unnecessary.

As people slowly resumed their daily routines, they did so in a city scarred, physically and emotionally, by what had happened. The correspondent for the *Times* reported that post-riot Belfast looked as though it had been 'sacked by a horde of banditti'.[80] The *Observer*, reflecting on the permanent damage done by the riots, was especially gloomy. 'The evil is a deep one,' it wrote, 'and a dangerous one, for when traced we find it firmly rooted in the very hearts of the people, bound up with their convictions, part and parcel of their principles and motives, and so inextricably associated with their thoughts and aims that it seems impossible to dissever it from their very existence.'[81] One of the most troubling developments in the immediate aftermath of the riots was a sharp rise in the incidence of workplace intimidation and expulsions, as workers from one religious group refused to allow the other to return to work. At a meeting of the Chamber of Commerce, William Thompson of Grimshaw's mill in Sandy Row stated that he had received a letter threatening to wreck the mill unless the owners dismissed all the Catholics in their employ. The mill's owner, Conway Grimshaw, also told the meeting how Sandy Row Protestants were preventing his Catholic workers from crossing the Boyne Bridge to come to work.[82] The *Newsletter*, the *Belfast Morning News*, the *Banner of Ulster* and the *Observer* all told similar tales. The latter claimed that there were 'no complaints that Catholics have endeavoured in any way to interfere with the employment of Protestants', a statement that received only slight qualifications in the other papers.[83] The mixed workplace, it seemed, was now going the way of the mixed working-class neighbourhood, largely at the behest of Protestant workers.

The restoration of ousted Catholic workers to their former jobs became one of the chief preoccupations of the so-called Peace Meetings that materialised in the last days of the riots. These meetings were organised by middle-class men on both sides – including some, such as the *Observer*'s editor, A. J. McKenna, who had been vocally encouraging the rioters only days before – with the stated purpose of using their 'influence' over the respective parties to restore peace. Aside from McKenna, other leading members of the Peace Meetings included Hugh Hanna, Bernard Hughes and the Liberal Presbyterian minister John Macnaughtan, who travelled to those mills and factories where workers were being expelled and tried to secure their return. Since most of the ousted workers were Catholics, the general pattern was for representatives of the Peace Meetings to broker deals whereby Catholics would be allowed to return to work so long as they pledged not to inform on their Protestant co-workers. It was a jury-rigged sort of a peace, one that relied upon both groups' willingness to let bygones be bygones and that assumed the law to be an obstacle to (rather than the dispenser of) justice, but in the short term these truces seem to have held.[84]

The post-riot atmosphere was especially poisonous in the shipyards. As noted earlier, fifty of the 850 workers at Harland and Wolff's shipyard were Catholics, most of them painters. During the riots these Catholics had been forced out by Protestant shipcarpenters who feared that they would act as 'spies' and report them to the police. After the riots, a Peace Committee comprised of Macnaughtan and the Catholic distiller Peter Keegan persuaded the shipcarpenters to allow the Catholics back to work, with the understanding that the Catholics would not inform on any of the Protestants.[85] Two weeks after the Catholics' return, however, two Protestant workers were arrested on riots charges, and the other Protestants, convinced that the Catholics had gone back on their word, refused to return to work unless the Catholics were fired.[86] On 16 September the Protestants sent a delegation to the mayor, who listened as a man named Stewart Craig read a memorial written on behalf of the Queen's Island shipcarpenters, the workers at McLaine's shipyard and the men of

Coates's foundry. The workers did not deny that some of their party had taken part in the riots, but they insisted that they had done so only to restore order. It was only after it had become clear that 'the town [was] in the hands of a lawless mob, whom the authorities could not, or, at least, did not quell' that the shipcarpenters decided to act, they said. Those Protestants currently sitting in jail were not rioters, therefore, but men who had intervened to 'prevent a lawless mob from injuring the persons and property, and disturbing the peace, not only of themselves, but other legal inhabitants'. The mayor assured the men that their co-workers would receive a fair and speedy trial, and within a few days most of the expelled Catholics returned to work at the shipyards, after once again swearing (this time in writing) that they would not inform on the Protestants.[87] Peace slowly returned to the shipyards, but the Protestant workers had clearly signalled that in the future they would be the ones regulating communal relations on the Queen's Island.

A final consequence of the 1864 riots was the abolition of the local Belfast police force and its replacement with an augmented force of Irish Constabulary. It was a change that had been a long time in coming, for the government had been aware of problems with the local force at least since 1857. Indeed, between 1858 and 1862 several governments had toyed with the idea of abolishing the force, but the Belfast Town Council opposed the idea and the proposals came to nothing.[88] When renewed accusations of police partisanship and ineptitude surfaced in 1864, however, it was clear that something had to be done. This time the denunciations came not only from local Catholics, but from the central government's own officials, who sent back damning reports of the local force's 'demoralization', 'incapacity' and 'partizanship in a high degree'.[89] These reports prompted Thomas Larcom and the new Chief Secretary, the young Robert Peel, to conclude, in Peel's words, 'that it would be far better for the town if the rubbishing local police were replaced by our more efficient constabulary'.[90]

Some of the most ardent denunciations of the local authorities were to be found in British newspapers. 'If the local authorities were weak, or partial, or incompetent, was there no power to supersede them at such a crisis?' asked the *Times*, 'Is municipal self-government invested with such a sacredness that murder and rapine are to be permitted within a city which possesses this much-prized but dangerous independence?'[91] For many British observers, the question of policing Belfast was closely tied to larger questions about the Irish national character and Britain's imperial obligations in the country, and it was clear that the central government needed to play a larger role. 'What sort of a country would Ireland be to live in if she were left wholly to her own devices,' asked the *Saturday*

Review, 'without the restraining and controlling influence of English law, English authority, and English opinion?'[92] The *Times* adopted a more petulant tone, insisting that Britain was doing all it could to stamp out religious intolerance in Ireland. 'These people are still in the 17th century', it said, and, if they chose to wallow in their 'childish and obsolete' feuds instead of partaking in the 'common liberty' offered by Britain, it was hardly the fault of Britain.[93] 'We suppose it must be always the same old story of the two parties in Ireland,' sighed the *Globe*, '"Fighting like devils for conciliation, and hating each other for the love of God," and all we can do from this side of the Channel is to supply troops to ward off some of the blows, and separate the combatants for the moment.'[94]

Belfast's Tory leaders, and even a few Liberals, opposed this erosion of their local autonomy and proposed several alternative measures that would have kept the local force intact, but to no avail.[95] In June 1865 Parliament passed the Belfast Police Act, which abolished the local police and provided Belfast with a permanent constabulary force of 450 men under a government-appointed Town Inspector.[96] As the *Dublin Evening Mail* pointed out, this made Belfast the most heavily policed town in Ireland, with one policeman for every 350 inhabitants.[97] According to Brian Griffin, the new constables received a 'guarded welcome' from many working-class Catholics, who appear to have accepted that this new force might be less anti-Catholic than the old one, but working-class Protestants were openly hostile.[98] Griffin lists some of the epithets by which Protestants addressed the constables in the coming years: '"Papist", "papish looking b[ugger]r", "fenian", "bloody lot of fenians", "popish rascal", "popish pig-drivers", "a parcel of ribbonmen", "papist pup", "papish brats", "a popish set". . .'[99] Over time, Protestant hostility to the constabulary – and nostalgia for the late-lamented local force – would grow stronger, and by 1886 relations between the Protestants and the constabulary had deteriorated so much that the city's worst riots of the century would be fought principally between Protestants and constables. The anti-state message of the 1862 riots and the McConnell funeral of 1864 had been but the first bold strokes in a long Protestant revolt that would define Belfast politics well into the twentieth century, and the constabulary, as the embodiment of the Protestants' weakening control over Belfast, bore the brunt of it.[100]

Conclusion

To say that the 1864 riots were Belfast's first truly urban riots is to say more than simply that they had encompassed a greater portion of the city's geography than earlier riots. It is also to say that the patterns of violence had themselves been shaped by Belfast's unique urban cultures, reflecting the emerging urban identities of the city's working-class inhabitants. The clearest example of this can be seen in the vigilante roles adopted by the navvies and the shipcarpenters. These groups could credibly act as communal defenders in 1864 because each of their respective communities had already developed a set of fiercely autonomous, insular, anti-state identities in the preceding decade. When the navvies exacted revenge for the attacks on Catholic women in Sandy Row, or when the shipcarpenters set out to restore 'order' by plundering shops and hunting down the 'lawless' navvies, they were acting in ways that reflected each side's imaginative relationship with the city itself. Other events during the riots – the McConnell funeral, the workplace expulsions, the blackmail exacted from the 'secret powers' on both sides – likewise reflected identities and interests that were intimately connected to people's places, real and imagined, in Belfast's urban cultures. The events of 1864 showed that Belfast's patterns of violence were developing a vitality and a relevance beyond the ritualised, rural-style battles of earlier years, and as these patterns evolved they were beginning to draw in an ever wider circle of participants from across the city.

Just as important was the way the riots contributed to the future development of both sides' urban identities. Individual resentments always piled up like paving stones after one of these conflicts, but the unusually spectacular and destructive nature of the 1864 riots meant that individual experiences of violence had a greater probability of becoming collective memories as tales about violence came to be told and retold in the coming years. One did not have to be a navvy, for instance, to feel the defeat at Thompson's Bank to be a defeat for one's community, just as one did not have to be a pupil at the Brown Street School to feel angry at the ruffians who had wrecked it. Moreover, because the riots had made such intimate use of the city's landmarks and contested spaces, collective memories of violence became attached to specific spots in the city's landscape in a particularly indelible way. Places like Thompson's Bank, the Brown Street School and the Boyne Bridge stood as constant reminders of the communal struggles that had taken place there, much as a building scarred by bullet holes becomes, in later years, a monument to the battle that scarred it. In the final chapter we will explore how each side's collective memories of the 1864 riots helped shape future outbreaks of violence, but before doing so it is instructive to pull back from Belfast momentarily and to consider its experience alongside that of a city that failed to develop the sorts of violent traditions I have been examining. The case of Glasgow, with its very different set of urban traditions and iden-

tities, provides an instructive contrast to the deepening violence of 1860s
Belfast.

Notes

1 *Ulster Observer*, 18 Aug. 1864.
2 *Northern Whig*, 18 Aug. 1864; Thomas Esmonde's report on the 1864 riots,
  NLI, Esmonde Papers, MS.5931/17–30; James Kennedy's evidence, *Report
  of the Commissioners of Inquiry, 1864, respecting the Magisterial and Police
  Jurisdiction Arrangements and Establishment of the Borough of Belfast*, HC
  1865 (3466) XXVIII (hereafter, *1864 Belfast Riots Inquiry*), 243; William
  Mullen's evidence, *ibid.*, 255.
3 Henry Murney, 'Report of the General Hospital on Riot Casualties', *Banner
  of Ulster*, 29 Nov. 1864.
4 *1864 Belfast Riots Inquiry*, 16–17; Sub-Inspector Harvey's report, Oct.
  1864, NAGB, Home Office Records, HO45/7649/106–7.
5 Dublin Castle denied this request. See Marquis of Donegal to Thomas
  Larcom, 18 Aug. 1864, and Larcom's replies, NLI, Larcom Papers,
  7626/28. The number of police and troops refers to 17 Aug., and it comes
  from *1864 Belfast Riots Inquiry*, Appendixes C and D, 362, Table B; and
  Northern Whig, 18 Aug. 1864.
6 Memorandum from Attorney General James Lawson, NLI, Larcom Papers,
  7627/4.
7 *Belfast Newsletter*, 1 Aug. 1864.
8 Letter from 'A Loyalist', *ibid.*, 4 Aug. 1864.
9 *Ibid.*, 6 Aug. 1864.
10 *Ulster Observer*, 12 Mar. 1864.
11 *Ibid.*, 30 July and 4 Aug. 1864.
12 *Ibid.*, 2, 4, 6 and 9 Aug. 1864.
13 *Ibid.*, 4 Aug. 1864.
14 *Freeman's Journal,* 9 Aug. 1864.
15 *Belfast Newsletter*, 9 Aug. 1864; *Ulster Observer*, 9 Aug. 1864.
16 *1864 Belfast Riots Inquiry*, 8; Edward Orme's evidence, *ibid.*, 13; Catherine Graham's evidence, *ibid.*, 32; *Banner of Ulster*, 9 Aug. 1864; *Northern
   Whig*, 9 Aug. 1864; *Belfast Newsletter*, 9 Aug. 1864.
17 *1864 Belfast Riots Inquiry*; Patrick McCabe's evidence, *ibid.*, p. 36; *Belfast
   Newsletter*, 10 Aug. 1864; *Banner of Ulster*, 11 Aug. 1864; *Ulster
   Observer*, 13 Aug. 1864.
18 *1864 Belfast Riots Inquiry*, 9; *Belfast Newsletter*, 11 Aug. 1864; *Banner of
   Ulster*, 11 Aug. 1864.
19 See *Freeman's Journal*, 17 and 18 Aug. 1864; *Dublin Evening Post*, 30 Aug.
   1864; *Times* (London), 18 Feb. 1865.
20 *Northern Whig*, 12 Aug. 1864.
21 In *1864 Belfast Riots Inquiry*, see James McCance's evidence, 145; Patrick
   Dorrian's evidence, 42; and William Kirkpatrick's evidence, 306. See also

Banner of Ulster, 13 Aug. 1864; *Ulster Observer*, 13 Aug. 1864; *Belfast Newsletter*, 13 Aug. 1864.

22 *Ulster Observer*, 13 Aug. 1864.

23 *Ibid.*, 13, 16 and 20 Aug. 1864.

24 *Ibid.*, 13 Aug. 1864; *1864 Belfast Riots Inquiry*, 10; Edward Orme's evidence, *1864 Belfast Riots Inquiry*, 26; 'Statistical Report of the Injures Sustained during the Riots in Belfast, from 8th to 22nd August, 1864', *1864 Belfast Riots Inquiry*, Appendix 18, 351–2.

25 Between 1861 and 1863, the number of buildings constructed annually rose from 730 to 1,260, or by nearly 73%. See *Ulster Observer*, 2 Jan. 1864.

26 Sean Farrell makes a similar claim about the 1857 Belfast riots, but the idea, as he puts it, that 'party passions' lacked space to 'dissipate' in the urban confines of Belfast is more appropriate to 1864 than to 1857. Sean Farrell, *Rituals and Riots: Sectarian Violence and Political Culture in Ulster, 1784–1886* (Lexington, Ky.: University Press of Kentucky, 2000), 149.

27 Very little research has been done on the place of bonfires and effigies in Irish popular culture, apart from two studies that consider the topic from the perspective of contemporary Northern Ireland. See Adam Gailey and G. B. Adams, 'The Bonfire in Northern Irish Tradition', *Folklore*, 88 (1977), 3–38; and Jack Santino, 'Light up the Sky: Halloween Bonfires and Culture Hegemony in Northern Ireland', *Western Folklore*, 55 (Summer 1996), 213–31.

28 David Cressy, *Bonfires and Bells: National Memory and the Protestant Calendar in Elizabethan and Stuart England* (Berkeley: University of California Press, 1989), 80–7, 179–84; Martin Ingram, 'Ridings, Rough Music, and the "Reform of Popular Culture" in Early Modern England', *Past and Present*, 105 (Nov. 1984), 79–113; Peter Burke, *Popular Culture in Early Modern Europe* (New York: Harper and Row, 1978); Natalie Zemon Davis, *Society and Culture in Early Modern France* (Stanford, Calif.: Stanford University Press, 1975), chs. 4–5; E. P. Thompson, *Customs in Common* (New York: The New Press, 1993), ch. 8.

29 *Freeman's Journal*, 19 Aug. 1864; *Banner of Ulster*, 23 and 25 Aug. 1864; *Daily Express*, 24 Aug. 1864; *Ulster Observer*, 25 Aug. 1864; *Irish Times*, 25 Aug. 1864; Kilkenny Resident Magistrate to Thomas Larcom, 26 Aug. 1864, NLI, Larcom Papers, 7626/61.

30 Catherine Hirst, *Religion, Politics, and Violence in Nineteenth-Century Belfast: The Pound and Sandy Row* (Dublin: Four Courts Press, 2002), 164 and 169–70.

31 For an example of evangelical objections to the crucifix, see Hugh Hanna's letter to the *Banner of Ulster*, 15 Sept. 1857.

32 Hirst's only other reason for arguing that these riots were 'predominately political' comes from a specious claim in a memoir by the Belfast Fenian Frank Roney that the revolutionary Fenian Brotherhood 'led' the Catholic rioters in 1864. In fact, Fenianism does appear to have existed in Belfast as early as 1862, but it was never more than a minor force in the city, and it appears to have been especially weak in this period. Moreover, Roney's

account, which was written some sixty years after the riots, wildly mis-
remembers several other aspects of the riots, claiming, for example, that
they lasted two months (rather than ten days) and that the government
declared martial law to end the riots (it did not). It also flatly contradicts
the strong denunciations of the riots found in the Fenians' own newspaper,
the *Irish People,* and the total silence regarding Fenian involvement in all of
the contemporary evidence. See Frank Roney, *Irish Rebel and California
Labour Leader: An Autobiography*, ed. Ira B. Cross (Berkeley, Calif.:
University of California Press, 1931), 51–60; and *Irish People*, 27 Aug.
and 10 Dec. 1864; John O'Leary, *Recollections of Fenians and Fenianism*,
vol. 1 (London: Downey & Co., 1896), 129; Thomas MacKnight, *Ulster as
it Is: or, Twenty-eight Years' Experience as an Irish Editor*, (London:
Macmillan and Co., 1896), vol. 1, 62–3; and Ambrose Macaulay, *Patrick
Dorrian: Bishop of Down and Connor, 1865–85* (Irish Academic Press:
Dublin, 1987), 184.

33 David Brooke, 'The "Lawless" Navvy: A Study of the Crime Associated
with Railway Building', *The Journal of Transport History*, 10 (Sept. 1989),
145–65; David Brooke, *The Railway Navvy: 'That Despicable Race of Men'*
(Newton Abbot: David & Charles, 1983), 108–22; James E. Handley, *The
Navvy in Scotland* (Cork: Cork University Press, 1970), 267–320.

34 George Stewart Hill's evidence, *Report of the Commissioners of Inquiry into
the Origin and Character of the Riots in Belfast, in July and September,
1857; together with Minutes of Evidence and Appendix,* HC 1857–58 (2309)
XXVI (hereafter, *1857 Belfast Riots Inquiry*), 157; *Northern Whig*, 15 Jan.
1859; Tom Garvin, 'Defenders, Ribbonmen and Others: Underground Political Networks in Pre-Famine Ireland', *Past and Present*, 96 (Aug. 1982),
149; Sybil Baker, 'Orange and Green: Belfast, 1832–1912', in *The Victorian City: Images and Realities*, ed. H. J. Dyos and M. Wolff (London:
Routledge & Kegan Paul, 1973), vol. 2, 795.

35 *Belfast Newsletter*, 20 Sept. 1862; *Banner of Ulster*, 23 Sept. 1862.

36 Brooke, *Railway Navvy*, 10–19.

37 This term was usually applied to all skilled shipyard workers without reference to their particular trades. It appears to date from the days of timber
ship construction, although by this period the shift to iron construction was
well underway. Other designations that appeared were 'ship wrights', 'ships'
carpenters' and, especially after the 1870s, 'the Islandmen', which referred
to the Queen's Island, the site of Belfast's principal shipyards.

38 Frank Wright, *Two Lands on One Soil: Ulster Politics before Home Rule*
(Dublin: Gill and Macmillan, 1996), 211–12; *Banner of Ulster*, 17 Sept.
1864. In Ulster generally, Catholics made up 28% of all shipyard workers
in 1861, a proportion that fell to 8% by 1911. See Sidney Pollard and Paul
Robertson, *The British Shipbuilding Industry, 1870–1914* (Cambridge,
Mass.: Harvard University Press, 1979), 67 n.37.

39 The ratio of skilled to unskilled workers in Belfast has not been calculated,
but it was probably similar to that in the Scottish shipyards, where it
remained 'fairly constant' between 1870 and 1900. In 1892, the proportions

were 66% skilled and 22% unskilled, with 12% employed as apprentices and in other miscellaneous positions. Translated to the Harland and Wolff shipyards of 1864, this would mean 561 skilled workers and 187 unskilled workers, with an additional 102 in miscellaneous positions. See Pollard and Robertson, *British Shipbuilding*, 152–3 and 156–63.

40 *Henderson's Belfast Directory, 1861* (Belfast: News-Letter Office, 1861) lists 102 ship carpenters, ship joiners, ship wrights and ship smiths. Almost without exception, they lived in an area bounded to the east by Corporation Street, to the west by North Queen Street to the north by Canning Street and to the south by Frederick Street. This area extended north from the city centre along the river, on the opposite side of town from Sandy Row, which lay to the south-west. In later decades, shipyard workers would settle more thickly in the Shankill Road area of west Belfast and across the river in east Belfast.

41 *Banner of Ulster*, 10 Sept. 1857; *1857 Belfast Riots Inquiry*, 12–13.

42 Wright, *Two Lands*, 243–5. Wright claims that the terms and 'ship carpenter' and 'navvy' were often used by observers 'to describe large gatherings of Protestants and Catholic workers arrayed for combat, sometimes without regard to their actual occupations'. This may have been true in some instances, but during this period most observers were quite ready to distinguish between these groups and their allies among the millworkers of west Belfast.

43 *Ulster Observer*, 13 Aug. 1864.

44 Edward Orme's evidence, *1864 Belfast Riots Inquiry*, 26. See also *Ulster Observer*, 16 Aug. 1864.

45 Thomas Donnellson's evidence, *1864 Belfast Riots Inquiry*, 229–30; *Belfast Morning News*, 18 Aug. 1864; *Belfast Newsletter*, 16 Aug. 1864.

46 Report of the Assizes, *Banner of Ulster*, 16 Mar. 1865; *Banner of Ulster*, 16 Aug. 1864; *Belfast Newsletter*, 16 Aug. 1864.

47 *Belfast Newsletter*, 17 Aug. 1864.

48 *Northern Whig*, 17 Aug. 1864; *1864 Belfast Riots Inquiry*, 11–12; *Belfast Morning News*, 18 Aug. 1864.

49 *1864 Belfast Riots Inquiry*, 12.

50 *Belfast Newsletter*, 17 and 18 Aug. 1864.

51 *Northern Whig*, 17 Aug. 1864.

52 Wright, *Two Lands*, 262. Elsewhere in its report of 17 Aug. the *Whig* noted that several of the leading shipcarpenters had actively restrained their fellows from wantonly destroying houses during their march.

53 *Belfast Newsletter*, 18 Aug. 1864.

54 *Northern Whig*, 19 Aug. 1864; *1864 Belfast Riots Inquiry*, 11–12.

55 *1864 Belfast Riots Inquiry*, 351–2.

56 *Northern Whig*, 17 Aug. 1864.

57 *Ulster Observer*, 16 Aug. 1864.

58 *Banner of Ulster*, 18 Aug. 1864.

59 *Northern Whig*, 18 Aug. 1864.

60 *1864 Belfast Riots Inquiry*, Appendix B, 362, Tables C and D.

61 *Banner of Ulster*, 18 Aug. 1864; *Northern Whig*, 18 Aug. 1864.
62 *Belfast Morning News*, 19 Aug. 1864.
63 Isaac Nelson's evidence, *1864 Belfast Riots Inquiry*, 272.
64 *Belfast Morning News*, 19 Aug. 1864; *Belfast Newsletter*, 18 Aug. 1864; *Banner of Ulster*, 18 Aug. 1864.
65 *Belfast Morning News*, 19 Aug. 1864.
66 Isaac Nelson's evidence, *1864 Belfast Riots Inquiry*, 271–2.
67 Thomas Esmonde's report on the 1864 riots, NLI, Esmonde Papers, MS.5931/17–30; Edward Orme's evidence, *1864 Belfast Riots Inquiry*, 19; *Banner of Ulster*, 18 Aug. 1864; George Nolan's evidence, *1864 Belfast Riots Inquiry*, 50–2; *Belfast Newsletter*, 18 Aug. 1864; *Northern Whig*, 18 Aug. 1864; *Ulster Observer*, 18 Aug. 1864. One of the most intriguing scraps of evidence to emerge from these events was the story told by Patrick McGrath, a local policeman who witnessed the fight and reported seeing a 'dark-complexioned man' drop to his knees and fire upon the navvies. 'I recollect going up beside the black fellow,' said McGrath, 'and saying he was a murdering rascal, and bidding him get up off his knees.' The identity of this 'black fellow' is not known. See the report of the Assizes in *Banner of Ulster*, 25 Mar. 1865.
68 *Belfast Newsletter*, 18 Aug. 1864.
69 Edward Orme's evidence, *1864 Belfast Riots Inquiry*, 19; *Ulster Observer*, 18 Aug. 1864; *Northern Whig*, 18 Aug. 1864.
70 *Banner of Ulster*, 20 and 23 Aug. 1864.
71 *Northern Whig*, 19 Aug. 1864; *1864 Belfast Riots Inquiry*, 11–12.
72 *1864 Belfast Riots Inquiry*, 13–14; Thomas Esmonde's report on the 1864 riots, NLI, Esmonde Papers, MS.5931/17–30; *Banner of Ulster*, 20 Aug. 1864; W. T. B. Lyons's evidence, *1864 Belfast Riots Inquiry*, 105.
73 *1864 Belfast Riots Inquiry*, 13–14 and William Burke's evidence, *ibid.*, 46–7; *Northern Whig*, 19 Aug. 1864.
74 W. T. B. Lyons's evidence, *1864 Belfast Riots Inquiry*, 106; *Northern Whig*, 19 Aug. 1864. One observer stated that the crowd was cheering not in welcome, but in defiance of the authorities. See the letter of H. N. Levinge in the *Times* (London), 25 Aug. 1864.
75 *Belfast Newsletter*, 19 Aug. 1864; *Northern Whig*, 19 Aug. 1864; *Banner of Ulster*, 20 Aug. 1864.
76 *Ulster Observer*, 20 Aug. 1864.
77 *Northern Whig*, 19 Aug. 1864; *Banner of Ulster*, 20 Aug. 1864; *1864 Belfast Riots Inquiry*, 14.
78 James Kennedy's evidence, *1864 Belfast Riots Inquiry*, 243.
79 William Mullen's evidence, *ibid.*, 255.
80 *Times* (London), 24 Aug. 1864.
81 *Ulster Observer*, 25 Aug. 1864.
82 *Ibid.*; *Belfast Newsletter*, 20 Aug. 1864. See also James Kennedy's evidence, *1864 Belfast Riots Inquiry*, 120.
83 *Ulster Observer*, 20 Aug. 1864; *Belfast Newsletter*, 29 Aug. 1864; *Belfast Morning News*, 22 Aug. 1864; *Belfast Newsletter*, 20 Aug. 1864.

84 *Banner of Ulster*, 19, 20, 23, 25 and 30 Aug. and 20 Sept. 1864; *Belfast Morning News*, 19 Aug. 1864; Wright, *Two Lands*, 264–8.

85 *Banner of Ulster*, 23 Aug. 1864.

86 *Belfast Newsletter*, 16 Sept. 1864; *Banner of Ulster*, 17 Sept. 1864.

87 *Banner of Ulster*, 17 and 20 Sept. 1864.

88 *1864 Belfast Riots Inquiry*, Appendixes 19 and 20, 353–5.

89 Thomas Esmonde's report on the Belfast riots, NLI, Esmonde Papers, MS.5931; Sub-Inspector Harvey to the Home Office, Oct. 1864, NAGB, Home Office Records, HO45/7649/79; Maxwell Hamilton to Larcom, 16 Sept. 1864, NLI, Larcom Papers, 7626/82; Report of the Assizes, *Banner of Ulster*, 28 Mar. 1865.

90 Peel to Larcom, 19 Aug. 1864, NLI, Larcom Papers, 7626/29.

91 *Times* (London), 20 Aug. 1864.

92 *Saturday Review*, 20 Aug. 1864.

93 *Times* (London), 24 Aug. 1864.

94 *The Globe*, 17 Aug. 1864 (extracted in *Dublin Evening Post*, 18 Aug. 1864).

95 Minutes of Belfast Police Committee, 24 Oct. 1864, PRONI, LA/7/10AB/1/5; *Belfast Newsletter*, 26 and 28 Nov., 1 and 7 Dec. 1864; *Banner of Ulster*, 3, 6 and 8 Sept., 3 Dec. 1864; William Mullen's evidence, *1864 Belfast Riots Inquiry*, 252; *Northern Whig*, 16 June 1865.

96 *Times* (London), 28 April 1865; Larcom to Sir George Grey, 21 Apr. 1865, NLI, Larcom Papers, 7627/38.

97 *Dublin Evening Mail*, 31 May 1865.

98 Brian Griffin, *The Bulkies: Police and Crime in Belfast, 1800–1865* (Dublin: Irish Academic Press, 1997), 140–1.

99 *Ibid.*, 139.

100 On policing in Belfast after 1864, see Mark Radford, 'The "Social Volcano": Policing Victorian Belfast', in *Politics and Power in Victorian Ireland*, ed. Roger Swift and Christine Kinealy (Dublin: Four Courts Press, 2006), 166–77.

7

Glasgow: sectarian détente

Even the boldest Belfast evangelical would have blushed at the audacity of it. In the summer of 1860, the Free Presbyterian Church opened a new church in the Glasgow slum of Bridgegate, an area well known for its large population of Irish Catholics.[1] The presence of a Protestant church in a Catholic neighbourhood would not normally have attracted much attention in Glasgow, where communal boundaries were often quite blurry, but this was no ordinary church. An outdoor pulpit, built of stone and facing the street, proclaimed the missionary intentions of the church's founders, and from this pulpit the church's minister, the Rev. McColl, began preaching that summer to the crowds passing below. Before long, teeming crowds of Protestants were gathering to hear McColl's Sunday evening services, and Catholics, who had to pass through the crowds to get to their own church, started to resent both the obstruction of the thoroughfare as well as the implicit insult to their religion. By way of protest some Catholics began hiring cabs and driving them through the crowds, setting off several scuffles that by late autumn threatened to escalate into a serious confrontation.[2]

Anxious to avert catastrophe, Glasgow's Catholic bishop, John Murdoch, informed the sheriff of Lanarkshire, Archibald Alison, of the situation. Alison, along with the Lord Provost, promptly sent a letter to McColl asking him to desist. When McColl refused, Alison and 200 local policemen arrived at the Bridgegate to force him to stand down. The scene that day would have been familiar to any Belfast magistrate: 'All the streets in the vicinity were choked with ardent multitudes,' Alison recalled, 'whose menacing looks bespoke their anxiety for strife. The Catholics from all parts of the city were assembled in great strength; the Orangemen had come in from Paisley and all the neighbouring towns, to support the cause of the Protestant faith against the assaults of the Popish idolaters, as they deemed them.' More than 40,000 men had gathered in the narrow streets, 'panting for the moment it was to begin', but before a fight could break out Alison swooped in with the policemen and dispersed the crowd. The next day Alison and the Lord Provost threatened to issue a legal interdict against McColl should he insist on preaching, and McColl, claiming that the weather had started to deteriorate anyway, agreed to suspend his services for the season.[3]

McColl did not relinquish his evangelical duty easily, however, and the following summer he announced that he would once again hold open-air services from his Bridgegate pulpit. The authorities now presented him with the legal interdict they had threatened him with the previous year. On 2 June, the day of the first scheduled service, Alison surrounded the area with 300 policemen, but McColl failed to appear, and 'the evening passed without any collision'.[4] At a hearing in the Sheriff Court a few days later, Alison explained that there were 'innumerable situations in Glasgow where open-air preaching can be carried on', but to preach in a Catholic area such as the Bridgegate was to endanger the public peace, and as such it could not be allowed.[5] Recalling this episode some twenty years later, Alison admitted that in issuing this proclamation he knew he was 'declaring open war on this point against the puritanical party of Scotland', but he refused to bow to their impassioned denunciations, and the uproar gradually subsided.[6]

The similarities between the Bridgegate affair of 1860–61 and the Belfast open-air preaching crisis of 1857 are tantalising. Both incidents were sparked by pugnacious evangelical ministers intent on holding religious services in contested spaces. Both drew upon a deep reservoir of sectarian feeling among the Protestant and Catholic working classes. Both forced the state to choose between an instinctual desire for order on the one hand and its constitutional obligation to preserve free expression on the other. But only the Belfast episode ended in violence and bloodshed, and in that fact lies an important truth about sectarian violence generally. This is, quite simply, that similar causes do not always produce similar effects. An understanding of context and agency – especially as they relate to the texture of relationships between and within social groups – is vital to understanding why sectarian violence emerges when and where it does. In this case, the Bridgegate affair failed to escalate into open violence primarily because important actors acted differently from their Belfast counterparts in 1857. The Glasgow authorities did not hesitate, as the magistrates did in Belfast, to curtail the abstract liberties of an evangelical minister in order to preserve peace. Glasgow evangelicals, likewise, conspicuously failed to offer any active assistance to their embattled colleague, as had Hugh Hanna, Henry Cooke and others in Belfast. Even the Catholic Church, which in Belfast was rarely able to curtail violence committed by its flock, appears to have been rather proactive in bringing the crisis in the Bridgegate to the authorities' attention. Clearly, important restraining forces were operating in Glasgow that were absent in Belfast.

'Sooner or later,' writes Ashutosh Varshney in his study of Hindu–Muslim riots in contemporary India, 'scholars of ethnic conflict are struck by a puzzling empirical regularity in their field. Despite ethnic diversity, some places ... manage to remain peaceful, whereas others experience enduring patterns of violence.'[7] In order to understand those places where violence becomes endemic, Varshney suggests, we must understand those where it does not. Glasgow presents just such an opportunity for the study of violence in Belfast. For the Bridgegate affair was indicative of a wider pattern: sectarian tensions, while strong, very rarely escalated into sectarian violence in Victorian Glasgow; much more often than those in Belfast, Glasgow's communal crises tended to fizzle out before they exploded.[8] In many other respects, however – including such potentially explosive areas as their demographic compositions and their ideological traditions – the two cities closely resembled one another. Glasgow therefore offers an ideal 'control' against which to test the explanations for Belfast's violence that I have developed thus far: their very similarities allow us to isolate those factors that made Belfast unique in its violence.[9]

In what follows I first establish the resemblances between mid-Victorian Belfast and Glasgow, with a particular eye on those elements that seemed to make the latter just as prone to sectarian violence as the former. The next three sections will return to those categories of analysis I have employed over the previous six chapters to trace the development of violence in Belfast. These categories are: (1) the nature of each side's pre-existing communal networks, especially the relative strength of their religious organisations; (2) the attitude and position of the state relative to the city's population; and (3) patterns of violence, which both foster and are reinforced by communal polarisation. In Belfast it was the way communal identities developed within these frameworks that gave rise to that city's violent traditions. If Glasgow was a more tranquil city during this period, then we might expect its experiences in these three areas to have been substantially different. My analysis will show that this was undoubtedly the case, and it will reinforce my larger argument that it was the complex patterns of social life – and not the abstract or inevitable clash of ideologies, faiths or ethnicities – that created Belfast's violent traditions.

For all this study's suspicion of tidy, unifying explanations of sectarian violence, however, one conclusion is inescapable. This is that, at a certain fundamental level, the differences between Belfast and Glasgow were differences in each city's experience of imperialism. Although the two cities were separated by a mere eight-hour steamer journey, the distance between Belfast and Glasgow was that between a colonial outpost and the imperial metropole. Glasgow's Protestants, unlike their Belfast counterparts, were secure in their positions and untroubled by any notion that Glasgow would cease to be a 'Protestant' city. Glasgow's Catholics, while certainly marginalised, did not experience the same alienation from state authority that was common in Belfast. Because both sides in Glasgow related to the imperial centre differently from their counterparts in Belfast, all sorts of things that were capable of causing violence in Belfast – evangelical anti-Catholicism, Tory populism, Catholic secret societies, heavy-handed policing, even residential segregation – were either greatly diluted or completely absent. The imperial context does not explain all of the differences in the sectarian experiences of both cities – it cannot account, for example, for the greater strength of the Catholic Church in Glasgow – but it does help to explain the greater urgency of sectarian antagonisms in Belfast. This urgency, born of both sides' anxieties about their place in the British imperial world, goes a long way towards explaining why sectarian tensions in Belfast so frequently flared into sectarian violence.

Cross-currents

People and goods have flowed freely between Ulster and Scotland since ancient times. The most consequential modern interaction was undoubtedly the Plantation of Ulster in the seventeenth century, when Scottish Presbyterians, along with English Protestants, came to Ulster as colonists. This migration gave to Ulster Protestantism its strong Presbyterian colouring (with all the complex blending of stern Calvinism and utopian radicalism that this implied), and, of course, it sowed the seeds of the Protestant–Catholic antagonism that was to trouble Ulster for centuries. But the flow of people was not all one-way, and, especially after the advent of cheap steam passages in the 1820s, thousands of Ulster workers migrated to Scotland to work as agricultural labourers or as operatives in the burgeoning industries of the lowlands.[10] As the pace of contact quickened, the dense thicket of intertwining religious traditions, local economies and population flows linking the two regions became denser. Indeed, to speak of Ulster and Scotland as separate, sharply bounded regions during this period is perhaps less accurate than to see them as a vast industrial archipelago held together by rapidly multiplying rail and steamer routes. This was especially true of Belfast and Glasgow, the industrial capitals of their respective regions, which by the early 1860s were linked by much more than the cheap ferries that plied the channel six days a week. If Scotland and Ulster were an industrial archipelago, then Belfast and Glasgow were its megalopolis, an urban expanse between whose halves economic, political and cultural currents flowed freely and swiftly. It is the strength of these cross-currents that makes a comparison of the communal relations in these two cities fruitful, for they show that many of the forces causing instability in Belfast were also present in Glasgow.

The communal balance

One factor that historians frequently point to in explaining Belfast's nineteenth-century violence is the rapid influx of poor Catholics into what had long been a predominately Protestant city.[11] This was undoubtedly a vital prerequisite for Belfast's sectarian polarisation – one can hardly have Protestant–Catholic riots without any Catholics – but the experience of Glasgow should caution us against positing any direct correlation between rising numbers of Catholics and increasing sectarian violence. Irish immigrants, most of them Catholics, had been arriving in Glasgow in increasing numbers since the start of that city's industrial expansion in the late eighteenth century, and, like those who migrated to Belfast, most came from rural Ulster to work in the textile industry. As early as 1831, 17.5% of Glasgow's population was Irish-born, and by 1834 Irish workers constituted a majority of Glasgow's textile workforce. As with the rest of Britain, the famine of 1845–49 greatly accelerated the pace of Irish immigration to Glasgow, boosting the city's Irish-born population to its peak level of 18.22% in 1851. Even more than before, the great bulk of these immigrants were poor and unskilled.[12]

There are two problems with these figures, however. First, not all Irish immigrants to Glasgow were Catholic, and, second, not all of Glasgow's Catholics were born in Ireland. Unfortunately, the nineteenth-century Scottish censuses did not record inhabitants' religions (as the Irish ones did from 1861), and so we are left to conjecture with woeful imprecision as to the region's precise religious makeup. Most scholars agree that Protestants made up between a third and a quarter of all Irish immigrants to Scotland, with the proportion probably being larger in the pre-famine years.[13] Contemporary estimates of the number of Catholics in Glasgow, taking into account Scottish-born Catholics of Irish descent, put their numbers as high as 100,000 in the immediate post-famine period, or roughly a quarter of the city's population.[14] This number may be somewhat exaggerated, but many Glasgow Catholics certainly believed this to be the case, proudly adopting the notion of 'one quarter' as a measure of their numerical strength in the city, and when one is studying sectarian conflict perceptions of this sort are often as important as reality.[15] Taken together, the evidence suggests a Catholic population of 20–5% in Glasgow at this time, a figure not too far below that of Belfast, which was roughly one-third Catholic in 1861. The remainder were Protestants of Irish and Scottish descent, creating the potential for conflict not only between Irish Catholics and Scots, but also between Irish Catholics and Irish Protestants.

The communal balance of power becomes clearer when we look at each group's place on the social scale. As in Belfast, Catholics tended to cluster near the bottom of Glasgow society, taking work as unskilled workers in the textile, construction, and shipbuilding industries and living in some of the city's worst neighbourhoods.[16] The skilled trades generally went to Scottish Protestants, although many Scots, especially Gaelic-speaking Highlanders, worked as unskilled labourers as well.[17] Irish Protestants, like their Catholic countrymen, also seem to have been clustered at the lower end of the economic scale, often competing with Catholics for unskilled work and, whenever possible, using the Orange Order to regulate entry to certain trades or workplaces.[18] Indeed, the arrival of the Orange Order in Glasgow in 1813 and its continued identification with Ulster (as distinct from native) Protestants throughout the nineteenth century clearly shows that some forms of Ulster sectarianism were capable of crossing the channel more or less intact.[19] As innumerable studies of the Irish in Britain have shown, moreover, sectarianism was by no means a monopoly of the Irish, and many unskilled Scots, nursing traditional anti-Catholic prejudices and worried that the Irish were dragging down wages and living standards, resented the influx of Irish Catholics.[20] Given these multiple fissures – Irish vs. Scots, Protestants vs. Catholic – there were plenty of axes along which violence might have developed in Victorian Glasgow, and it would have done so among roughly similar social groups as those responsible for violence in Belfast, i.e. unskilled and skilled workers.

Economic structures

If Glasgow's religious balance appeared to make it susceptible to sectarian violence, then so, too, did its economic structure. This had less to do with the nature of the Glasgow economy itself, which was highly diverse and not easily given to rigid sectionalism, than with the extensive connections it developed with the Belfast economy, where sectionalism and sectarianism were rife. These connections were possible because of the two cities' complementary economic structures and the many opportunities for labour migration that developed between them. The frequent movement of Belfast workers to Glasgow, and of Glasgow workers to Belfast, promoted a sort of sectarian cross-fertilisation between the two cities, ensuring that Glasgow was heavily exposed to the polarising currents sweeping through Belfast's industries.

Although Glasgow industrialised earlier than Belfast, and its economy was both larger and more diverse, the two cities generally followed similar paths of economic development. From the late eighteenth century, textile production was the engine driving both economies, and it remained the largest single employer in both cities for most of the nineteenth century. In the early part of the century both economies ran primarily on cotton, but just before Glasgow's cotton industry reached its peak in the 1830s, Belfast's entrepreneurs made the fateful leap to linen, a decision that made possible Belfast's phenomenal post-famine boom. Whether it was cotton or linen, however, it was the textile industry's enormous demand for unskilled labour that propelled the massive migration that was such an important feature of both societies, and it was this sector of the economy that created the appalling living conditions endured by both cities' inhabitants (although those in Glasgow probably had it worse). The success of the textile industry spawned important ancillary industries in both cities, including engineering and construction, and by the middle of the nineteenth century both cities were becoming important centres of shipbuilding. Like textiles, shipbuilding took off first in Glasgow (in the 1830s and 1840s) before getting underway in Belfast (in the late 1850s), and well into the next century shipbuilding and the subordinate industries it spawned would be centrepieces of both economies.[21]

All these structural similarities created multiple opportunities for labour migration between the two cities, and there is considerable evidence that certain sectors shared a common labour pool. When depression hit Glasgow's sewed muslin industry in late 1857, for example, a number of female muslin spinners travelled to Belfast looking for work, although they soon found conditions there to be just as bad.[22] Other groups, including those involved in Belfast's sectarian broils, also migrated between the two cities. As I noted in the previous chapter, during the 1864 Belfast riots many Catholic navvies were reported to have taken the steamer to Glasgow in order to avoid detection by the ship-carpenters or the police, and there is also a possibility that some of these men returned to Belfast several years later as Fenian agitators.[23] Shipbuilding was another Belfast industry in which sectarian attitudes were strong, and here there is even stronger evidence of labour migration. When, for example, the great Belfast shipbuilder Edward Harland (himself a veteran of the Glasgow shipyards) needed skilled workers to break a strike on the Queen's Island in 1854, he brought over workers from the Clyde (Glasgow's main river) whom he expected to be more amenable to his rigorous management style.[24] As late as the 1880s, skilled

Clydeside workers were travelling to Belfast during downturns in Glasgow's economy while unskilled Belfast workers, Protestant and Catholic, often took the boat to Glasgow to take advantage of the higher wages there.[25] One important 'cultural transmission' from all this labour migration was Orangeism. Long a fixture of the Belfast shipyards, Orange lodges slowly began to take hold on the Clydeside docks as well, and, as in Belfast, they heavily coloured employment patterns in the region.[26]

Rural violence

For proof that the combined forces of Irish immigration, economic competition and Orangeism could, indeed, produce sectarian violence in Scotland, we need look no further than the towns and villages of Glasgow's industrial hinterland. Places like Greenock, Coatbridge, Airdrie and Paisley all experienced serious, sometimes deadly sectarian riots during this period. Plentiful work in industries such as sugar refining, railroad construction, mining, shipbuilding and textile manufacturing drew the Irish to these areas, and, as in Glasgow, Protestant and Catholic Irish tended to take unskilled jobs while the skilled trades went to native Scots.[27] Violence born of economic competition was most common, therefore, between different groups of Irish migrants, although violence between Irish and Scots was not unknown.[28] Many riots occurred during Orange marches that sought to regulate territorial boundaries between different groups of Irish immigrants. These were especially common during downturns in the business cycle, and they clearly demonstrated that Scotland was not immune to the sorts of ritualised violence that plagued rural Ulster.[29]

Events in the Lanarkshire mining villages of Coatbridge and Airdrie were indicative of the general pattern. This district, which lay no more than a dozen miles east of Glasgow, was heavily populated by Irish immigrants 'of the most vicious, turbulent, & disaffected character', as one local magistrate described them.[30] Between 1848 and 1869, according to Alan Campbell, no fewer than thirty-six sectarian incidents took place here, ranging in severity from the use of insulting 'party expressions' to full-blown riots.[31] One of the worst outbreaks happened at the Airdrie racetrack in August 1854, where tents had been set up to sell drinks to thirsty miners. When a number of 'party tunes' began emanating from a tent known to be frequented by Orangemen, a band of Irish Catholics attacked the offending party, and the ensuing affray left one Protestant dead.[32] Three years later, another riot broke out in Coatbridge when thirty or forty Orangemen, returning from a Twelfth of July demonstration in Garnkirk, were attacked by 1,200 to 1,500 Catholics described variously as 'Ribbonmen' and 'navvies'. More than twenty Catholics were arrested in this incident, and the guilty were sentenced to a relatively severe term of four years in prison.[33]

Like sectarian riots in rural Ulster, these Scottish outbreaks tended to be male-dominated affairs occurring at public events such as Orange marches and fairs. They were often fuelled by drink and nearly always of limited scope and duration. Deaths did occur, but these were uncommon, largely because firearms were rarely used. Because they usually involved Irish Protestants and Irish Catholics, these outbreaks also had little direct impact on the surrounding population, apart from reinforcing certain stereotypes about drunken and rowdy Irishmen. Moreover, unlike those in Belfast itself, sectarian tensions in the Scottish countryside tended to die away over time – nowhere did a protracted, endemic tradition of violence take hold as it did in Belfast. Still, the presence of sectarian violence on Glasgow's doorstep suggests that there was nothing peculiar about Scotland that prevented sectarian rioting from occurring here. If Glasgow managed to remain largely tranquil, it was partly because these patterns of violence failed to migrate from the countryside to the city.

Religious traditions

A final strand connecting Belfast and Glasgow could be found in the cities' shared religious traditions. As I noted above, the seventeenth-century Scottish migration to Ulster had introduced Presbyterianism to Ireland, and in the centuries that followed there remained an intimate and fruitful relationship between Irish and Scottish Presbyterians.[34] One of the most important beliefs connecting Presbyterians in Ulster and Scotland at this time was the gospel of civic evangelicalism. In fact, Glasgow evangelicals, led by the energetic reformer Thomas Chalmers, had pioneered the sorts of 'moral reform' bodies that were to become so important in Belfast, in most cases building organisations that were older and bigger than their Belfast counterparts and just as vital to the city's civic culture.[35] Anti-Catholicism was also an important component of Glasgow evangelicalism, and, as in Belfast, it received a significant fillip in the middle of the nineteenth century. Like their Ulster cousins, Glasgow's anti-Catholic agitators were spurred to action by the twin threats of Catholic immigration at home and high papal politics abroad, and they adopted similar techniques to shore up the Protestant defences. These ranged from officially sponsored protests against 'papal aggression' to groups such as the Glasgow Protestant Laymen's Association, founded in 1852 to 'combat and expose, by every legitimate means, the pretensions and claims of the Papacy, as opposed to God's truth and the civil and religious liberty of mankind'.[36] Anti-Catholic periodicals such as the *Bulwark* and *The Scottish Protestant* printed lurid descriptions of the depravity of Popery, their efforts complemented by book-length studies such as the Rev. Robert Gault's *Popery, the Man of Sin and the Son of Perdition*, a 400–page screed which, for sheer vehemence, rivalled anything published anywhere in the British Isles at this time.[37]

By mid-century aggressive anti-Catholic displays and disputations had acquired a prominent place in the city's public sphere. Alessandro Gavazzi, a former priest who lectured almost wholly in Italian, managed to pack Glasgow City Hall twice, in 1851 and 1860, with his stirring denunciations of the Papacy and praise for the Italian nationalists of the Risorgimento.[38] Glasgow Green, in the heart of the city, was probably the most famous arena of evangelical anti-Catholicism in Glasgow, providing a public platform for the controversialist lectures of men like H. A. Long, who also spread his message via cheap pamphlets exposing the fallacies of transubstantiation and predicting the imminent downfall of Rome.[39] In 1857 Hugh Hanna himself, fresh from his open-air preaching triumph in Belfast, arrived to deliver lectures on 'The Spirit and Policy of Popery' in Glasgow City Hall and the Stockwell Free Church.[40] It is unclear whether Hanna's appearance at the Stockwell Church, which stood a few streets away from the Bridgegate, helped to inspire the construction of the Rev. McColl's controversial outdoor pulpit in 1860, but it is clear that both men were acting from the same impulses.

In a number of ways, then, Glasgow appeared to have all the necessary ingredients for serious sectarian violence during these years. High levels of Irish Catholic migration, coupled with a considerable Ulster Protestant presence, created opportunities for violence either between Irish and Scots or between Catholic and Protestant Irish. The complementary economic structures of Belfast and Glasgow, which brought a regular flow of workers from one city to the other, made Glasgow vulnerable to the same occupational and economic rivalries that developed in Belfast. The recurrence of serious riots in Glasgow's immediate hinterland, often fuelled by Orange demonstrations, likewise showed that Irish migrants did not abandon their sectarian attitudes at the Scottish border. Finally, the centrality of evangelicalism and the prominence of belligerent anti-Catholicism in Glasgow seemed to offer plenty of opportunity for communal antagonists to join battle, as indeed they almost did during the Bridgegate affair of 1860–61. To determine why this constellation of forces failed to produce the same violent polarisation that emerged in Belfast, it is necessary to look a little closer at the relationships that existed among different segments of Glasgow's population.

Communal networks

Throughout this study, I have argued that some of the most powerful determinants of Belfast's patterns of violence were the communal networks that bound (or failed to bind) different sectors of the city's Protestant and Catholic populations together. On the Protestant side, the loose alliance between evangelical ministers, local state officials and the Protestant working classes created a support structure that allowed working-class Protestants to feel assured of their special place in the city. On the Catholic side, such networks tended to be weaker, since both the clergy and the lay middle classes failed to forge strong relationships with poor Catholics. Other networks – those between Catholic navvies and 'mill girls', for example, or between Protestant shipcarpenters and the operatives of Sandy Row – were also important, enabling the most violent elements on each side to act not as solitary individuals but as part of a larger community whose interests they could claim to be defending and on whose support they could rely. The situation in Glasgow was quite different. For a variety of reasons, those individuals with sectarian attitudes – and there were plenty – were unable to count upon the same degree of external support as their Belfast counterparts, and this meant that sectarian violence, when it did happen, tended to be localised and short-lived. It also meant that communal crises, such as the Bridgegate affair of 1860–61, were unlikely to escalate to the point of open violence before someone stepped in to stop it. 'Let us assume', Steve Bruce writes, 'that bigots remain bigots so long as they find satisfying outlets for, and rewards from, their bigotry, and that what we need to examine are the structures which provide, or fail to provide, opportunities for sectarian actions.'[41] Part of what accounts for the absence of serious violence in Glasgow, I want to suggest here, is precisely that its bigots remained marginalised.

To begin with the Protestants, one of the most striking differences between Belfast and Glasgow was that in Glasgow belligerent anti-Catholicism, although undoubtedly a vocal presence, was not nearly the central cultural force that it was in Belfast. Men like Robert Gault, H. A. Long and the Rev. McColl certainly caused great excitement with their 'No Popery' antics, but they received little active support from their colleagues, and in most instances they stood well outside the mainstream of their own churches. By and large, it was the evangelicalism of Thomas Chalmers – a proponent of Catholic Emancipation, a defender of congregational democracy and a vigorous advocate of 'moral reform' among the urban poor – that the Glasgow middle classes tended to emulate. When Glasgow's civic leaders did raise their voices against Popery, as during the 'papal aggression' controversy, their grievances tended to be directed against the Pope's political machinations, not individual Catholics.[42] Poor Catholics, safely hidden in their urban slums or toiling away in the factories, tended not to arouse too much passion or anxiety.

The story of Robert Gault's ill-fated Anti-Popish Mission demonstrates just how hard it was to get the Glasgow middle classes excited about aggressive anti-Catholicism. In 1856 the Ulster-born Gault persuaded the Glasgow Free Presbytery to endorse the Anti-Popish Mission that he had started in his own capacity as a Free Presbyterian minister. The Presbytery set up a committee and declared its 'unabated interest in the objects of that Mission', and over the next seven years it instructed that funds be collected in its churches to support Gault's mission.[43] This did not necessarily reflect overwhelming support for Gault's anti-Catholic crusade, however: as Bruce has observed, 'setting up a committee is often a very simple way of sidetracking an enthusiast who threatens to disrupt the organisation's routine business with his magnificent obsession'.[44] In 1860 the General Assembly of the Free Presbyterian Church declined Gault's request that it officially endorse the Anti-Popish Mission, and in 1862 the mission found itself in serious financial difficulty after several Glasgow congregations stopped sending it money. In October 1862 the Glasgow Free Presbytery cut its ties with Gault, promising to continue supporting him for three years but declaring that he and his congregation should 'become self-supporting as soon as possible'.[45] Cut off from official support, Gault's Anti-Popish Mission withered, and Gault turned his energies to supporting the Orange Order, becoming one of the few Glasgow clergymen to patronise that organisation.[46]

The chequered career of the Scottish Orange Order likewise shows how reluctant the Scottish elite were to support belligerent anti-Catholicism. Elaine McFarland has argued that the Orange Order never attained the privileged status in Scotland that it enjoyed in Ulster largely because the Scottish elite, unlike their Ulster counterparts, refused to patronise a body that they saw as unrespectable and alien. Composed mostly of Ulster Protestants, frequently associated with sectarian disorder and burdened with a reputation for drunkenness, Orangeism failed to win many adherents among the sober and upright Scottish bourgeoisie. The Scottish clergy and gentry also remained aloof, and Scottish magistrates approached the Order with what McFarland calls 'outraged and contemptuous neutrality'.[47] Native Scottish workers, though often sympathetic to anti-Catholicism in principle, also kept their distance, seeing little need for the Order's ritualised displays of Protestant superiority in a country where Catholics did not present a serious threat.[48] Ironically, much of this Scottish contempt for Orangeism was fuelled by anti-Irish prejudice. The

North British Daily Mail, commenting on an 1859 riot in Paisley, expressed the prevailing view when it declared that Orangeism had been brought to Britain 'by ignorant and bigoted Irishmen, just as any filthy distemper might be carried from one country to another . . .'.[49] The scarcity of Scottish workers within the Orange ranks only reinforced the notion that Orangeism was a fundamentally un-Scottish institution, and the legitimacy of all forms of belligerent anti-Catholicism, Orange or not, tended to suffer by association.

There were other reasons for the failure of aggressive anti-Catholicism to capture the imagination of Glaswegians. One was that Glasgow Presbyterians were far more preoccupied with their own internal rifts during this period than with waging war against the Papacy.[50] In 1843 Chalmers and his evangelical followers had split from the established Church of Scotland to form the Free Presbyterian Church, a rupture that reflected the social divisions within Scottish society (the Church of Scotland was supported by the gentry and rural poor, the Free Church represented the new middle classes and many Highlanders) and helped to create what Bruce has called a '*de facto* pluralism' in Scotland, eventually spawning many new evangelical groupings that vigorously competed with one another for followers. 'The various Presbyterian groupings were unable to attack convincingly the rights of Roman Catholics while simultaneously defending their own rights to full religious, civil, and political liberties', says Bruce.[51] This situation was strengthened by the overwhelming Liberalism of nearly all the Scottish churches, which placed a high premium on religious tolerance, something that many Belfast Protestants spoke about but which they were often unwilling to extend to the 'intolerant' Catholic Church.

There was, finally, a larger circumstance underlying the weakness of anti-Catholicism in Glasgow. This was the absence of any serious Catholic threat to Protestants or Protestantism in Scotland. In Belfast, where the old Ascendancy structures were crumbling and 'Protestant liberties' seemed to be under relentless attack from a resurgent Catholic nationalism and a conciliating Irish Executive, anti-Catholicism had a powerful resonance even among those liberal, middle-class Protestants who cared little for the histrionics of men like Hugh Hanna or Thomas Drew. The Glasgow middle classes, on the other hand, experienced no such anxieties. Safely located on the British mainland, where the overwhelming Protestantness of society could be taken for granted, and enjoying, as we shall see, a large degree of autonomy over their own local affairs, the Glasgow elite found themselves in a much more secure position than their Belfast counterparts. Individual working-class Scots may have felt threatened, at times, by competition from Irish Catholics willing to work for lower wages, but the Glasgow middle classes – and the bulk of the skilled workers also – had little reason to fear them.[52]

The difference, as I suggested above, lay in the respective elites' relationships with the imperial centre. In Belfast, the Protestant elite considered themselves to be what, in many respects, they were: an embattled settler class in a hostile land. For many Presbyterians, in particular, it was precisely their Scottish heritage that helped to define their place in Ireland. 'We have in Belfast numerous descendants of the old Covenanters', declared the *Banner of Ulster* during the Belfast open-air preaching controversy in 1857,

> – of those hardy men against whom fire and faggot were tried in vain, and whose love of the truth withstood all the demons of persecution. In the veins of these people runs a portion of the blood that once warmed the hearts of the numberless fugitives who, more than 'two hundred years ago,' peopled the hill-sides of Down, and by their industry rendered fertile the wildest vales of Antrim.[53]

In such circumstances anti-Catholicism, always a latent component of Presbyterianism, acquired an urgency that simply did not exist in Scotland itself. And as the threat of Irish Catholic self-rule grew over the years, even Belfast's Liberal Presbyterians exhibited a degree of anti-Catholicism that was not normally seen in Glasgow. 'It did not occur to Mr. Macnaughtan,' recalled the *Northern Whig* editor, Thomas MacKnight, of one of Belfast's leading Liberal Presbyterians,

> it did not occur to any of the Ulster Liberals, that the time would ever come when a policy of setting up an Irish Parliament and Executive, in which the Catholics would inevitably have an enormously preponderant power in the representation and in the administration, would be supported by many Scotch Liberals, by many Scotch Presbyterians, in defiance of the almost unanimous protests of their Presbyterian kinsmen in Ulster, whose forefathers had been induced to settle there and to carry out a work of colonisation and civilisation on the faith of the English Government.[54]

Belfast Presbyterians stood on the frontier of an empire that they had once been sent to colonise. Glasgow Presbyterians, on the other hand, were not so much the British Empire's vanguard as its architects, partners with England in a global project of which they were both the directors and the beneficiaries. So long as the fundamentals of this relationship did not change, the latent anti-Catholicism of Glasgow Presbyterianism could remain muted.

There was also a Catholic side to this equation, of course, and here, too, we find an absence of the sorts of communal networks that facilitated violence in Belfast. As was often the case in cities with high levels of Irish immigration, the Catholic Church in Glasgow initially struggled to accommodate Irish migrants. By 1835, after several decades of intensive Irish migration, there were still only four priests in the city, or one for every nine to eleven thousand Catholics, and there were just three Catholic Churches in the entire Glasgow area before 1840. During this early period the state of Catholicism in Glasgow resembled the atrophy and disarray of Belfast Catholicism under Bishop Denvir, but things began to change in the 1840s and 1850s. Although the waves of famine refugees arriving in Glasgow initially overwhelmed the city's flimsy Catholic infrastructure, they also invigorated those efforts already underway to build a stronger institutional Catholic presence. Bernard Aspinwall describes this as a period of 'devotional revolution' in Scottish Catholicism comparable to that which happened elsewhere in the Catholic world during these years. Among the first groups to arrive in Glasgow were the Sisters of Mercy, who came in 1849 to care for the destitute refugees and to set up day and Sunday schools. They were followed two years later by the Sisters of Our Lady of Charity of the Good Shepherd, who founded a home for fallen women. Men's orders came next: the Marist Brothers set up a boys' school at St Mungo's in 1858; the Jesuits began their Glasgow mission that same year; the Vincentians arrived in 1859; and the Passionists came in 1865. Lay organisations also came to Glasgow during these years, as did a tremendous number of new churches: between 1841 and 1860 fourteen new Catholic churches were built in Glasgow and its suburbs, bringing the total in the area to seventeen.[55] All this occurred while Bishop Denvir was either failing to support or actively discouraging similar initiatives in Belfast. By 1860, if the contemporary estimates of 100,000 Catholics living in Glasgow are correct, there was one church for every 5,882 Catholics in Glasgow; in Belfast, where there were just four churches, the ratio was one to 10,352.[56]

In short, what emerged in Glasgow during the post-famine years was a sizeable institutional Catholic support network designed to succour the poor, preserve their faith and insulate them from the host society.[57] It was not a completely airtight system, but it was a much larger and more visible network than anything that existed in Belfast until at least the late 1860s. It was also well attuned to the Catholic grassroots. Glasgow's growing number of priests, for instance, lived among the poor on a working man's wage of £40 a year, enjoying a degree of influence among the poor that was unmatched even by many Protestant ministers.[58] The intimacy of these connections enabled Glasgow's Catholic leadership to act as a moderating influence among working-class Catholics in a way that those in Belfast could not. Time and again, as we have seen, the Catholic clergy in Belfast had urged their people to acquiesce in the face of provocation, and time and again their pleas had either been ignored or drowned out by louder, more militant voices. In Glasgow, where priests and other Catholic leaders were thicker on the ground, working-class violence could be more easily contained.

Perhaps the best illustration of the moderating power of Glasgow's Catholic infrastructure can be seen in the St Vincent de Paul Society. Established in Glasgow in 1848, the society met a pressing need at a time of massive famine migration, becoming a sort of lay adjunct to the priesthood in many Glasgow slums. Between 1848 and 1852 members of the society distributed material and spiritual relief to some 746 people a week, and by 1858 it had fourteen conferences in Glasgow with 131 active members.[59] In addition to providing 'vital personal aid at critical times', as Aspinwall notes, the society 'prevented any significant penetration of the Catholic body by proselytism', thereby averting the need for Glasgow Catholics to resist evangelical proselytism with violence, as Belfast Catholics were sometimes wont to do.[60] A striking instance of the society's moderating influence occurred during an anti-Catholic open-air sermon in the heavily Catholic Gorbals district one Sunday in July 1851. Several priests at nearby St John's Catholic Church had urged their congregation to ignore the sermon, but they were unable to prevent some five thousand people from gathering outside the church to oppose the preacher. Acting together with the priests, several members of the Society went in among the crowd and persuaded the crowd to disperse, managing to prevent any violence apart from a few 'scuffles'.[61] In Belfast, where moderate lay leaders were few and priests even fewer, Catholic restraining mechanisms like this just did not exist.

The state

One of the reasons why sectarian extremists failed to acquire power in Glasgow, then, was that religious institutions and other communal networks allowed them little room to do so. Another, equally important reason for this marginalisation of violence was that the state's legitimacy was never really in question in Glasgow. Unlike in Belfast, there was neither any pronounced conflict between the central government and the local Glasgow elite, nor any widespread anti-state sentiment among the city's inhabitants. There were few displays of overwhelming force by state officials, and even fewer allegations that state agents were acting solely in the interests of one religious group or the other. Once again, the difference here had to do with the two cities' positions relative to the imperial centre. Because Glasgow sat in the metropole rather than on the frontier, there was no settler elite to agitate for lost or disappearing 'liberties', no ethnic underclass resentful of the chauvinism of the local elites and very little tendency on the part of the central authorities to flood this British city with overwhelming force to put down trouble. Allegiance, if not always obedience, to the law characterised the relationship between the people and the state in Glasgow, and this was reciprocated by a government that treated Glasgow not as a subordinate territory to be ruled by force but as a part of the British nation to be governed by consent.

Before I consider the state's role in Glasgow itself, a few general points must be made. First, as I noted in Chapter 4, government in Victorian Britain was a somewhat more decentralised affair than it was in Ireland. Local magistrates, town councils and other local officials had considerably more autonomy in Britain than in Ireland, where the persistent threat of disorder led the central government to intervene much more regularly in local affairs. This was especially true when it came to policing. There was no equivalent in Victorian Britain to the centrally controlled Irish Constabulary, for example, nor did the central government have much interest in directing local policing arrangements. The Home Office, which officially oversaw policing throughout Britain, preferred to leave the details (and expense) of policing to local officials, restricting itself to offering advice and, if absolutely necessary, troops to combat disorder.[62] During the many sectarian riots that broke out in mid-Victorian England, including the notorious Murphy Riots that convulsed northern England for several years, the Home Office consistently deferred to local officials in a manner that was quite unknown in Ireland.[63]

The essentially local nature of government in nineteenth-century Britain was especially evident in Scotland, although here there was an additional administrative layer in the Lord Advocate's office at Edinburgh. In a sense, the separate state structure of Scotland resembled that of Ireland: like the Irish Chief Secretary, the Lord Advocate was a political appointee, and he, in turn, was responsible for the appointment (in consultation with local elites) of Scotland's highest county officials, the Sheriffs. These Sheriffs (and their deputies) were also paid agents of the state, and in this sense their position resembled that of the Resident Magistrates in Ireland.[64] But here the resemblance between Irish and Scottish structures of government ends. For one thing, the running of Scotland was left almost wholly to these intermediary officials, with very little interference from the centre. 'So much did the Home Secretary keep out of the politics of those bodies for which he was theoretically responsible', writes Lindsay Paterson, 'that they had to remind him what they were for whenever they had occasion to make contact with him.' The same was true of Scottish legislation, which was usually debated by Scottish MPs in a separate 'sub-parliament' before being submitted to the imperial

Parliament, where Scottish members usually decided the bill's fate.[65] Aside from appointing and paying the authorities at the top rungs of Scottish government, the central government 'developed an attitude of "benign neglect" which allowed the Scots to find their own solutions to their own particular problems'.[66]

Of course, the central government could be neglectful of Ireland's internal affairs as well, but the difference was that the state had much faster recourse to coercion in Ireland than in Scotland. Because Scotland presented little threat to the security of England, and because it experienced little of that collective unrest that British officials in Ireland so frequently mistook for rebellion, the central authorities saw no need to exercise in Scotland the sort of coercive control that was institutionalised in Ireland.[67] When, for example, a magistrate in Airdrie wrote to the Home Office in the turbulent year of 1848 warning of an imminent insurrection from the area's Irish colliers, the Home Office coolly denied his request for arms, noting that 'arms are never furnished to the special constables, and never to the Police except for extraordinary occasions and when the force is properly disciplined or trained'.[68] That very year, however, the Irish Executive had armed *Orange lodges* in Dublin for the express purpose of fending off a nationalist rebellion, paying little heed to whether the Orangemen were 'properly disciplined or trained'.[69] Coercive state actions that in Scotland would have been unthinkable, even in the face of serious disorder, were an integral part of the state's repertoire in Ireland.

The most important government officials in Scotland were the Sheriffs and the Sheriffs Substitute, who, as centrally appointed and paid officials, had ultimate authority over the policing arrangements in each county. But unlike in Ireland, where local elites often challenged the power of the Resident Magistrates in their localities, Scottish Sheriffs exercised unambiguous control over their districts. Bruce speculates that the presence of these 'cosmopolitan' officials helped to override whatever sectarian attitudes may have existed among less enlightened local officials.[70] Certainly the Sheriffs and their subordinates strove to maintain a scrupulous impartiality in dealing with sectarian conflict, seeing themselves as modern, liberal men who had little time for the atavistic wrangling of poor Protestants and Catholics, whatever their nationality. This attitude was most evident in their handling of Orange processions, which they routinely prohibited despite the fact that there was no legislative ban on them in Scotland.[71] Archibald Alison, the Sheriff of Lanarkshire, was perhaps the most vigorous opponent of Orangeism at this time, and after violence attended an Orange march in Airdrie in 1848 he issued a blanket prohibition on all Orange marches in the county that lasted into the 1860s.[72] In

Ulster, as we have seen, the state's ban on party processions was met by howls of protest not only from Orange marchers but also from their patrons among the rural and urban elite. In Scotland, Alison's actions, which were emulated by other lowland Sheriffs, encountered very little opposition.[73]

Turning now from Scotland generally to Glasgow in particular, one is initially struck by the similarities between local government there and in Belfast. Like the Belfast Town Council, the Glasgow City Council was dominated by Protestants who allied themselves closely with the city's various evangelical groups.[74] There was not a single Catholic magistrate in Glasgow before 1903, and when the first Irishman was elected to the Glasgow City Council in 1893, he was not a Catholic but the Protestant radical John Ferguson.[75] Their lack of local representation was something of which Glasgow's Catholics were not unaware. 'You are not represented in the Parliament of the empire,' the Catholic *Glasgow Free Press* reminded its readers in 1857, 'nor on the bench of this city; nor in any of the Public Boards, or Institutions, of Glasgow. You have not a Catholic magistrate, nor a Catholic Town Councillor, nor a Catholic Manager of the Poor, among the hundred thousand of your body in the city Parish.'[76] This situation would remain largely unchanged for most of the nineteenth century, and it meant that, in a formal sense, Catholic political power-lessness was even greater in Glasgow than in Belfast.

There was one significant difference between local government in Glasgow and Belfast, however. Whereas Belfast was dominated by a tight-knit Tory–Protestant clique, mid-Victorian Glasgow was a thoroughly Liberal city.[77] This was true not just of the City Council, but of the polit-ical culture of Glasgow generally, which shared with the rest of Scotland a widespread belief in 'free trade, free speech and religious rectitude' of such intensity that Liberalism was 'as much a national crusade as a matter of politics'.[78] Between 1832 and 1874, every single MP elected for Glasgow was a Liberal; the Tories, especially after the 1846 repeal of the Corn Laws, were 'an impotent rump' here even longer than they were in England.[79] Indeed, during the middle of the century the Glasgow Tories were far weaker than the Belfast Liberals, and Glasgow's electoral contests, like those in the rest of Scotland, were frequently fought not between Liberals and Tories but between different segments of the Liberal party, principally along lines laid down by the 1843 split in the Church of Scotland. The different churches' positions on issues like state educa-tion and temperance reform, along with the differing approaches to political and social reforms advocated by various branches of the Liberal party, formed the political fault lines in mid-Victorian Glasgow.[80] More-over, later in the century Protestants and Catholics frequently made common cause on issues such as labour reform and Irish Home Rule, and it was partly on the strength of such non-sectarian alliances that Glasgow developed one of the most vigorous labour movements in the United Kingdom at the turn of the century.[81] Again, the contrast with Belfast is stark.

We might attribute the different political climate in Glasgow once again to the absence of any significant threat to 'Protestant liberties' here. As the experience of Belfast suggests, Liberalism and anti-Catholicism were by no means incompatible, but because the essential Protestantness of Glasgow society was more or less assured, the eternal struggle between Protestantism and Catholicism assumed a much less prominent role in Glasgow's political discourse than it did in Belfast's. This difference was particularly evident in the electoral politics of both cities, as the example of the 1857 general election illustrates. In that year Belfast's two Parliamentary seats were contested by two Tories and three Liberals. Both of the Tory candidates explicitly pledged themselves to defending Protestantism; the Orange Order made its familiar appeal for Protestant electors to vote for those candidates who would resist 'Romanism'; and the Liberal vote was split between the two pro-Catholic Liberals and the anti-Catholic one, who had secured the endorsement of Hugh Hanna, among others.[82] In Glasgow, three Liberals ran for the city's two seats. The only explicit references to Protestantism on the hustings had to do with internal differences between Presbyterians, principally regarding the issue of denominational education, and 'Protestant liberties' were generally left to look after themselves as candidates talked about extending the franchise and undertaking social reforms.[83] It was a matter of no little significance that the election in Belfast, like elections there for so much of the century, was marked by fierce rioting among the partisans of the Tories and the pro- and anti-Catholic Liberals, riots that included attacks on clergymen's homes, churches and other religious institutions.[84] In Glasgow, by contrast, election day was so peaceful that Sheriff Alison felt moved to congratulate the candidates in particular, and the city in general, 'for the very orderly manner in which this contest has been conducted'.[85]

One important by-product of Glasgow's relatively tranquil politics was that policing was a much less contentious issue here than in Belfast. In Belfast, working-class alienation from the police – whether the local police or the Irish Constabulary – stemmed from a deeper distrust of the government bodies that controlled them, and it was this alienation that fed working-class vigilantism on both sides. The situation was different in Glasgow for a number of reasons. First, there was only one police force in Glasgow to command the inhabitants' allegiance. Established in 1800, the Glasgow police force was among the first professional forces in the country, and, although it was sometimes assisted by the military and special constables during periods of unrest, it generally remained the sole peace-keeping force in the city.[86] Second, the Glasgow force appears to have been open to more segments of the population than was the Belfast force. During a five-and-a-half month period in 1847, for example, it admitted eighty-six Irish recruits alongside seventy-nine Scots and eight Englishmen.[87] It is unclear whether any of these Irishmen were Catholics, but, given the widespread presence of Irish Catholics in police forces throughout Britain and the United States at the time, this seems likely.

A third reason for the lack of substantial working-class alienation from the police was the determinedly impartial attitude of high-ranking law enforcement officials in Glasgow. On the one hand, as both James Handley and Tom Gallagher have argued for Scotland generally, it seems likely that individual policemen sometimes acted in an anti-Catholic manner; indeed, it would be remarkable if, given the working-class backgrounds of policemen, they failed to share the prejudices common to others of their class.[88] On the other hand, as Bruce suggests, the isolated newspaper reports cited by Gallagher and Handley as evidence of police anti-Catholicism do not necessarily indicate a widespread trend, and the local elite's overwhelming desire for order undoubtedly discouraged anti-Catholic activities by individual policemen.[89] Certainly, as the Bridgegate affair and other near-misses indicate, law enforcement officials in Glasgow were just as eager to curtail provocative sectarian displays as were officials in the countryside. A typical instance occurred in 1867, when a planned Fenian procession in Glasgow threatened to provoke an Orange counterdemonstration. Although Orange processions had often been prohibited in the past, the legality of banning a Fenian procession that did not in itself constitute a threat to the peace troubled Glasgow officials, and so the Lord Advocate wrote to the Home Office for advice.[90] The reply was typically diffident. After noting that 'A very large discretion is ... always left in the hands of the local Authorities' and insisting that the Home Secretary 'does not take upon himself in any way to limit such discretion or to prescribe any absolute course of action', the Home Office suggested that the Fenian procession might be prohibited if that was the only way to prevent a breach of the peace.[91] Glasgow officials accordingly banned the procession, and neither the Fenians nor the Orangemen took to the streets that day.[92]

I do not wish to suggest here that working-class Glaswegians demurely accepted the authority of policemen in their neighbourhoods. Like working-class people everywhere, they undoubtedly resented the policemen's interference with their 'rowdy' street culture, and there is some reason to suspect that the Glasgow police were more interventionist than most.[93] The point is simply that working-class hostility to the police had little political or religious basis; no single group felt persecuted or unprotected because of their religious identity. Had riots been more common in Glasgow – had Glasgow's Catholics, for instance, had more opportunities to observe police behaviour and to infer anti-Catholic prejudice in their actions – then alienation similar to that which prevailed in Belfast might have emerged. But riots were uncommon in Glasgow, in part, precisely because there was little disagreement as to the legitimacy of the state among Protestants and Catholics.

Communal polarisation

One lesson that emerges from the study of communal rioting in Belfast is that violence itself is a polarising phenomenon. During and after Belfast's riots, mutual recriminations multiplied as previously submerged communal tensions burst to the surface. Working-class denunciations of the police became louder, conflict among co-workers became more intense, residential boundaries hardened, and many people who had taken no part in the originating conflict began, wittingly or not, to take sides. In Glasgow, however, the relative absence of violence meant that polarisation of this sort was rare. At first glance, this appears to raise the question of the chicken and the egg: was communal polarisation weak in Glasgow because riots did not happen, or did riots fail to happen because polarisation was weak? Violence and polarisation are self-reinforcing phenomena, of course, and we might define their relationship by suggesting that violence helps to solidify what would otherwise remain fluid and uneven sectarian tendencies – like heat applied to wet clay. If Catholics in Belfast tended to settle near each other before a riot, for example, then after a riot the 'Catholic' identity of their neighbourhood became even stronger, as outsiders were expelled, neutral non-combatants gravitated towards their more militant neighbours and boundaries between the 'Catholic' streets and the 'Protestant' streets became more strictly enforced.[94] In Glasgow, where such violence was rare, we would expect communal boundaries to be much more fluid.

A glance at Glasgow's residential patterns confirms this point. Although Irish Catholics, like Irish immigrants everywhere, tended to cluster together in the city's poorer neighbourhoods, these neighbourhoods were never monolithically Catholic. Writing of the Bridgegate area in 1851, the Rev. Robert Buchanan of Tron Church observed, 'though the Wynds may be said to be the headquarters of Irish Popery in this city, the population is scarcely more than one-half Popish after all'.[95] From their earliest enclaves in the old city centre, Irish immigrants spread steadily outwards in all directions, and by the 1880s Irish-born people were living all over the city: 30% of them in the east end of Glasgow, 20% along the city's north-south axis, and the other 50% scattered throughout the remainder.[96] In some places, such as the shipbuilding areas west of the city, Irish Protestants and Catholics do appear to have reproduced the patterns of residential segregation with which they had been familiar in Ulster, and, especially in the later decades of the century, some localised skirmishes did take place when one side attempted to transgress the other's territory.[97] In general, however, the trend was towards residential integration; there were no Irish or Irish-Catholic ghettoes in Glasgow of the sort that existed in Belfast, Liverpool or Manchester.[98]

Evidence of workplace segregation in Glasgow is less well documented, but it seems that the general trend was the same. In their study of Glasgow in the late 1880s, John Foster, Muir Houston and Chris Madigan find that Glasgow's labour market was much more fluid than Belfast's, where discrimination was 'sectoral' and Catholics 'were excluded from whole industries'. Unlike those in Belfast, Catholic shipyard workers in Glasgow were able to advance to skilled positions partly because the labour market was larger and more diverse, and partly because the Orange Order was relatively weak as a mechanism of exclusion.[99] Whether Glasgow Protestants attempted, like Belfast Protestants, to prevent employers from hiring unskilled Catholics in textile mills and factories is unknown, but here again the weakness of the Orange Order and the absence of any rioting that might have exacerbated sectarian tensions suggests that this was unlikely.

The extent of intercommunal cooperation in Glasgow between Protestants and Catholics at the level of social organisation, political mobilisation and everyday interactions is something that requires considerably more research, but here, too, the overall picture of substantial communal integration appears the same.[100] Certainly, as Martin Mitchell has shown for the early nineteenth century, and as Joan Smith's study of Glasgow's 'Labour tradition' in the late nineteenth century suggests, Irish Catholics were heavily involved in working-class political movements in Glasgow and the west of Scotland generally.[101] The absence of residential segregation in Glasgow suggests, furthermore, that everyday interaction between working-class Protestants and Catholics was more common there than in Belfast, where periodic purges of 'outsiders' from neighbourhoods and workplaces prevented normal social contact across the religious divide.

One final difference between the two cities may be noted, even if it is entirely unmeasurable. Communal memories of violence, which in Belfast formed an integral part of Protestants' and Catholics' emerging identities, were almost entirely absent in Glasgow. The innumerable stories of violence, the grudges and the settling of scores, the landmarks and commemorations and re-enactments of violence that became such a vital part of Belfast's working-class cultures did not exist in Glasgow, unless they were carried there by Ulster immigrants themselves. When Ulster immigrants did try to carry on the traditions of violence with which they were familiar, moreover, their energies quickly dissipated amid the very different cultural forces at work in Glasgow. The next chapter will explore the persistence of Belfast's own traditions of violence over the course of several decades; in Glasgow, such traditions never had a chance to emerge.

Conclusion

Perhaps the worst of Glasgow's communal disturbances occurred in the summer of 1875. Two Irish nationalist demonstrations – one sponsored by the clergy, one by a more radical group of Fenian sympathisers – had taken place in Glasgow to commemorate the centenary of Daniel O'Connell's birth. On their return to the shipbuilding district of Partick, a group of Catholics came under attack from the Orangemen who lived in the area. Several days of rioting ensued before the authorities managed to restore calm. At one point, in a move 'significant of the relationship which the Order imagined it could and should have with the authorities', the Orangemen asked to be appointed special constables to help put down the disturbances, but the authorities graciously declined.[102] As the rioting continued, a thousand armed Catholics set out from Maryhill to avenge the rumoured death of a Catholic in Partick. Before they could reach the scene of battle, however, a priest intercepted the crowd and, warning them of the dire consequences for their souls if they joined in the riots, persuaded them to turn back. There was, in fact, no dead Catholic to be avenged, for no one was killed during the entire 'extended weekend' of rioting.[103]

This chapter has sought to understand the emergence of communal violence in mid-Victorian Belfast by looking at the parallel, but largely tranquil, experience of Glasgow. As the 1875 O'Connell riots indicate, Glasgow was not without its sectarian tensions, but even when these tensions exploded into open violence the fighting failed to attain the massive proportions of a Belfast riot. Important restraining mechanisms, exemplified here by the Maryhill priest and the local government's refusal to countenance sectarian activities, were present in Glasgow that were missing in Belfast. In the absence of any significant external support for sectarian violence and of a broad alienation from the state on the part of ordinary Protestants and Catholics, the extremists on both sides failed to gain that hegemony in Glasgow that their counterparts enjoyed in Belfast. Part of the reason for this difference, as we have seen, had to do with each city's relationship to the British government: Glasgow Protestants were not an embattled settler minority in a frontier society, and Glasgow Catholics were not a resurgent people determined to reclaim their rights to equal protection under the law. The state, moreover, was not fractured in Glasgow between a chauvinist local elite and a coercive central government. Those imperial structures of domination and belief that created so much tension in Belfast found very little purchase in the Scottish metropolis.

Notes

1 The Bridgegate had been associated with Irish Catholics since at least the 1830s. See William Sloan, 'Religious Affiliation and the Immigrant Experience: Catholic Irish and Protestant Highlanders in Glasgow, 1830–1850', in *Irish Immigrants and Scottish Society in the Nineteenth and Twentieth Centuries: Proceedings of the Scottish Historical Studies Seminar, University of Strathclyde, 1989–90*, ed. T. M. Devine (Edinburgh: John Donald, 1991), 72–3.

2 Archibald Alison, *Some Account of My Life and Writings*, (Edinburgh: William Blackwood and Sons, 1883), vol. 2, 292–4.

3 *Ibid.*, 295–6.

4 *Ibid.*, 311.

5 *Glasgow Daily Herald*, 6 June 1861.

6 Alison, *Some Account*, vol. 2, 312–13.

7 Ashutosh Varshney, *Ethnic Conflict and Civic Life: Hindus and Muslims in India* (New Haven: Yale University Press, 2002), 5–6.

8 Tom Gallagher, *Glasgow, The Uneasy Peace: Religious Tension in Modern Scotland, 1819–1914* (Manchester: Manchester University Press, 1987), 3.

9 Contemporary scholars of communal violence have recognised the value of comparing Protestant–Catholic relations in Ulster and Scotland, but for the most part their analyses have concentrated on the twentieth century. See Graham Walker, *Intimate Strangers: Political and Cultural Interaction between Scotland and Ulster in Modern Times* (Edinburgh: John Donald, 1995); and Steve Bruce, *No Pope of Rome: Anticatholicism in Modern Scotland* (Edinburgh: Mainstream Publishing, 1985). The one sustained comparison of Belfast and Glasgow is also weighted towards the twentieth century: Ian Budge and Cornelius O'Leary, *Belfast: Approach to Crisis* (London: Macmillan, 1973).

10 James Edmund Handley, *The Irish in Scotland, 1798–1845* (Cork: Cork University Press, 1945), 23–30.

11 Budge and O'Leary, *Belfast*, 33; Sybil Baker, 'Orange and Green: Belfast, 1832–1912', in *The Victorian City: Images and Realities*, ed. H. J. Dyos

and M. Wolff (London: Routledge & Kegan Paul, 1973), vol. 2, 793; Fred Heatley, 'Community Relations and the Religious Geography, 1800–86', in *Belfast: The Making of the City, 1800–1914*, ed. J. C. Beckett et al. (Belfast: Appletree Press, 1983), 129–42.

12 Brenda Collins, 'The Origins of Irish Immigration to Scotland in the Nineteenth and Twentieth Centuries', in *Irish Immigrants and Scottish Society in the Nineteenth and Twentieth Centuries: Proceedings of the Scottish Historical Studies Seminar, University of Strathclyde, 1989–90*, ed. T. M. Devine (Edinburgh: John Donald, 1991), 1–18; Bernard Aspinwall, 'A Long Journey: The Irish in Scotland', in *The Irish World Wide: History, Heritage, Identity*, vol. 5, *Religion and Identity*, ed. Patrick O'Sullivan (London: Leicester University Press, 1996), 155; Martin Mitchell, *The Irish in the West of Scotland 1797–1848: Trade Unions, Strikes, and Political Movements* (Edinburgh: John Donald, 1998), 23–5.

13 Graham Walker, 'The Protestant Irish in Scotland', in *Irish Immigrants*, ed. Devine, 49–50; E. W. McFarland, *Protestants First: Orangeism in Nineteenth Century Scotland* (Edinburgh: Edinburgh University Press, 1990), 104.

14 In 1857, Glasgow's city chamberlain, John Strang, estimated that there were 105,691 Catholics in the Glasgow area, or roughly a quarter of the city's population. See James Edmund Handley, *The Irish in Modern Scotland* (Cork: Cork University Press, 1947), 46. Strang's figures are not entirely accurate, however (the 1861 census, for instance, showed that Glasgow had a total population of 395,503, not the 403,142 that Strang had estimated in 1857). More recently, the historian John McCaffrey, using parish registers from 1883 to 1887, has estimated the total number of Catholics within the Glasgow boundaries during this later period at 70,000, or 14% of the city's 1881 total, although he admits this may be an underestimate. John McCaffrey, 'The Irish Vote in Glasgow in the Later Nineteenth Century: A Preliminary Survey', *Innes Review*, 21 (1970), 30–1.

15 See e.g. the Catholic *Glasgow Free Press*, 6 June and 24 Oct. 1857.

16 Gallagher, *Glasgow*, 14; Mitchell, *Irish*, passim; Irene Maver, *Glasgow* (Edinburgh: Edinburgh University Press, 2000), 37–58.

17 Joan Smith, 'Labour Tradition in Glasgow and Liverpool', *History Workshop*, 17 (Spring 1984), 48; Maver, *Glasgow*, 84.

18 John Foster, Muir Houston and Chris Madigan, 'Distinguishing Catholics and Protestants among Irish Immigrants to Clydeside: A New Approach to Immigration and Ethnicity in Victorian Britain', *Irish Studies Review*, 10 (Aug. 2002), 171–92. This study challenges earlier historians' assumptions that Irish Protestants enjoyed greater social mobility than Catholics by examining surnames and census rolls in order to identify the religion of Irish immigrants in late nineteenth-century Glasgow. Its conclusions, therefore, apply to a later period than the one I am considering, but the trends it identifies were in all probability present in the earlier period as well.

19 McFarland, *Protestants First*, 47–69.

20 Very little research has been done into the reaction of unskilled Scots to

Irish immigrants in the post-famine period, but most historians detect a generalised anti-Irish/anti-Catholic sentiment among Scottish workers at this time. See e.g. Bruce, *No Pope*, 24–5; Gallagher, *Glasgow*, 10; Handley, *Irish in Modern Scotland*, 93–121; and McFarland, *Protestants First*, 97–100. See also the literature on Liverpool, esp. Frank Neal, *Sectarian Violence: The Liverpool Experience, 1819–1914* (Manchester: Manchester University Press, 1988); and P. J. Waller, *Democracy and Sectarianism: A Political and Social History of Liverpool, 1868–1939* (Liverpool: Liverpool University Press, 1981).

21 R. A. Cage, 'Population and Employment Characteristics', in *The Working Class in Glasgow, 1750–1914*, ed. R. A. Cage (London: Croom Helm, 1987), 25; John Butt, 'Belfast and Glasgow: Connections and Comparisons, 1790–1850', in *Ireland and Scotland, 1600–1850*, ed. T. M. Devine and David Dickson (Edinburgh: John Donald, 1983), 198–201. On the economic history of Glasgow during this period, see John Butt, 'The Industries of Glasgow', in *Glasgow: 1830 to 1912*, ed. W. Hamish Fraser and Irene Maver (Manchester: Manchester University Press, 1996), 96–140; and Maver, *Glasgow*, 37–58. On the similarities between the two cities' economies in the early twentieth century, see A. C. Hepburn, *A Past Apart: Studies in the History of Catholic Belfast, 1850–1950* (Belfast: Ulster Historical Foundation, 1996), 205–7.

22 *Banner of Ulster*, 19 Nov. and 3 Dec. 1857.

23 Thomas MacKnight, *Ulster as it Is: or, Twenty-eight Years' Experience as an Irish Editor* (London: Macmillan and Co., 1896), vol. 1, 62–3.

24 Michael Moss and John R. Hume, *Shipbuilders to the World: 125 Years of Harland and Wolff, Belfast, 1861–1986* (Belfast: Blackstaff Press, 1986), 15–16.

25 Foster et al., 'Distinguishing', 175–6.

26 I. G. C. Hutchison, *A Political History of Scotland: 1832–1924* (Edinburgh: John Donald, 1986), 123–4. See also Foster, 'Distinguishing', 179.

27 Tony Clarke and Tony Dickson, 'Class and Class Consciousness in Early Industrial Capitalism: Paisley, 1770–1850', in *Capital and Class in Scotland*, ed. Tony Dickson (Edinburgh: John Donald, 1982), 24–5; R. D. Lobban, 'The Irish Community in Greenock in the Nineteenth Century', *Irish Geography*, 6 (1971), 270–81; Alan B. Campbell, *The Lanarkshire Miners: A Social History of their Trade Unions, 1775–1974* (Edinburgh: John Donald, 1979), 180.

28 In 1850, for example, Scottish workers in the town of Dumfermline, near Edinburgh, forced Irish colliers and weavers from their homes for driving down wages. NAS, Lord Advocate's Papers, AD58/75. See also Campbell, *Lanarkshire*, 181–2.

29 Elaine McFarland, 'Marching from the Margins: Twelfth of July Parades in Scotland, 1820–1914', in *The Irish Parading Tradition: Following the Drum*, ed. T. G. Fraser (New York: St Martin's Press, 2000), 62–5; Lobban, 'Irish', 277–8; Gallagher, *Glasgow*, 20; Campbell, *Lanarkshire*, 185–91.

30 MacCallum to Home Office, 7 Aug. 1848, NAS, Lord Advocate's Papers, AD58/68/1.

31 Campbell, *Lanarkshire*, Appendix III, 316–19.

32 *North British Daily Mail*, 5 Aug. 1854; NAS, Lord Advocate's Papers, AD14/54/272–273.

33 Archibald Alison to Lord Advocate, 16 July 1857, NAS, Lord Advocate's Papers, AD56/309/3; *Glasgow Free Press*, 25 July and 10 Oct. 1857.

34 See e.g. Ian McBride, 'The School of Virtue: Francis Hutcheson, Irish Presbyterians and the Scottish Enlightenment', in *Political Thought in Ireland since the Seventeenth Century*, ed. D. George Boyce, Robert Ecclehall and Vincent Geoghegan (London: Routledge, 1993), 89.

35 Stewart J. Brown, 'Chalmers, Thomas (1780–1847)', *Oxford Dictionary of National Biography* (Oxford: Oxford University Press, 2004); Laurance James Saunders, *Scottish Democracy, 1815–1840* (Edinburgh: Oliver and Boyd, 1950), 208–21; Callum G. Brown, *The Social History of Religion in Scotland since 1730* (London: Methuen, 1987), 17; *Annual Report of the Glasgow Young Men's Christian Association, Year 1861–1862* (Glasgow: James Cameron, 1862); *The Forty-first Annual Report of the Glasgow University Missionary Association. April, 1862* (Glasgow: James MacNab, 1863).

36 *Ninth Annual Report of the Glasgow Protestant Laymen's Association* (Glasgow: Thomas Smith, 1862).

37 Robert Gault, *Popery, the Man of Sin and the Son of Perdition* (Glasgow: W. R. McPhun, 1853). On anti-Catholic periodicals in Scotland, see Handley, *Irish in Modern Scotland*, 99–111.

38 Handley, *Irish in Modern Scotland*, 97–99. Gavazzi was also a perennial favourite in Belfast. See *The Orations of Father Gavazzi, delivered in Belfast on the 3rd, 4th, and 5th November, 1852* (Belfast: William McComb, 1852); *Belfast Weekly Mail*, 12 May 1854; *The Presbyterian Magazine*, 1/4 (Apr. 1859), 94; and *Belfast Newsletter*, 8 Sept. 1862.

39 H. A. Long, *Transubstantiation: Being the substance of what was advanced thereupon, in the late discussions, when disputing with the Roman Catholics on Glasgow Green, on certain evenings immediately after the fair of 1864* (Glasgow: Wm. Macrone, 1864); H. A. Long, *Mene: The Numeration of Babylon Mystical. A Tract for the Times, on the Coming Fall of the Papacy* (Glasgow: William Macrone, 1865).

40 *Banner of Ulster*, 17 and 24 Nov., 1 Dec. 1857.

41 Steve Bruce, 'Comparing Scotland and Northern Ireland', in *Scotland's Shame? Bigotry and Sectarianism in Modern Scotland*, ed. Tom Devine (Edinburgh: Mainstream Publishing Company, 2000), 135.

42 See e.g. the report of the Glasgow anti-papal meeting in the *North British Daily Mail*, 20 Mar. 1851.

43 Minutes of Glasgow Free Presbytery, 1856–63, ML, Glasgow City Archives, CH3/146/36.

44 Bruce, *No Pope*, 34.

45 Minutes of Glasgow Free Presbytery, 1856–63, ML, Glasgow City

Archives, CH3/146/36. For a discussion of the Scottish anti-Catholic agitators James Begg and John Hope, whose 'magnificent obsessions' likewise met with official indifference, see Bruce, *No Pope*, 31–9.

46 McFarland, *Protestants First*, 123; Gallagher, *Glasgow*, 27.
47 McFarland, *Protestants First*, 52.
48 *Ibid.*, 86–88, 111; Smith, 'Labour Tradition', 47–8.
49 *North British Daily Mail*, 14 July 1859. Similar passages from the Scottish press are quoted in McFarland, *Protestants First*, 52, 107–11.
50 Gallagher, *Glasgow*, 34.
51 Steve Bruce, 'Protestantism and Politics in Scotland and Ulster', in *Prophetic Religions and Politics: Religion and the Political Order*, ed. Jeffrey K. Haddon and Ason Shupe (New York: Paragon House, 1986), 416.
52 Bruce, *No Pope*, 149; Bruce, 'Protestantism', 420–2.
53 *Banner of Ulster*, 8 Sept. 1857.
54 MacKnight, *Ulster As It Is*, vol. 1, 40–1.
55 Bernard Aspinwall, 'The Formation of the Catholic Community in the West of Scotland: Some Preliminary Outlines', *Innes Review*, 33 (1982), 46–51; Sloan, 'Religious Affiliation', 69–70; Aspinwall, 'Long Journey', 155 and 159; Bernard Aspinwall, 'The Welfare State Within the State: The Saint Vincent de Paul Society in Glasgow, 1848–1920', in *Voluntary Religion: Papers Read at the 1985 Summer Meeting and the 1986 Winter Meeting of the Ecclesiastical History Society*, ed. W. J. Shiels and Diana Wood (Oxford: Basil Blackwell, 1986), 456.
56 The Catholic population of Belfast in 1861 was 41,406.
57 W. M. Walker, 'Irish Immigrants in Scotland: Their Priests, Politics and Parochial Life', *The Historical Journal*, 15 (1972), 649–67; Bernard Aspinwall, 'The Catholic Irish and Wealth in Glasgow', in *Irish Immigrants*, ed. Devine, 91–115; Gallagher, *Glasgow*, 18.
58 Andrew L. Drummond and James Bulloch, *The Church in Victorian Scotland, 1843–74* (Edinburgh: Saint Andrew Press, 1975), 74.
59 Aspinwall, 'Welfare State', 446.
60 *Ibid.*, 447–8.
61 *Glasgow Free Press*, 2 Aug. 1851.
62 R. Quinault, 'The Warwickshire County Magistracy and Public Order, c.1830–1870', in *Popular Protest and Public Order: Six Studies in British History, 1790–1920*, ed. R. Quinault and J. Stevenson (London: George Allen & Unwin Ltd., 1974), 181–214.
63 On the Murphy riots, see Walter L. Arnstein, 'The Murphy Riots: A Victorian Dilemma', *Victorian Studies*, 19 (Sept. 1975), 51–70; Donald Richter, *Riotous Victorians* (Athens, O.: Ohio University Press, 1981), 35–49; and Donald M. MacRaild, *Culture, Conflict and Migration: The Irish in Victorian Cumbria* (Liverpool: Liverpool University Press, 1998), 177–83. On policing riots in Liverpool, see Anne Bryson, 'Riotous Liverpool, 1815–1860', in *Popular Politics, Riot, and Labour*, ed. John Belchem (Liverpool: Liverpool University Press, 1992), 98–134. See also the following Home Office reports at the NAGB: HO45/3140 (Birkenhead riot, 1850),

HO45/3472M (Liverpool Orange procession, 1851), HO45/4085F (Liverpool Orange procession, 1852), HO45/5128Y (Walshall anti-Catholic lecture, 1853, and Murphy Riots) and HO45/7326 (Birkenhead riot, 1862).

64 Ann E. Whetstone, *Scottish County Government in the Eighteenth and Nineteenth Centuries* (Edinburgh: John Donald, 1981), 22–5.

65 Lindsay Paterson, *The Autonomy of Modern Scotland* (Edinburgh: Edinburgh University Press, 1994), 49.

66 Whetstone, *County Government*, p. x. See also Paterson, *Autonomy*, 48.

67 Paterson, *Autonomy*, 50; T. M. Devine, 'Unrest and Stability in Rural Ireland and Scotland, 1760–1840', in *Economy and Society in Scotland and Ireland, 1500–1939*, ed. Rosalind Mitchison and Peter Roebuck (Edinburgh: John Donald, 1988), 126–39.

68 NAS, Lord Advocate's Papers, AD58/68/1–4.

69 See Frank Wright, 'Protestant Ideology and Politics in Ulster', *European Journal of Sociology*, 14 (1973), 252; Hereward Senior, 'The Early Orange Order 1795–1870', in *Secret Societies in Ireland,* ed. T. Desmond Williams (New York: Barnes and Noble, 1973), 44; and Frank Wright, *Two Lands on One Soil: Ulster Politics before Home Rule* (Dublin: Gill & Macmillan, 1996), 153.

70 Steve Bruce, Tony Glendinning, Iain Paterson and Michael Rosie, *Sectarianism in Scotland* (Edinburgh: Edinburgh University Press, 2004), 24; Whetstone, *County Government*, 27–60, 95–115.

71 McFarland, 'Marching', 64, and *Protestants First*, 54–5.

72 Alison, *Some Account,* vol. 1, 606–8; *Glasgow Daily Herald*, 6 June 1861.

73 For similar bans on Orange processions in Ayrshire, see NAS, Lord Advocate's Papers, AD58/70 and AD56/309/3. In Renfrewshire, authorities failed to prohibit an Orange procession in 1859, and the Paisley area consequently saw serious rioting. After that, Orange processions were prohibited here as well. See *North British Daily Mail*, 13 and 14 July 1859; 13 July 1860; 14 July 1862.

74 C. Brown, *Social History*, 132; Paterson, *Autonomy*, 56–9; Geoffrey Best, 'The Scottish Victorian City', *Victorian Studies*, 11 (Mar. 1968), 340–1; Maver, *Glasgow*, 89–92.

75 I. G. C. Hutchison, 'Glasgow Working-Class Politics', in *Working Class in Glasgow*, ed. Cage, 130–1; Elaine McFarland, *John Ferguson, 1836–1906: Irish Issues in Scottish Politics* (East Linton, East Lothian, Scotland: Tuckwell Press, 2003), 245–9.

76 *Glasgow Free Press*, 6 June 1857.

77 Maver, *Glasgow*, 78–80, 143–8.

78 Paterson, *Autonomy*, 48.

79 Hutchison, *Political History*, 84.

80 *Ibid.*, 59–102; Irene Maver, 'Glasgow's Civic Government', in *Glasgow: 1830 to 1912*, ed. W. Hamish Fraser and Irene Maver (Manchester: Manchester University Press, 1996), 441–85.

81 Smith, 'Labour Tradition', 47. On the significant support among some Glasgow Protestants for Irish Home Rule, see McFarland, *Ferguson*, esp.

49–66; Maver, *Glasgow*, 145–6, 153; and MacKnight, *Ulster as it Is*, vol. 1, 40–1.

82 *Ulsterman*, 25 Mar. 1857; *Banner of Ulster*, 2 and 4 Apr. 1857; *Belfast Newsletter*, 31 Mar. 1857.

83 *North British Daily Mail*, 31 Mar. 1857; Hutchison, *Political History*, 80–3.

84 *Belfast Daily Mercury*, 3, 4 and 6 Apr. 1857.

85 *North British Daily Mail*, 2 Apr. 1857. The absence of violence on this occasion was typical of elections in nineteenth-century Scotland generally. See Hutchison, *Political History*, passim; W. Ferguson, 'The Reform Act (Scotland) of 1832: Intention and Effect', *Scottish Historical Review*, 45 (Apr. 1966), 105–14; Michael Dyer, '"Mere Detail and Machinery": The Great Reform Act and the Effects of Redistribution on Scottish Representation, 1832–1868', *Scottish Historical Review*, 72 (Apr. 1983), 17–34.

86 Douglas Grant, *The Thin Blue Line: The Story of the City of Glasgow Police* (London: John Long, 1973), 15, 30–5.

87 Grant, *Thin*, 29. It is also worth noting, in relation to the number of men in each force, that the ratios of policemen to inhabitants in both cities were roughly the same. In 1864, Belfast had one policeman for every 590 inhabitants, while Glasgow had one for every 530. *Report of the Commissioners of Inquiry, 1864, respecting the Magisterial and Police Jurisdiction Arrangements and Establishment of the Borough of Belfast* HC 1865 (3466) XXVIII, Appendix 26, 357.

88 Handley, *Irish in Modern Scotland*, 117; Tom Gallagher, 'The Catholic Irish in Scotland: In Search of Identity', in *Irish Immigrants*, ed. Devine, 23.

89 Bruce et al., *Sectarianism*, 20–4.

90 Draft letter from Lord Advocate to Home Office, 11 Dec. 1867, NAS, Lord Advocate's Papers, AD56/309/1.

91 Home Office to Lord Advocate, 12 Dec. 1867, NAS, Lord Advocate's Papers, AD56/309/1.

92 *North British Daily Mail*, 16 Dec. 1867.

93 Grant, *Thin*, 37–9.

94 Hepburn, *Past Apart*, 121–2.

95 Quoted in Handley, *Irish in Scotland*, 248.

96 John McCaffrey, 'Political Reactions in the Glasgow Constituencies at the General Elections of 1885 and 1886', unpublished Ph.D. thesis, University of Glasgow, 1970, 9–10. For a comparison of both cities' residential patterns in the Edwardian period, see Hepburn, *Past Apart*, 207–8.

97 Foster et al., 'Distinguishing', 182–3; McFarland, 'Marching', 70.

98 Smith, 'Labour Tradition', 49; Maver, *Glasgow*, 84; M. A. Busteed and R. I. Hodgson, 'Irish Migrant Responses to Urban Life in Early Nineteenth-Century Manchester', *The Geographical Journal*, 162 (July 1996), 139–53; and Gallagher, *Glasgow*, 37. Although Gallagher does periodically use the term 'ghetto' to describe the Catholics in Glasgow, he does so primarily to point out the rigour with which the clergy sought to limit interactions between Catholics and the rest of society, not to indicate strict residential segregation.

99 Foster et al., 'Distinguishing', 186.
100 For Varshney, this is the most important category of analysis one might employ in comparing peaceful places with violent ones. See Varshney, *Ethnic Conflict*, 9–18.
101 Mitchell, *Irish*, 11–12; Smith, 'Labour Tradition'.
102 Ian Wood, 'Irish Immigrants and Scottish Radicalism, 1880–1906', in *Essays in Scottish Labour History*, ed. Ian MacDougall (Edinburgh: John Donald, 1978), 69.
103 *Ibid.* See also Handley, *Irish in Modern Scotland*, 117–18; and McFarland, *Protestants First*, 178–9.

8

Memories of violence, 1864–86

Up comes the man
With the shovel in his hand.
    (from a Belfast children's song, c. 1930[1])

I know this labyrinth so well – Balaclava, Raglan, Inkerman, Odessa Street –
Why can't I escape? Every move is punctuated. Crimea Street. Dead end again.
    (from 'Belfast Confetti' by Ciaran Carson, 1990[2])

In his memoir of growing up on Belfast's Shankill Road in the 1920s, John Simms recalls coming upon a political firebrand haranguing the Protestants of his neighbourhood about the glories of their forefathers and the dangers of Popery. Simms, stirred by the patriotic display but perplexed by 'the Popery bit', turned to his father. 'Why is it da that the Catholics are always fighting?' 'Och son,' replied the father, 'they are still flaming mad because we gave them a good hiding at the Boyne. It gets their goat up to be reminded of them days, especially when we sing the songs.' The young Simms eventually learned the songs, but he got no more history lessons from his father. 'All that had gone,' Simms recalls. 'The songs were all he knew.'[3]

It is an archetypal Belfast story, one that conveys both the crushing grip of history upon its people as well as the supposed hollowness of their historical understanding. 'These people are still in the 17th century', the *Times* had pronounced during the riots of 1864, and this judgement has echoed down the years in countless analyses of Ulster's troubles.[4] Sometimes, as in the studies of Andrew Boyd and A. T. Q. Stewart, tradition and memory obtain an almost autonomous existence in these discussions, propelling communal discord regardless of changes in Ulster's political, social or economic circumstances.[5] Thus Boyd, writing at the start of Northern Ireland's recent 'Troubles', confidently declares that 'religious violence in Northern Ireland arises today from the same sources as the many disturbances of the past', while Stewart, writing in the dark days of the 1970s, traces the region's violence to the 'atavism' and 'folk-memory' of its people.[6] More recently, scholars such as Neil Jarman and Dominic Bryan have proposed a more complex understanding of the role of memory in contemporary Northern Ireland, demonstrating how each rival community adapts its expressions of collective memory to suit its contemporary aspirations.[7] Where Boyd and Stewart see memory as a prison, Jarman and Bryan see it as an imaginative space that can be made and remade, within certain limits, to fit the needs of the group. All agree, however, that collective memory has played an indispensable role in shaping the competing identities of the people of Ulster. Indeed, in a society forged by conflict, it could hardly be otherwise.

By way of concluding this study, I want to re-examine this question of collective memory and its role in perpetuating conflict in Belfast in the years after 1864, and to suggest some ways in which we might refine and expand our understanding of how memories of violence have operated in the city. On the one hand it is absolutely necessary to recognise, with Jarman and Bryan, that collective memory is a continually evolving, dynamic relationship between social groups and the past. Memories are no more immune to the vicissitudes of time and space than are other social and psychological relationships, and it is a mistake to dismiss either group's actions as evidence that they are simply 'trapped in the past' or 're-enacting' earlier battles, despite what Boyd and Stewart have suggested. On the other hand, we must also begin looking for evidence of collective memory in realms of civic life that many scholars, including Jarman and Bryan, tend to ignore. For it is not simply the endless processions, banners, murals and songs recalling grand historical events – the Battle of the Boyne, the Easter Rising, the Battle of the Somme – that transmit and preserve collective memory. These heavily studied 'sites of memory' (to borrow Pierre Nora's phrase) undoubtedly help to bind together geographically dispersed groups across Ulster and the world, but when we narrow our focus to the level of the neighbourhood, or the workplace or the home, a more intimate – one is tempted to say parochial – sort of collective memory begins to emerge.[8] In Belfast, this was most often seen in people's memories of specific riots.

For example: in the Shankill Road of John Simms's boyhood, many Protestants may have been vague about the details of the Williamite wars, but there were some collective memories that had much greater resonance. Describing a funeral procession from the Shankill to the Milltown cemetery, Simms recalls that in order to get to the cemetery one had to pass through the Catholic Falls Road. As a matter of course, most Protestant mourners turned back before they arrived at the Falls, shaking hands and wishing the family well just before the casket passed into enemy territory. On this occasion, however, Simms and a friend decided to risk following the procession all the way to the cemetery. 'Weaned on tales of demonic priests and bloody accounts of the 1922 riots, the rumblings of which still echoed across the Belfast of my childhood', Simms recalls, he and his friend knew that the Falls 'was a place to be avoided if at all possible.' On arriving there, however, Simms was surprised to see people who looked just like his own, the barefooted children trundling hoops, the women in shawls and the men doffing their caps as the procession passed.[9] For Simms, what inspired fear of the Falls was not some distant memory of a seventeenth-century battle, but rather the recent memory of the colossal riots of 1920–22, which accompanied the partition of Ireland. This observation holds true, I would suggest, for most inhabitants of Belfast's sectarian neighbourhoods stretching back to the mid-Victorian years: if they were reluctant to cross communal boundaries, it was not because of what King William had done at the Boyne, but because of what their rivals had done, within living memory, in the very streets they now inhabited.

In a sense, what I am describing is the difference between historical memory and autobiographical memory as outlined by the French sociologist Maurice Halbwachs.[10] I will say more about Halbwachs below; here, I want simply to suggest that autobiographical memory – that is, the memory of events directly experienced by individuals or groups – can be just as potent as historical memory – that of distant events transmitted through texts, images and oral traditions – in shaping communal identities. If we recognise this, then we can begin to understand how the tradition of violence that began in Belfast in the 1850s and 1860s operated and, in particular, how it created the conditions for future violence. It was not the case, as Stewart claims, that each of Belfast's riots was 'unaltered by the current political circumstances, the ululation of politicians and clergy, or the military strength used to suppress it', but it is undoubtedly true that memories of earlier riots helped to propel and to shape future outbreaks.[11] They did so not only by providing people with a model of how they should act when communal tensions began to escalate, but also by solidifying a type of communal identity that had violence at its core. Fear and hatred of the other, coupled with a glorification of one's own communal heroes, were the messages carried by both sides' collective memories of violence, and this made future riots more likely.[12] In the pages that follow, I shall first offer a few theoretical reflections on the relationship between collective memory and place, suggesting that the environment each group inhabited in Belfast helped greatly to transmit and preserve memories of violence. Next, I examine some of the artefacts of memory that emerged in the immediate aftermath of the 1864 riots, items that helped to transform individual memories of violence into collective narratives that encapsulated the communal identities of both sides. I conclude with brief sketches of the two major riots of the next two decades, those of 1872 and 1886, with an eye on how earlier patterns of rioting persisted and how they changed over time.

Place and memory

'Welcome to the memory industry', writes Kerwin Lee Klein in his cautionary survey of the recent rise of 'memory studies' in historical scholarship.[13] Klein is rightly critical of the ways historians have begun to employ memory as a category in their analyses, often utilising a sort of 'Memory with a capital *M*' that seems to operate independently of human action.[14] The danger of attributing a quasi-mystical agency or autonomy to 'Memory' is especially great when we discuss collective memory, says Klein, for then the concept threatens to become a post-modern stand-in for discredited notions such as 'soul' or 'nature'. To guard against this tendency, it is necessary to delineate precisely what we mean when we speak of collective memory; specifically, we must make clear where it resides, how it persists, and what role it plays in historical change.

The modern study of collective memory derives largely from the ideas of Maurice Halbwachs.[15] For Halbwachs, all memory is essentially social: that is, each individual's memories have meaning only in relation to that person's social relationships. Collective memory, as distinct from individual memory, is that which resides within each group's 'social frameworks', or the web of relationships that tie groups together in space and time. Far from positing a mysterious, Jungian 'collective unconscious', however, Halbwachs argues that individual memories become collective memories through the social acts of communication and commemoration, and in the process the past itself becomes a social construct. Groups adjust their collective memories to accommodate their present circumstances and aspirations, and the strength of their memories depends on the current needs of the group as well as the strength of the 'social frameworks' that bind them.

One important aspect of Halbwachs's work is the significance he gives to objects generally, and to places specifically, as receptacles of collective memory. In their recent discussion of Halbwachs, David Middleton and Steven Brown point out that objects – possessions, commodities, landmarks – play a special role in Halbwachs's conception of collective memory, insofar as they 'act not merely as symbolic tokens on which are projected the desires and concerns of groups, but also as mediators of relationships between people'. Objects, for Halbwachs, 'serve as the means of coordinating and stabilising social practices and the remember-

ing activities that are threaded through them'.[16] In this sense, objects are
not merely prompts for memory, but rather the sites of memory, those
things without which shared memories between people would be impossible. For this reason a group's physical environment (the streets and
buildings in which they live out their daily lives) is especially important,
for it literally contains collective memory, transmitting individual experiences from person to person and generation to generation through the
daily interactions between people and their environment.

In the last few decades dozens of cultural theorists, public and archi-
tecture historians and social scientists have confirmed and further
delineated the intricate relationship between the physical environment and
a society's collective memories.[17] In her study of nineteenth-century
Paris, for instance, Priscilla Ferguson has suggested that that city's public
spaces acted as a sort of 'text' in which writers and revolutionaries alike
'read' and 'wrote' the ideas of revolution. By renaming streets, appropri-
ating buildings and landmarks and even transforming the topography of
Paris, a collective vision of 'revolution' emerged that both encapsulated
collective memories and shaped collective identities.[18] Social psycholo-
gists have likewise spoken of the 'city as living memory', a space where
the physical structure reinforces and encourages group cohesion. For
Eugene Rochberg-Halton, 'the city is itself a vast means of externalized
memory, a concrete and tangible storehouse of experiences, achievements,
of whole lifetimes given to the embodiment of dreams and purposes'.[19]
When a group occupying a specific place is sharply defined religiously,
politically or ethnically, then we might expect the places in which they
interact to be especially heavy with such memories.

These ideas have obvious implications for the study of collective
memory in Belfast. As the history of Belfast's mid-Victorian riots shows,
communal conflict often took the form of disagreements over each group's
place – literally and imaginatively – in the city. Hugh Hanna's 1857
demonstration showed the close connection between claiming a central
piece of the city's geography and making a moral claim about one's own
centrality in the broader civic culture. The processionists in the
McConnell funeral of 1864, by marching through the principal streets of
the city, made a similar point. Even more consequential were the residential expulsions that took place during these riots, for violence of this
sort was explicitly designed to carve out a piece of 'pure' communal space
in which both groups could exist without the presence of the other.
Moving within their own carefully patrolled enclaves, working-class
Protestants and Catholics in the post-riot city developed an intense identification with their neighbourhoods.

O, Sandy Row! O, Sandy Row!
My heart is there where'er I go;
Life's currents all shall cease to flow,
Ere I forget thee, Sandy Row.

Thus had the Rev. Thomas Drew, returning to Belfast after moving to Loughlinisland, flattered his audience at the Botanic Gardens demonstration of 1862, shortly before riots erupted in Sandy Row and elsewhere.[20] Another ditty, which conveys something of the venom that often seeped into these local loyalties, was overheard during the 1857 riots:

Hurrah for Mullan's corner,
And to hell with Sandy Row;
And the Devil build Sandy-row up.[21]

This fierce localism inevitably became a major component of the 'social frameworks' of collective memory on both sides. Forged through violent expulsions, Belfast's segregated neighbourhoods owed their communal identity to the city's mid-Victorian riots. The spots where violence occurred became constant reminders of the treachery of which one's enemies were capable, or, alternatively, of the valour displayed by one's own side. Seen in this light, the description of Belfast offered by James Winder Good in 1919, to which I referred at the very beginning of this study, acquires substantial significance.

Belfast is a raw new city, and out of its broils it evolves the legend which is as essential to new cities as old. One generation points out to another a gate still riddled with bullet-holes; a corner, famous for the operations of a sniper . . . ; a *cul-de-sac* into which a body of dragoons were lured and had to fight their way out with stones rattling off their brass helmets as riveters' hammers clang on steel plates in the shipyards. Naturally youngsters, to whom these tales and a thousand others are told, make for themselves holy places like the Mohammedans, and vow, after the fashion of Indian braves, that when their turn comes they will prove not unworthy of the traditions they have inherited.[22]

Increasingly prone to live their lives in segregated urban enclaves, both groups found themselves surrounded by streets and houses that were heavily laden (in some cases, quite literally etched) with such memories. Violence, in a sense, became a permanent feature of the city's landscape, continually present even when the streets themselves were quiet.

Remembering 1864

The interaction between place, memory and communal identity becomes clearer when we examine the cultural artefacts of the 1864 riots. Here I shall examine two sorts of artefacts: sketches, sold as souvenirs, that depicted scenes from the riots, and ballads, sold as broadsides, that discussed a broad array of riot-related topics. These items tell us not only how Protestants and Catholics understood the events of the riots, but also how they remembered them, for each sketch and song was also a powerful mnemonic device capable of articulating and transmitting a particular interpretation of the riots within both groups' 'social frameworks'. In many of these artefacts the sectarian geography of Belfast occupied a prominent place, and if we look closely we can catch a glimpse of the process by which each side's 'holy places' were becoming mythologised even at this early date.

The most striking artefacts of the 1864 riots are two sketches depicting the riots' most famous scenes, the 'Battle of the Navvies' on 17 August and the McConnell funeral on 18 August. The first sketch (Figure 8.1) shows shipcarpenters standing and crouching near the edge of the water at Thompson's Bank. At least eight of the men can be seen pointing and firing their guns into the water, where several dozen dark figures, representing the vanquished navvies, flail about.

Figure 8.1 The battle of the navvies

The other sketch (Figure 8.2) shows the corner of Hercules Street and Castle Street just as the McConnell procession approaches from Donegall Place. Several of the men in the procession are openly brandishing firearms, while crowds rush in from the left, from the direction of the Pound, and gather menacingly on the right, at the entrance to Hercules Street. The large building in the centre is the Catholic Institute.

Although one of the sketches appeared in the *Illustrated Times* shortly after the riots, the principal mode by which these images became known in Belfast was through sepia-toned *cartes de viste* (non-postable precursors to the modern postcard) sold in the city's bookshops.[23] A brief notice in the *Belfast Weekly News* identified Messrs. Philips & Sons, of Bridge Street, as the publishers of the images.[24] The newspaper offered no information about the identity of the artist, but it did provide a sense of how these images were received in Belfast, at least by those who shared the *Weekly News*'s ultra-Protestant opinions. Referring to the McConnell sketch, the writer noted with approval the artist's depiction of several shots coming from the Catholic Institute, 'a fact of which there is no longer any doubt'. The image of Thompson's Bank met with less

Figure 8.2 The McConnell funeral

approval, for, according to the writer, eyewitnesses saw only three guns among the shipcarpenters. Moreover, 'it is not the fact that they took "pot-shots" at the navvies as they struggled through the mud. If they did they are but indifferent marksmen, as no gunshot wound was inflicted by them.' On the whole, however, the writer was pleased with the images, concluding that 'the localities are admirably represented, and the photographs will long be treasured up as mementoes of the unfortunate scenes they more or less accurately depict'.[25]

What are we to make of these strange 'mementoes'? For one thing, there is little obvious partisan commentary in them. As the response of the *Weekly News* suggests, the sketch of the 'Battle of the Navvies' differed from the prevailing Protestant narrative of this event, which maintained that the shipcarpenters had not engaged in the unmanly activity of firing upon the defenceless navvies. On the other hand, this scene clearly showed the navvies in an unflattering light, floundering in the water as faceless, vaguely pitiful objects struggling under the shipcarpenters' overpowering might. The sketch of the McConnell funeral, in which the *Weekly News* observed smoke coming from the Catholic Institute (something that is not apparent in the image reproduced here), was likewise ambiguous in its sympathies. Once again foregrounding the Protestants, it showed the funeral party clearly defying the law by waving their firearms in the air, an accusation that some Protestant sources disputed. However, there was little to suggest that the artist's sympathies were with the Catholics, who were depicted as indistinct, lurking threats to the funeral procession. In a society overflowing with partisan icons that might easily have been appropriated to tell the story of the riots, the artist opted instead for a sort of rough-hewn realism, apparently concerned more with reporting the events than with commenting upon them.

If the sketches themselves offer little clue as to their function, then the medium through which they circulated tells us considerably more. Printed and sold as *cartes de viste*, the sketches were reproduced with the simple expectation that people would buy them, that there was a market for 'mementoes' of the riots. It is extremely difficult to imagine Catholics purchasing such images; even though both scenes could be taken as confirmation of the iniquities of the Protestants and their unjust persecution of Catholics, the images fit uneasily with the dominant Catholic narratives that praised the navvies' courage and manliness. Instead, it is likely that Protestants were the primary consumers, especially since both sketches depicted events generally held by Protestants to be great communal victories. In this respect, the idea of place as a marker of a group's territorial as well as moral dominance becomes significant. In both scenes Protestants are the central figures, masters both of the city's topography and of the viewer's gaze, while Catholics lurk or flounder as an undifferentiated, peripheral mass. Both images seem, therefore, to offer a graphic illustration of Protestants' desire to retain control over Belfast; this is especially strong in the funeral scene, where the figures on horseback, representing the magistrates who accompanied the procession, appear to provide official sanction to the processionists' actions.

Unfortunately, it is impossible to know how many people purchased these *cartes de viste*, nor is there any way to discover how long they kept them, where they displayed them or, ultimately, what they thought of them. As pieces of mass-produced popular art, the images resembled nothing so much as the imperial battle scenes and other images of empire that would become ubiquitous later in the century and which appeared on such varied items as cigarette cards, advertising posters and food canisters.[26] Like these later images, the sketches of the 1864 riots offered those who had not taken part in these events a chance to experience them vicariously. Put another way, they had the ability to transform what was the collective memory of a small group of people (the men at Thompson's Bank, the participants in the McConnell funeral) into a symbolic narrative that could be understood and 'remembered' by those who had only heard about the events.[27] We may imagine that this function was especially important for the illiterate and semi-literate workers of west Belfast, for whom a pictorial sketch of the riots was much more powerful than any newspaper report could be. This group was also more likely to purchase the sketches than were the Protestant middle classes, who outwardly condemned social disorder. Whether they were sold in significant numbers is unknown, although the fact that the images were picked up and publicised by the *Weekly News*, one of the city's more populist ultra-Protestant newspapers, suggests that they received some considerable publicity in the riots' immediate aftermath.

Another form of popular culture that took up the subject of the 1864 riots was the broadside ballad, a number of which were collected by the magistrates and sent to Dublin Castle in the months after the riots.[28] Typically sold in the streets and often performed by street singers for large crowds, broadside ballads were an important form of popular entertainment in nineteenth-century Ireland, their attractions considerably enhanced by their low cost, which was usually a penny or less.[29] They often told sensational or exaggerated versions of current events, translating the complex verbiage of newspaper stories into a memorable and easily accessible form, much in the way of the music hall ditty or tabloid of later years.[30] Much more openly partisan than the *cartes de viste*, the Belfast ballads covered a range of topics, from the parliamentary inquiry to the major battles of the riots. Many of the broadsides were quite crude, peppered with typographical errors and strained rhyme schemes, although a few were rather more sophisticated. I have included each of the surviving 1864 ballads in the Appendix; here I shall briefly examine a handful of them that demonstrate the varied ways in which people had begun to remember 1864.

Three of the ballads, all written from a Protestant perspective, told the story of the battle between the navvies and the shipcarpenters at Thompson's Bank. All three depicted the navvies as savage beasts whose unmanly assault on the Brown Street schoolchildren prompted the shipcarpenters to inflict a just punishment, with the implication that the state itself had become helpless to restore order. 'The Battle of the Navvies', a ballad set to the tune of the Orange standard 'The Battle of the Diamond', was typical.[31] Opening with an account of the burning of the O'Connell effigy, the ballad declares that 'ten thousand people' rejoiced to see 'the Bully Beggarman' set alight, believing 'That we were crushed by government, while petted were our foes.' Witnessing these insults, 'Mick Kenna' (A. J. McKenna, editor of the Catholic *Ulster Observer*) urges the navvies to retaliate, and these men then terrorise the town 'like demons of misrule' before pausing 'to show their valour deside [sic] an infant school'. After the wrecking of the Brown Street School, the shipcarpenters sweep forward 'like a bounding avalanche' to put down 'The assassins of the children – the despoilers of the town.' At Thompson's Bank, the navvies 'scramble through the mud' at the onslaught of the shipcarpenters. With the navvies thus vanquished, the ballad ends with lines that celebrate the Protestant ethos of self-reliance, restraint, and orderliness:

> And now that they have fled away, to keep our fair renown,
> We'd help the Special Constables, and gentlemen of town,
> To crush those fearful riots, which we are bound to say
> Were started up by Mick Kenna and the Navvies in his pay.

The other Protestant ballads dealing with these events, 'The Glorious Orange Victory at the Belfast Riots' and 'Sandy Row', likewise exalt the gallantry of the Protestants, who are commended for upholding 'the laws of King William' and subduing the cowardly navvy 'rebels'. In each of these narratives, the battle at Thompson's Bank is presented as a contest of masculine prowess, and, in their victory, the Protestants show that it is they who enjoy the preponderance of strength, judiciousness and chivalry in Belfast.[32]

None of the surviving ballads provides a Catholic perspective on the events at Thompson's Bank, but one, 'The Navvies Victory at the Belfast Riots', offers a general assessment of the navvies' conduct during the riots. Like the Protestant ballads, this ballad was obviously the work of someone intimately familiar with the working-class life of the city, and the broadside's considerable crudity suggests that it was not the work of a professional hack (like some of those discussed below) but of a working-class Catholic for whom the riots were a matter of great personal importance.[33] Also like the Protestant ballads, 'The Navvies Victory' is concerned chiefly with demonstrating the manliness of one's own side and the cowardice of the other. In this version of events, the navvies are roused to action by the Protestant weavers' assaults upon a Catholic church and innocent Catholic women: 'They could not meet us man to man I give you for to know – / But to strip and beat poor mill girls they're fit in Sandy row.' These assaults inspire the navvy attack on Brown Square, and in the ensuing tumult the Protestants repeatedly fail to defeat the navvies, even when the navvies are greatly outnumbered. This narrative, though somewhat divorced from reality, is consistent with the idea I introduced in Chapter 6 that what motivated the navvies was a sense that Protestants were threatening Catholic womanhood. By praising the navvies' manliness, this ballad was able to overcome, albeit rhetorically, the very real vulnerability of Catholic men in Belfast. Unskilled, economically weak and objectively less powerful than their Protestant counterparts, Catholic men could nevertheless reaffirm their stature by becoming defenders of even more vulnerable Catholic women.

There is a second aspect of 'The Navvies Victory' that merits attention. As in several other ballads, a strong geographical consciousness pervades the narrative. 'The Herclus [sic] Street and Smithfield men, and the Loney boys also' are celebrated for their ability 'to tame poor Sandy-row', while the Protestant weavers of Tea Lane and Purple Row are told to 'bow their heads, / For stripping of poor mill girls and burning a man that's dead'. In the ballad's most arresting geographical allusion, the singer declares that the Boyne Bridge – which had served for years as the battleground between the Pound and Sandy Row – 'has lost its name' and will now be called the Navvy Bridge. Several Protestant ballads mention the Boyne Bridge as well, celebrating it as the place where the O'Connell effigy was burned. Significantly, these Protestant ballads also allude to the historic Battle of the Boyne, drawing an implicit comparison between that seventeenth-century Protestant victory and their recent communal triumphs. In these passages, therefore, we can see something of the interplay between collective memory and the everyday urban environment; indeed, in the case of the Boyne Bridge, it is difficult to imagine a landmark that more perfectly embodies both the deep, historical memories of religious warfare and the more immediate, autobiographical memories of communal violence that motivated both sides.[34]

In addition to these crude partisan ballads, the magistrates also collected a number of slightly more sophisticated, though no less opinionated, compositions. 'Barney's Evidence' was a Protestant response to the testimony of Bernard Hughes, the wealthy Catholic baker, at the 1864 riots commission. Sarcastically affecting the brogue of the stage Irishman, the singer addresses himself directly to Hughes, making frequent allusions to his reputation as a baker and a champion of Catholic causes. In an extraordinary passage that reveals the author's familiarity with the published report of the 1857 riots commission, the lyrics mention specific pages from the 1857 report that refute Hughes's 1864 testimony:

> I find on the page markèd 241 –
> This is a Report Smythe and Lynch sat upon:
> Here Barney yer axed by Returney M'Lean –
> When ye give him that answer, then what did ye mane?

A second ballad, 'Nolan's Advice to Barry & Dowse', appears to have been written by the same author.[35] Also affecting a mocking brogue, this ballad offers a more comprehensive picture of the 1864 riots, discussing the testimony of several witnesses and punctuating its observations with venomous asides about 'The brave Navvie fellows who blow the Papal bellows', 'Mick-Kenna', and the Pope. Also of this genre was 'The Marquis & The Mayor', which commented upon the public controversy that raged between Mayor John Lytle and the Marquis of Donegall after the Marquis accused the mayor of abandoning Belfast during the riots to take his holiday at Harrogate. Finally, there is 'The Good Old Orange Magistrate', a Catholic indictment of W. T. B. Lyons, the local magistrate who commanded the government's forces during the McConnell funeral. In the course of attacking Lyons for his supposed Orange sympathies, this ballad takes the unusual step of providing a footnote that refers the reader to the 30 August edition of the *Ulster Observer*. Clearly, the author had something more in mind than mere street performance for this particular composition.

Perhaps the most important function of this second group of ballads was to educate the public about the riots' central events. By providing a sensational and highly partisan gloss upon information that was otherwise accessible only through newspapers or parliamentary reports, these ballads offered the illiterate and semi-literate an opportunity to learn about what was happening in the political life of the city. At the same time, a few of them also seem to have been aimed at a more 'respectable' audience; although the middle classes normally looked down upon broadside ballads as low plebeian doggerel, it was not uncommon during periods of high political excitement for ballad sellers to attract prosperous customers, provided their purchases could be made discreetly.[36] For literate people of all classes, of course, to own a broadside ballad was not just to own the words and the tune; it was also to own a physical object. It was, as Mark Booth says, 'less like owning a fact-sheet than it is like owning a book of pin-up photographs or dirty stories, to which one returns at will for the excitation of a special state of feeling'.[37] In England, weavers commonly decorated their walls with framed broadsides, and it is reasonable to suppose that many ballad purchasers in Belfast did the same, especially with those ballads that contained complex information that could not easily be remembered.[38]

By packaging riot stories into easily accessible forms, then, ballads became ideal transmitters of collective memories of violence. As with the riot sketches, it is difficult to measure the precise impact these ballads had, but an extraordinary piece of oral history – conducted more than sixty years after the 1864 riots – confirms that such ballads did, indeed, lodge in people's memories for a very long time. In 1930 Cahal Bradley, a journalist for the Catholic *Irish News*, wrote a series of articles entitled 'Stories of the 1864 Riots' for which he interviewed a number of elderly people who had been children during the riots. Incredibly, several of them were able to recall quite detailed fragments of songs from 1864. One fragment was from a Catholic ballad that Bradley calls 'Toner's Navvy Song':

On the 15th of last August, it was Our Lady's Day,
To St. Malachy's Roman Catholic Church to hear Mass we took our way,
Where thousands there assembled to pull our chapel down, . . .
Our navvies they struck right and left, both bricks and stones did throw.[39]

Another fragment, this one adopting a Protestant perspective, described the shipcarpenters' search for the navvies on 16 August:

For when the carpenters came out
No navvies could be found;
They ran to hide their carcasses
In the dump-pits of the Pound.
Hurrah, my lads! the Island boys
Have placed the name once more
Of William – the immortal –
Far above each Fenian door.[40]

The most interesting fragment came from a Catholic ballad in which the singer offers a detailed description of the Catholic portion of Belfast's sectarian geography.

The Smithfield boys I can't forget, they were ready for the call;
There was a man supplied them with plenty of powder and ball.
The matchless men of Hercules Street, of Mill Street and the Pound
Of Hamill Street and Irvine Street, and neighbouring streets around:
With one consent away they went prepared to meet the foe –
To put right down each silly clown that came from Sandy Row.[41]

Although none of these lyrics come from the surviving broadsides of 1864, it is clear that some, at least, of the sectarian tunes circulating through Belfast in the post-riot period enjoyed a very long life indeed.

The 1872 riots

Part of the reason memories of violence remained strong in Belfast was that new riots kept coming along to refresh them. After 1864 slowly simmering violence continued to be a constant presence in the city, with particularly severe outbreaks in 1872 and 1886 that in many ways exceeded anything that happened in the immediate post-famine years. Although each successive outbreak was shaped by different external and internal forces, the patterns the outbreaks followed showed an undeniable continuity with earlier riots. In this and the next section, I shall suggest some ways in which each side's memories of the riots of the 1850s and 1860s informed its actions during these later outbreaks. Often we can see the power of such memories in the styles of violence adopted on both sides; sometimes references to earlier riots appeared in the observations of journalists and politicians; and sometimes, on a few rare occasions, the actors in this ever-evolving conflict explicitly indicated that they were motivated by memories of earlier riots.

The 1872 riots began with the usual patterns of provocation and retaliation. The Party Processions Acts had been repealed earlier that year, and in July the Belfast Orangemen, like their brethren throughout the country, celebrated with a large, but mostly peaceful, procession. The following month a group of Catholic nationalists led by the radical town councillor Joseph Biggar decided to hold their own procession to support amnesty for Irish political prisoners. The day chosen was 15 August, Lady Day, the date on which the navvies had wrecked Brown Square in 1864. As Catholics gathered in west Belfast to march to Hannahstown, a short distance north of the city, Hugh Hanna urged local Protestants to gather near his new church at Carlisle Circus to protect it from attack.[42] Neither the outbound nor the return procession attracted much violence, for a large troop of constabulary was on hand to keep the two crowds separate, but that night several attacks occurred in the Shankill and Falls

Roads. The people of those neighbourhoods, recognising the signs of an imminent riot, began putting out the street lamps and pulling up the cobbles from the streets, just as they had done in years past.[43]

The rioting began in earnest the following day, and as the 'disturbed districts' once again descended into turmoil, the old patterns began to re-emerge. Once again the major objective on both sides was to engage the other in battle without the interference of the police, and this time the major theatre of conflict was the brick-fields that spanned the distance between the Shankill and Falls Roads. These neighbourhoods, which lay north and west of the Pound and Sandy Row, were now becoming the undisputed centre of gravity for Belfast's sectarian brawls as the city's population expanded outwards.[44] Even more important than the set-piece battles, however, was the unprecedented number of residential expulsions carried out by militant extremists wishing to purge these newly settled areas of outsiders.[45] According to the government's official figures, in one week rioters wrecked or damaged some 247 houses and forced 837 families to leave their homes.[46] In some cases people had to flee their homes simply to make room for refugees arriving from other districts.[47] In 1864 the Falls and Shankill areas had started down the path towards complete communal homogeneity much in the manner of the Pound and Sandy Row; after 1872, the 'purifying' of both neighbourhoods was largely complete.[48]

Expulsionist violence and set-piece battles were not the only echoes of past riots to be heard in 1872. The 'old plan of levying black mail', reported the *Newsletter*, also reappeared, as extremists began extorting money from their neighbours.[49] The customary gendered division of labour, whereby women supplied the men with arms, kept watch, and vocally encouraged the rioters, also returned.[50] Even the shipcarpenters put in a brief appearance, leaving work at the Queen's Island one day to attack the offices of the Catholic *Daily Examiner*.[51] In all of this, rioters implicitly adhered to the patterns established in the 1850s and 1860s; indeed, on some occasions, memories of those earlier riots became explicit. In the Catholic slum of Smithfield, a man named Rodgers received a letter 'to the effect that, owing to the part which he had taken in the 1864 riots, they could not allow a spy like him to remain in his present residence'. Another Smithfield man received a similar letter written in the same hand.[52]

Despite these continuities, however, there were also signs that the city's patterns of rioting were continuing to evolve. Much had changed in Belfast since 1864. For one thing, the Catholic Church was now much stronger than it had been eight years earlier, and it therefore had a greater number of priests on hand to restrain Catholic rioters.[53] In a report to

Dublin, the magistrates commended the priests for using their influence 'over (even) the very lowest of the members of their faith' to promote peace.[54] Another change from earlier riots was that policing was now entirely in the hands of the Irish Constabulary, the local police having been abolished in 1865. This had the effect both of strengthening anti-police violence on the part of Protestants and of enabling more aggressive policing tactics by the authorities. An especially ugly instance of the former occurred on 20 August, when a Protestant crowd invaded the home of a Catholic constable and beat him.[55] Reciprocal violence between Protestants and constables also became more frequent and more intense. On one occasion besieged constables fired over sixty rounds into an attacking crowd, reportedly killing four rioters and wounding ten.[56] The only officially reported deaths, however, were those of a constable shot by a Protestant and a rioter killed by a constable's sword.[57]

At the same time, the central authorities continued to refine their doctrine of overwhelming force. 'When once Belfast gets excited it is a difficult place to cool down', observed the Lord Lieutenant, Earl Spencer, (mis)remembering the '3 weeks' of rioting that had occurred in 1864.[58] Drawing on their prior experiences of Belfast's riots, the authorities sent more than 2,000 constables and soldiers to the city, and immediately after the riots the Chief Secretary increased the permanent constabulary force in Belfast from 420 to 650.[59] In some ways the 1872 riots were a test of Dublin Castle's ability to police Belfast without the aid of a local police force, and the lesson it learned from this outbreak was that more, not less, coercive force must be employed in the future. In particular, officials determined that the constabulary must have faster recourse to deadly force in order to overawe the rioters.[60] Writing to Lord Halifax, the Lord Lieutenant admitted 'that much as I dislike the idea of killing men in a crowd, I think it often would save great loss of property & life if at the outset after due warning an effective volley were fired'.[61] Reports of police over-reaction prompted the Belfast Town Council to call for a commission to investigate the policing of these riots, insisting 'that it is not an increase in the Police force of the Borough that is required so much as a complete change in the semi-military character, arms, discipline, and management of the present force'.[62] Such observations were directly at odds with the Castle's longstanding faith in the discipline and efficiency of the constabulary, however, and the government refused either to reconsider its policing tactics or to initiate yet another riots inquiry.

Although the 1872 riots were considerably less bloody than those of 1864, their long-term consequences were probably even more profound. By forcing an unprecedented transfer of people in west Belfast, communal extremists created an unambiguous demarcation between Protestant and Catholic streets that remains in place to this day. After the riots residential expulsions became much less common, a fact that suggests that communal boundaries were being even more vigorously policed than they had been before.[63] The riots also marked an important shift in the alignment of the warring parties: as working-class Catholics came more and more under the restraining influence of their priests, violence between working-class Protestants and the constabulary became more common. Like earlier riots, this outbreak also created new sets of memories that were capable of fuelling future hostilities. In an uncharacteristic burst of melancholy, the *Newsletter* reflected, 'The remembrance of these events will rankle in the people's minds through an entire generation; and things trivial and unimportant in themselves may easily lead to consequences the most disastrous. A deeply-rooted sense of injury seems to pervade the community.'[64] The coming years would largely vindicate this assessment.

The 1886 riots

The 1870s and 1880s were turbulent decades in Ireland. For the first time since the famine, a constitutional movement for Irish autonomy (now called Home Rule) operated alongside an openly revolutionary movement (the Fenians) to push the Irish question to the forefront of British politics. In Belfast, Protestants and Catholics eagerly joined the political fray, and as the stakes grew higher both sides kept up a steady drumbeat of violence. Annual processions of Protestant schoolchildren, led by Hugh Hanna and invariably accompanied by burly Protestant 'bodyguards', frequently degenerated into violence.[65] Catholic Lady Day processions, which after 1872 became a regular part of the sectarian calendar, were another source of recurring conflict.[66] Indeed, between the Orange celebrations in July and the Lady Day demonstrations in August, summers in Belfast were becoming increasingly tense. During these months orange and green arches sprouted overnight in the working-class neighbourhoods, visibly reinforcing a sectarian landscape that was by now deeply entrenched. One summer, in 1885, Catholics in the Pound hoisted an arch facing Sandy Row that showed images of Robert Emmet, Archbishop Croke and Charles Parnell and proclaimed 'Remember 1864'.[67]

Major rioting broke out once again in the summer of 1886. The Liberal government's introduction of a Home Rule bill in April, along with some trenchant oratory from pro- and anti-Home Rule politicians in Belfast, had packed the powder keg tighter than it had been at least since 1864. The spark came in early June, while the Home Rule bill was being debated in Parliament. When a Protestant navvy working on the new Alexandra Dock objected to the manner in which a Catholic navvy was cutting a drain, the Catholic replied, 'It won't be long until none of your sort will be allowed to earn a loaf of bread in this country.' A scuffle broke out, and the next day more than a thousand shipcarpenters and 'rivet boys' from the Queen's Island marched to the dock, 'there to repeat on the navvies the cruel treatment to which they subjected them during the great riots of 1864'.[68] As before, the Catholic navvies found themselves heavily outnumbered, and, as before, a number of them fled into the water for safety. One Catholic, a young man named Curran, died in the affray, and his funeral on 6 June became a great Catholic demonstration involving several thousand people. As the funeral passed by the brick-fields that had been the site of the 1872 riots, violence flared.[69]

This was the start of more than four months of protracted violence in Belfast, during which at least thirty-two people died and many more were injured. Much has been made of the political background of the 1886 riots to show that they were essentially 'political' in nature, but this is only part of the story.[70] To be sure, disagreements over Home Rule framed much of the violence, and, crucially, the widespread anti-Home Rule sentiments of the Protestant elite undoubtedly led them to offer tacit support to Protestant rioters. But from the beginning it was evident that these riots were driven as much by Belfast's own internal quarrels as by external political forces. 'The Home Rule business', recollected an old Protestant shipyard worker interviewed by Cahal Bradley in 1930,

> had us worked up terribly, and the talk about fighting had us ready to kill anybody. Unfortunately . . . there was a kind of historic headline in 'the yard' then about attacking navvies. We had old men who remembered the '64 battles with them, and the younger ones who recalled the '80 fight, so that it seemed to be an accepted precedent for future copy.[71]

Expanding on the 'yardman's' observations, Bradley wrote, 'No doubt the older and also experienced younger men must have talked. The stories of the earlier conflicts were listened to between the clangs of the hammer or at meal hours. The inexperienced possibly envied those of us who had "come through it." When would their time come? they no doubt wondered.'[72] Contemporary evidence confirms that the 1864 riots were on the shipcarpenters' minds the day the riots began. At the trial of one of the men charged with assaulting the navvies, a witness told the court that as the shipcarpenters ran towards the docks, he could hear them shouting, 'Where are the navvies' and vowing that 'they would make them remember '64'.[73]

In the months of violence that followed, observers frequently looked back upon Belfast's earlier riots to make sense of what was happening. When looting and wrecking broke out on the newly settled Springfield

Road in August, for example, the *Whig* noted that the attacks 'reproduce exactly' the 'awful scenes' of earlier riots, which 'remain as vivid reminiscences with many of our townspeople'.[74] In the House of Commons, the Nationalist west Belfast MP Thomas Sexton insisted that the present riots were not motivated by Home Rule as such, but rather by the same forces that had caused the riots of 1857, 1864 and 1872: Protestant provocation.[75] Hugh Hanna, now a leading Unionist organiser, wrote to the *Times* refuting Sexton's interpretation of these events. Recalling his part in the 1857 riots, Hanna rehearsed the arguments he had made thirty years earlier, explaining how he had 'declined to accept the will of Mr. Sexton's mob as the measure of my liberty' and declaring of his defiant stand in Corporation Square that year, 'there has been no event in my life that I regard with greater satisfaction'. As for the 1864 riots, Hanna reminded the *Times* of the navvies' 'savage attack on a school in the district, particularly on the "infant department"'. Noting that the cause of the present riots 'was somewhat similar', Hanna said, 'If the coming inquiry took in the past 40 years of our history, we would prove that in every instance Roman Catholics have been the aggressors when the public peace was disturbed.'[76]

While they were clearly shaped by memories of earlier conflicts, however, the 1886 riots differed from earlier riots in several important ways. For one thing, Catholics played a less central role in the summer's violence than they had on previous occasions. This was partly attributable to the Catholic clergy, who, as in 1872, 'laboured persistently in the cause of peace, and who exercised over their people a great and beneficial influence'.[77] Another difference was that direct confrontations between Catholics and Protestants had become more difficult to orchestrate: the constabulary force was too large, and the rival neighbourhoods too homogeneous, to allow hostile crowds much chance to come into conflict with each other, although on several occasions they managed to do so. Instead, the most serious violence in 1886 arose from clashes between Protestants and the constabulary. At the start of the riots, consistent with its doctrine of overwhelming force, the government flooded Belfast with constables from all over Ireland. Protestants, convinced that the government 'was packing the town of Belfast with Catholic policemen, carefully selected from certain southern counties, and charged with the duty of shooting down the Protestants', responded violently.[78] Facing relentless attacks in the streets and in their barracks, the constables made free use of their firearms, sometimes opening fire under rather dubious circumstances. The scale of the repression only exacerbated Protestant hostility, and for a time the Shankill area became wholly off limits to the constabulary. Some 371 of the 2,000 constables in Belfast received injuries and two were killed. It is not known exactly how many Protestants died. By the time order was restored in October, Protestant alienation from the forces of law and order was as strong as had ever been the case among the Catholics during the era of the local police.[79]

The 1886 riots dramatically illustrated the shortcomings of the central government's response to rioting in Belfast. More than twenty years after the abolition of the local police, the riots inquiry found that the constabulary in Belfast was still unable to act as a civil police force, recommending 'that they should be taught the art of dealing discreetly and with tact with an urban population – to rely, save in the last extremity, on the baton, instead of the rifle'.[80] For nearly thirty years, however, Dublin Castle's policy had tended in precisely the opposite direction: the use of overwhelming force, often implemented over the objections of local officials and despite a demonstrated tendency to excite rather than alleviate tensions, had long been the Executive's standard reaction to Belfast's violence. After the fiasco of 1886 the state scaled back its coercive presence in Belfast, but the profound crisis of legitimacy that had opened up between Protestants and the constabulary never quite disappeared.[81] Like the warring communities themselves, the state had played no small part in forging the tradition of violence that, by the end of the century, seemed to be an indelible part of Belfast's civic life.

Conclusion

Throughout this study, I have argued against those who see Belfast's riots as simply a series of unending variations upon the same dreary theme. As we have seen, the tradition of violence that by the twentieth century had come to appear timeless and inevitable was in fact a constructed condition that arose from concrete historical circumstances. Protracted violence was no more inevitable in Belfast than it was in Glasgow; rather, it took a set of precise social and political relationships to bring about the city's mid-Victorian riots. The networks of association linking working-class people to each other and to the elite, the actions (and inactions) of the state and its relationship with the inhabitants of the city and the peculiar patterns of rioting that evolved during the 1850s and 1860s all conspired to create the tradition of violence that defined Protestant–Catholic relations in Belfast. Tensions between Protestants and Catholics in Belfast may well have been unavoidable, but entrenched violence was not.

Nevertheless, once this tradition of violence began to emerge, it acquired a place in each side's collective memories that profoundly influenced their future actions. These memories, firmly rooted in both groups' physical and imaginative relationship with the city, provided a template for later violence that was most clearly evident in the riots of 1872 and 1886. As Protestants and Catholics commemorated, commodified and rehearsed particular moments of violence over the years, conflict between their two communities came to seem deeply and indisputably normal. Memories of violence wove themselves into each side's collective identities, and the eternal conflict between Protestants and Catholics in Ireland acquired a terrible banality that, for the inhabitants of Belfast, was a central part of their conflicting urban cultures. Over time, as new generations became initiated to this tradition of violence, it became difficult to imagine how things could ever have been otherwise.

Notes

1 Cahal Bradley, 'Stories of the 1864 Riots', *Irish News*, 1 Nov. 1930.
2 Ciaran Carson, 'Belfast Confetti', in Ciaran Carson, *The Ballad of HMS Belfast* (Loughcrew, Ireland: The Gallery Press, 1999), 23.
3 John Young Simms, *Farewell to the Hammer: A Shankill Boyhood* (Belfast: The White Row Press, 1992), 21–2.
4 *Times* (London), 24 Aug. 1864.
5 A. T. Q. Stewart, *The Narrow Ground: Aspects of Ulster, 1609–1969* (London: Faber, 1977); Andrew Boyd, *Holy War in Belfast* (Tralee: Anvil Books, 1969). See also Oliver MacDonagh, *States of Mind: A Study of Anglo-Irish Conflict, 1780–1980* (London: George Allen & Unwin, 1983), 1–14.
6 Boyd, *Holy War*, preface (n. p.); Stewart, *Narrow Ground*, 185.
7 Neil Jarman, *Material Conflicts: Parades and Visual Displays in Northern Ireland* (Oxford: Berg, 1997); Dominic Bryan, *Orange Parades: The Politics of Ritual, Tradition, and Control* (London: Pluto Press, 2000). A similar approach is taken by most of the contributors to the most recent study of memory in Ireland, north and south, Ian McBride, ed., *History and Memory in Modern Ireland* (Cambridge: Cambridge University Press, 2001).
8 Pierre Nora, 'Between Memory and History: Les lieux de mémoire', *Representations*, 26 (Spring 1989), 7–24.
9 Simms, *Farewell*, 75–6.
10 Lewis A. Coser, 'Introduction: Maurice Halbwachs, 1877–1945', in M. Halbwachs, *On Collective Memory*, ed. and trans. Lewis A. Coser (Chicago: University of Chicago Press, 1992), 1–34.
11 Stewart, *Narrow Ground*, 148.
12 This is similar to what Paul Connerton, following Henri Bergson, has called 'habit-memory'. See his *How Societies Remember* (Cambridge: Cambridge University Press, 1989). A similar observation, albeit concerning a quite different society, has been made by Patricia A. Gossman, *Riots and Victims: Violence and the Construction of Communal Identity among Bengali Muslims, 1905–1947* (Boulder, Colo.: Westview Press, 1999).

13 Kerwin Lee Klein, 'On the Emergence of Memory in Historical Discourse', *Representations*, 69 (Winter 2000), 127–50.
14 *Ibid.*, 135.
15 In this paragraph I draw principally from Coser's introduction to Halbwachs, *On Collective Memory*.
16 David Middleton and Steven D. Brown, *The Social Psychology of Experience: Studies in Remembering and Forgetting* (London: Sage Publications, 2005), 50.
17 See e.g. David Lowenthal, *The Past is a Foreign Country* (Cambridge: Cambridge University Press, 1999); Yi-Fu Tuan, *Space and Place: The Perspective of Experience* (Minneapolis: University of Minnesota Press, 1977); and Sarah Farmer, *Martyred Village: Commemorating the 1944 Massacre at Oradour-sur-Glane* (Berkeley: University of California Press, 1999).
18 Priscilla Parkhurst Ferguson, *Paris as Revolution: Writing the Nineteenth-Century City* (Berkeley: University of California Press, 1994).
19 Eugene Rochberg-Halton, *Meaning and Modernity: Social Theory in the Pragmatic Attitude* (Chicago: University of Chicago Press, 1986), 207.
20 *Belfast Newsletter*, 13 Aug. 1862.
21 Jonathan Jones's evidence, *Report of the Commissioners of Inquiry into the Origin and Character of the Riots in Belfast, in July and September, 1857; together with Minutes of Evidence and Appendix*, HC 1857–58 (2309) XXVI, 100. Mullan's Corner was a place at the border between the Pound and Sandy Row that became famous in 1857 as the spot from which Catholic snipers operated.
22 James Winder Good, *Ulster and Ireland* (Dublin: Maunsel and Co., 1919), 259–60.
23 Both matted *cartes de viste* are held at PRONI, D/2930/6/84/1–2.
24 *Belfast Weekly News*, 15 Oct. 1864; *Henderson's Belfast Directory, 1861* (Belfast: News-Letter Office, 1861).
25 *Belfast Weekly News*, 15 Oct. 1864.
26 John M. MacKenzie, *Propaganda and Empire: The Manipulation of British Public Opinion, 1880–1960* (Manchester: Manchester University Press, 1984), 16–38.
27 See Bernard Rimé and Véronique Christophe, 'How Individual Emotional Episodes Feed Collective Memory', in *Collective Memory of Political Events: Social Psychological Perspectives*, ed. James W. Pennebaker, Dario Paez and Bernard Rimé (Mahwah, NJ: Lawrence Erlbaum Associates, Publishers, 1997), 131–46.
28 All nine broadsides are held in the NLI, Larcom Papers, 7626/106. Two of the broadsides, 'The Battle of the Navvies' and 'The Navvies Victory', are also held at the NAI, CSORP (1864) 18631.
29 Georges Denis Zimmermann, *Songs of Irish Rebellion: Irish Political Street Ballads and Rebel Songs, 1780–1900*, 2nd ed. (Dublin: Four Courts Press, 2002), 22–3; Anthony Bennett, 'Broadsides on the Trial of Queen Caroline: A Glimpse at Popular Song in 1820', *Proceedings of the Royal Musical*

Association, 107 (1980–81), 72; J. S. Bratton, *The Victorian Popular Ballad* (London: The Macmillan Press Ltd, 1975), 24.

30 Mark W. Booth, *The Experience of Songs* (New Haven: Yale University Press, 1981), 98–113; Alan Bold, *The Ballad* (London: Methuen & Co., 1979), 66–82.

31 This ballad was subsequently reprinted in *Orange Songs,* 'New Edition', Part II (Armagh: Armagh Standard, n.d.), alongside Orange standards such as 'The Protestant Boys' and 'Dolly's Brae'.

32 In this, they resembled the more broadly nationalist and imperialist 'heroic ballads' popular in Victorian England. See Bratton, *Victorian*, 37–88.

33 See Zimmermann, *Songs*, 21–2.

34 On the important relationship between toponymy – or the ways in which items in the landscape are named – and memory, see P. Ferguson, *Paris*, 12.

35 Charles R. Barry and Richard Dowse were the government's commissioners heading the 1864 riots commission.

36 Bennett, 'Broadsides', 77–8.

37 Booth, *Experience*, 108.

38 Zimmermann, *Songs*, 21.

39 *Irish News*, 27 Oct. 1930.

40 *Ibid.*, 1 Nov. 1930.

41 *Ibid.*

42 A statue of Hanna stood in Carlisle Circus from 1894 until the early years of the recent 'Troubles', when it was destroyed by an IRA bomb.

43 *Belfast Newsletter*, 17 Aug. 1872; *Freeman's Journal*, 21 Aug. 1872; Catherine Hirst, *Religion, Politics, and Violence in Nineteenth-Century Belfast: The Pound and Sandy Row* (Dublin: Four Courts Press, 2002), 170–1; Frank Wright, *Two Lands on One Soil: Ulster Politics before Home Rule* (Dublin: Gill and Macmillan, 1996), 372–3.

44 *Belfast Newsletter,* 19 Aug. 1872.

45 *Ibid.*, 20 Aug. 1872; *Freeman's Journal*, 22 Aug. 1872; *Times* (London), 22 Aug. 1872.

46 *Freeman's Journal*, 14 Jan. 1873.

47 *Daily Express*, 22 Aug. 1872.

48 The baptismal records of St Peter's Catholic Church suggest that the Protestant nature of the Shankill Road was much more absolute after the 1872 riots than before. Between October 1866 and 12 August 1872 a total of forty-five baptisms (1.2% of all baptisms) took place in St Peter's for families listing their residence as the Shankill Road. In the same period the Falls Road had seventy-one children baptised at St Peter's (1.9% of the total). In the three years after the 1872 riots, however, the Falls had twenty-nine children baptised in St Peter's (1.9% of the total again) but the Shankill had only 5 (0.3% of the total). St Peter's Church Baptismal Records, Oct. 1856 to Feb. 1875, PRONI, MIC/1D/64. Owing to the poor state of the registers, these figures can only be approximate, and they cover only the most prominent streets in each district.
     Protestant church records support the notion that substantial residential

integration existed in these areas before 1872. The baptismal register of the Anglican Christ Church (which ends in 1871) shows at least 142 baptisms (0.9% of all baptisms) performed for families residing in the Falls Road between January 1858 and October 1871 (Christ Church records, PRONI, MIC/583/25–27). The communicant roll of the Albert Street Presbyterian Church, meanwhile, shows at least eighteen communicants living in the Falls Road or Divis Street (at the eastern end of the Falls Road) between 1853 and 1865, whereas the Shankill Road and Agnes Street (another major road passing through the Shankill area) had only eleven communicants (Albert Street Presbyterian Church Records, PRONI, MIC/1P/16/2). Again, these figures are approximate and cover only the main roads in each area.

49 *Belfast Newsletter*, 21 Aug. 1872.
50 See e.g. *ibid.*, 19 Aug. 1872.
51 Report of Assistant Inspector General Duncan, 5 Nov. 1872, NAI, CSORP (1873) *17338*.
52 *Weekly Northern Whig*, 24 Aug. 1872.
53 In 1857, there was only one priest for every 4,601 Catholic inhabitants. By 1871, this number had been reduced to 2,416. A. C. Hepburn, *A Past Apart: Studies in the History of Catholic Belfast, 1850–1950* (Belfast: Ulster Historical Foundation, 1996), 129.
54 Orme and O'Donnell to Dublin Castle, NAI, CSORP (1873) *14541*.
55 Report of Assistant Inspector General Duncan, 5 Nov. 1872, NAI, CSORP (1873) *17338*.
56 Lord Spencer to Lord Halifax, 26 Aug. 1872, BI, HALIFAX/A4/110A.
57 The death of the constable was the only official death during the riots. See *Freeman's Journal*, 14 Jan. 1873. The death of the rioter at the hands of the police is reported *ibid.*, 19 Aug. 1872.
58 Lord Spencer to Lord Halifax, 19 Aug. 1872, BI, HALIFAX/A4/110A.
59 *Freeman's Journal*, 14 Jan. 1873.
60 Draft letter from Lords Justice to Inspector General of Constabulary, 30 Sept. 1872, NAI, CSORP (1872) 15087.
61 Lord Spencer to Lord Halifax, 26 Aug. 1872, BI, HALIFAX/A4/110A.
62 The Mayor and Aldermen and Burgesses of Belfast to the Lord Lieutenant, 16 and 21 Jan. 1873, DDC, typescript copy of Special Letter Book, 1867–1879, Belfast City Hall, L.114.
63 During the 1886 riots, for instance, only twenty-nine homes were damaged in four months of intense rioting, as compared with the 247 houses damaged during one week in 1872. *Report of the Belfast Riots Commissioners. Minutes of Evidence and Appendices.* HC 1887 (4925–I) XVIII, 576.
64 *Belfast Newsletter*, 23 Aug. 1872.
65 Hirst, *Religion*, 182–3.
66 Neil Jarman and Dominic Bryan, *From Riots to Rights: Nationalist Parades in the North of Ireland* (Coleraine: Centre for the Study of Conflict, University of Ulster, 1998), 15.
67 *Northern Whig*, 13 July 1885. Hirst (*Religion*, 169–70) claims that this arch shows that the residents of the Pound had 'forgotten' the rout of the navvies

in 1864, but I am inclined to believe the opposite. For these Catholics, it was most probably their past suffering at the hands of the Protestants, symbolically reinforced by the Twelfth of July parades, that was being remembered.

68 *Weekly Northern Whig*, 12 June 1886.
69 *Ibid.*; *Report of the Belfast Riots Commissioners*, 1887, 5–6.
70 Hirst, *Religion*, 174–82. See also Sean Farrell, *Rituals and Riots: Sectarian Violence and Political Culture in Ulster, 1784–1886* (Lexington, Ky: University Press of Kentucky, 2000), 183.
71 *Irish News*, 10 Nov. 1930.
72 *Ibid.*
73 *Weekly Northern Whig*, 3 July 1886.
74 *Ibid.*, 21 Aug. 1886.
75 *Times* (London), 2 Sept. 1886.
76 *Ibid.*, 6 Sept. 1886.
77 *Report of the Belfast Riots Commissioners*, 1887, 12; Hirst, *Religion*, 176.
78 *Report of the Belfast Riots Commissioners*, 1887, 17. The religious composition of the constabulary force permanently stationed in Belfast was more or less even at 300 Protestants to 268 Catholics.
79 *Ibid.*, 8–9; Thomas Sexton's speech in the House of Commons, *Times* (London) 6 Sept. 1886; Hirst, *Religion*, 175–81; Sybil Baker, 'Orange and Green: Belfast, 1832–1912', ed., *The Victorian City: Images and Realities*, ed. H. J. Dyos and M. Wolff (London: Routledge & Kegan Paul, 1973), vol. 2, 799.
80 *Report of the Belfast Riots Commissioners*, 1887, 19.
81 Baker, 'Orange and Green', 799.

Epilogue

It is tempting to see Belfast's nineteenth-century riots as precursors to the more recent violence that has torn apart Northern Ireland. When I began research for this project, back in 2002, Northern Ireland was limping its way through the aftermath of the Belfast Agreement of 1998 and the thirty years of warfare, known as the 'Troubles', that preceded it. The Irish Republican Army (IRA) was beginning to dispose of its arms, but slowly. A new, avowedly non-sectarian police force, the Police Service of Northern Ireland, had been set up, but republicans remained aloof and distrustful. A Northern Ireland Assembly, the province's first serious experiment in communal power sharing, had been established at Stormont, but it was dissolved in October 2002 after the discovery of an alleged republican spy ring. Things remained uncertain and unsettled, and it seemed to be a good time to look into Belfast's past for some understanding of how the people of this one city had become so entangled in hatred, bitterness and fear. I wanted to show that there was nothing natural or inevitable about their conflict – that it was rooted in a definable historical moment – that, when we make bland pronouncements about the 'weight of history' in Northern Ireland, we essentialise Ulster's people and their past, sealing them off in a sectarian twilight zone where communal rivalries never die and history endlessly repeats itself.

But it is for this very reason that these early riots cannot be used to explain the 'Troubles' of the twentieth century, or at least not to explain very much. A strong case can be made, as the research of Alan Parkinson has suggested, that the bloody clashes surrounding the partition of Northern Ireland in 1921 echoed Belfast's Victorian riots, and memories and stories about the Victorian riots may even have had some influence on the tremendous riots of 1935.[1] But I suspect that the long period of relative peace that prevailed from the 1930s to the late 1960s greatly attenuated the old traditions, so that what were once autobiographical memories slowly became less immediate, historical memories that had little direct relevance for people's everyday lives. Radically new influences, such as the civil rights movement in the United States, Third World liberation movements, utopian Marxism, romantic Irish nationalism, advanced weapons technologies, deindustrialisation, drug smuggling and overseas financial contributions all made the post-1960s 'Troubles' a profoundly different sort of conflict. The IRA's paramilitary campaign – with its bombings, assassinations, ambushes and hunger strikes, to say nothing of its nationalist and even internationalist aspirations – had no precedent in Victorian Belfast, and insofar as this campaign was largely responsible for propelling the violence for the better part of thirty years, it is inaccurate to see this later period as a mere continuation of the Victorian-era conflicts that we have been examining. Moreover, the 'Troubles' were a province-wide phenomenon (indeed, at times the theatre of war extended to Britain and the Irish Republic as well) in which Belfast was but one field of battle, albeit a central one. To explain the 'Troubles' in terms of this single city's nineteenth-century traditions of violence is to commit an error of geography as well as chronology.

And yet some dots beg to be connected. The Unionist leader Ian Paisley, for instance, has loudly (and self-consciously) echoed Belfast's Victorian 'political parsons' with his powerful blend of loyalist politics and 'No Popery' evangelicalism, and his ideas and influence have been of decisive importance throughout the 'Troubles'.[2] The communal extremists of the mid-Victorian years – the Ribbonmen, Orangemen, shipcarpenters and navvies – likewise had their descendants among the working-class paramilitaries of the Belfast slums; the parallels are especially clear among those loyalist groups who justified their existence by presenting themselves as adjuncts to the state whose only desire was to preserve order in the face of Catholic violence. The vicious communal purges during the early years of the 'Troubles', when rioters set ablaze whole blocks of Victorian-era tenements, had ample precedent in the previous century, as did the massive funeral processions for dead paramilitaries and civilians on both sides. Even the recent dispute between republicans and loyalists surrounding children travelling to the Holy Cross School recalled the violence that attended Hugh Hanna's children's processions in the 1870s and 1880s.

Perhaps the most striking parallels concern the state. At the beginning of the 'Troubles' Catholics, like their Victorian ancestors, faced discrimination from a sectarian local government (now based at Stormont) and police force (the Royal Ulster Constabulary and the 'B' Specials), and this led many to take up defensive positions to protect their communities once the violence broke. The British government's dismantling of Stormont and imposition of direct rule in 1972 likewise resembled the centralising and rationalising agendas of the Victorians, and had similar consequences. As before, the British state tried to position itself as an impartial referee between the two sides; as before, it relied very heavily on overwhelming force to put down violence; and, as before, neither its professed impartiality nor its (often excessively) coercive measures did much to alleviate the violence or to prevent the state itself from becoming a belligerent in the war.[3] The result was an even greater crisis of state legitimacy than that which pertained in the Victorian period, and it is only now, in 2009, that Northern Ireland appears finally to have obtained a government that can rule with the consent of a substantial majority of the population.

These parallels – one might even say continuities – are significant, for they suggest that certain structural conditions remained in place in Ulster from the Victorian period to the last decades of the twentieth century. Imperialism, with the problems of legitimacy, power and resistance that it engenders, surely helps to explain many of these continuities. It helps to explain, for instance, the tendency of successive British governments to misunderstand Irish realties, their reflexive resort to coercive force when handling Irish disorder and their failure to construct a 'neutral' version of the state on which all sides could agree. Whether we choose to believe that Britain's motives were benign or malignant in this respect, its presence in Ulster has been of central importance. The settler ideology of Ulster Protestantism, with its siege mentality and ethos of self-reliance, has also remained important, as have the historic grievances of Catholics, often presented by twentieth-century republicans as outgrowths of a malicious imperialism that put their struggle on the same plane as anti-colonial liberation movements around the world.[4] Insofar as questions of state legitimacy are central to the colonial condition, then, a shared imperial framework does indeed seem to tie the Victorian era to the later 'Troubles'.

If Belfast's Victorian riots can tell us anything useful about Ulster's more recent violence, however, the lessons are in the generalities, not the details. Violent extremists who create ethnically pure neighbourhoods while cowed non-combatants watch in fear; ordinary people drawn into a conflict in which they initially had no interest, and who slowly adopt the prejudices of those who preach communal hatred; a powerful external (imperial) force adopting a stance of impartiality and seeking to contain communal violence, only to find that violence cannot be contained with overwhelming force alone; religious fanaticism; a local government in which a significant minority have little faith – all these elements were present in mid-Victorian Belfast, and most have been in evidence, in one form or another, not only in late twentieth-century Northern Ireland, but also in places like Bosnia, Sri Lanka, northern India and – most recently – Iraq. To understand how these societies became violent we must be attuned not only to the structural and ideological forces framing the violence, but also to how human beings experienced and responded to violence as individuals and as groups. The emotions and memories brought on by violence, solidified and preserved in the stories people tell themselves, form the core of communal identity in divided societies. In Victorian Belfast these identities were embedded and expressed in a decades-long tradition of violence whose ghosts linger still. To understand the size, shape and colour of those ghosts is to take the first step toward exorcising them.

Notes

1 Alan F. Parkinson, *Belfast's Unholy War: The Troubles of the 1920s* (Dublin: Four Courts Press, 2004), 14–16.

2 Ian Paisley, *The 'Fifty Nine' Revival: An Authentic History of the Great Ulster Awakening of 1859* (Belfast: Nelson & Knox, 1958).

3 For an insightful critique of Britain's security policies in the twentieth century, see Mike Tomlinson, 'Walking Backwards into the Sunset: British Policy and the insecurity of Northern Ireland', in *Rethinking Northern Ireland: Culture, Ideology, and colonialism*, ed. David Miller (London: Longman, 1998), 94–122.

4 For a critical assessment of these positions, see Stephen Howe, *Ireland and Empire* (Oxford: Oxford University Press, 2000), esp. chs. 9 and 10.

APPENDIX: 1864 riot ballads

THE BATTLE OF THE NAVVIES

By One of the Carpenters – Air – 'Battle of the Diamond'.

We burnt the Bully Beggarman – for him our scorn expressed,
And at the gate of Friar's-bush we laid him down to rest,
And from ten thousand people an indignant cry erose,
That we were crushed by government, while petted were our foes.

And when we burnt the Beggarman, we thought it well to join
And raise a noble monument for William of the Boyne:
But angry grew Mick Kenna, and he wrote his anger down,
That he might raise the Navvies then to desolate the town.

And soon the navvies left their work; and then the raging crew
Went marching up and down the street with pike and pistol too
There was danger in their faces, by sectariun nature nursed,
And horror went before them like a cloud about to burst.

The shops were closed for safety in the middle of the day,
The streets were near deserted – people dreaded an affray,
But onward went the Navvies like demons of misrule,
And they paused to show their valour deside an infant school.

And there they fired their pissols, and heaps of stones they flung
Right through the school-house windows to massacre the young:
And they only paused from ruin when they seen the gallant foe
Rush like molten iron from the foundry of Soho.

They fled like demons to their dens – in running they excel –
But forth again they issued when the evening shadows fell;
And many an honest citizen was reft of all he had,
By the brutal plundering Navvies, by Mick Kenna driven mad,

Oh, shame upon Mick Kenna, he's a stranger to our town;
He's disloyal to his Clergy, and disloyal to the Crown;
His tongue like a malaria, sends a poison with his breath;
It was he who fired the Navvies to ruin and to death.

But woe to you, ye Navvies, for before another sun,
You will sup a heap of sorrow for the ruin you have done,
We'll come upon you like a storm or like a sudden flood,
And send you helter-skelter writhing, wriggling through the mud.

They sent unto the Island and they challenged us that day;
For they had guns and pistols to begin a blaody fray,
Our arms – we had to find them, but we didn't dally long,
And we rushed upon the Navvies in three columns stout and strong.

Brave Charley led us onward bold Dick and gallant Roe,
And like a bounding avalanche we swept upon the foe,
The Navvies fought like bull-dogs but we swore to put them down,
The assassins of the children – the despoilers of the town.

Some struggle in a deadly grip some load away and fire
Ho, ho, the Navvies show their backs and down the bank retire,
Some leap into the river some scramble through mud,
And our noble follows follw to the margin of the flood.

They scatter o'er the mob-land – too warm behind to stay –
They struggle onward o'er the slime and fling their guns away.
They call upon the holy saints to help them in their flight,
And all along the banks our boys were bursting at the sight.

'Tis not for us to claim the prais – we'll leave it to the town,
To tell by true acknowledgment who put the Navvies down.
But many good fols do confess our work was done in time,
To stay the murderous Navvies in theirt course of blood and crime.

And now that they have fled away, to keep our fair renown,
We'd help the Special Constables, and gentlemen of town,
To crush those fearful riots, which we are bound to say
Were started up by Mick Kenna and the Navvies in his pay.

SANDY ROW

By a Cavan Anti-Forester.

The demonstration's over – the great event is past,
And Romanists returning at eve approach Belfast;
O'erhead, illumed in splendour, appears some fiery mass,
Upon the Boyne Bridge hoisted, as underneath they pass:
The Liberator! could it be? in flames enveloped so;
None would this do but men so true – the Boys of Sandy-row.

A shout of wild defiance goes up with evening's air,
The Pound-street rebels for attack on Orangemen prepare;
But happily they must contend with men of courage tried,
Who routed and confused them, and burned Dan with pride.
That night upon the Boyne Bridge they made a gallant show,
They proved Belfast true to the last, the Boys of Sandy-row.

The Pound-street miscreants sally forth, our window-panes to break;
They little know that Sandy-row such insults will not take:
Resolved each man to bury Dan, our Orangemen agree
To raise a stir – they will inter his charcoaled effigy:
To bury him they now intend, in Stygian depths below,
And form a demonstration in loyal Sandy-row.

The rebels smash, we hear the crash of glass on every side;
Determined then, our Orangemen with missiles are supplied;
In the Nunnery transparency soon lost its crystal light –
Their Bishop too our courage knew, combined with orange might.
Pound rebels fled – on every had a mark we did bestow;
In each affray we gained the day – success to Sandy-row!

Queen's Island carpenters came forth in artizan array;
Through every alley that they passed they did their 'footing pay;'
In Townsend-street and Peter's-hill, and other nooks around,
Thro' Hercules and North streets, chased rebels from the Pound.
They fought them with a right good will, and made them onward go,
With twice one hundred Orangemen, from loyal Sandy-row.

The police and soldiery arrive in martial trim,
But Protestants were not afraid to venture life and limb;
On every way the wounded lay, like Boyne's proud fight of yore,
We made them feel our Orange steel in August, Sixty-four:
Whilst William's sons can use their guns, we'll give them blow for blow,
And let them see the bravery of dauntless Sandy-row.

The rioting continued from eighth to seventeenth day,
At length Queen's Island men were called to fight without delay:
Wild Navvies, armed for the attack with pistol, pike, and spade,
Thus thought by their appearance to make our boys afraid.
But soon they fly, wading breast-high where Lagan's waters flow;
Queen's Island braves thus chased the knaves, and succoured Sandy-row.

The riots now are ended, and party strife near o'er;
Our faith we have defended in August, Sixty-four.
Now a health to Enniskillen, and to each Orangeman,
And may the green at length be seen reposing with old Dan.
In every street let Brothers meet, and face the wily foe,
And in each fight maintain the right, like men of Sandy-Row.

THE GLORIOUS ORANGE VICTORY AT THE BELFAST RIOTS

Over the Navvies and Pound Loaning Men.

All you Orangemen I hope you'll draw near,
Of the riots in Belfast I'll soon let you hear,
How the Navvies turned out and away the did go,
For to wreck all Brown Square and destroy Sandy Row.

Chorus – Derry down, down, all you Navvies lie down

You poor Navvies and threshers that murder by night.
Sure when danger is at hand you are all in a fright.
Not like the sons of King William who ne'er were afraid,
For to meet in daylight with their Orange cockade.

Now the Navvies turned out with their shovels and spades
For to kill our Orangemen and make them afraid,
But upon the Boyne Bridge, where our Orangemen did stand,
And that very same night we set fire to Dan.

The great fame of the Navvies these threshers did boast
They were cursing King William and all the Orange host
While the sticks, stones, and weapons did darken the air,
And the swore that none of our Orangemen they would spare.

But when our Ship Carpenters heard of the news,
To befriend Sandy Row sure they did not refuse,
While the men of the Foundry and Brown Square did join,
And we played them the tune that we played at the Boyne.

Sure they shot John M'Connell, a true Orangeman,
For nothing but burning the model of Dan,
But if the provoke us we'll tell them in plain,
We'll banish the navvies and burn him again.

We went down to the docks when the tide was on flood
And we hunted the navvies right into the mud;
When the smelt Orange powder they daren't look back,
For in gutters and mud they were up to the neck.

So you mud-larks and navvies I pray you beware,
And of our Ship Carpenters I hope you'll take care,
For the laws of King William they'll die to a man,
They can conquer the navvies and all of their clan.

To the memory of William we all do incline,
When we think on the day that he fought at the Boyne,
To praise the Ship Carpenters in duty we're bound,
For they conquered the navvies and subdued the Pound.

THE NAVVIES VICTORY

At the Belfast Riots.

You Romans all of Belfast town I hope you will attend,
I call your kind attention to those lines I've lately penned,
For the burning of that effigy I'll give you for to know
How the navvies and Pound Loaning boys repaid Sandy row

Chorus. – Long life attend our navvies, while assisted by the Pound
They're able when they're called upon to keep the beagles down.

Those orange monsters gathered round as yod may understan
But they would not meet our navvies yet or fight them hand to hand.
For when our navvies did appear we drove them to despair –
And they caused the weavers to run that das, and leave Brown's Square.

These cowardly orange ruffians now for plunder they are bent,
And to wreck the blessed house of God it was their intent.
They could not meet us man to man I give you for to know –
But to strip and beat poor mill girls they're fit in Sandy row.

With hatchets sticks and hammers the orange cubs did apear
But how soon they ran and left the way when our Navvies gave a cheer.
We put them out of Brown's street till not one there could be found
And for all they number ten to one they dare not meet the Pound.

The scrubs of the Queen's Island, when our Navvies they did see –
Sure they would not close upon them nor fight us 1 to three.
But we will not let them off my boys, like in the days of yore
And we'll shew they're never able to burn brave Dan no more

The Herclus Street and Smithfield men, and the Loney boys also,
Is very fit and able to tame poor Sandy-row.
Sura they never came before us yet ten minutes could us stan
For on any ground we meet them we can beat them 10 to 1.

But I hold you they are settled that they shant annoy the town
After all the mill girls they did beat, they dare not face the pound.
For our Navvies they are alwass fit to give the weavers play
And we'll hunt them out of Sandy-row before the next 12th day.

Let all our Roman members come fill a flowing glass,
With a health unto our navvy boys that's fit to rule Belfast.
For if we knew the weaver's minds you find they rue the day,
They'll say no more about Belfast till the navvies go away.

The Boyne bridge it will be called no more, for it has lost its name,
We'll christen it the natvy bridge – they're men of mighty fame,
Tea Lane and Purple row for shame must bow their heads,
For stripping of poor mill girls and burning a man that's dead

Bat weat could be expected from that bloody Tory crew,
For their church aefore them was false and her hearers are not true,
But if they annop us any more I'll have you for to know
We'll close some day upon them and drive them from Sandy-row.'

BARNEY'S EVIDENCE

Och, Barney, dear Barney – och, what made you say,
In answer to questions of boul' Johnny Rea,
That the Cawthlicks of Belfast were loyal and true,
And that you ne'er called them 'the bone and s*inew*'?

Try and mind '57 – purty Barney, *do* try,
For I'm under in*flu*ence you've tould a big lie:
You tould the Commissioners then, it is true,
That in Belfast *your sort* were the bone and sin*ew*.

Now lend me yer lugs, my brave Cawtholick cock:
On the day of the fight I was down at the Dock,
And I'm under inflúence no blank shots were fired,
Till *my* brother Navvies t' the mudbank retired.

Then afther the chase shure I wint away home;
So angry was I, man-alive, I did foam,
To see these poor fellows far out in the mud –
For that same I would walk knee-deep in Orange blood.

I met Mister Loyons – so proudly he paced,
And horsemen with prisoners tied to each baste;
A man wint up to him – I did it all see –
So then he giv ordhers a prisoner to free.

The thruth I am spakin' – I'll swear it, by Dan;
Mister Loyons, I know, is a foine gintleman,
And what I have stated he will not deny –
Och, look at him, Barney – he's likin' to cry.

I've left my first question, and wandered away,
But I'm under inflúence you will nothing say;
So look at the words here – och, what's yer mishap?
Why, Barney, yer face is as white as a bap.

I find on the page markèd 241 –
This is a Report Smythe and Lynch sat upon:
Here Barney yer axed by Returney M'Lean –
When ye give him that answer, then what did ye mane?

And here again, Barney, page 242,
(Bedad I could wish that it hadn't been you,)
Mr. Purcel has axed it agin – see it there:
Now, Barney, explain it – for why do you stare?

Another lafe over, page 243,
Och, och, what is this here again that I see?
I'm under the influence you're in a mess;
Och, Barney, run fast to the praste, and confess.

Dear Sir, I am sorry you've met sich disgrace,
And tould a big lie to the gintlemen's face,
But I hope they will strive, fur to solace yer care,
To set up yer sponge fur a justice or mayor.

Did the Local Police e'er do you any harm?
Did they ever swallow your dough or your barm?
Do you think it was them to your trade put a stop,
When the weevilly biscuit was sould in yer shop?

Och, Barney, I wish you had stayed at yer buns,
Or that you were sweetly immured with the Nuns;
For I'm under the notion, from hearing ye spake,
That our cause, like our wealth, is exceedingly wake.

I know, Barney dear, none yer bread can impeach,
It is yer invintion, and fine as yer speech,
But *I* have a notion – and I'm not alone –
That *our sort* here will ne'er be the sinew and bone.

NOLAN'S ADVICE TO BARRY & DOWSE.

Dear Dowse and Barry who in Belfast tarry,
    And from Mick and Larry bring knowledge out;
Won't your foine decision prevint all collision,
    And a state elysian at last bring about?

You have found how hearty each different party
    Do hate each other in their separate ends;
But it is no fable for to think you're able
    To write a label that will make them friends.

You are both so cliver! and the State has niver
    Such larned kimmisioners to haythens sint;
You will put down riot, and you'll keep us quiet,
    Or very nigh it, by Act o' Parleymint.

You heerd our Barney wid his honest blarney,
    And our Docthor Marney, wid Loughran's jaw;
And won't you make thim, ere you do forsake thim,
    All mighty magistrates fur to give us law.

There is Brokey Ross, too, and 'twould be a loss, too,
   If his noble larnin' didn't grace the Binch;
So condescind – he'll our cause befrind,
   And you may depind Brokey wudn't flinch.

And there's M'Cann, sirs – a Ribbonman, sirs,
   He will plot and plan, sirs, against William's sons;
He will say and swar too, what no other daur do,
   As he did declaur too, about Ingram's guns.

The brave Navvie fellows who blow the Papal bellows,
   We do hope you'll tell us you will find them bread;
They wud make foine Polis, and 'twud be a solace
   If the bould Mick-Kenna was stuck at their head.

Och, it will be jolly fur to see our folly
   Become a whip fur to lash our foes;
And it will be splindid, when all is inded,
   Fur to see us minded in mate and clothes.

That gaynius Hagan, unmatched by saint or Pagan,
   He is a-plaguin' all our inimies:
And we won't say 'Oh no,' if Pio Nono
   Should sind him straight to glory whene'er he dies.

Now shure we've rayson, in this thryin' sayson,
   Fur to be a-praisin' the Vargin bright;
We may look defiance at oul' Turnip Lyons,
   For O'Donnell's science is our shield in flight.

Now, boys, be joyous, fur nought kin annoy is,
   When Papa Pius of our bravery sings;
We are making way, boys – hooray, hooray, boys,
   We may lift our heads now like oul' Irish kings.

THE MARQUIS & THE MAYOR.

Over the sea, with the absentees,
Our Marquis was merry, and lived at ease:
With lords and with ladies, so gay and bold,
He spent his time, and his Irish gold.

Back he came to our Irish land
For the Masons to make him their Master Grand;
And with him his lady, so fair to view,
And pure as a snowdrop in morning de.

Brave was the Marquis long long ago,
When he gladdened the echoes of old Ormeau;
But time is the worker of changes vast,
It has changed his lordship, and changed Belfast.

Who would have thought, in his life's long track,
He would shoot his lance in his victim's back;
Who would have thought he would ever dare
For to bespatter our gallant Mayor.

Ah, my lord! you have surely won
A title of honour for labour done:
Good you did us – but should we pause
To give you credit, and ask the cause?

We have been raising with steady toil,
A noble city upon your soil;
You have been claiming for many a day,
Your legal rights, while we worked away.

Take the credit, and all the fame
That duty allies with your noble name;
Your smallest merit we'll praise as rare,
But won't you be merciful to our Mayor?

For what are we to your high estate –
Our Mayor is little and you are great;
He is a merchant, and you a peer,
But whom have we reason to love more dear?

Sad was the greeting that met your view –
Riot, disorder, and murder too;
But why should your lordship explode the gun
Of your arrogant deputy, Ferguson?

Petty and sordid, with all his pelf,
He would try to make you resemble himself;
If his breast had been warmed with the fervid tone
Of a patriot's zeal, 'twould have fired your own.

But now you're of Masons the Master Grand,
And your bosom with Charity will expand;
And Hope and Faith will exalt your mind,
O'er the creeping malice of humankind.

Scorn the seducer – he turns aside,
Groaning in secret with wounded pride;
Soiled by associates, let him blow
His sulphrous fumes in the shades below.

And you, as you value the high renown
You claim in your interest for the town,
Will learn the maxim we now declare –
Insult the people, insult the Mayor.

THE GOOD OLD ORANGE MAGISTRATE

Composed on William Thomas Bristow Lyons, Esq. J. P., Belfast
Air – 'The Good Old English Gentleman'.

I'll sing you a good new song, and the truth I mean to state,
Of a good old Belfast gentleman – an Orange magistrate,
Who gallops upon horseback at a very furious rate,
Keeping Papists in subjection, at an early hour and late,
Like a good old Orange magistrate – one of the present time.

He makes himself conspicuous in many ways beside,
And in actions most ridiculous he seems to take a pride;
He is partial to the Orangemen, unless he is belied,
And they cheer him when they meet him, and surround him e'ery side,
Like a good old Orange magistrate – one of the present time.

He is hated in Pound-Loaning, but he's loved in Sandy-Row,
To the latter he is partial, to the former he's a foe.
The Papists hiss and groan at him, I'm bound to let you know,
But he's greeted by the Orangemen, as onward he doth go,
Like a good old Orange magistrate – one of the present time.

Some say that he's a fanatic, and some that he's 'not wise;'
And, as regards these sayings, I am sure they are no lies.
And, hence, we're bound by charity with him to sympathise;
But sympathy from Papists he'd indignantly despise,
Like a good old Orange magistrate – one of the present time.

He daily sits upon the Bench the law for to dispense,
But knows no more of justice than he does of common sense,
And when Papists come before him, he regards not their defence,
But provides them long with lodgings 'at her Majesty's expense,'
Like a good old Orange magistrate – one of the present time.

When the Orangemen are rising, he makes a deal to do,
And commands as proud as Wellington, who fought at Waterloo.
Many Papists are led captive, but the Orangemen are few,
For the Papists are the party he's determined to subdue,
Like a good old Orange magistrate – one of the present time,

When cars of gallant Orangemen came into Belfast town,
With guns and pistols well prepared to shoot the Papists down,
* Said the cavalry, 'These men shall we make prisoners of the Crown'?
'Oh no,' said he, 'they'll quiet be,' while he answered with a frown,
Like a good old Orange magistrate – one of the present time,

And they residing out of town, and might not know the way,
To Sandy-row head-quarters where their Orange brethren lay,
Or that a Romish mob might dare their progress to delay,
With Soldiers he conducted them, and rode along the way,
Like a good old Orange magistrate – one of the present time.

To signify that they had come, some Papist blood to spill,
They fired their guns and pistols, and the shots were loud and shrill,
And as they boldly passed along, they cheered him with good will,
For protecting them thus nobly, though the Tagues they came to kill,
Like a good old Orange magistrate – one of the present time.

And when three thousand Orangemen all armed did invade
The Popish streets of Belfast, then he likewise brought them aid,
He led in front the Cavalry, lest ought should them impede,
And rode himself the foremost, for he never was afraid,
Like a good old Orange magistrate – one of the present time.

The Orangemen encouraged thus by him they love so dear,
And seeing by his conduct they had no cause to fear,
They fired into each Papist house and passed it with a cheer,
While their brave protector led them on and did not interfere,
Like a good old Orange magistrate – one of the present time,

As William rode across the Boyne he could not have more pride,
Than had this brave old gentleman as onward did he ride,
He sat with such a kingly air his thoughts he could not hide,
And he looked with admiration at his friends on every side
Like a good old Orange magistrate – one of the present time,

But, now, my song I must conclude, perhaps you'll think it time,
And if it has not pleased you why the fault is none of mine,
The truth I've merely told you though my muse is not sublime,
But the truth in certain cases is regarded worse than crime,
By those good old Orange magistrates – all of the present time.

* See letter of 'Sergeant J. J. Depot, – Regt. 14 D. B., Belfast', in the 'Ulster Observer' of 30th August, 1864

THE BELFAST SPECIAL BOBBIES AND KING MOB

An Original Ballad composed by One of the Belfast Specials.
Copyright!

Search Ireland again,
Over hill and over glen,
And you cannot find a finer company of men:
Our favour they command,
They are such a gallant band:
And then their only weapons are the batons in their hand.

When Riot in the town
Did trample Order down;
Our noble Mayor could trust in the lovers of the Crown:
For Church and State they stand;
They're a most devoted band;
And then their only weapons are the batons in their hand.

There is Charley, Tom, and Dick,
Who can use their bit of stick,
Ned Luke and Andy Gilmore – we needn't mention *Mick*:
And Father Mackey too,
Who's the boy could chase a few;
All noble valiant fellows when there's any work to do.

See them doing up and down
In those districts of the town
Where the frantic mob were furious as devils in a poun'!
How gallant is their mien,
When one or more is seen
To seize and take the offender to McKitterick or Green!

Fell Bigotry and Hate
The bitterest feuds create,
But the Specials are no bigots – they are pillars of the State:
They are loyal to the Crown;
They are valiant for the town;
They will wipe away the stigma from its eminent renown.

Ah, brothers! one and all,
Upon you with hope we call,
To bring the fiend of Riot to its everlasting fall:
Let the first town of the land
As the first for order stand,
And more and more our Arts and Commerce will expand!

Then Andy, Dick, and Ned,
Let your kindling fervour spread,
And all our worthy citizens no more may terror dread;
As your fervour will increase,
So the Bigot's powers will cease,
He who goads the mob to frenzy, then chatters for a peace.

Let praises fill the air
For our Magistrates and Mayor,
And for all the men who laboured our order to repair!
King Mob they trampled down,
Gave repose unto the town:
In life may they be honoured, and immortal their renown!

Printed for the Author by Thomas Henry, 7 Pottinger's Entry.

Source: NLI, Larcom Papers, *7626/106*. All spelling and typographical errors in
the originals have been retained .

Bibliography

Primary sources

Manuscript sources
Borthwick Institute of Historical Research, University of York
Halifax papers.

Cardinal Tomás O Fiaich Library, Armagh
Archbishop Joseph Dixon papers.

Diocese of Down and Connor Archives
Denvir Papers.
Typescript copy of Special Letter Book, 1867–79, Belfast City Hall.

Grand Orange Lodge of Ireland
Orange Registry of Warrants for the Belfast district, 1856.

Linen Hall Library, Belfast
Minutes of the Proceedings of the General Assembly of the Presbyterian Church in Ireland, vol. 2 (1851–60).

Mitchell Library, Glasgow
Minutes of Glasgow Free Presbytery, 1856–63, Glasgow City Archives.

National Archives, Kew
Home Office Records.

National Archives of Ireland, Dublin
Chief Secretary's Office Registered Papers (CSORP), 1857–65, 1872.

National Archives of Scotland, Edinburgh
Lord Advocate's Papers.

National Library of Ireland, Dublin
Esmonde Papers.
Grand Orange Lodge meeting minutes.
Larcom Papers.
Mayo Papers.

Public Record Office of Northern Ireland, Belfast
A. McIntyre, diary.
Albert Street Presbyterian Church Records.
Annals of Christ Church.
Belfast Police Committee minutes.
Cartes de viste of Belfast riots.
Census of Christ Church, 1852.
Christ Church records.
Colonial Office records on Ribbonism.
James MacAdam, diary.
St Peter's Church Baptismal Records, Oct 1856 to Feb 1875.
William Johnston, diary.

Newspapers and periodicals

Banner of Ulster
Belfast Daily Mercury
Belfast Mercantile Journal
Belfast Morning News
Belfast Newsletter
Belfast Weekly Mail
Belfast Weekly News
Daily Express
Daily Telegraph
Dublin Evening Mail
Dublin Evening Post
Evening Post
Freeman's Journal
Glasgow Daily Herald
Glasgow Free Press
The Globe
Irish News
Irish People
The Irish Presbyterian

Irish Times
Limerick Reporter and Tipperary Vindicator
North British Daily Mail
Northern Whig
Punch
Saturday Review
Times (London)
Ulsterman
Ulster Observer
Weekly Northern Whig

Parliamentary papers

Bill to restrain Party Processions in Ireland, HC 1850 (519) V.

The Census of Ireland for the year 1861. Part IV. Report and Tables relating to the Religious Professions, Education, and Occupations of the People, HC 1863 (3204–III) LIX, vol. 1.

Copies of any Instructions issued to the Magistrates or Constabulary in Ireland relative to the Processions Act, between 1860 and 1864, both inclusive: – And, of the Commissions of Inquiry at Belfast in 1857 and 1864, HC 1865 (134) XLV.

Papers relating to an Investigation Held at Castlewellan into the occurrences at Dolly's Brae, on the 12th July, 1849, HC 1850 (331) LI.

Report of the Belfast Riots Commissioners. Minutes of Evidence and Appendices. HC 1887 (4925–I) XVIII.

Report of the Commissioners Appointed to Inquire into the State of the Municipal Affairs of the Borough of Belfast, in Ireland, with Appendices and Minutes of Evidence, HC 1859, session 1 (2470) XII.

Report of the Commissioners of Inquiry, 1864, respecting the Magisterial and Police Jurisdiction Arrangements and Establishment of the Borough of Belfast, HC 1865 (3466) XXVIII.

Report of the Commissioners of Inquiry into the Origin and Character of the Riots in Belfast, in July and September, 1857; together with Minutes of Evidence and Appendix, HC 1857–8 (2309) XXVI.

Report to the Lord Lieutenant of Ireland by Messrs. Fitzmaurice and Goold, with the Minutes of the Evidence taken by them at the Inquiry into the Conduct of the Constabulary during the Disturbances at Belfast in July and September, 1857, HC 1857–58 (333) XLVII.

Returns of the number of convictions for assaults on the agents of the Irish Church Missionary Society, in the city of Kilkenny, for the last twelve months; of the number of additional police force lately introduced into Kilkenny; Copies of reports and correspondence on the subject of the increased police force; and resolutions of the grand jury to the Lord Lieutenant, and his Excellency's reply, HC 1856 (517) LIII.

Published sources: books, pamphlets, proceedings, etc.

Alison, Archibald. *Some Account of My Life and Writings*. 2 vols. Edinburgh: William Blackwood and Sons, 1883.

Annual Report of the Glasgow Young Men's Christian Association, Year 1861–1862. Glasgow: James Cameron, 1862.

Archer, William. *Orange Melodies, Occasional Verses, Stanzas for Music, Notes*. Dublin: James Forrest, 1869.

The Belfast Almanac 1864. Belfast: Alexander Mayne, 1864.

The Belfast and Province of Ulster Directory for 1858–9. Belfast: James Alexander Henderson, 1858.

Belfast Politics and Parliamentary Elections. Belfast: Banner of Ulster Office, 1865.

Carson, Ciaran. *The Ballad of HMS Belfast*. Loughcrew, Ireland: The Gallery Press, 1999.

Cooke, Henry. *The Papal Aggression! Lecture by the Rev. H. Cooke, D.D., LL.D., on the Present Aspect and Future Prospects of Popery*, 2nd ed. Belfast: William McComb, 1851.

Drew, Thomas. *A Sermon, Preached in Christ Church, Belfast, on the evening of November 5, 1856, being the Anniversary of the Deliverance from the Popish Gunpowder Plot, and also of the Arrival of William III., Prince of Orange, before the Assembled Orangemen of Belfast.* Belfast: A. Welsh, 1856.

Edgar, John. 'The Cry from Connaught'. In *Select Works of John Edgar, D.D., LL.D*, 481–92. Belfast: n.p., 1868.

——. *The Dangerous and Perishing Classes. A paper read before the Statistical Section of the British Association, at Belfast, September 3, 1852*. Belfast: Belfast Social Inquiry Society, 1852.

The Forty-first Annual Report of the Glasgow University Missionary Association. April, 1862. Glasgow: James MacNab, 1863.

Gault, Robert. *Popery, the Man of Sin and the Son of Perdition*. Glasgow: W. R. McPhun, 1853.

Good, James Winder. *Ulster and Ireland*. Dublin: Maunsel and Co., 1919.

Grand Orange Lodge of Ireland. *Report of the Proceedings of the Grand Orange Lodge of Ireland, at the Special Meeting, held in the General Central Committee Rooms, 45, Molesworth St., Dublin, On Tuesday, the 3rd, Wednesday, the 4th, Thursday, the 5th, and Friday, the 6th days of November, 1857; and at the Adjourned Special Meeting, Held in the Protestant Hall, Belfast, On Wednesday, the 20th, and Thursday, the 21st days of January, 1858*. Londonderry: Sentinel Office, 1858.

Henderson's Belfast Directory, 1861. Belfast: News-Letter Office, 1861.

Long, H. A. *Mene: The Numeration of Babylon Mystical. A Tract for the Times, on the Coming Fall of the Papacy*. Glasgow: William Macrone, 1865.

——. *Transubstantiation: Being the substance of what was advanced thereupon, in the late discussions, when disputing with the Roman Catholics on Glasgow Green, on certain evenings immediately after the fair of 1864*. Glasgow: Wm. Macrone, 1864.

MacKnight, Thomas. *Ulster as it Is: or, Twenty-eight Years' Experience as an Irish Editor*. 2 Vols. London: Macmillan and Co., 1896.

Malcolm, A. G. *The Sanitary State of Belfast, With Suggestions for its Improvement, a Paper Read before the Statistical Section of the British Association, at Belfast, September 7, 1852*. Belfast, Henry Greer, 1852.

McComb, William. *The Repealer Repulsed*, ed. Patrick Maume. Dublin: University College Dublin Press, 2003.

'Nemo' [F. S. Gordon]. *St Enoch's Church, Belfast, and Rev. Dr. Hanna. Historical Sketch*. Belfast: Whiffin & Hart, 1890.

Ninth Annual Report of the Glasgow Protestant Laymen's Association. Glasgow: Thomas Smith, 1862.

O'Brien, R. Barry. *Dublin Castle and the Irish People*. London: Kegan Paul, Trench, Trübner & Co., Ltd., 1909.

O'Hanlon, W. M. *Walks Among the Poor of Belfast, and Suggestions for Their Improvement*. Belfast: H. Greer, 1853.

O'Leary, John. *Recollections of Fenians and Fenianism*. Vol. 1. London: Downey & Co., 1896.

Orange Songs. 'New Edition,' Part II. Armagh: Armagh Standard, n. d.

The Orations of Father Gavazzi, delivered in Belfast on the 3rd, 4th, and 5th November, 1852. Belfast: William McComb, 1852.

Presbyterian Church of Ireland. *Reports of the Berry Street Congregation*. Belfast: Banner of Ulster Office, 1853.

Report of the Belfast Students' Missionary Association, for the year ending 31st January, 1857. Belfast: Banner of Ulster Office, 1857.

Roney, Frank. *Irish Rebel and California Labour Leader: An Autobiog-raphy*, ed. Ira B. Cross. Berkeley, Calif: University of California Press, 1931.

Sagitarius. *Orangeism Versus Ribbonism: A Statement on behalf of the Orange Institution*. Dublin: Roe and Brierley, 1852.

Simms, John Young. *Farewell to the Hammer: A Shankill Boyhood*. Belfast: The White Row Press, 1992.

The Town Council in Chancery. The case of the Attorney General at the relation of John Rea, Esq., v. the Belfast Municipal Corporation heard before the Lord Chancellor of Ireland, June, 1855. Belfast: Northern Whig Office, 1855.

Weir, John. *The Ulster Awakening: Its Origin, Progress, and Fruit. With notes of a tour of personal observation and inquiry.* London: Arthur Hall, Virtue, & Co., 1860.

Secondary sources

Adams, J. R. R. *The Printed Word and the Common Man: Popular Culture in Ulster, 1700–1900.* Belfast: Queen's University Institute of Irish Studies, 1987.

Anderson, David M., and David Killingray, eds. *Policing the Empire: Government, Authority, and Control, 1830–1940.* Manchester: Manchester University Press, 1991.

Armstrong, D. L. 'Social and Economic Conditions in the Belfast Linen Industry, 1850–1900', *Irish Historical Studies*, 7 (1950–51), 235–69.

Arnstein, Walter L. 'The Murphy Riots: A Victorian Dilemma', *Victorian Studies*, 19 (Sept. 1975), 51–70.

Aspinwall, Bernard. 'The Catholic Irish and Wealth in Glasgow'. In *Irish Immigrants and Scottish Society in the Nineteenth and Twentieth Centuries: Proceedings of the Scottish Historical Studies Seminar, University of Strathclyde, 1989–90*, ed. T. M. Devine, 91–115. Edinburgh: John Donald, 1991.

——. 'The Formation of the Catholic Community in the West of Scotland: Some Preliminary Outlines', *Innes Review*, 33 (1982), 44–57.

——. 'A Long Journey: The Irish in Scotland'. In *The Irish World Wide: History, Heritage, Identity*. Vol. 5, *Religion and Identity*, ed. Patrick O'Sullivan, 146–82. London: Leicester University Press, 1996.

——. 'The Welfare State Within the State: The Saint Vincent de Paul Society in Glasgow, 1848–1920.' In *Voluntary Religion: Papers Read at the 1985 Summer Meeting and the 1986 Winter Meeting of the Ecclesiastical History Society*, ed. W. J. Shiels and Diana Wood, 445–59. Oxford: Basil Blackwell, 1986.

Baker, Sybil. 'Orange and Green: Belfast, 1832–1912'. In *The Victorian City: Images and Realities*, Vol. 2, ed. H. J. Dyos and M. Wolff, 787–815. London: Routledge & Kegan Paul, 1973.

Bardon, Jonathan. *Belfast: An Illustrated History.* Belfast: The Blackstaff Press, 1982.

Beames, M. R. 'The Ribbon Societies: Lower-Class Nationalism in Pre-Famine Ireland', *Past and Present*, 97 (Nov. 1982), 128–43.

Bebbington, D. W. *Evangelicalism in Modern Britain: A History from the 1730s to the 1980s.* Winchester, Mass.: Allen & Unwin, 1989.

Beckett, J. C. 'Belfast to the End of the Eighteenth Century'. In J. C. Beckett et al., *Belfast: The Making of the City, 1800–1914*, 13–26. Belfast: Appletree Press, 1983.

—— et al. *Belfast: The Making of the City, 1800–1914*. Belfast: Appletree Press, 1983.

Belchem, John. 'Ribbonism, Nationalism and the Irish Pub'. In John Belchem, *Merseypride: Essays in Liverpool Exceptionalism*, 67–100. Liverpool: Liverpool University Press, 2000.

Belfast County Grand Lodge. *Centenary Official History, 1863–1963*. Newtownabbey: Universal Publishing Company, 1963.

Bennett, Anthony. 'Broadsides on the Trial of Queen Caroline: A Glimpse at Popular Song in 1820', *Proceedings of the Royal Musical Association*, 107 (1980–81), 71–85.

Bernstein, Iver. *The New York City Draft Riots: Their Significance for American Society and Politics in the Age of the Civil War*. New York: Oxford University Press, 1990.

Best, G. F. A. 'The Scottish Victorian City', *Victorian Studies*, 11 (March 1968), 329–58.

Blackstock, Allan. '"The Invincible Mass": Loyal Crowds in Mid Ulster, 1795–96', in *Crowds in Ireland, c. 1720–1920*, ed. Peter Jupp and Eoin Magennis, 83–114. New York: St Martin's Press, 2000.

Bohstedt, John. *Riots and Community Politics in England and Wales, 1790–1810*. Cambridge, MA: Harvard University Press, 1983.

Bold, Alan. *The Ballad*. London: Methuen & Co., 1979.

Booth, Mark W. *The Experience of Songs*. New Haven: Yale University Press, 1981.

Bowen, Desmond. *History and the Shaping of Irish Protestantism*. New York: Peter Land, 1995.

——. *Paul Cardinal Cullen and the Shaping of Modern Irish Catholicism*. Dublin: Gill and Macmillan, 1983.

——. *The Protestant Crusade in Ireland, 1800–70: A Study of Protestant–Catholic Relations between the Act of Union and Disestablishment*. Dublin: Gill and Macmillan, 1978.

Boyd, Andrew. *Holy War in Belfast*. Tralee: Anvil Books, 1969.

Brasted, Howard. 'Indian Nationalist Development and the Influence of Irish Home Rule, 1870–1886', *Modern Asian Studies* 14 (1980), 37–63.

Bratton, J. S. *The Victorian Popular Ballad*. London: The Macmillan Press Ltd, 1975.

Brewer, John D., with Gareth Higgins. *Anticatholicism in Northern Ireland, 1600–1998: The Mote and the Beam*. London: Macmillan Press, 1998.

Brooke, David. 'The "Lawless" Navvy: A Study of the Crime Associated with Railway Building', *The Journal of Transport History*, 10 (Sept. 1989), 145–65.

——. *The Railway Navvy: 'That Despicable Race of Men'*. Newton Abbot: David & Charles, 1983.

Brooke, Peter. *Ulster Presbyterianism: The Historical Perspective, 1810–1970*. Belfast: Athol Books, 1994.

Brown, Callum G. *The Social History of Religion in Scotland since 1730*. London: Methuen, 1987.

Brown, John. 'Part 2: From the Diamond to Home Rule, 1795–1886.' In M. W. Dewar, John Brown and S. E. Long, *Orangeism: A New Historical Appreciation*, 81–144. Belfast: Grand Orange Lodge of Ireland, 1967.

Brown, Stewart J. 'Chalmers, Thomas (1780–1847).' *Oxford Dictionary of National Biography*. Oxford: Oxford University Press, 2004.

Bruce, Steve. 'Comparing Scotland and Northern Ireland.' In *Scotland's Shame? Bigotry and Sectarianism in Modern Scotland*, ed. Tom Devine, 135–42. Edinburgh: Mainstream Publishing Company, 2000.

——. *No Pope of Rome: Anticatholicism in Modern Scotland*. Edinburgh: Mainstream Publishing, 1985.

——. 'Protestantism and Politics in Scotland and Ulster.' In *Prophetic Religions and Politics: Religion and the Political Order*, ed. Jeffrey K. Haddon and Ason Shupe, 410–29. New York: Paragon House, 1986.

——, Tony Glendinning, Iain Paterson, and Michael Rosie, *Sectarianism in Scotland*. Edinburgh: Edinburgh University Press, 2004.

Bryan, Dominic. *Orange Parades: The Politics of Ritual, Tradition, and Control*. London: Pluto Press, 2000.

Bryson, Anne. 'Riotous Liverpool, 1815–1860.' In *Popular Politics, Riot, and Labour*, ed. John Belchem, 98–134. Liverpool: Liverpool University Press, 1992.

Budge, Ian, and Cornelius O'Leary. *Belfast: Approach to Crisis*. London: Macmillan, 1973.

Burke, Peter. *Popular Culture in Early Modern Europe*. New York: Harper and Row, 1978.

Burrows, Montagu. 'Larcom, Sir Thomas Askew, First Baronet (1801–1879)', *The Dictionary of National Biography*, Vol. 11. London: Oxford University Press, 1921–22.

Busteed, M. A., and R. I. Hodgson. 'Irish Migrant Responses to Urban Life in Early Nineteenth-Century Manchester', *The Geographical Journal*, 162 (July 1996), 139–53.

Butt, John. 'Belfast and Glasgow: Connections and Comparisons, 1790–1850.' In *Ireland and Scotland, 1600–1850*, ed. T. M. Devine and David Dickson, 193–203. Edinburgh: John Donald, 1983.

——. 'The Industries of Glasgow.' In *Glasgow: 1830 to 1912*, ed. W. Hamish Fraser and Irene Maver, 96–140. Manchester: Manchester University Press, 1996.

Cage, R. A. 'Population and Employment Characteristics'. In *The Working Class in Glasgow, 1750–1914*, ed. R. A. Cage, 1–28. London: Croom Helm, 1987.

Campbell, Alan B. *The Lanarkshire Miners: A Social History of their Trade Unions, 1775–1974*. Edinburgh: John Donald, 1979.

Chatterji, Joya. *Bengal Divided: Hindu Communalism and Partition, 1932–1947*. Cambridge: Cambridge University Press, 1994.

Clarke, Tony, and Tony Dickson. 'Class and Class Consciousness in Early Industrial Capitalism: Paisley, 1770–1850'. In *Capital and Class in Scotland*, ed. Tony Dickson, 8–60. Edinburgh: John Donald, 1982.

Clayton, Pamela. *Enemies and Passing Friends: Settler Ideologies in Twentieth Century Ulster*. London: Pluto Press, 1996.

Cohn, Bernard. 'The Census, Social Structure, and Objectification in South Asia'. In *An Anthropologist among the Historians and Other Essays*, ed. Bernard Cohn, 224–54. Delhi: Oxford University Press, 1987.

Collins, Brenda. 'The Origins of Irish Immigration to Scotland in the Nineteenth and Twentieth Centuries'. In *Irish Immigrants and Scottish Society in the Nineteenth and Twentieth Centuries: Proceedings of the Scottish Historical Studies Seminar, University of Strathclyde, 1989–90*, ed. T. M. Devine, 1–18. Edinburgh: John Donald, 1991.

Comerford, R. V. *The Fenians in Context*. Dublin: Wolfhound Press, 1985.

——. 'Patriotism as Pastime: The Appeal of Fenianism in the Mid-1860s', *Irish Historical Studies*, 22 (Mar. 1981), 239–50.

Connerton, Paul. *How Societies Remember*. Cambridge: Cambridge University Press, 1989.

Cook, Scott B. 'The Irish Raj: Social Origins and Careers of Irishmen in the Indian Civil Service, 1855–1914', *Journal of Social History* 20/3 (Spring 1987), 507–30.

Coser, Lewis A. 'Introduction: Maurice Halbwachs, 1877–1945.' In M. Halbwachs, *On Collective Memory*, ed. and trans. Lewis A. Coser. Chicago: University of Chicago Press, 1992.

Cressy, David. *Bonfires and Bells: National Memory and the Protestant Calendar in Elizabethan and Stuart England*. Berkeley: University of California Press, 1989.

Cronin, Mike, and Daryl Adair. *The Wearing of the Green: A History of St. Patrick's Day*. London: Routledge, 2002.

Crossman, Virginia. 'Local Government in Nineteenth-Century Ireland'.

In *Was Ireland a Colony? Economics, Politics, and Culture in Nine-teenth-Century Ireland*, ed. Terrence McDonough, 102–16. Dublin: Irish Academic Press, 2005.

——. *Local Government in Nineteenth-Century Ireland*. Belfast: Queen's University Institute of Irish Studies, 1994.

——. *Politics, Law and Order in Nineteenth-Century Ireland*. Dublin: Gill & Macmillan, 1996.

Curtin, Nancy J. *The United Irishmen: Popular Politics in Ulster and Dublin, 1791–1798*. Oxford: Clarendon Press, 1994.

Davis, Natalie Zemon. *Society and Culture in Early Modern France*. Stanford, Calif.: Stanford University Press, 1975.

Devine, T. M. 'Unrest and Stability in Rural Ireland and Scotland, 1760–1840'. In *Economy and Society in Scotland and Ireland, 1500–1939*, ed. Rosalind Mitchison and Peter Roebuck, 126–39. Edinburgh: John Donald, 1988.

Dolan, Jay P. *The Immigrant Church: New York's Irish and German Catholics, 1815–1865*. Baltimore: Johns Hopkins University Press, 1975.

Doyle, Mark. 'Fighting like the Devil for the Sake of God: Protestants, Catholics, and the origins of violence in Belfast, 1850–1865'. Unpublished Ph.D. thesis, Boston College, 2006.

——. 'Visible Differences: The 1859 Revival and Communal Identity in Belfast.' In *Irish Protestant Identities*, ed. Mervyn Busteed, Frank Neal and John Tonge. Manchester: Manchester University Press, 2008.

Drummond, Andrew L., and James Bulloch. *The Church in Victorian Scotland, 1843–74*. Edinburgh: Saint Andrew Press, 1975.

Dunlop, Robert. 'The Famine Crisis: Theological Interpretations and Implications'. In *'Fearful Realities': New Perspectives on the Famine*, ed. Chris Morash and Richard Hayes, 164–74. Dublin: Irish Academic Press, 1996.

Dye, Ryan. 'Catholic Protectionism or Irish Nationalism? Religion and Politics in Liverpool, 1829–1845', *The Journal of British Studies*, 40 (July 2001), 357–90.

Dyer, Michael. '"Mere Detail and Machinery": The Great Reform Act and the Effects of Redistribution on Scottish Representation, 1832–1868', *Scottish Historical Review*, 72 (Apr. 1983), 17–34.

Elliott, Marianne. *The Catholics of Ulster: A History*. London: Penguin Books, 2000.

Farmer, Sarah. *Martyred Village: Commemorating the 1944 Massacre at Oradour-sur-Glane*. Berkeley: University of California Press, 1999.

Farrell, Sean. *Rituals and Riots: Sectarian Violence and Political Culture in Ulster, 1784–1886*. Lexington, Ky: University Press of Kentucky, 2000.

Ferguson, Priscilla Parkhurst. *Paris as Revolution: Writing the Nine-teenth-Century City.* Berkeley: University of California Press, 1994.

Ferguson, W. 'The Reform Act (Scotland) of 1832: Intention and Effect', *Scottish Historical Review*, 45 (Apr. 1966), 105–14.

Foley, Tadhg, and Maureen O'Connor, eds. *Ireland and India: Colonies, Culture, and Empire.* Dublin: Irish Academic Press, 2006.

Foster, John, Muir Houston and Chris Madigan. 'Distinguishing Catholics and Protestants among Irish Immigrants to Clydeside: A New Approach to Immigration and Ethnicity in Victorian Britain', *Irish Studies Review*, 10 (Aug. 2002), 171–92.

Fraser, Derek. *Power and Authority in the Victorian City.* New York: St Martin's Press, 1979.

Gailey, Adam, and G. B. Adams. 'The Bonfire in Northern Irish Tradi-tion', *Folklore*, 88 (1977), 3–38.

Gallagher, Tom. 'The Catholic Irish in Scotland: In Search of Identity'. In *Irish Immigrants and Scottish Society in the Nineteenth and Twenti-eth Centuries: Proceedings of the Scottish Historical Studies Seminar, University of Strathclyde, 1989–90*, ed. T. M. Devine, 19–43. Edin-burgh: John Donald, 1991.

——. *Glasgow, The Uneasy Peace: Religious Tension in Modern Scotland, 1819–1914.* Manchester: Manchester University Press, 1987.

Garrard, John. *Leadership and Power in Victorian Industrial Towns, 1830–80.* Manchester: Manchester University Press, 1983.

Garvin, Tom. 'Defenders, Ribbonmen and Others: Underground Political Networks in Pre-Famine Ireland', *Past and Present*, 96 (Aug. 1982), 133–55.

Gibbon, Peter. *The Origins of Ulster Unionism: The Formation of Popular Protestant Politics and Ideology in Nineteenth-Century Ireland.* Manchester: Manchester University Press, 1975.

Gilley, Sheridan. 'Catholic Faith of the Irish Slums: London, 1840–70'. In *The Victorian City: Images and Realities*, Vol. 2, ed. H. J. Dyos and M. Wolff, 837–53. London: Routledge & Kegan Paul, 1973.

——. 'Protestant London, No Popery, and the Irish Poor: II (1850–1860)', *Recusant History*, 11 (Jan. 1971), 21–56.

Gooptu, Nandini. *The Politics of the Urban Poor in Early Twentieth-Century India.* Cambridge: Cambridge University Press, 2001.

Gossman, Patricia A. *Riots and Victims: Violence and the Construction of Communal Identity among Bengali Muslims, 1905–1947.* Boulder, Colo.: Westview Press, 1999.

Grant, Douglas. *The Thin Blue Line: The Story of the City of Glasgow Police.* London: John Long, 1973.

Gray, Peter. *Famine, Land and Politics: British Government and Irish*

Society, 1843–1850. Dublin: Irish Academic Press, 1999.

Griffin, Brian. *The Bulkies: Police and Crime in Belfast, 1800–1865*. Dublin: Irish Academic Press, 1997.

Handley, James E. *The Irish in Modern Scotland*. Cork: Cork University Press, 1947.

——. *The Irish in Scotland, 1798–1845*. Cork: Cork University Press, 1945.

——. *The Navvy in Scotland*. Cork: Cork University Press, 1970.

Harrison, Mark. *Crowds and History: Mass Phenomena in English Towns, 1790–1835*. Cambridge: Cambridge University Press, 1988.

Hawkins, Richard. 'The "Irish Model" and the Empire: A Case for Reassessment'. In *Policing the Empire: Government, Authority, and Control, 1830–1940*, ed. David M. Anderson and David Killingray, 18–32. Manchester: Manchester University Press, 1991.

Heatley, Fred. 'Community Relations and the Religious Geography, 1800–86'. In J. C. Beckett et al., *Belfast: The Making of the City, 1800–1914*, 129–42. Belfast: Appletree Press, 1983.

Hempton, David. 'Belfast: The Unique City?' In *European Religion in the Age of Great Cities, 1830–1930*, ed. Hugh McLeod, 145–64. London: Routledge, 1995.

——. 'Evangelicalism in English and Irish Society, 1780–1840.' In *Evangelicalism: Comparative Studies of Popular Protestantism in North America, the British Isles, and Beyond, 1700–1990*, ed. Mark A. Noll, David W. Bebbington and George A. Rawlyk, 156–76. Oxford: Oxford University Press, 1994.

——, and Myrtle Hill, *Evangelical Protestantism in Ulster Society, 1740–1890*. New York: Routledge, 1992.

Hepburn, A. C. *A Past Apart: Studies in the History of Catholic Belfast, 1850–1950*. Belfast: Ulster Historical Foundation, 1996.

Hill, Jacqueline. 'The Meaning and Significance of "Protestant Ascendancy", 1787–1840'. In *Ireland after the Union: Proceedings of the Second Joint Meeting of the Royal Irish Academy and the British Academy, London, 1986*, 1–22. Oxford: Oxford University Press, 1989.

Hill, Myrtle. *The Time of the End: Millenarian Beliefs in Ulster*. Belfast: The Belfast Society, 2001.

Hilton, Boyd. *The Age of Atonement*. Oxford: Clarendon Press, 1988.

Hirst, Catherine. *Religion, Politics, and Violence in Nineteenth-Century Belfast: The Pound and Sandy Row*. Dublin: Four Courts Press, 2002.

Hobsbawm, Eric, and Terence Ranger, eds. *The Invention of Tradition*. Cambridge: Cambridge University Press, 1983.

Holmes, Finlay. *Henry Cooke*. Belfast: Christian Journals Limited, 1981.

Holmes, Janice. 'The Role of Open-Air Preaching in the Belfast Riots of 1857'. In *Proceedings of the Royal Irish Academy*, 102C (2002), 47–66.

Hoppen, K. Theodore. *Elections, Politics, and Society in Ireland, 1832–1885.* Oxford: Clarendon Press, 1984.

Howe, Stephen. *Ireland and Empire: Colonial Legacies in Irish History and Culture.* Oxford: Oxford University Press, 2002.

Hutchison, I. G. C. 'Glasgow Working-Class Politics'. In *The Working Class in Glasgow, 1750–1914*, ed. R. A. Cage, 98–141. London: Croom Helm, 1987.

——. *A Political History of Scotland: 1832–1924.* Edinburgh: John Donald, 1986.

Ingram, Martin. 'Ridings, Rough Music, and the "Reform of Popular Culture" in Early Modern England', *Past and Present*, 105 (Nov. 1984), 79–113.

Jackson, Alvin. 'Ireland, the Union, and the Empire, 1800–1960'. In *Ireland and the British Empire*, ed. Kevin Kenny, 123–53. Oxford: Oxford University Press, 2006.

Jackson, J. A. *The Irish in Britain.* London: Routledge and Kegan Paul, 1963.

Jarman, Neil. *Material Conflicts: Parades and Visual Displays in Northern Ireland.* New York: Berg, 1997.

——. and Dominic Bryan. *From Riots to Rights: Nationalist Parades in the North of Ireland.* Coleraine: Centre for the Study of Conflict, University of Ulster, 1998.

Jeffery, Keith, ed. *'An Irish Empire'? Aspects of Ireland and the British Empire.* Manchester: Manchester University Press, 1996.

Jenkins, Brian. *Era of Emancipation: British Government of Ireland, 1812–30.* Kingston: McGill-Queen's University Press, 1988.

Jordan, Alison. *Who Cared? Charity in Victorian and Edwardian Belfast.* Belfast: Queen's University Institute of Irish Studies, 1993.

Jordan, Thomas E. *An Imaginative Empiricist: Thomas Askew Larcom (1801–1879) and Victorian Ireland.* Irish Studies, vol. 5. Lampeter, Wales: The Edwin Mellen Press, 2002.

Karsten, Peter. 'Irish Soldiers in the British Army, 1792–1922: Suborned or Subordinate?' *Journal of Social History* 17/1 (Fall 1983), 31–64.

Kenny, Kevin. *The American Irish: A History.* New York: Longman, 2000.

——, ed. *Ireland and the British Empire.* Oxford: Oxford University Press, 2006.

Kerr, Donal. *Peel, Priests and Politics: Sir Robert Peel's Administration and the Roman Catholic Church in Ireland, 1841–1846.* Oxford: Clarendon Press, 1982.

Kerr, Peter. 'Voluntaryism within the Established Church in Nineteenth Century Belfast'. In *Voluntary Religion: Papers Read at the 1985 Summer Meeting and the 1986 Winter Meeting of the Ecclesiastical History Society*, ed. W. J. Shiels and Diana Wood, 347–62. Oxford: Basil Blackwell, 1986.

Killen, W. D. *Memoir of John Edgar, D.D., LL.D.* Belfast: William Mullan, 1869.

Kinealy, Christine, and Gerard MacAtasney. *The Hidden Famine: Poverty, Hunger, and Sectarianism in Belfast, 1845–1850.* London: Pluto Press, 2000.

Kirk, Neville. 'Ethnicity, Class and Popular Toryism, 1850–1870.' In *Hosts, Immigrants and Minorities: Historical Responses to Newcomers in British Society 1870–1914*, ed. Kenneth Lunn, 64–106. New York: St Martin's Press, 1980.

Klein, Kerwin Lee. 'On the Emergence of Memory in Historical Discourse', *Representations*, 69 (Winter 2000), 127–50.

Larkin, Emmet. 'The Devotional Revolution in Ireland, 1850–75', *The American Historical Review*, 77 (June 1972), 625–52.

——. *The Making of the Roman Catholic Church in Ireland, 1850–1860.* Chapel Hill, NC: University of North Carolina Press, 1980.

—— and Herman Freudenberger, eds. *A Redemptorist Missionary in Ireland, 1851–1854: Memoirs by Joseph Prost, C. Ss. R.* Cork: Cork University Press, 1998.

Lee, J. 'The Ribbonmen.' In *Secret Societies in Ireland*, ed. T. D. Williams, 75–91. Dublin: Gill and Macmillan, 1973.

Lobban, R. D. 'The Irish Community in Greenock in the Nineteenth Century', *Irish Geography*, 6 (1971), 270–81.

Loughlin, James. 'Parades and Politics: Governments and the Orange Order, 1880–86.' In *The Irish Parading Tradition: Following the Drum*, ed. T. G. Fraser, 27–43. New York: St Martin's Press, 2000.

Lowe, W. J., and E. L. Malcolm. 'The Domestication of the Royal Irish Constabulary, 1836–1922', *Irish Economic and Social History*, 19 (1992), 27–48.

Lowenthal, David. *The Past is a Foreign Country.* Cambridge: Cambridge University Press, 1999.

Macaulay, Ambrose. *Patrick Dorrian: Bishop of Down and Connor, 1865–85.* Dublin: Irish Academic Press, 1987.

MacDonagh, Oliver. *States of Mind: A Study of Anglo-Irish Conflict, 1780–1980.* London: George Allen & Unwin, 1983.

MacKenzie, John M. *Propaganda and Empire: The Manipulation of British Public Opinion, 1880–1960.* Manchester: Manchester University Press, 1984.

MacRaild, Donald M. '"Abandon Hibernicisation": Priests, Ribbonmen and an Irish Street Fight in the North-East of England in 1858', *Historical Research*, 194 (Nov. 2003), 557–73.

——. *Culture, Conflict and Migration: The Irish in Victorian Cumbria*. Liverpool: Liverpool University Press, 1998.

Madden, Kyla. *Forkhill Protestants and Forkhill Catholics, 1787–1858*. Montreal and Kingston: McGill-Queen's University Press, 2004.

Magee, Hamilton. *Fifty Years in 'The Irish Mission'*. Belfast: Religious Tract and Book Depot, 1905.

Magee, Jack. *Barney: Bernard Hughes of Belfast, 1808–1878*. Belfast: Ulster Historical Foundation, 2001.

Maguire, W. A. 'Lords and Landlords: The Donegall Family'. In *Belfast: The Origin and Growth of an Industrial City*, ed. J. C. Beckett and R. E. Glasscock, 27–40. London: British Broadcasting Corp., 1967.

Maver, Irene. *Glasgow*. Edinburgh: Edinburgh University Press, 2000.

——. 'Glasgow's Civic Government.' In *Glasgow: 1830 to 1912*, ed. W. Hamish Fraser and Irene Maver, 441–85. Manchester: Manchester University Press, 1996.

McBride, Ian. 'The School of Virtue: Francis Hutcheson, Irish Presbyterians and the Scottish Enlightenment.' In *Political Thought in Ireland since the Seventeenth Century*, ed. D. George Boyce, Robert Ecclehall and Vincent Geoghegan, 73–99. London: Routledge, 1993.

——, ed. *History and Memory in Modern Ireland*. Cambridge: Cambridge University Press, 2001.

McCaffrey, John. 'The Irish Vote in Glasgow in the Later Nineteenth Century: A Preliminary Survey', *Innes Review*, 21 (1970), 30–6.

——. 'Political Reactions in the Glasgow Constituencies at the General Elections of 1885 and 1996'. Unpublished Ph.D. thesis, University of Glasgow, 1970.

McClelland, Aiken. *William Johnston of Ballykilbeg*. Lurgan, Northern Ireland: Ulster Society (Publications) Limited, 1990.

McDonaugh, Terrence, ed. *Was Ireland a Colony? Economics, Politics, and Culture in Nineteenth-Century Ireland*. Dublin: Irish Academic Press, 2005.

McDowell, R. B. *The Irish Administration, 1801–1914*. London: Routledge & Kegan Paul, 1964.

McFarland, Elaine. *John Ferguson, 1836–1906: Irish Issues in Scottish Politics*. East Linton, East Lothian, Scotland: Tuckwell Press, 2003.

——. 'Marching from the Margins: Twelfth of July Parades in Scotland, 1820–1914.' In *The Irish Parading Tradition: Following the Drum*, ed. T. G. Fraser, 60–77. New York: St Martin's Press, 2000.

——. *Protestants First: Orangeism in Nineteenth Century Scotland*. Edinburgh: Edinburgh University Press, 1990.

Middleton, David, and Steven D. Brown. *The Social Psychology of Experience: Studies in Remembering and Forgetting*. London: Sage Publications, 2005.

Miller, David W. 'The Armagh Troubles, 1784–95'. In *Irish Peasants: Violence and Political Unrest, 1780–1914*, ed. Samuel Clark and James S. Donnelly, Jr., 155–91. Dublin: Gill and Macmillan, 1983.

——. 'Presbyterianism and "Modernization" in Ulster', *Past and Present*, 80 (Aug. 1978), 66–90.

——. *Queen's Rebels: Ulster Loyalism in Historical Perspective*. Dublin: Gill and Macmillan, 1978.

——, ed. *Peep O'Day Boys and Defenders: Selected Documents on the Disturbances in County Armagh, 1784–1796*. Belfast: Public Record Office of Northern Ireland, 1990.

——, ed. *Rethinking Northern Ireland: Culture, Ideology, and Colonialism*. London: Longman, 1998.

Miller, Kerby A. 'Belfast's First Bomb, 28 February 1816: Class Conflict and the Origins of Ulster Unionist Hegemony', *Eire-Ireland*, 39 (Spring–Summer 2004), 262–80.

Mitchell, Martin. *The Irish in the West of Scotland 1797–1848: Trade Unions, Strikes, and Political Movements*. Edinburgh: John Donald, 1998.

Moss, Michael, and John R. Hume. *Shipbuilders to the World: 125 years of Harland and Wolff, Belfast, 1861–1986*. Belfast: Blackstaff Press, 1986.

Muenger, Elizabeth A. *The British Military Dilemma in Ireland: Occupation Politics, 1886–1914*. Lawrence, Kan.: University Press of Kansas, 1991.

Murphy, David. *Ireland and the Crimean War*. Dublin: Four Courts Press, 2002.

Murray, A. C. 'Agrarian Violence and Nationalism in Nineteenth-Century Ireland: The Myth of Ribbonism', *Irish Economic and Social History*, 13 (1986), 56–73.

Nagai, Kaori. *Empire of Analogies: Kipling, India, and Ireland*. Cork: Cork University Press, 2006.

Neal, Frank. *Sectarian Violence: The Liverpool Experience, 1819–1914*. Manchester: Manchester University Press, 1988).

Nora, Pierre. 'Between Memory and History: Les Lieux de Memoire', *Representations*, 26 (Spring 1989), 7–24.

Norman, E. R. *The Catholic Church and Ireland in the Age of Rebellion, 1859–1873*. Ithaca, NY: Cornell University Press, 1965.

O'Leary, Cornelius. 'Belfast Urban Government in the Age of Reform'.

In *The Town in Ireland: Papers Read before the Irish Conference of Historians, Belfast, 10 May – 2 June 1979*, ed. David Harkness and Mary O'Dowd, 187–202. Belfast: Appletree Press, 1981.

Ollerenshaw, Philip, 'Industry, 1820–1914'. In *An Economic History of Ulster, 1820–1940*, ed. Liam Kennedy and Philip Ollerenshaw, 62–108. Manchester: Manchester University Press, 1985.

Paisley, Ian. *The 'Fifty Nine' Revival: An Authentic History of the Great Ulster Awakening of 1859*. Belfast: Nelson & Knox, 1958.

Palmer, Stanley H. *Police and Protest in England and Ireland, 1780–1850*. Cambridge: Cambridge University Press, 1988.

Pandey, Gyanendra. *The Construction of Communalism in Colonial North India*. Delhi: Oxford University Press, 1990.

Parkinson, Alan F. *Belfast's Unholy War: The Troubles of the 1920s*. Dublin: Four Courts Press, 2004.

Paterson, Lindsay. *The Autonomy of Modern Scotland*. Edinburgh: Edinburgh University Press, 1994.

Patterson, Henry. *Class Conflict and Sectarianism: The Protestant Working Class and the Belfast Labour Movement, 1868–1920*. Belfast: Blackstaff Press, 1980.

Pollard, Sidney, and Paul Robertson. *The British Shipbuilding Industry, 1870–1914*. Cambridge, Mass: Harvard University Press, 1979.

Price, Richard. *British Society, 1680–1880: Dynamism, Containment and Change*. Cambridge: Cambridge University Press, 1999.

Quinault, R. 'The Warwickshire County Magistracy and Public Order, c.1830–1870'. In *Popular Protest and Public Order: Six Studies in British History, 1790–1920*, ed. R. Quinault and J. Stevenson, 181–214. London: George Allen & Unwin, 1974.

Radford, Mark. 'The "Social Volcano": Policing Victorian Belfast'. In *Politics and Power in Victorian Ireland*, ed. Roger Swift and Christine Kinealy, 166–77. Dublin: Four Courts Press, 2006.

Richter, Donald. *Riotous Victorians*. Athens, O.: Ohio University Press, 1981.

Rimé, Bernard, and Véronique Christophe. 'How Individual Emotional Episodes Feed Collective Memory'. In *Collective Memory of Political Events: Social Psychological Perspectives*, ed. James W. Pennebaker, Dario Paez and Bernard Rimé, 131–46. Mahwah, NJ: Lawrence Erlbaum Associates, 1997.

Robinson, Ronald. 'Non-European Foundations of European Imperialism: Sketch for a Theory of Collaboration'. In *Studies in the Theory of Imperialism*, ed. Roger Owen and Bob Sutcliffe, 117–42. London: Longman, 1972.

Rochberg-Halton, Eugene. *Meaning and Modernity: Social Theory in the*

Pragmatic Attitude. Chicago: University of Chicago Press, 1986.

Rogers, P. *St. Peter's Pro-Cathedral, 1866–1966.* Belfast: Howard Publications, 1966.

Rudé, George. *The Crowd in History: A Study of Popular Disturbances in France and England, 1730–1848.* New York: Wiley, 1964.

Santino, Jack. 'Light up the Sky: Halloween Bonfires and Culture Hegemony in Northern Ireland', *Western Folklore*, 55 (Summer 1996), 213–31.

Saunders, Laurance James. *Scottish Democracy, 1815–1840.* Edinburgh: Oliver and Boyd, 1950.

Senior, Hereward. 'The Early Orange Order 1795–1870.' In *Secret Societies in Ireland*, ed. T. Desmond Williams, 36–45. New York: Barnes and Noble, 1973.

——. *Orangeism in Ireland and Britain, 1795–1836.* London: Routledge and Kegan Paul, 1966.

——. *Orangeism: The Canadian Phase.* Toronto: McGraw-Hill Ryerson Limited, 1972.

Seymour, W. A., ed. *A History of the Ordnance Survey.* Folkestone, Kent: Wm. Dawson & Sons, 1980.

Shirlow, Peter, 'Ethno-Sectarianism and the Reproduction of Fear in Belfast', *Capital and Class*, 80 (Summer 2003), 77–94.

——. '"Who Fears to Speak": Fear, Mobility, and Ethno-Sectarianism in the Two "Ardoynes",' *The Global Review of Ethnopolitics*, 3 (Sept. 2003), 76–91.

Sibbett, R. M. *For Christ and Crown: The Story of a Mission.* Belfast: 'The Witness' Office, 1926.

——. *Orangeism in Ireland and Throughout the Empire.* Vol. 2. London: Thynne & Co., 1914.

Silvestri, Michael. '"The Sinn Fein of India": Irish Nationalism and the Policing of Revolutionary Terrorism in Bengal', *The Journal of British Studies*, 29 (Oct. 2000), 454–86.

Sloan, William. 'Religious Affiliation and the Immigrant Experience: Catholic Irish and Protestant Highlanders in Glasgow, 1830–1850.' In *Irish Immigrants and Scottish Society in the Nineteenth and Twentieth Centuries: Proceedings of the Scottish Historical Studies Seminar, University of Strathclyde, 1989–90*, ed. T. M. Devine, 67–90. Edinburgh: John Donald, 1991.

Smith, Joan. 'Labour Tradition in Glasgow and Liverpool', *History Workshop*, 17 (Spring 1984), 32–56.

Stewart, A. T. Q. *The Narrow Ground: Aspects of Ulster, 1609–1969.* London: Faber, 1997.

Storch, Robert. 'The Plague of Blue Locusts: Police Reform and Popular

Resistance in Northern England, 1840–1857', *International Review of Social History*, 20 (1975), 61–90.

——. 'The Policeman as Domestic Missionary: Urban Discipline and Popular Culture in Northern England, 1850–1880', *Journal of Social History*, 9 (Summer 1976), 481–509.

Thompson, E. P. *Customs in Common*. New York: The New Press, 1993.

Tomlinson, Mike. 'Walking Backwards into the Sunset: British Policy and the Insecurity of Northern Ireland'. In *Rethinking Northern Ireland: Culture, Ideology, and Colonialism*, ed. David Miller, 94–122. London: Longman, 1998.

Townshend, Charles. *Political Violence in Ireland: Government and Resistance since 1848*. Oxford: Clarendon Press, 1983.

Tuan, Yi-Fu. *Space and Place: The Perspective of Experience*. Minneapolis: University of Minnesota Press, 1977.

Varshney, Ashutosh. *Ethnic Conflict and Civic Life: Hindus and Muslims in India*. New Haven: Yale University Press, 2002.

Walker, Graham. *Intimate Strangers: Political and Cultural Interaction between Scotland and Ulster in Modern Times*. Edinburgh: John Donald, 1995.

——. 'The Protestant Irish in Scotland'. In *Irish Immigrants and Scottish Society in the Nineteenth and Twentieth Centuries: Proceedings of the Scottish Historical Studies Seminar, University of Strathclyde, 1989–90*, ed. T. M. Devine, 44–66. Edinburgh: John Donald, 1991.

Walker, W. M. 'Irish Immigrants in Scotland: Their Priests, Politics and Parochial Life', *The Historical Journal*, 15 (1972), 649–67.

Waller, P. J. *Democracy and Sectarianism: A Political and Social History of Liverpool, 1868–1939*. Liverpool: Liverpool University Press, 1981.

Weber, Max. 'Politics as a Vocation'. In *From Max Weber: Essays in Sociology*, trans. and ed. H. H. Gerth and C. Wright Mills, 77–128. New York: Oxford University Press, 1946.

Whetstone, Ann E. *Scottish County Government in the Eighteenth and Nineteenth Centuries*. Edinburgh: John Donald, 1981.

Wood, Ian. 'Irish Immigrants and Scottish Radicalism, 1880–1906.' In *Essays in Scottish Labour History*, ed. Ian MacDougall, 65–89. Edinburgh: John Donald, 1978.

Wright, Frank. 'Communal Deterrence and the Threat of Violence in the North of Ireland in the Nineteenth Century.' In *Political Violence: Ireland in a Comparative Perspective*, ed. John Darby, Nicholas Dodge and A. C. Hepburn, 11–28. Belfast: Appletree Press, 1990.

——. *Northern Ireland: A Comparative Analysis*. Dublin: Gill and Macmillan, 1987.

Bibliography

——. 'Protestant Ideology and Politics in Ulster', *European Journal of Sociology*, 14 (1973), 213–80.

——. *Two Lands on One Soil: Ulster Politics before Home Rule*. Dublin: Gill and Macmillan, 1996.

Zimmermann, Georges Denis. *Songs of Irish Rebellion: Irish Political Street Ballads and Rebel Songs, 1780–1900*. 2nd ed. Dublin: Four Courts Press, 2002.

Index

Act of Union (1801) 4
Airdrie 199, 209
Albert Street Presbyterian Church
   23, 248n.48
Alison, Archibald 192–3, 209–10,
   211
Anglican Church *see* Church of
   Ireland

ballads 233–8
Ballymacarrett 53, 179, 180
Bates, John 111, 119
Belfast Domestic Mission 16, 23
Belfast General Hospital 24, 160,
   167–8, 177
Belfast Parochial Mission 89, 91–2
Belfast Police Act (1865) 184
Belfast Town Mission 23, 35, 88–9
Belfast Daily Mercury 104n.69
Belfast Newsletter 22
   criticisms of central government
     152, 153
   and O'Connell procession (1864)
     162–3
   praise of shipcarpenters 174
   views on open-air preaching
     37–8, 90–1, 139–40
Berry Street Presbyterian Church
   23, 34–5, 152

   see also Hanna, Hugh
Biggar, Joseph 238
Botanic Gardens demonstration
   (1862) 149–52
Bourke, Richard, 6th Earl of Mayo
   (Lord Naas) 144–6
Boyd, John 98, 103n.43
Boyne Bridge 76, 88, 144, 164,
   175, 178, 181, 182, 185, 235
Brady, W. Maziere 140–1
Bridgegate 192–4, 201, 213
Brown Square 122, 173

Cairns, Hugh McCalmont 70n.6,
   92–3, 103n.43, 141–2, 149
Carlisle, Lord *see* Howard, George,
   7th Earl of Carlisle
cartes de viste 230–3
Catholic Church (Belfast)
   church construction 3, 52–3
   efforts to restrain violence 167,
     175, 179, 206–7, 239–40, 243
   weakness 23, 51–5
   see also Catholics; Denvir,
     Cornelius; Dorrian, Patrick
Catholic Emancipation Act (1829)
   26, 81, 111, 132, 202
Catholic Gun Club 68, 107–9, 129,
   144

Catholic Institute 58–60, 175, 180, 231–2

Catholics
Belfast police and 118–23
bourgeois leadership in Belfast 55–60, 109
marginal status in Belfast 7–8, 48–50, 57–8, 113numbers in Belfast 22, 50
response to open-air preaching 91–3
see also Catholic Church; Hughes, Bernard; Ribbon societies

census returns *see* population figures

central government
Belfast Protestants and 130–1, 136–42, 147–54, 178, 184, 243–4
contrasting attitudes toward Ireland and Britain 208–9
Irish Constabulary 116, 118, 134, 184, 240, 243–4
reforming agenda of 131–6
Resident (Stipendiary) Magistrates 134–6
use of overwhelming force 4, 88, 142–8, 152–3, 175–6, 240, 243–4
see also imperialism

Chalmers, Thomas 200, 202, 204

Christ Church 22, 76–8, 84, 164, 248n.48
see also Drew, Thomas

Christ Church Protestant Association *see* Drew, Thomas – political activities of

church construction *see individual denominations*

Church of Ireland
church construction 23
and evangelicalism 19–20

see also Drew, Thomas; McIlwaine, William

Clarke, John 94, 152

class conflict 7, 114–15

Coatbridge 199

Coates, William 43n.48, 94, 103n.43, 177, 182–3

Cole, William Willoughby, 3rd Earl of Enniskillen 141–2

collective memory *see* memory

'communal deterrence' 8–9, 10, 95–6

Conservative Party
in Belfast *see* local government
in Britain 114–15, 132–3, 142, 210

Cooke, Henry 19, 25–6, 112, 150
and open-air preaching 91
response to Birkenhead riots 22

Crimean War (1854–56) 6, 26–7, 92

Cullen, Paul 53–4
Protestant anxieties about 20–1, 90, 162

Custom House 89–93 *passim*, 100

Davison, Richard 43n.48, 70n.6, 103n.43, 112

Defenders 4, 61, 108
see also Ribbon societies

Denvir, Cornelius 52–5, 206

Derry *see* Londonderry

'devotional revolution' *see* Cullen, Paul

Dixon, Joseph 53–4

Dolly's Brae 82–3, 98, 135

Donegall family 110–11

Donegall Place 56, 94, 179–80, 231

Dorrian, Patrick 54–5, 59–60, 167, 175

Drew, Thomas
and 1858 Belfast riots 147
anti-Catholic rhetoric of 16–17, 27, 84–5

and open-air preaching 93
and Orangeism 29, 76–8, 84
political activities of 26–7, 112, 229
Dublin Castle *see* central government
Durham Street 76, 120, 129, 152, 166, 168, 179

economic development
  government support for 113–14
  linen manufacturing 4, 6, 148
  migration and 4, 5, 80, 198–9
  shipbuilding 6, 171, 182–3, 198
  trade 3
  see also employment patterns
Edgar, John 32, 39, 113
education 54, 56
  see also literacy
Eglinton, Lord *see* Montgomerie, Archibald, 13th Earl of Eglinton
elections 29, 112–13, 211
employment patterns 4, 49, 98, 181–2
  see also millworkers; navvies; shipcarpenters
Enniskillen, Lord *see* Cole, William Willoughby, 3rd Earl of Enniskillen
Evangelical Alliance 37
evangelicalism (Protestant) 19–21
  anti-Catholicism of 8, 19, 39–40
  in Belfast civil society 23–4, 103–4n.43, 113
  controversialism 33–6
  missionaries
    domestic 5, 16, 23–4
    Irish and foreign 32
  'moral' vs. 'political' forms 17
  open-air preaching 36–40, 78–9, 88–94, 100, 137–40, 192–3

proselytism among Catholics 31–6, 54–5
revival of 1859 34–5
see also networks (social); religion; *and under individual churches, ministers and organisations*

Falls Road 38–9, 176, 225–6, 238–9
famine, Irish (1845–49) 5–6, 31–2
Feast of the Assumption (Lady Day) 172, 237, 238, 241
Fenian Brotherhood 187–8n.32, 198, 212, 215, 241
Friar's Bush Burying Ground 144, 164
funeral processions
  during 1858 riots 144–5
  during 1886 riots 242
  McConnell funeral, Belfast (1864) 178–81, 228, 236
  McManus funeral, Dublin (1861) 149
  for O'Connell effigy (1864) 164
  in twentieth-century Belfast 225–6, 251

Gault, Robert 201, 203
Gavazzi, Alessandro 201
gender relations 30–1, 97–9, 167, 235, 239
Getty, Samuel G. (S. G.) 125n.24, 139, 152
Glasgow
  anti-Catholicism in 200–1, 202–5, 212
  Catholic Church in 192–3, 205–7, 215
  economic structure 197–9
  employment patterns 197–9, 214
  evangelicalism in 192–3, 200–1, 202–4

Irish settlement in 196–7
labour movement in 114, 210–11, 214
links with Belfast 177, 195–201
local government 210–11
Orange Order in 197, 199, 203, 212, 214, 215
policing 192–3, 209–10, 211–13
residential patterns 192, 213–14
state legitimacy in 207–13, 215–16
Good, James Winder 1, 229
Grand Orange Lodge *see* Orange Order

Hacket, John 68, 107, 144
Halbwachs, Maurice 226, 227–8
see also memory
Hanna, Hugh
and 1857 riots 79, 92–4, 100, 137–9, 228
and 1862 riots 150, 152
and 1864 riots 182
and 1872 riots 238
and 1886 riots 243
in Glasgow 201
proselytising activities of 33–5
and Protestant shipcarpenters 171–2
schoolchildren processions 241, 251
Harland and Wolff shipyards *see* economic development – shipbuilding
Hercules Street 4–5, 58, 64, 180–1, 231, 235, 238
Hill, George Stewart 62–3, 66–7, 68
Holland, Denis 55–8 *passim*, 108–9
see also Ulsterman
Home Rule *see* nationalism – Home Rule
Howard, George, 7th Earl of

Carlisle 139–40, 144
Hughes, Bernard 48–50, 55, 56
and 1864 riots 182, 236
bakery 68, 107, 126n.34, 144, 145, 152, 180
philanthropic activities of 53, 163

imperialism
evangelical support for 25, 84
as explanation of violence 12, 130–1, 133–4, 194–5, 205, 207–8, 216, 252
see also central government; Crimean War; India
India 65, 130–1, 148
Irish Church Missionary Society 36
Irish Constabulary *see* central government
Islandmen *see* shipcarpenters
Italy 6, 142, 201

Johnston, William (of Ballykilbeg) 150–1
Johnston, William (of Belfast) 38–9

Kilkenny 37, 169

'Lady Day' processions *see* Feast of the Assumption (Lady Day)
Lanyon, Charles 103–4n.43, 151–2
Larcom, Thomas 134–5, 139, 144–8 *passim*, 183
Liberal Party
in Belfast 111–16 *passim*, 205, 211
in Scotland 205, 210–11
see also local government
Limerick 37
linen industry *see* economic development – linen manufacturing
Lisburn 5, 83
literacy 14n.16, 70n.3, 233, 236

Liverpool 114–15
local government
  Botanic Gardens demonstration
    (1862) and 151–2
  Catholics and 107–10, 112–13,
    118–23
  Conservative domination of
    110–16
  Justices of the Peace (local
    magistrates) 50, 136, 140–2,
    153
  local police 7, 50, 86–8, 117–22,
    136–7, 183–4
  open-air preaching and 137–40
  Town Council 50, 111, 116
Londonderry 168
Long, H. A. 201
Lyons, William Thomas Bristow
  (W. T. B.) 103n.43, 179–81,
  236
Lytle, John 125n.24, 166, 182–3,
  179, 236

McConnell, John 175, 178
  see also funeral processions
McIlwaine, William 33, 89, 138,
  144–5
McIntyre, Andrew 16–18, 19, 24
McKenna, Andrew Joseph (A. J.)
  58–9, 182, 234, 236
  see also Ulster Observer
MacKnight, Thomas 151, 205
Mateer, John 90
Maynooth (Catholic seminary) 53,
  132–3, 150
memory
  autobiographical vs. historical
    224–6, 235, 250
  as explanation of violence 226
  place and 1, 185, 214–15, 227–9,
    235, 238
Methodist Church 23, 38
Miller, Thomas 28, 103n.43, 152

millworkers 98–9, 167, 181–2
missionaries *see* evangelicalism
  (Protestant)
Montgomerie, Archibald, 13th Earl
  of Eglinton 144, 146–7

Naas, Lord *see* Bourke, Richard,
  6th Earl of Mayo (Lord Naas)
nationalism
  and 1872 riots 238
  and Belfast Catholic bourgeoisie
    57, 60, 163
  as explanation of violence 169,
    242
  Home Rule 211, 241–3
  and Ribbon societies 61–2, 64–6,
    69
  see also Fenian Brotherhood;
    Society of United Irishmen
navvies 63, 170–1
  and 1862 riots 152
  and 1886 riots 241–2
  attack on Brown Square 172–3,
    237, 243
  battle with shipcarpenters (1864)
    177–8, 185, 230–5
Nelson, Isaac 176
networks (social) 9–10, 18, 40, 50,
  69–70, 202–7
  see also evangelicalism
    (Protestant); gender relations;
    millworkers; navvies; Orange
    Order; religion; Ribbon
    societies; shipcarpenters; *and
    under individual churches*
newspapers *see under individual
  newspapers*
Northern Ireland *see* 'Troubles'
Northern Whig 17, 145, 174

O'Connell, Daniel 25–6, 57, 65, 132
  centenary celebration in Glasgow
    215

Dublin statue and Belfast riots
(1864) 162–4, 168–9, 178,
234–5
O'Hanlon, W. M. 21
open-air preaching *see*
evangelicalism (Protestant) –
open-air preaching
Orange Order
in Belfast police force 119–21
central government and 140–2,
209
growth in Belfast 28
as link between elite and poor
28–9, 82, 93, 112–13, 149–52
origins 27, 81
processions 5, 76–8, 81–3, 98,
135–6, 150–1, 199–200,
209–10, 238
Ribbonism and 69
in Scotland 192, 197, 199–200,
203–4, 209–10, 212, 214, 215
social function of 29–31
see also Drew, Thomas
Orme, Edward 166, 172

Paisley 192, 199, 203–4, 221n.73
Paisley, Ian 79, 251
Palmerston, Lord *see* Temple,
Henry John, 3rd Viscount
Palmerston
'papal aggression' controversy 5,
20, 29, 202–3
see also Cullen, Paul;
evangelicalism (Protestant)
Partick 215
Party Emblems Act (1860) *see* Party
Processions Acts (1850 & 1860)
Party Processions Acts (1850 &
1860) 135–6, 149–51, 162,
169, 178, 238
see also Johnston, William (of
Ballykilbeg); Orange Order
Peace Meetings (1864) 182

Plantation of Ulster 3, 130, 195,
205
policing *see* local government;
central government
Poor Law Union 24, 49
population figures 4, 6, 21, 41n.18
Pound, the 5, 49, 53, 73n.53, 76–9,
85–8, 94, 107, 122, 145, 152,
164–8, 170–1, 173, 237–8, 241
Presbyterian Church (Ulster)
church construction 22–3
and evangelicalism 19
links with Scotland 195, 200–1,
205
and open-air preaching 38–9
see also Cooke, Henry; Edgar,
John; Hanna, Hugh
Presbyterians
see Presbyterian Church (Ulster);
Test Act (1704)
Protestant Ascendancy 26, 110–12,
130–1, 133, 142, 204
Protestant Defence Association
129–30, 147–8
Protestants *see under individual
denominations*

Queen's University Belfast 54

Rea, John 64, 116, 119–21
religion
as explanation of violence 7–8,
17–18, 83–4, 169
as social network 18, 40
see also evangelicalism
(Protestant); networks (social);
and under individual churches

Ribbon societies 58, 60–70, 92,
107, 123, 170, 251
riots
Belfast
(1813) 4–5, 83

(1857) 76–80, 83–101, 118,
121, 129, 138–9, 143–4,
229
(1858) 118, 144–8
(1862) 152–4, 229
(1864) 162–86, 230–8
(1872) 238–41
(1886) 241–4
(1920–22) 1, 225–6, 250
England 22, 208
Glasgow 215
rural Scotland 199–200
rural Ulster 4, 80–3, 135
ritualised violence 79, 81–2, 86–7,
94, 163–6, 168–9, 199–200
see also funeral processions; riots
Roney, Frank 187–8n.32

St Malachy's Catholic Church 52,
94, 145, 172, 237
St Mary's Catholic Church 52–3
St Patrick's Catholic Church 52,
145
St Patrick's Day banquets 56–7
St Peter's Catholic Church 53, 55,
247n.48
St Vincent de Paul Society 52, 207
Saltwater Bridge *see* Boyne Bridge
Sandy Row 5, 16–18, 22, 30, 49,
76–9, 85–8, 94–5, 98–9, 122,
129, 144, 152, 163–9, 171–3,
177, 180–2, 229, 235, 238
Seaver, Charles 89–90
secret societies *see* Defenders;
Fenian Brotherhood; Orange
Order; Ribbon societies
Sexton, Thomas 243
Shankill Road 145, 176, 189n.40,
224, 225–6, 238–9, 243
shipbuilding *see* economic
development – shipbuilding
shipcarpenters 171–2
and 1857 riots 94

and 1858 riots 145
and 1872 riots 239
and 1886 riots 242
politicisation of 8
rivalry with navvies (1864)
173–5, 177–8, 182–3, 185,
230–5, 237, 241–2
Sisters of Mercy 54, 167, 206
Smithfield 5, 39, 63, 74n.60, 107,
180, 235, 238, 239
social conditions 21–2, 114
Society of United Irishmen 3–4
state
see central government;
imperialism; local government

Temple, Henry John, 3rd Viscount
Palmerston 141–2
Test Act (1704) 3
Thompson's Bank 177, 185, 230–2,
234
Times (London) 148, 183–4
Tory Party *see* Conservative Party
Tracy, William 62, 86, 87, 89, 99,
105n.88, 117–18, 138, 139,
143–4, 145–6, 153
'Troubles' 7, 224–5, 250–3

Ulsterman
on Catholic secret societies 65
on disorganisation of Belfast
Catholics 57–8
hostility to Belfast police 120–1
responses to evangelicalism 33,
35–6, 37, 91, 93
see also Holland, Denis
Ulster Observer 58–60
and O'Connell monument 163
see also McKenna, Andrew
Joseph (A. J.)
unionism 28, 150, 241–2
United Irishmen *see* Society of
United Irishmen

United Protestant Committee 156
United States Civil War (1861–65)
6, 148
urban space 87, 168, 178, 180,
184–5, 213–15
see also memory – place and;
*and under individual
neighbourhoods and streets*

Verner, William 141, 150

visual culture *see cartes de viste*

Watson, William 55–8 *passim*,
87–8
Wesley, John 19, 36
William III
effigies of 166, 168–9
proposed statue of 162
'wrecking' 82, 87–8, 94–8, 176,
239, 251